Penguin Books

THE PENGUIN NEW WRITING

John Frederick Lehmann was born in June 1907 and educated at Eton and at Trinity College, Cambridge. In the course of a highly distinguished career he has been partner and general manager of the Hogarth Press (1938–46); advisory editor to the *Geographical Magazine* (1940–45); editor of 'New Soundings', 1952 (BBC Third Programme) and of the *London Magazine* (1945–61); chairman of the British Council's editorial advisory panel (1952–8); managing director of John Lehmann Ltd (1946–52); founder and editor of *New Writing* (1936–50) and of *The Penguin New Writing* (1940–50); president of the Royal Literary Fund (1966–76) and president of the Alliance Française in Great Britain (1955–63). He has also been invited as a visiting professor to several American universities. He has received many honours, among them the CBE (1964) and the Queen's Silver Jubilee Medal (1977). A Fellow of the Royal Society of Literature, he is a prolific author and has written and edited books on a wide range of subjects. His most recent publications are *Rupert Brooke: His Life and His Legend* (1980); *The English Poets of the First World War* (1981) and *Three Literary Friendships* (1983).

Roy Fuller was born in Failsworth in 1912. A famous poet and author, he has had a distinguished career both as a solicitor for the Woolwich Equitable Building Society, of which he is now a director, and as Professor of Poetry at the University of Oxford (1968–73). He is now a vice-president of the Building Societies Association and has edited *The Building Societies Acts*. From 1941 to 1946 he served in the Royal Navy, becoming a lieutenant in 1944. Among his many publications are *Savage Gold* (1946); *With My Little Eye* (1948); *Fantasy and Fugue* (1954); *Image of a Society* (1956) and *The Father's Comedy* (1961), all of which have been published by Penguin. His last novel was *The Carnal Island* (1970); more recently he has published three volumes of autobiography: *Souvenirs*, *Vamp Till Ready* and *Home and Dry*.

Roy Fuller has been a governor of the BBC and is a Fellow of the Royal Society of Literature. He was awarded the CBE and the Queen's Gold Medal for Poetry in 1970. He is married and has one son, the poet and author John Fuller, whose *Flying to Nowhere* is published by Penguin.

THE PENGUIN

NEW WRITING

An Anthology edited by
John Lehmann in association with Roy Fuller

Penguin Books

Penguin Books Ltd, Harmondsworth, Middlesex, England
Viking Penguin Inc., 40 West 23rd Street, New York, New York 10010, U.S.A.
Penguin Books Australia Ltd, Ringwood, Victoria, Australia
Penguin Books Canada Ltd, 2801 John Street, Markham, Ontario, Canada L3R 1B4
Penguin Books (N.Z.) Ltd, 182–190 Wairau Road, Auckland 10, New Zealand

First published in *Penguin New Writing* between 1940 and 1950
This anthology first published 1985

Made and printed in Great Britain by
Cox & Wyman Ltd, Reading

Photoset in Linotron Sabon by
Rowland Phototypesetting Ltd
Bury St Edmunds, Suffolk

Contents

CONTENTS

III   STORIES, MEMOIRS, IMPRESSIONS

IV   THE CRITICAL ESTIMATE

INTRODUCTION

The history of *Penguin New Writing* was a success story that surprised and delighted not only Allen Lane and myself, but also that core of enthusiasts which had formed round the original hardback bi-annual volumes of *New Writing* that had started publication only a few years before – in 1936. But could the series survive war conditions? I was doubtful, even though I had redesigned them as *Folios of New Writing*, something smaller and less ambitious than the original volumes, but retaining as far as possible their distinctive character.

It was therefore with some excitement that I found a letter from Allen Lane in May 1940, suggesting that I should follow up the Pelican *New Writing in Europe*, which he had recently commissioned, with a selection of the best contributions from the pre-war volumes of *New Writing* which had originally been backed by Lane himself just before he broke away from Bodley Head to found his Penguins. I agreed with alacrity, and before another month had passed he told me that his editorial committee had approved, and he would come to see me at once about details. In an extremely harmonious and sanguine discussion we agreed about everything, his mood being buoyed up by the great success Penguins were having under wartime conditions. It was not difficult to persuade him that at least two selections could be made out of the abundant first-class material which had appeared in the old volumes. I set to work at once, and had the two selections drafted out in a few weeks. The first was due to appear early in November 1940, though it was in fact delayed till December.

But the second selection never appeared as planned. Things began to move very fast during the summer. I pressed on with the work with a sense of urgency, inspired partly by the idea at the back of everybody's mind that an invasion was imminent, and partly by the fear that I myself might be called up at any moment. During our discussion Lane had tentatively mentioned that Penguins might start a monthly literary magazine. The more I thought about this, the clearer it seemed to me that in Penguin's selections from *New Writing* he already had a magazine in embryo. Why shouldn't the selections appear each month, but with half of every number consisting of *new* contributions, stories, poems and articles? I believed I could organize that, the war permitting; and the moment the idea crystallized in my mind, I wrote off to Lane. It was more than I had dared to hope, that an almost immediate reply arrived from Lane, saying that he thought the scheme was excellent and would I go ahead with it at once. The details were settled with what seems to me now incredible speed, and by the end of October I had a new contract in my hands for the first six numbers of a monthly.

I realized that in these new circumstances I should have to jettison the second number as originally planned, and re-design the series altogether. The first of the new monthly series was planned to appear in January 1941, by which time No. 1 had had a runaway success and sold out two printings, making 80,000 in all. In the Foreword to No. 2 I wrote, with heady confidence in spite of the nightly bombardment of London which had succeeded the Battle of Britain: 'Beginning with this January number, the *Penguin New Writing* will appear as a monthly, and will consist not merely of reprints of the best contributions selected from the old volumes, but also of new features specially written for us by well-known authors, many of which will have a more topical bent. There will be a series of articles by Stephen Spender about the place of books in our lives and what literature can mean to us during this war. There will also be a feature entitled 'The Way We Live Now', in which each month a different worker, or soldier, or someone "in the thick of it" will describe and discuss his (or her) recent experiences. Other regular contributors will include Rosamond Lehmann; Robert Pagan, who is a new author with something lively and unexpected to say; and Fanfarlo. This is the *nom de guerre* which conceals the identity of a young writer who has already made his name, though in a rather different branch of journalism. Fanfarlo's comments on our life today, and the account of his distressing adventures, will have a highly individual flavour, and will certainly not appeal to anyone who lacks a sense of humour.

'But in addition to these features, and to the outstanding stories, poems and sketches of past *New Writing* authors, both British and foreign, we also intend in due course to print other original contributions and not least by young and unknown authors: we hope no budding poet or story-writer who feels that our pages are just the right place for his first efforts will hide his light under a bushel.'

Fanfarlo was the name adopted by George Stonier, a contributor to the *New Statesman*; knowing him personally, I felt that he had more in him than his work for that weekly had yet shown: a strain of wit and fantasy to which I encouraged him to give full scope in the light-hearted series which we decided to call 'Shaving Through the Blitz'. Fanfarlo's identity was a closely kept secret which few guessed even after he disappeared, to reappear as Joseph Gurnard. Not so Robert Pagan, in whose contributions a number of readers very soon spotted the highly individual style and tone of voice of William Plomer: he had chosen a pseudonym because he had become a temporary civil servant working in the Admiralty, and wanted to have the freedom to poke fun when occasion arose at the solemnities and eccentricities of the war bureaucracy. I don't think more than two or three of his intimates in the Department knew of his double life, and they kept very mum.

The new monthly's immediate success ran into difficulties at once; partly financial, partly due to the war. More money was needed on the editorial side, as the flood of manuscripts offered to us steadily mounted. All had to be stored, sifted, carefully read and, if rejected – and that was the inevitable fate of most of them – sent back with as kindly a note as possible. Cupboards, drawers, suitcases bulged with them; postal costs swelled week by week; new auxiliary readers had to be enrolled – and paid. It was soon clear that the advances originally promised me by Penguin Books were going to dwindle to vanishing point and leave nothing for the editor himself. Still in the most buoyant of moods, Lane was not difficult to convince of the need for further finance.

But finding money was by no means the only problem. We were not far into the New Year before the full extent of the damage caused by the blitz to production in Britain became starkly apparent. Printing works were not spared; and as Allen Lane had a great many books beside *Penguin New Writing* to look after, we had to take our turn, though I fought hard for at least a semi-priority. The other problem was harder to resolve. Paper rationing had begun to bite; warning letters arrived from Harmondsworth; and I remember a night on Home Guard duty during which I rehearsed all the arguments I could muster for a crucial meeting with Lane on the morrow, while the anti-aircraft guns banged away all down the valley. In the end I came away with at least a partial victory. Five tons of paper a month – roughly the whole of the ration of the Hogarth Press for a year – was allocated to *Penguin New Writing*, which it was estimated would produce about 75,000 copies of each number.

As everybody knows, the blitz did not let up until May 1941, when Hitler turned all his forces against the Soviet Union. The delays from the printing works became more important than the paper ration. Impatient clamour from the addicts grew louder, but the gap between the appearance of the still ostensibly monthly numbers steadily widened, until, after No. 12, we took the only sensible course open to us, and decided to call *Penguin New Writing* what it had in fact become – a quarterly. But as its popularity had not decreased, and the first nine numbers were already impossible to obtain except in remote bookshops where the odd copy still lingered, we decided to compensate to some extent by increasing its scope. Each volume, to begin with, was to be slightly larger; more important, new features were to be introduced. First of all, a series of articles by recognized experts, but writing anonymously, on wartime developments in Britain in theatre, ballet and cinema. And further, to support these, a regular supplement of photogravure illustrations was to appear in each number, a development in which we also felt we had got one ahead of our friendly rival, *Horizon*, which still managed to keep (more or less) to its monthly time-table. We had found that the critical articles on books were extremely popular, and so we enlarged that feature to include three or four articles in each number, one of which was 'A Reader's Notebook', to give space for comment on current literary developments that I thought would be of special interest to *PNW*'s readers. The writer called himself Jack Marlowe (who was in fact myself). Finally, we abolished the series 'The Way We Live Now' and started in its place 'The Report on Today', to give room for more of those topical reflections and sketches which were coming to us in increasing numbers, and were more and more often distinctly a cut above the ordinary reportage of wartime experience. In the first three quarterly numbers, for instance, we printed *The Sky Makes Me Hate It* by William Chappell, in peace time a ballet dancer and stage-designer; Christopher Isherwood's account of his experiences with Quaker pacifists in a seminar at La Verne; Henry Green's luridly brilliant description of a fire-fighting experience, *Mr Jonas*; and *Y List*, a highly characteristic piece, reportage on the edge of fiction, by a new writer, Julian Maclaren-Ross.

These new features went down very well, or so it seemed from the letters that came in from all over the world where English-speaking soldiers, sailors and airmen were fighting the war. The airgraph had been invented, and half our correspondence consisted of these little photographs which arrived much faster than any other form of communication could have in war conditions, but with odd irregularity, so that, for example, the end of a poem from East Africa arrived before its beginning. We were being read in remote camps in the jungles of Asia; Auden and Spender were being discussed in the fo'c'sles of warships protecting the convoys to the Arctic; and gradually the little volumes, passed from hand to hand in fighter pilots' messes or from bunk to bunk, disintegrated, soaked in machine-oil or salt water. The illustrations of new ballets and theatrical productions in London went down particularly well, I thought, keeping the nostalgic wearers of battledress and bell-bottoms in touch with the faraway world of the living arts they were missing so much. By a curious and fruitful chance, I was soon able to add contemporary painting and drawing to ballet, theatre and film. A man I had not heard of before sent me in a sketch he had written of unloading the wounded from a Red Cross train. As soon as I started to read it I was deeply struck by the quiet compassion it expressed and the seemingly experienced use of words it revealed. I wrote at once to the author and asked him to tell me about himself. I was intrigued to learn that he thought of himself rather as an artist than as a writer: he enclosed some sepia drawings he had made of army life, which have haunted me ever since. His name was Keith Vaughan; and through him I was eventually put in touch with that group of artists, now called neo-romantics, and including John Minton, Leonard Rosoman, John Craxton and Michael Ayrton, who are all so highly prized today.

While 1943 moved into 1944, and the gaps between even the quarterlies increased, owing to the ravages of the call-up in the already sufficiently ravaged printing works, we did our best not to let *PNW* stagnate but introduced more new features and adapted old features to the always changing situation. As the months went by we found that the number of publishable poems we had accepted was steadily increasing, and we therefore started a series of occasional poetry supplements. The number of contributions in each issue reprinted from the hardback volumes dwindled to two or three; we added Radio Critic and Music Critic to the other critics; and included portraits of authors in the photogravure illustrations. And finally, as 1945 arrived with peace, colour reproductions began to be included with the photogravure.

But peace, and the slow lifting of restrictions, also brought its problems as well as opportunity and relief. Gradually more new books were being produced, more reprinted; while more opportunities arose for spending one's money on travel and cars and other leisure pursuits. The boom in books and periodicals began to fade; the circulation of *Penguin New Writing* began to fall off. We decided to call it a day in 1950, and in my Foreword to No. 40, I said farewell. 'For a magazine carrying no advertising, the steady increase in costs and the post-war decline in all periodical sales has been too severe a test. Though its circulation is still remarkably high for a publication exclusively devoted to literature and the arts, it is not high enough to make both ends meet.' I concluded my nostalgic valedictory remarks with the following paragraph: 'Finally, we make a bow of thanks to our most faithful readers, still to be numbered in thousands; one to our faithful contributors, promising poems and stories even before their conception and providing articles just in time in the most trying circumstances; one to the discerning enthusiasts who have not ceased to spread a tale of our virtues and one to the unwearying objectors who always found time to excoriate our faults; one to the great organization of Allen Lane's Penguin Books, who took our bundle of scored typescripts, drawings and photographs forty times, and each time turned it into a neat little book with a bright cover; and the deepest one of all to our patient editorial assistants and advisers among whom we have been honoured to number at various times Virginia Woolf, E. M. Forster, Rosamond Lehmann, Christopher Isherwood, Stephen Spender, Demetrios Capetanakis and Keith Vaughan, and all the time of nine years, Barbara Cooper.'

John Lehmann

Select Biographical Glossary

GEORG ANDERS was the pen-name of Jura Soyfer, an Austrian writer who died in a concentration camp in Germany just before the war. *Song of the Austrians in Dachau* was memorized by one of his fellow prisoners when about to be released and so was brought out of the camp. Soyfer's plays subsequently became famous in Austria.

EARLE BIRNEY was born in Canada in 1904. He served in the Canadian Army overseas from 1942 to 1945, and has since become well known in Canada as a poet, short-story writer and teacher of English in Canadian universities. He now lives in Toronto.

NORMAN CAMERON, born in 1905, was a poet and translator of Rimbaud, Villon, Voltaire and other French writers. He died in 1953.

DEMETRIOS CAPETANAKIS, a Greek poet and philosophical writer born in Smyrna in 1912, came to England in 1939 and died in Westminster Hospital in 1944. During those years he wrote poems and critical studies in English.

LOUIS CLAMORGAN was the pen-name of a French writer, author of several novels, who served with the Free French Navy during the war and was killed in action at the age of twenty-five.

JOHN CORNFORD, born in 1915, took a leading part in left-wing politics in Cambridge in the Thirties. He died in the Spanish Civil War in 1936.

DENIS GLOVER was born in 1912 in New Zealand where, in 1936, he founded the Caxton Press and published much important New Zealand writing. During the war he served in the Royal Navy. He died in 1980.

J. C. HALL was born in London in 1920. As a result of the essay reprinted here he met Edwin Muir and later edited his *Collected Poems*. Hall's own *Selected Poems 1939–84* has recently been published. He lives in London and works in publishing.

DENYS L. JONES was born in 1916 in Cardiff. After serving in the army during the war he went into teaching, from which he has recently retired. He is a poet and author of two novels, both about Africa: *Look Not Upon Me* and *Hand of the Wind*.

JULIAN MACLAREN-ROSS, a prolific short-story writer, novelist, radio playwright and film scriptwriter, was born in London in 1912 and died in 1964. His *Memoirs of the Forties* has recently been reissued.

R. D. MARSHALL, born in 1917, was twice wounded in the desert, and wrote this story in convalescence after losing an arm.

J. E. MORPURGO, born in 1918, served in the Far East, the Middle East and Europe as an officer in the R.A. After the war he joined the staff of Penguin Books where he was editor of the Penguin history series and of *Penguin Parade*. He has also been director-general of the National Book League and latterly Emeritus Professor of American literature at the University of Leeds. He is the author of books on a variety of subjects, including a biography of Allen Lane.

JIŘÍ MUCHA, son of the Czech artist Alphonse Mucha, was born in Prague in 1916. He came to England during the war as a member of the Free Czech Forces, and has since published several novels and short stories. He now lives in Prague.

DOUGLAS NEWTON was born in 1920 in the Malay States, came to England in 1927 and had four years of land work during the war. He has been co-editor of two anthologies, and has published poems and criticism in various English and American periodicals.

YURI OLYESHA, born in 1899 in Elizabetgrad (Kirova), was one of the most original Russian writers of his generation. He later fell foul of the Russian authorities.

J. F. POWERS, born in 1917, is one of the most distinguished of American short-story writers. His collection of stories *Prince of Darkness* was published in England in 1948.

ALAN ROSS was born in Calcutta and educated at St John's College, Oxford. Editor of the *London Magazine* since 1961, he is the author of several volumes of poetry, a biography of the cricketer Ranji and a study of Second World War art, *Colours of War*.

WILLIAM SANSOM was born in London in 1912. A short-story writer and novelist, he was also a night-club pianist and at one time a director of radio programmes. He died in 1976.

FRANK SARGESON was born in Hamilton, New Zealand, in 1903. Though he qualified as a solicitor and spent brief periods working as a market gardener, milkman and journalist, he devoted most of his time to writing novels and short stories, a collection of which has recently been published. He died in 1982.

IAIN SCOTT-KILVERT was born in 1917. He served during the war in the Intelligence Corps in the Middle East and in Greece. He was director of the Literature Department of the British Council from 1962 to 1977 and is general editor of the *Writers and Their Work* series to which he contributed studies on A. E. Housman and John Webster. He has translated three volumes of Plutarch's *Lives* for the Penguin Classics and also Polybius' *The Rise of the Roman Empire* and Dio Cassius' *The Reign of Augustus*.

E. J. SCOVELL was born in Sheffield in 1907, has lived in Oxford since 1939 and is married to the ecologist Charles Elton. She has published four collections of poetry, the latest, *The Space Between*, in 1982.

JOHN SOMMERFIELD was born in 1908. He was in the International Brigade in the Spanish Civil War and served in the R.A.F. during the Second World War. He has been a film scriptwriter and has written eight novels and many short stories. He now lives in Oxford.

GEORGE STONIER, born in 1903, was a regular contributor to the *New Statesman* from 1925 to 1963, first as assistant literary editor and later as film reviewer under the name 'Whitebait'. In 1968 he left England to live in Rhodesia where he died in 1985.

JOHN SHORT was born in Westmorland, a county which provided the setting for his volume of poetry, *The Oak and the Ash*, published in 1947. During the war he served in the army and later was engaged in adult education.

ONE

THE PANORAMA OF WAR

JOHN SOMMERFIELD

THE WAY WE LIVE NOW

Everpresent and unheard is the voice of aero engines. From a distance
the drome sounds like a zoo of hungry animals, loud with confused
roarings and growlings.

There are many hangars, huge, dark within, their echoing gloom
broken by pools of bluish light, in which bathe the sleek forms of
aircraft. They crowd close together, and give out a peculiar smell,
sweetish and oily, like the breath of cattle mingled with exhalations of
machinery.

Here planes are dismantled and overhauled. Little fighters, with
fish-shaped bodies, have their sides laid open, disclosing elegant and
complex silvery bones. Multi-coloured electric cables branch and
ramify like a nervous system amongst the bewildering confusion of
tightly packed metallic entrails. The oily fingers of mechanics delve
into these intricacies, removing them part by part. And when each part
is opened up and dissected nothing remains but a jigsaw collection of
accurately-shaped fragments, a jigsaw in three dimensions that somehow comes to life when fitted together. Tenderly, intently, surgeons
operating with spanners, the mechanics replace each reassembled
organ into the plane's body-cavities, put back the dural skin, and
make ready for the moment of re-awakening. The cylinders inhale
petrol breaths, the propellers turn, oil circulates through copper
arteries, wires are charged with nervous energy, and a powerful
creature roars with a hungry voice, moves, and flies. (The pilot
socketed into his tiny cockpit, hands and feet fitted to controls, eyes
linked with dials and gauges, seems only the final piece that completes
the puzzle.)

These are first impressions. You forget them. Aircraft that infest the
sky by day become as unremarkable as traffic passing outside a house
in which you have lived for years. Your nose grows accustomed to the
strange vegetable smell of aviation spirit that cloys the air like a jungle
scent. The war and flying go on all the time, forgotten reasons for our
presence here.

*

A wide plain of mud, streaked with concrete roads, dotted with camouflaged huts and workshops, is the setting for our jobs. The mud is toffee-coloured, with the texture of lumpy porridge. Gumbooted, in once-blue dungarees, we wade, heads down into the wind, the damp and gusty wind that blows for three days out of four. On the shoulders of the tunics beneath our overalls are twin eagle's wings. We are aircraftsmen, general duties, the unskilled labour of the Air Force.

Our objective is a bomb dump, beside which stands a muddy lorry. The bombs – five-hundred pounders – are stacked in neat piles, their blunt, destructive shapes painted a brownish yellow. When we reach them we stand staring, as if it was the first time we had ever seen such things. But it is only a few weeks since we built the dump. Now we have to take it down and rebuild it two hundred yards away. Why? No one seems to know. No one cares. No one is ever surprised. Things like this often happen to us.

The late, wintry dawn is breaking. A huge sky, pink as tinned salmon, arches over the wind-blown waste of the flying field. And we stand and shiver, indifferent to the threatening glories of the sunrise, until our corporal says half-heartedly, 'Come along, lads, time we got a start on.'

No one moves for a little. Then Tich languidly extends his large hard hand and rests it on one of the bombs. The metal is damp with icy dew, repulsive to the touch, and Tich snatches his arm away.

'Come on,' says the corporal in a sleepy voice. 'We can't stand here all day.' At this some begin to move away, looking as if they had just remembered something important that had to be done. The corporal gets into the driving cab of the lorry, produces yesterday's *Daily Mirror*, and goes to sleep behind it. Eventually, because it is even more unpleasant to stand about doing nothing than to work, four of us lay hold of one of the bombs and lift it. It is smooth, very slippery, very cold, and horribly heavy. It wrenches our numb fingers, and as we slip and stagger in the porridgy mud our arms feel as if they were being dislocated. A final agonized heave lands the bomb with a crash in the lorry, splintering one of the floor boards. The driver bounces out, cursing.

'Get stuffed,' says Taff. 'Get knotted,' he adds. The conversation proceeds on well worn lines.

Six times we agonize across the mud with the bombs. Six is a lorry load. Our noses drip, eyes water in the wind, numb hands turn blue under coats of freezing mud. The interval between each journey is long. No one cares to be the first to lay hold of the next bomb, so each stands ruminatively shivering, waiting for someone else to take the initiative.

The pink has faded from the sky, which is now a uniform grey. 'Going to rain,' says one. ''Course it's going to rain,' says Tich. 'Y'oughter 'ave enough sense to know it always —— well rains when we're —— bomb dumping!'

When the lorry starts its wheels whizz round impotently, scattering brownish spray into our faces. The corporal, rubbing his eyes, leans out of the cab and urges us to shove.

We shove. More mud-splashing, more slipping and panting and straining, to the accompaniment of a monotonous recitation of obscenities, uttered without meaning or conviction.

Suddenly we stop shoving, put hands in pockets and stare at the lorry, intently, despondently, just as we stand and stare at the bomb dump each time we return to it, as if we were waiting for some word to be uttered, some move to be made, that will deliver us from responsibility.

No one says anything for a little. The morning roar of aero engines enfolds us like silence. 'I'm browned off,' announces Taff. 'I'm cheesed.' He walks away and relieves himself against a bomb.

The lorry wheels buzz round again in a frantic spasm of activity that, surprisingly, sends it skittering off under its own power. We follow, wading deliberately.

Later a fine, cold drizzle sets in. One sings 'A little rain must fall'. 'The hell it must,' says another.

'Why don't Jerry come over and drop a load on the dump?' says Tich. 'Think of the trouble it'd save.'

'Fix your bloody constipation it would, man,' says Taff.

'Fix it for good and all.'

Leaning against the lorry, passively suffering the unremitting rain, we debate with gloomy bawdiness the favourite themes of death and excretion.

'D'you remember,' says Sam. 'D'you remember the raid when we first came here . . .'

A falling bomb makes a tearing noise, the sound of a great sheet of air being ripped through, and then there's the crash, the explosion flowering into smoke shapes that drift up and away from a smashed building. The crash and smoke and destruction is the purpose intended for these yellow iron shapes that we curse and carry. We forget it, think only of the weight, cold and mud and aching limbs, and how long it is to knocking off time. The bombs that fall on the towns where we were born were also thus. But we don't think about it. Now the chaps talk of afterwards, of when the war is over. 'I've had enough,' says Taff. 'I've had e-bloody-nough. No more hard graft for me. A rich cow I'll find, and —— for a living.'

'There's a good job waiting for me,' says Tich.

'There's plenty who said that last time, and got the —— dole.'

'What's wrong with dole, anyway? Better than this.'

'I'll be O K,' says Tich. 'I'm in the building trade. Tiler and slater, that's me. Plenty of graft for us afterwards.'

'I'd bloody steal,' says Taff. 'Any bloody thing.'

'There's one thing certain. It won't go back to being the same.'

'I don't see why not . . .'

Silence. Rain. Flying has stopped. You can hear the sigh of the wet wind. The chaps' faces have unfrozen, are reflective, human. Thinking what? Of afterwards, homes and wives, lit streets and shop windows, football matches, jobs, Sunday mornings in bed, the pains and pleasures of domesticity? Or of ruined towns, the difficulties of earning a living, and the end of irresponsibility?

The corporal reappears. (He had been to get a cup of tea in the canteen; we know this, but he doesn't know that we know it.) 'Scrounging!' he says indignantly. 'It's always the bloody same. Soon as my back's turned you all begin to scrounge.' No one says anything. He sees the look on our faces and changes the subject. 'Now come on,' he says. 'You can knock off when you've done three more loads. So get cracking.'

Something rather odd happens now. We really do get cracking. The work goes with a swing. Song scraps are shouted, we laugh, joke, despise rain, wind and cold. A warm current of friendship bears us along and unites us, a wonderful feeling of comradeship and freedom. It is a mood distilled from hardship and lack of responsibility, boredom and shortage of women, the mood that makes men sentimentalize about their war experiences. It's a fine mood, and while it lasts we don't give a —— for anything or anybody.

At night things are different. Limitless seems the flying field, a formless blackness in which swim long, unthreaded necklaces of little red and yellow lights. The drone of bombers warming up sounds menacing out of invisibility. Coming out of the village pubs you can hear them in the distance, and the bar-room mood is blurred.

For us, in the night, there are guard duties. We patrol in twos, with rifles, bayonets, tin hats, and cartridges slung round us. At first the bitterness of being torn from the warm oblivion of sleep renders us speechless. Gradually the cold night air dissolves away the stickiness of our fatigue, and we talk. This is the time when we talk of girls, of leave, of home, in voices that are low and confidential. Each is really speaking to himself, reminding himself of dreams, longings, memories, that are made more real by being uttered aloud, even though they are only hinted at, by indirect allusions. Of food we speak, of peace-time luxuries that, being no longer attainable, have become the symbols of our nostalgia.

Thus, soliloquizing to one another, we pace up and down the edge of the flying field, occasionally halting and challenging figures that loom anonymously in the darkness.

One by one the bombers taxi into position for the take-off, darting out long, narrow beams of bluish light that wheel through wide arcs of misty air, sometimes shooting clear of the ground altogether and grazing the mottled camouflage of hangars and workshop buildings, then swinging across the field and throwing into abrupt violent relief the irrelevant shapes of petrol wagons or the figures of men walking steadily through a bluish nothingness.

Then, roaring hungrily, pale flames spouting from red-hot exhausts, the bombers leave, black shapes vanishing into blackness. (Seen near at hand the exhaust flames have a strange beauty. They are like great, luminous flower buds, whose delicate lilac petals enfold a glowing, incandescent core.)

After the cold darkness and the impersonal austerities of night flying, the guardroom seems another world, its air confined, smelling of sweat, tobacco and sleep, its sounds of low voices and men breathing. Fully clothed we lie down on the straw palliasses, and abandon ourselves to the stealthy onrush of our fatigue. Outside the wind rubs itself against the wooden walls of the hut. Someone snores. Another mutters to himself. This short sleep is precious. Waking and stumbling bad-temperedly out to patrol again we yearn for its prolongation.

The bombers are returning. First each is visible as a little moving constellation of coloured lights (red, green and yellow, with the tiny pulsing glow of the exhaust flames showing faintly pink). The remote engine roar grows louder and more distinct. Then the stars wheel, begin to dip, and suddenly, dramatically, the landing lights flash out, twin rods of icy brilliance stabbing down from the sky to earth. Engines cough, splutter a few times, and cut out. The last act of the descent is accomplished in silence, a hovering glide whose apparent hesitancy and slowness is denied by the steady swooping onrush of landing lights across the ground. Wheels skim the tops of the tallest grasses for a moment, and then the plane is no longer flying; engines lift their voices in a final triumphant roar, and the flight is over.

'Half-past four,' says my mate, who keeps looking at his wrist-watch. 'Hour and a half to go yet.' It is another day already, but the long night still stretches far ahead of us.

[*PNW* 4, 1941]

FANFARLO

SHAVING THROUGH THE BLITZ

The guns have started almost at once. Down we shuffle, grim and gay, into our cellar. It is very tiny, with a low ceiling which makes us walk like mourners. 'Poop! poop!' whispers Mr Stevens at my back. He never fails to warm up in this way; Mrs Stevens tells me that all through the years of peace he was poop-pooping to keep life going. 'Don't, dear,' says Mrs Stevens, 'you encourage them.' 'Poop, poop!' repeats her husband aloud and this time in reply there's a wail, piercingly close.

We halt.

'Good God!' says Jimmy, 'it's coming.'

Mrs Greenbaum gasps wheezily, Mr and Mrs Stevens hold hands, Mary presses against the wall, I remain stiffly where I am, with one foot advanced, as though caught by the camera.

But Lizzie has pounced in the darkness. 'Little Skinny!' she exclaims. 'And has he been here all alone, waiting for the horrid Nazis to begin! Has he been wondering if they'd forgotten him! What's the matter, tell Aunty!'

We relax. We continue our march. Little Skinny is a Blitz orphan, whose mother ran away to join the Wrens and whose father is a City fireman. His alphabet begins with Anti-Aircraft Guns and leaves off somewhere about S with Spitfires; he is a nervous child except where raids are concerned. We had forgotten about little Skinny.

He goggles at us balefully in the lamplight. 'Wanter grow up and go and live in a big shelter! Ow!'

'So you shall, ducky, in good time. The war isn't over yet.'

We grope about feebly. There are seven of us, eight counting the orphan. Two-thirds of a mattress, built up with rugs and blankets, is the allotment of each. Only Mrs Greenbaum has a mattress to herself.

'Mrs Stevens,' says Lizzie decidedly, 'you go there, with Mr Stevens of course, and next to Mrs Greenbaum, who finds you such a comfort. Mary, you stay by the boiler, and tell me if it wants anything; and you can take out little Skinny too when he asks, he's sure to have forgotten. Jimmy, you'd better come over here with Bob and me. Now let's close up a little so that we can all get in. Oh Bob, don't stand about like that pretending there's only standing room. You needn't be depressing.'

For a while we crawl over one another like kittens, then the general flux ceases, to be replaced by individual movements as we settle in.

'Wanter hear the guns!'

Little Skinny's voice has become drowsier, contented. There is a moment's hush while he is held up to listen to the guns. 'Is that the Barker?' he insists, 'the big new naval gun?'

'Poop! poop!' says Mr Stevens approvingly. 'Now you can go to sleep like a good boy.'

My evening meal (this begins to nag at me) has consisted of two slices of ginger-cake. But I have swallowed a capsule containing Vitamins A, B_1, B_2, C and D, and this has changed a crumby snack into a dish of fresh fruit and vegetables.

Theoretically, that is sound. Still, I feel I have missed something, something more than a little roughage. It has been one of those days when my inattention has fed the rapacity of others. I have left an almost full packet of cigarettes on a park seat, where perhaps in the black-out it still is; that is not the sort of gift one remembers with pleasure. When I came home Jimmy had already finished the kedgeree. I shouldn't have been surprised, because I know how Jimmy gets carried away by what he is eating, and probably he thought that he had carte-blanche; but expecting kedgeree and finding ginger-cake, I naturally felt cheated.

Now that I come to think of it I didn't have any lunch either. When Lizzie produces the paste sandwiches and tea from the thermos at eleven, I shall swallow a second capsule.

The rumours of gas (Mrs Greenbaum has just found another on her back page) are disturbing. Our cellar isn't meant to protect against gas, but against splinters. It is the worst possible place in the house for gas. We almost need oxygen as it is.

However, no one takes gas quite seriously, possibly because gas-masks are so awkward to carry round. Invasion is much more in the air. When the moon and the tides are right, and the papers report calm weather in the Straits, one expects the invader from hour to hour. On Sunday mornings it seems almost a certainty. Why aren't they here? When will the bells ring out? But you open the papers, and Mme Tabouis says, 'No, not this week; Hitler must wait till next.'

On the French coast the Invasion has gone into rehearsal as usual. The barges that have put out in the early hours turn back and make a dawn landing. Aeroplanes tow trains of gliders. Parachutists drop into villages and then walk on as if nothing had happened. Officers practise reading *Punch* and ordering whiskies and sodas, while in fog-filled rooms sit the shock-troops, who for days have fed on nothing but poached eggs and tea and lukewarm stew.

All the details of infiltration and penetration, I am told, have been worked out. There are to be innumerable Boy Scouts picked for their rosy looks, whose presence in woods and on commons will not attract attention. Other units include a scarlet-coated Hunt, for wrecking activities in the shires, and travelling theatrical companies which will stick up bills announcing the arrival of *Chu Chin Chow*. In addition, of course, there will be the main contingent of clerks, tube-squatters, soldiers, modistes, unemployed, road-hogs, policemen, etc., whom one expects to see in ordinary times.

The idea that the Nazis will make things easy by all being British soldiers is, I hold, dangerously wrong. Mr Stevens takes the narrow, the military, view. But what is the use of arguing from 1914, when this is 1941?

Today's invasion odds, says Jimmy, are 15–7 against. But this price may be expected to shorten before the week-end.

Jimmy, it seems, is a mass-observer.

'Do tell us,' says Lizzie, clasping her knees, 'what do you do exactly? Follow people?'

'We're scientists, not 'tecs,' retorts Jimmy. 'People have to be taught how they think and behave. I bet no one here knows which boot they put on first or how many puffs they take to a cigarette! That's the sort of thing we're after.'

We look at one another suspiciously. We begin to see ourselves, for a moment, as others see us.

Jimmy's outlook has quite changed since his conversion. Nothing, now, he says, is irrelevant. All men are equally interesting. He even prefers bad books to good ones, because they are more typical. He goes a lot to pubs, as he always did, but now – like a bird-watcher in a swamp – it is with the object of investigating Drinking Habits. 'You can't imagine what it's like to come back after a good day's hunting, to sit down, still in your field-clothes and the heat of the chase, and make out your report.'

'It sounds fun,' agrees Lizzie doubtfully.

Today he has been listening to Invasion Talk. He taps the notebook in his pocket, and gives me a meaning glance.

When the Day comes, he hopes to be one of the intrepid interviewers whose task it will be to cross-examine parachutists when they land. He will ask some searching questions. Among other things: (7) Is this your first visit to England? (8) Do you carry a picture of the Führer? (98) Do you approve of: mirrors, all-in wrestling, jazz, polygyny, hot or cold baths?

Mr Stevens glares at Jimmy with the fury of a Home-Guardsman bilked.

'There is a new world,' concludes Jimmy, 'of which most people aren't neatly enough aware. We are building up a conscious humanity. We are the shock-troops of civilization . . . While we've been talking I've noticed here a pronounced agoraphobia.'

A hurricane lamp hangs from a nail. Looking round in the phossy light one gets the impression of an opium den, without the opium.

Now and then a sleeper stirs and grumbles incomprehensibly. Morpheus gently tortures his prisoners, tickling noses and soles of feet, twisting an arm here – 'Ah, ah!' – inducing a victim there to raise himself, only to find that he is bound fast.

To some extent, through sleeping here night after night, I share their dreams. Mrs Greenbaum is the most persistent dreamer. At one time she seems to have been concerned with moving house in Poland, and when she wags her head from side to side, and struggles to speak, it is almost certain that the piano has stuck again while being lowered from the window in the snow. 'It'll never manage,' she gasps; and it never does, for at that moment inevitably she wakes. Oh what? Where? Ah, dear me, oh dear! She groans, she frets, she flutters her fingers, then her breathing irons out and she's off again, this time into regions where, even if I wished, I cannot follow.

The moon's up, and I rise to the surface to see how things are going. I must say my local patriotism rises too. Herpes Street in the moonlight looks magnificent.

I call to the others. Instead of Lizzie, as I expect, wearing her Finnish hood, or Mr Stevens sucking at a pipe, Mrs Greenbaum lumbers up.

'It's so quiet, I don't understand,' she complains. Then, 'What you doing, looking at the stars? I wonder is there anything in that – the stars, I mean, and influencing people?'

'There are many strange influences, Mrs Greenbaum. I wonder what makes some people like cats –'

'That's what I say!' (She makes a gesture of sweeping things off a table.) 'I used to say to my husband – he was a socialist, you understand – well, we don't know what influences there may be, and certainly those astrologers are very wise fellers. They foretold the war, didn't they? And isn't Hitler himself an astrologer?'

'Almost. At least they say he employs one.'

'There you are! And if he's ruled by the stars, a man like him, what chance have you and I got? I went to a lady friend of mine who does charts, and she told me some funny things. Mind you, I'm not believing all those things. But blue's my unlucky colour, she said, and the night we had the landmine I was wearing blue. Then she told me I'm an Arian – born under Aries that is – and my good shopping days, and warned me against walking near gasworks on a Friday. That's not so easy when you live next to one, but perhaps she only meant not to *walk*, so Fridays I stay at home. Oh, and she told me a heap of things, things I nearly didn't know had happened myself. And she kept saying, It's not me, it's the stars. Do you know the stars, Mr F?'

'Only by sight, Mrs Greenbaum, I'm afraid.'

Jimmy steps into the moonlight beside us.

Jimmy: 'Hullo, spotted something?'

Fanfarlo: 'We were looking at the stars. Mrs Greenbaum and I were just discussing astrology.'

Jimmy: 'Piffle.'

He walks across the road into the shadow, whistling.

Mrs Greenbaum: 'He's rather hasty, that young feller. What did he say he was, when he was telling us?'

Fanfarlo: 'A mass-observer.'

Mrs Greenbaum: 'That's bad. Can't you break him of it? My little nephew was a terrible mass-observer, too, before he got married. There's the planes again, we better be going back.'

At the height of the raid, with Mr Stevens poop-pooping like mad and everyone being very brave, there is a clatter and a rattle of glass.

'We've been hit,' exclaims Lizzie. Jimmy and I go to look. We climb three flights of stairs and then a ladder jutting through a black square into the loft. We crawl from joist to joist; one false move and our knees would be through the plaster. There are a couple of holes in the roof, and after feeling our way round we find half a brick and a lump of weedy clay. These trophies are borne down.

'Did they come all this way to drop that?' asks Mrs Stevens. 'Do you suppose it's poisoned?'

Mr Stevens: 'Don't be stupid, Ada. This is debris, part of someone's garden.'

Whose garden? we wonder for an instant, then sigh thankfully because it isn't ours.

But Lizzie is dissatisfied. *Go and try again,* her eyes signal, while she says something off-hand about incendiaries and time-bombs.

So I trudge upstairs, this time taking with me Mr Stevens, who flashes a torch round the webby rafters. 'Ah!' He darts forward; but it is only an empty paint-pot, with a cutlet-bone inside. Mr Stevens seems puzzled, and looks from the paint-pot to me and finally at the cutlet-bone, but such things should be taken for granted. One of the holes in the roof is just large enough for me to poke my head out. Millions of stars, thousands of constellations? And among them – but where, I wonder? – Mrs Greenbaum's Aries.

[*PNW* 5, 1941]

GRAHAM GREENE

MEN AT WORK*

Richard Skate had taken a couple of hours away from the Ministry to see whether his house was still standing after the previous night's raid. He was a thin, pale, hungry-looking man of early middle-age. All his life had been spent in keeping his nose above water, lecturing at night-schools and acting as temporary English master at some of the smaller public schools, and in the process he had acquired a small house, a wife and one child – a rather precocious girl with a talent for painting who despised him. They lived in the country, his house was cut off from him by the immeasurable distances of bombed London – he visited it hurriedly twice a week, and his whole world was now the Ministry, the high heartless building with complicated lifts and long passages like those of a liner and lavatories where the water never ran hot and the nailbrushes were chained like Bibles. Central heating gave it the stuffy smell of mid-Atlantic except in the passages where the windows were always open for fear of blast and the cold winds whistled in. One expected to see people wrapped in rugs lying in deck-chairs, and the messengers carried round minutes like soup. Skate slept downstairs in the basement on a camp-bed, emerging at about ten o'clock for breakfast, and these imprisoned weeks were beginning to give him the appearance of a pit-pony – a purblind air as of something that lived underground. The Establishments branch of the Ministry of Propaganda thought it wise to send a minute to the staff advising them to spend an hour or two a day in the open air, and some members did indeed reach the King's Arms at the corner. But Skate didn't drink.

And yet in spite of everything he was happy. Showing his pass at the outer gate, nodding to the Home Guard who was a specialist in early Icelandic customs, he was happy. For his nose now was well above water: he had a permanent job, he was a Civil Servant. His ambition had been to be a playwright, and one Sunday performance in St John's Wood had enabled him to register as dramatist in the Central Register,

---

* The individuals in this realistic study are purely fictitious characters.

and now that the London theatres were most of them closed, he was no longer taunted by the sight of other men's success.

He opened the door of his little dark room. It had been built of plywood in a passage, for as the huge staff of the Ministry accumulated like a kind of fungoid life – old divisions sprouting daily new sections which then broke away and became divisions and spawned in turn – the five hundred rooms of the great university block became inadequate: corners of passages were turned into rooms, and corridors disappeared overnight.

'All well?' his assistant asked: the large-breasted young woman who mothered him, bringing him cups of coffee when he looked peaky and guarding the telephone.

'Oh, yes, thanks. It's still there. A pane of glass gone, that's all.'

'A Mr Savage rang up.'

'Oh, did he? What did he want?'

'He said he'd joined the Air Force and wanted to show you his uniform.'

'Old Savage,' Skate said. 'He always was a bit wild.'

The telephone rang, and Miss Manners grasped it like an enemy.

'Yes,' she said, 'yes, R.S. is back. It's H.G.,' she explained to Skate. All the junior staff called people by initials: it was a sort of social compromise, between a Christian name and a Mr. It made telephone conversations as obscure as a cable in code.

'Hello, Graves. Yes, it's still standing. Will you be at the Book Committee? I simply haven't got any agenda. Can't you invent something?' He said to Miss Manners, 'Graves wants to know who'll be at the Committee.'

Miss Manners recited quickly down the phone, 'R.K., D.H., F.L., and B.L. says he'll be late. All right, I'll tell R.S. Good-bye.' She said to Skate, 'H.G. asks why you don't just put Report on Progress down on the agenda.'

'He will have his joke,' Skate said miserably. 'As if there ever is any progress.'

'You want your tea,' Miss Manners said. She unlocked a drawer and took out Skate's teaspoon. No teaspoons had been supplied in the Ministry after the initial loss of 6,000 in the opening months of the war, and indeed it was becoming more and more necessary to lock everything portable up. Even the blankets disappeared from the A R P shelters. Like the wreck of a German plane the place seemed to be the prey of relic-hunters, so that one could foresee the day when only the heavy Portland stone structure would remain, stripped bare, scorched by incendiaries and pitted with bullet-holes where the Home Guard unloaded their rifles.

'O dear, O dear,' Skate said, 'I must get this agenda done.' His worry was only skin deep: it was all a game played in a corner under the gigantic shadow. Propaganda was a means of passing the time: work was not done for its usefulness but for its own sake – simply as an occupation. He wrote wearily down 'The Problem of India' on the agenda.

Leaving his room Skate stood aside for an odd little procession of old men in robes, led by a mace-bearer. They passed – one of them sneezing – towards the Chancellor's Hall, like humble ghosts still carrying out the ritual of another age. They had once been kings in this place, the gigantic building had been built to house them, and now the civil servants passed up and down through their procession as though it had no more consistency than smoke. Long before he reached the room where the Book Committee sat he heard a familiar voice saying, 'What we want is a really colossal campaign . . .' It was King, of course, putting his shoulder to the war-effort: these outbreaks occurred periodically like desire. King had been an advertising man, and the need to sell something would regularly overcome him. Memories of Ovaltine and Halitosis and the Mustard Club sought an outlet all the time, until suddenly, overwhelmingly, he would begin to sell the war. The Treasury and the Stationery Office always saw to it that his great schemes came to nothing: only once, because somebody was on holiday, a King campaign had really got under way. It was when the meat ration went down to a shilling; the hoardings all over London carried a curt King message: 'DON'T GROUSE ABOUT MUTTON. WHAT'S WRONG WITH YOUR GREENS?' A ribald Labour member asked a question in Parliament, the posters were withdrawn at a cost of twenty thousand pounds, the Permanent-Secretary resigned, the Prime Minister stood by the Minister who stood by his staff ('I consider we are one of the fighting services'), and King, after being asked to resign, was instead put in charge of the Books Division of the Ministry at a higher salary. Here it was felt he could do no harm.

Skate slid in and handed round copies of the agenda unobtrusively like a maid laying napkins. He didn't bother to listen to King: something about a series of pamphlets to be distributed free to six million people really explaining what we were fighting for. 'Tell 'em what freedom means,' King said. 'Democracy. Don't use long words.'

Hill said, 'I don't think the Stationery Office . . .' Hill's thin voice

35

was always the voice of reason. He was said to be the author of the official explanation and defence of the Ministry's existence: 'A negative action may have positive results.'

On Skate's agenda was written:

1. Arising from the Minutes.
2. Pamphlet in Welsh on German labour conditions.
3. Facilities for Wilkinson to visit the A T S.
4. Objections to proposed Bone pamphlet.
5. Suggestion for a leaflet from Meat Marketing Board.
6. The Problem of India.

The list, Skate thought, looked quite impressive.

'Of course,' King went on, 'the details need working out. We've got to get the right author. Priestley or somebody. I feel there won't be any difficulty about money if we can present a really clear case. Would you look into it, Skate, and report back?'

Skate agreed. He didn't know what it was all about, but that didn't matter. A few minutes would be passed to and fro, and King's blood would cool in the process. To send a minute to anybody else in the great building and to receive a reply took at least twenty-four hours: on an urgent matter an exchange of three minutes might be got through in a week. Time outside the Ministry went at quite a different pace. Skate remembered how the minutes on who should write a 'suggested' pamphlet about the French war-effort were still circulating indecisively while Germany broke the line, passed the Somme, occupied Paris and received the delegates at Compiègne.

The committee as usual lasted about an hour – it was always, to Skate, an agreeable meeting with men from other divisions, the Religions Division, the Empire Division and so on. Sometimes they co-opted another man they thought was nice. It gave an opportunity for all sorts of interesting discussions – on books and authors and artists and plays and films. The agenda didn't really matter: it was quite easy to invent one at the last moment.

Today everybody was in a good temper: there hadn't been any bad news for a week, and as the policy of the latest Permanent-Secretary was that the Ministry should not do anything to attract attention, there was no reason to fear a purge in the immediate future. The decision, too, eased everybody's work. And there was quite a breath of the larger life in the matter of Wilkinson. Wilkinson was a very popular novelist who wanted to sound a clarion-note to women, and he had asked permission to make a special study of the A T S. Now the military authorities refused permission – nobody knew why. Speculation continued for ten minutes. Skate said he thought Wilkinson was a bad writer and King disagreed – that led to a general literary discussion: Lewis from the Empire Division, who had fought at Gallipoli during the last war, dozed uneasily.

He woke up when they got on to the Bone pamphlet. Bone had been asked to write a pamphlet about the British Empire: it was to be distributed, fifty thousand copies of it, free at public meetings. But now that it was in type, all sorts of tactless phrases were discovered by the experts. India objected to a reference to Canadian dairy-herds, and Australia objected to a phrase about Botany Bay. The Canadian authority was certain that mention of Wolfe would antagonize the French-Canadians, and the New Zealand authority felt that undue emphasis had been laid on the Australian fruit-farms. Meanwhile the public meetings had all been held, so that there was no means of distributing the pamphlet. Somebody suggested that it might be sent to America for the New York World Fair, but the American Division then demanded certain cuts in the references to the War of Independence, and by the time those had been made the World Fair had closed. Now Bone had written objecting to his own pamphlet which he said was unrecognizable.

'We could get somebody else to sign it,' Skate suggested – but that meant paying another fee, and the Treasury, Hill said, would never sanction that.

'Look here, Skate,' King said, 'you're a literary man. You write to Bone and sort of smooth things over.'

Lowndes came in then hurriedly, smelling a little of wine. He said, 'Sorry to be late. Had to lunch a man on business. Seen the news?'

'No.'

'Daylight raids again. Fifty Nazi planes shot down. They are turning on the heat. Fifteen of ours lost.'

'We must really get Bone's pamphlet out,' Hill said.

Skate suddenly, to his own surprise, said savagely, 'That'll show them,' and then sat in humble collapse as though he had been caught out in treachery.

'Well,' Hill said, 'we mustn't get rattled, Skate. Remember what the Minister said: It's our duty just to carry on our own work whatever happens.'

'Yes, I didn't mean anything.'

Without reaching a decision on the Bone pamphlet they passed on to the Meat Marketing Leaflet. Nobody was interested in this, so the matter was left in Skate's hands to report back. 'You talk to 'em,

Skate,' King said. 'Good idea. You know about these things. Might ask Priestley,' he vaguely added, and then frowned thoughtfully at that old-timer on the minutes, 'The Problem of India'. 'Need we really discuss it this week,' he said. 'There's nobody here who knows about India. Let's get in Lawrence next week.'

'Good chap, Lawrence,' Lowndes said. 'Wrote a naughty novel once called *Parsons' Pleasure*.'

'We'll co-opt him,' King said.

The Book Committee was over for another week, and since the room would be empty now until morning, Skate opened the big windows against the night's blast. Far up in a pale enormous sky little white lines, like the phosphorescent spore of snails, showed where men were going home after work.

[*PNW* 9, 1941]

KEITH VAUGHAN

THE WAY WE LIVE NOW

It was long after midnight when the train came in. Word had come through earlier that the first casualties from France were expected that evening, and we were told to stand by. Time lay heavily, dry and still over the hot afternoon. About nine we drove the ambulances down to the station and lined them up along the far siding where the cattle were usually unloaded. We prepared the stretchers and blankets, and then stood about in groups, talking and smoking cigarettes. A small crowd collected on the bridge and looked down on us, idly, to see what was going on. Traffic moved carefully about the town as the light faded. Then the searchlights went up and gleaned the last thin clouds out of the sky and went out and the crowd wandered away one by one and we were left alone with the night and the tiny points of our cigarettes pricking the darkness.

The moon was high and full and clear and the night still. We walked up and down the tracks, past cattle boxes, and looked out beyond the signals and sheds trying to distinguish the first signs of smoke against the horizon. For a long time there was nothing but the empty moonlit rails and a dull stain in the sky where the sun had set. People yawned and kicked at the rags of paper and rubbish lying about the tracks.

As soon as we forgot to think about it the train was there, a long shadow creeping quietly, carefully up the siding, avoiding hurry. The first windows slid past, overcrowded with heads like family photographs. Sparks of words caught at us out of the darkness and drew us to them. The engine closed against the buffers with a soft compressed sigh, then greetings and the click of buffers broke thunderously about our heads. Hands reached up and met hands, exchanging cigarettes, matches; faces were lit here and there in momentary smiles; questions, shouts, laughter, poured over us from the windows; but some kept silent, leaving others to speak for them, content to rest their faces against the glass and gaze out on a night miraculously free from treachery.

Further down, the carriages stood immensely high above us, steel walls without windows, the red crosses dim beneath layers of soot and dirt. We talked and waited with our attention narrowed to the paper edge of light beneath the doors; to the buried murmur and hurrying within. The doors swung back suddenly, and doused us in light, as though a portable aseptic heaven had opened in the darkness. We drew in like moths, blinking at the whiteness. Hands helped us aboard and we climbed from the night into a warm smell of wool and urine and sickly sweet flesh.

Three tiers of bunks lined the white walls, each with a face that stared out quietly and expressionless, like the eyes of an animal caught for a moment in a car's headlights. We felt strange and helpless with men remote from us in experience. Some turned to look at us, visitors out of the night, from another planet. Others were still locked in their prisons of pain, where we had no admittance. No one spoke. We drew on our stretchers and began the routine of unloading, glad of the work that would let us forget our awkwardness.

The stretchers were held up level against the bunks and the men coaxed, like animals, to brave the crossing on to their steel meshes. They dragged across those parts of their bodies they were able, the rest we carried for them, grotesque shapes of wool and splint and bandage, joined to them only by pain. Some moved suddenly and clumsily, hoping to make the journey before pain had observed their going. Others, like children impatient to shew their ability, would begin lowering themselves gleefully before we were ready, their white woolly feet swinging down everywhere from the white ceiling. As each stretcher was filled it was lowered to the floor, arranged with blankets and launched out into the sea of arms and anxious upturned faces waiting below in the darkness.

In the bunk near the door was a mild, timid youth of eighteen or nineteen with thick lenses roped to his face with black string. He was a German. His eyes followed each stretcher as it went out, a smile behind his lips ready to be released at the first hint of friendliness or recognition. 'Leave Fritzie – there's a special ambulance for him later,' an orderly said. We took the boy from the bunk above him.

He watched our approach with an open, curious gaze. He was so pale that it seemed to be only a pair of eyes that looked at us from the white pillow. When he saw we were coming for him he turned his face away quickly. A nurse came up and leant over him and whispered something in his ear and wiped his forehead with some wool. We asked him if he could ease himself across a bit. He tried and couldn't and looked miserably at us. 'It's his leg, poor laddie,' the nurse said and gave him a quick little pat and a smile. We drew back the blankets and saw that his arms finished at the wrists in two logs of yellow stained wool and bandage. His right leg was a shapeless embalment of bandage and lay supported on pillows. He worked himself across slowly on his elbows, balancing the pain precariously on his endurance while we gathered up the leg gently to bring with him. He moved a little way and then froze suddenly rigid and we lowered the leg quickly on to the pillows. He lay back a moment with closed eyes and lips trembling on despair. Then drawing together the last fibres of courage, forced himself too quickly on to the stretcher so that the leg twisted in our arms and broke open his face into silent tears. We reached for the pillows, quickly, to take the weight of the leg, but the nurse came up and told us no pillows could leave the train. We looked at her helplessly, holding the bones and flesh and bandage in our arms. 'Sorry, it's an order.' She picked up his kit-bag and neatly patted its lumpiness into place where the pillows should be, 'There, try that,' she said, her cuffs clicking with authority. Obediently we lowered the leg, knowing it was cruelty. But he had no strength to protest. Pain too long endured bent him backwards like a strung bow, fretting his face with sweat. We covered him up, miserably; there were others waiting, and he went out over the dark shoulders of the bearers into the subaqueous glow of the ambulance.

As each carriage was emptied we moved to the next, leaving the orderlies dazed with sleeplessness leaning on their brooms amidst the white ruins of bedding, and lighting up the stub ends of cigarettes. We worked on through the night, through each intimate and infinite tragedy, not noticing when it turned to day. Above the last stretcher the sky was already blue and adorned with morning. The doctors made a last round of the ambulances, checking forms, adding signatures – final instructions. The train lay behind us, a hollow, picked carcase, the whiteness of the carriages now grey and dirty in the morning light.

We started out through the town, through the early traffic. Women with perambulators stopped to gaze anxiously at the frosted mystery of our windows. News-boys shouted the morning news, the Cabinet was hopeful, the line held near Châlons – enormous losses had been inflicted on the enemy – our own casualties were not large considering the numbers involved. The drivers sweated with anxiety at each scar in the tarmac that might hold a fresh pocket of agony for the men behind. We left the town and moved on into the country; beneath the mounting sun, between fields heavy and still with the green abundance of summer.

[PNW 12, 1942]

WILLIAM CHAPPELL

THE SKY MAKES ME HATE IT

I

How do you feel after sixteen months of army life? I asked myself. Exactly how do you feel? Stop now, I said, before I could begin to answer. You were going to reply without thinking or considering. Why not? I said. I can reply without thinking and without considering; and I can give you three answers. All of them would be correct, though none of them would describe exactly how I feel. Today it is no longer possible to be exact about the way one feels.

I could say –
I feel much better, thank you,
or
I do not feel at all, thank you,
or
I feel quite differently, thank you very much.

Don't thank me, I said to myself. You are so ridiculous with words. You do not understand how to handle or present them; and you know, one does not really give question and answer in the mind. Particularly your mind, I said. Your consciousness is never consecutive. You have no real stream of thought; only a slow circular movement that changes form, and is sometimes globular, sometimes elliptical. It churns round and round; pauses and churns on. Through it, and across it, small flashing things move; passing so rapidly it is difficult to tell what shape they are.

Each one of your separate thoughts has nine hundred and ninety-nine little off-shoots, trailing inelegantly out of its small, fecund inside. One thousand births a second, each like a kitten that is drowned before it can open its staring blue eyes.

It is a miracle that you do not appear a kind of cretin to the world; making grunting sounds, lolling your head, and unable to read or spell.

Don't you quite often despair?

Yes, I said. Not so much, however, as I did during my first six months, and when I despair now it is in a different way. Of course, before the war, I did not know how to despair. My life being free, I did not have to think at all. These days I think all the time, and so deeply that I find I am paying no attention to what people are saying to me, though I can feel my face set in an expression of unreal interest as I continue to answer them. It is almost as though it were being done for me by a familiar spirit, so that I might lean back into the warm darkness of my head, and busy myself with the important work of tracking and listening to my thoughts. My mind is altering. Whether it is due to army life, or whether my mental condition is a general one, a world war-mind, I cannot decide. When I first joined the army I could understand my vague, muddled way of thinking. Now, I cannot understand it at all. I might have undergone a very delicate operation, and been given an unused brain, in which to find my way about. I have to learn to know it and to discover how it functions.

I did not alter during my first few months in the army. I could not even change, as most of the recruits did, that is, by losing weight and looking healthier. My body has always been hard and strong, and I was sunburnt all over a deep golden brown. There was nothing to affect me adversely about my surroundings. I was stationed by the coast on the edge of a town where I had friends. It was summer and the weather was hot, and when it is hot I can be more or less contented anywhere. It was later, at the beginning of the winter, when I was moved to another unit, inland, that I became rather unhappy. It was an unhappiness I could cope with, as I could see all the reasons for it. I was unhappy because I was uncomfortable, and nearly always cold; and I disliked sleeping in one hut with twenty-eight other men; and the food was ugly and unappetizing, and I was tired all the time, and had to do mathematics, which I hated.

II

It was shortly after my arrival at the new station that I began, periodically, to undergo a peculiar new mental condition in which I would suddenly feel as though I were no longer myself. I might be drilling or sitting in the crowded Naafi with people talking all round me and the piano playing; or be on guard, alone in a steely night; or just walking by day through the camp; when abruptly, inside my clothes, my body would dissolve, and harden again to a thin glass centre. My glass bones, and my glass flesh, fragile and brittle, would creep away into a central thinness, avoiding all contact with the outer shell of my clothing. My heavy boots would crash like thunder as I moved. Out of my transparent head, I would look down, and see my boots advancing, neatly, one after the other, with the toes turned in a little; but the feet beneath the polished leather had no substance, and though I could still feel the blisters on my heels, I knew that the feet inside the boots were as unsubstantial as the mists that filled the hollows of the country, and made Japanese landscapes round the camp in the early winter mornings. These strange moments occurred frequently for about six or eight months, and then gradually ceased.

III

Later, I discovered that it made me strangely sad to look at the sky. During the weeks I had spent on the coast it had never affected me deeply, though it had always been a source of pleasure to my eyes. It was there, before me. Like a stage backcloth with pretty lighting effects, it hung behind the edge of the grey horizon.

When I joined my new unit I found the sky immensely important. It dominated the landscape completely, and seemed higher and vaster than I had ever known it. I realized it as an element, aloof, distant, limpid and unsoilable; and so far removed from this small dirty world, whirling like a pebble through space, with the small dirty people balanced on it, wrangling and gesticulating with infinitesimal gestures.

I can remember how I sometimes stood at the first parade, in the still bitter air of the winter dawn, waiting for the command to fall in, changing my rifle from hand to hand to avoid its chill touch that crept through my woollen gloves and froze my fingers. I can remember standing there, shifting my numb feet, and staring down at the floor of the parade ground shaded umber and indigo and thinly sheeted with ice. After a time my reluctant eye would lift its lid of flesh, letting the sight travel forward across the frosted grass, till it climbed the edges of the squat corrugated-iron huts and mounted into the sky. There, like a seeing mouth, my eye would peer and nibble at the marbled clouds, seeking a life-vein of light, an artery that it might tear with its probing glance, to suck the gushing radiance from the new-risen sun. It hurt me to look, because I simultaneously desired and dreaded this bright food for my sight.

Now the marbled surface of the sky began to stir, and the night-drowsed men around me moved with it, breaking their muttering groups to re-form into orderly files. The sergeants shouted; a few rifle butts clattered, slipping through numb fingers, and the icy ground rang like iron.

Frozenly 'at ease' I stood, my greedy eyes fixed again on the sky, searching for the heart of the morning to stab it and gulp the life-light blood. The rosy marble cracked. Its patterns dissolved and changed, edges appeared, entrances to cool tunnels of space and beyond them, a piercing distance, now filled with light.

Break — marble paving! My heart cried out. Break? Floor of the gods. And release my sustenance. This glittering poison that I need and hate.

How high is the sky! How far! How delicate! My eyes and my heart exclaimed in thin, jangling whispers. The morning rose, bringing with it a wind that dragged the clouds apart, and as they sank into colourless wisps, drained of their rosy blood (a quota of it swallowed by my sight), a blinding radiance drowned my preying eyes. High up in the magic architecture of the heavens, a flock of starlings wheeled, competing noisily with a distant aeroplane for possession of the morning.

Oh, sweet denizens of space! Winged with speed! cried the heart. Let me into the skies. Better not to look upwards said the mind, dashed to despair by the glory above it. Drag down the feasting glance and bury it here, in this soiled and injured world that dims and swallows all exultation. I will look down and never up, for the sky makes me feel, and then I hate the earth I move on.

Nevertheless, and inevitably, the sky draws my gaze, and I cannot avoid it, for here it is spread in infinite arcs from horizon to horizon. I can watch the storms gather and break, and take their way around the edge of the distance. The looming mulberry-coloured clouds, dragging behind them trains of rain, pass slowly by, avoiding the centre where I stand. Above my head, day and night, the sky spreads its ethereal canopy, shot with colour and stained with light, patterned with star and cloud, and burnt by the rising and setting of the sun. It points all my moods, lifts up my heart, and underlines my despair.

IV

Before the war, and during my first months in the army, my thoughts streamed from me in a jerky rhythm, outwards, into the world. Now they turn inwards, probing; and I feel in my brain that an endless transformation scene is taking place. A pantomime transformation in which curtains of membrane that are patterned with my life endlessly dissolve and part. My thoughts peck and knock at things which stir somewhere behind the furthest curtains. My mind knows that there is something more than it was aware of to be found behind itself. It claws and scratches gently at the walls of its dimly-lighted caves, sensing, more than seeing, a thin music of words it has never heard before. Suspecting, more than seeing, a suggestion of forms it cannot picture, they are so distant, remote, and unknown. Perhaps, lurking there, is the enormous comprehension that humanity needs; the lack of which makes so pitiful its efforts to manage itself. To tackle decently the handling of its relationships, its loves, lifes and deaths.

This turning inwards of my thoughts cannot be happening only to me. I look avidly into the faces of the men who fill the camps and barracks in the district; the faces that crowd my sight in the streets of the town, in the pubs and restaurants and cinemas and on the buses; faces oafish, brutal, cunning, noble, sensitive and beautiful.

In the cathedral I see soldiers moving under the high arches, holding their caps in their hands, with faces solemn because they are in church. Their eyes rove, and their sight climbs from them, like birds, into the vaulted roof. They sit, too, in the back seats, beside the tall pillars, at Evensong. Sometimes praying or singing, or just resting their faces in their hands, staring quietly before them, their eyes sightless with thought, and I feel that in all their minds, whether they realize it or not, something is happening, as in mine.

No one can be genuinely happy at this time. War, as it welds the people of a nation together, makes every life an isolated life. Everyone is lonely. More lonely than they have ever been before in the life of the world. We have all become strangers; and when the war is over we shall have to start learning once more to know each other. The picture I hold, painted on my mind, of people, things and places is the pre-war picture. When I go on leave there is an air of strangeness about everything and everybody, and I cannot fully enjoy the companion-ship of my friends and my family, for our lives no longer mix. They run for a while parallel; thin, dusky-coloured streams with a narrow space between them. The mind cannot make the stupendous effort needed to bridge the gap; nor can it do anything to stop the running of the stream when it diverges from its place beside the others, and moves off quietly into a deserted country.

The life I lead in the army gives me nothing. My freedom is restricted, my privacy torn, my comfort abolished. New friendships are almost an impossibility, hardly can the first gestures be made before one or the other of the two people involved are moved away and a crowd of strange faces hem each one about. Army life lacks everything, particularly in a static unit. People do not realize it is worse for the spirit to be dreary than endangered; that boredom is more deadly than bombs.

Even in its fighting aspects, the army has none of the terrible beauty of the airman's flight to the stars and his battles in high space. None of the plunging splendour of the sailors' life in the vast steel ships that cut the spreading seas. And army death is sad: a heap of mutilated bodies, littering the scarred earth in ugly anonymity. Yet this life, that is not an individual's life, is making me more of an individual, driving my thoughts into deeper, rarer places than they have visited before. I wait for them to bring up to the surface of my consciousness the knowledge that my mind desires. Behind the self that goes about my army duties, I am occupied feverishly, searching to find this new mind that is forming somewhere within me.

I hate to think that war can do anything good for me, yet it has reached into me and made my thoughts, which were moving quietly in a known direction, turn on themselves and move another way, inwards this time, listening; and then down to my heart, whispering, at present so quietly that I cannot hear the words. It makes me restless and uncomfortable not to recognize the meaning, or the shape, of those words. I cannot tell if the other eyes I see hide the same turmoil that my calm gaze protects from the people around me. It seems to be such a very personal thing. One cannot talk of it, or explain it, even to one's friends. It has to be understood and explained by oneself to oneself.

This chaos within my head is bringing about a ruin of the brain that will eventually disclose a place where order and comprehension have always existed. The mind is being wrecked to reveal the foundations on which it can be rebuilt in clear and understandable patterns.

So I find that I accept this life. Accept the loss of my home, the collapse of my career, the bomb that injured my mother, the wide scattering and disintegration of the web of friendship I had woven so painstakingly for myself; accept it all with an equanimity that amazes me. I have always had a character chameleon-like in its capacity for adjustment to new surroundings. This is more than adjustment. It is an intense preoccupation with my innermost being that protects me from everything, without making me self-centred or egotistical in the smallest degree.

This concentrated stirring of thought continues the whole time. Above it, my life moves quietly as before. I still want the same things.

More chocolate; longer hours in bed; easily acquired hot baths; delicious, varied and delicate food; all my own possessions around me. I still do the same things. I read, and talk, and sit in the cinema watching gangsters, palm trees, machines of war, and Marlene Dietrich with equal interest. I am bothered by my feet, sick of khaki, bored and annoyed by my companions, and all the monotonous, slow, fiddle-de-dee of army life. I long for it all to be finished with, and sometimes vaguely envy those who have gone. I suffer the same desires, disappointments and frustrations as all my fellows. I wonder if they partake with me of this inward life that murmurs without cease, its busy, urgent humming, in the hidden places of the brain; and draws me at all times and between the thoughts that run my daily life, into itself?

Sometimes, at night, my mind calls halt to my thoughts and each one becomes immobilized; imprinted on the backs of my eyes as the people and objects one sees through the window of a moving train, are left in the mind's eye, struck to stone in the one gesture that was seen as the train rattled past. The child that climbs a fence and waves a hand; the long grass blown sideways by the wind; the curtain that billows from an open window; the woman in the suburban garden who lifts her arms to the washing-line; the man who pauses on the street corner to light his pipe; the horse in the field that tosses its head; and the girl who moves, bent forward a little, up the side of the hill. As they are caught and immortalized by the mind, so my surface thoughts stand still; I wait, straining my ears, longing and hoping to hear the small cry that will tell me of the birth of my new self. This self which must struggle its way up from the darkness and out of me, reaching immediately forward with clawing hands, its clear, serene, wide-open eyes, reflecting and understanding all the distance of the sky. No longer saddened, but enraptured and possessed, by those crystal heights.

[*PNW 13*, 1942]

Henry Green

Mr Jonas

Above us, in the night, as we drew up, in the barrage, the sky, from street level, seemed to be one vast corridor down which, with the speed of light, blue double wooden doors as vast were being slammed in turn. From outside the fire station, at which we were waiting to be ordered on to a particular address, that is to the next blaze on the list, we could see three fires, one of which was unattended yet.

The rain was in full swing. Already it would have been possible to read in the reddish light spread by a tall building sixty yards away, the top floors of which, with abandon, in recklessness, with fierce accept-ance had exchanged their rectangles for tiger-striped hoops, great wind-blown orange pennants, huge yellow cobra tongues of flame. Three thin, uncoloured plumes of water were being played on to the conflagration by firemen in the street. The extremities of these jets were broken into zigzags, moving up and down as the force of gravity overcame the initial pressure at the nozzle. This gave the effect of three flags of water rippling in a breeze. The plumes, when all pressure was spent, dipped weakly to those flames in a spatter of drops. It was as though three high fountains which, through sunlight, would furl their flags in rainbows as they fell dispersed, had now played these up into a howling wind to be driven, to be shattered, dispersed, no longer to fall to sweet rainbows, but into a cloud of steam rose-coloured beneath, above no wide water-lilies in a pool, but into the welter of yellow banner-streaming flames.

Accustomed, as all were, to sights of this kind, there was not one amongst us who did not now feel withdrawn into himself, as though he had come upon a place foreign to him but which he was aware he had to visit, as if it were a region the conditions in which he knew would be something between living and dying, not, that is, a web of dreams, but rather such a frontier of hopes or mostly fears as it may be in the destiny of each, or almost all, to find, betwixt coma and the giving up of living.

Violence was there in so strange a shape as to appear a lamb, and danger also, but, in the extravagance by which this was displayed, it seemed no more than a rather deadly warmth we could feel, and which, at the distance, was all that remained of that heat, which turned those fountains into steam.

The breaking pattern of rings which rain, lost in colour, can form on the surface of water, was no more likely than this other, blasted white into clouds. But the black goldfish gulping at the drops, were more conscious than firemen, unafraid, seated hands on knees, silent beneath that awful, the wide magnificence of that sight.

Not many minutes had gone by before one of our crew had criticized the way in which these three jets were being played, so far below the fire that there was no force left behind them. He said they should have been taken to a neighbouring roof from which they could be directed down in a torrent into the flames. He pointed. Looking up again, we saw the writhing mass, the pointed tongues had leapt still higher, huge sparks now flew out in showers and there was more black smoke than steam. This, as it rolled away, was coloured on the under side a darker red, the purple of a fire momentarily beyond control.

More pumps drew up. Those who manned them began, in the half dark, to look about for friends. Then, from out of the fire station, some five or six came trotting. These were the number ones, those in charge of each unit, coming back to their pumps with the address to which each had been ordered. Not able to distinguish crews quickly in this light they were calling out the numbers of their own sub-stations. It was hard to realize all the noise which was made by those pumps already at work, the roaring of the fire, and that continuous battering up above until we had noticed how difficult it was for these men to make themselves heard, shouting, as they passed, into the backs of the tenders.

When he found us our man shouted the address, then climbed in front with the driver. As we drove off, we asked each other which street he had named, but no one behind had heard. And taking, as we did, the first turn to the left, then right, we were far enough from the blaze to lose all sight of it. We did not know where we might be. We had drawn up no more than ninety yards away, but the only sign of what we had left was in the pink roofs of an office building opposite, glowing in the reflection. The noise was so much less.

We had come to a very different problem.

There was almost quietness as we got down. It was very dark. All I could see was a thick mass of smoke or steam, it was impossible to tell one from the other, surging heavy from a narrow passage. We were told to run hose out, up this alley. One man took a length, snapped the coupling in, laid out the fifty foot and went back for more, while another snapped his coupling in where the first had ended, went on, and, while he in his turn was back to get a second length, yet another went on from where the second had finished. The hose was laid without the men taking in their surroundings.

Some living things turn to the light, we went by instinct into the deepest dark. I hurried, stumbled, into this pall of smoke and steam, when suddenly, after my boots had crunched on grit, I came to the debris.

What I saw, a pile of wreckage like vast blocks of slate, the slabs of wet masonry piled high across this passage, was hidden by a fresh cloud of steam and smoke, warm, limitless dirty cotton wool, disabling in that it tight bandaged the eyes. Each billow, and steam rolls unevenly in air, islanding a man in the way that he can, to others, be isolated asleep in blankets. Nor did the light of a torch do more than make my sudden blindness visible to me in a white shine below the waist. There was nothing for it but to go on towards the voices out in front, but climbing, slipping up, while unrolling the hose, I felt that I was not a participant, that all this must have been imagined, until, in another instant, a puff of wind, perhaps something in the wreckage which was alight below the surface, left me out in the clear as though in, and among, the wet indigo reflecting planes of shattered tombs deep in a tumulus the men coughing ahead had just finished blasting.

It was impossible to work fast. The number one was shouting for that last connection, into which he could snap the nozzle, long before we could get it to him. In the struggle, with the directions we yelled at each other, the scene came real again. But when everything was laid out, and word had been sent back to turn the water on, a vault quiet fell once more as we stood waiting in smoke which came by waves, hot, acrid, making the eyes run, and bringing on a cough that hurt the lungs.

Water is never got quickly, perhaps because it seems so long to wait before the fire. This I could not see yet from the place I had reached, on top of the wreckage, beyond the steam at last but into smoke, and, as I could now realize in the intervals of sight, on a mass of rubble about fifteen foot up from the roadway. Below, to my left, a Rescue Squad was silently getting into the escape shaft of a basement shelter, climbing one by one into the earth, as it might be into the lower chamber of a tomb. On my right, the steam, which had bothered us as we climbed, was still belching out. There must have been a gas main alight beneath the debris for whitish yellow flames were coming out, as I could now see five yards away round a great corner, in darker blue, of sculptured coping stone, curved in an arc up which this yard-high maple leaf of flame came flaring, veined in violet, then died, then flared again.

In the quiet, I could not believe. The guns had given up firing. There were no aeroplanes. Another few moments drowned in smoke and then I could make out, forward, a concentration of torches in an archway five foot above where I stood, in what might have been a door when the ruins had been an office building, and figures that moved, but were too flat, too indistinct to seem real. I was wringing wet with sweat. At that minute there was absolute silence, I struggled closer. Broken gas pipes caught at my rubber boots, wires at my helmet, jagged spars of wood lunged at my flanks, and at my lungs writhed briars of smoke. I heard a man steadily coughing. Then I could see the top of him. He was sitting in that archway, in battledress, I thought, a mug between his hands, and coughing, coughing. In everything but sound it was too vague. He seemed, by the light of the torch on his belt, to be sitting on a taut sheet of steam.

The number one took it into his head I had a message from the pump. He wanted to know about the water, why it still had not come. We both had a fit of coughing. When he could, he told me the Rescue people had a man in under there, pointing to where the smoke was a rising wall. I was sure the individual sitting on his sheet, still coughing hopelessly, on and on, while every now and then he retched, was someone who had been brought out. Then he spoke. With difficulty he said they would have to have oxygen breathing apparatus, that it was too thick without. I realized that he must be the leader. Again he began to cough. My number one went back to order on the oxygen. Taking his place, I came up to another member of our crew. He told me, between his spasms, that this man was trapped at the bottom of a small jagged hole at our feet, and that before the Rescue Squad had been driven out, they had just been able to see him.

There was a shout of 'water' behind, the hose kicked once or twice and then jumped tight, the jet sprang out solid, white. The leader got up. He stood. His legs were still hidden but I could now see they were in steam which was drawn in by the draught of the doorway, steam running compactly like a swollen brook. He said, 'Not too near or you'll drown him, he's just below you there, play it over here against this wall, the fire's creeping along from behind. Come on, he's alive.' We played the water where he said and then were blotted out immediately in more than night, a forgetting, a death of black, the thick smoke, it let no air in, of a fire smacked out below, but which, we knew, would be up again if we did not almost flood it. 'By Christ, you'll drown him,' he shouted. But we judged, at the depth that man must be lying, that we should get more steam and smoke than he would get water. Now everything became too real in our fight for breath, too solid in the heavy river pressing without weight, in the enemy that seeks out to weaken, to dam life out from the source.

When we had had enough we raised the nozzle. We played our jet farther away. In under a minute we were breathing air, a little more and the leader was visible again, attended by three others. Smoke is in a hurry to get away, all we had to contend with now was steam, the smoke was whirling off that wreckage and coming back above our heads, we were clear. He asked us to keep our water still farther off while he got down to find out if he could still hear the man below. It was plain he did not think that he would get an answer. He got into the hole and the smoke. He disappeared, it was deeper than I had thought. His companions crowded round, shining their torches down on the rising well of smoke and steam. He called out, incongruously, 'Can you hear me, Mr Jonas?' We waited.

'He's all right,' he called back to us, 'but we've got to be quick.' The others climbed half-way down. The torches made it seem as though these men were fighting, half drowned, against a source of water, the smoke came up so solid there.

They began handing back single pieces of wreckage to others by me whom I had not seen come up, bits of wood, slats, parts of a chair. They talked about where to shine their torches. They were all coughing again. They worked in silence for some time. Then the leader said, 'Here, here.' Then he said, 'Careful now, up here.' Then he said, 'Towards that light.' Another man said, 'A bit to the left, take it easy,' and I saw a bald head, then khaki shoulders. He was not coughing. He was getting up alone. Then I saw he was smothered in dust. He was bone dry. It was Mr Jonas. As he came up and out, almost without assistance, we all began talking to him, telling him where to tread. He said absolutely nothing. He climbed right into that archway and disappeared. Coughing, the Rescue men climbed out. They thanked us. There were no more victims below. They also went out through the arch by which we could hear, but not see, others getting Mr Jonas off. Then we were alone.

Then the firing began again overhead. And then we settled down to the next four hours we reckoned it would take us to put the fire out, or, if not to extinguish it, to leave the job in such a state that it would not break out before we could be relieved. But in spite of anything we could do, it spread. In half an hour the deep corner, out of which they had got this man, was a mass of flames. By morning forty pumps were on the job. After twelve hours we were relieved, at half-past nine in the morning. When the other crew took over we had fought our way back to exactly the same spot above that hole out of which, unassisted once he had been released, out of unreality into something temporarily worse, apparently unhurt, but now in all probability suffering from shock, had risen, to live again whoever he might be, this Mr Jonas.

[*PNW 14*, 1942]

J. MACLAREN-ROSS

Y LIST

It started with a pain in my side. I didn't know I had pneumonia; nobody told me. We were out on the square, first period, 06.55 hours. Arms drill. The CSM himself was taking us. He looked browned off: I don't believe he liked it any more than we did. Drilling before breakfast's a bugger, believe me.

That morning I just couldn't do anything right. I felt sick and also I had this pain. It caught me every time I breathed: you know, like when you've been running and you get a stitch. Only worse than that, of course. At last I couldn't stand it any longer. I thought I was going to be sick over the man in front of me, so I committed a terrible crime: I broke the ranks.

The CSM was outraged. At first he couldn't speak at all when he saw me walking across the square towards him. He went scarlet and his face swelled up. Then he found his voice and shouted: 'Go back! Fall in! What the hell you think you're doing?'

'I'm sick, sir,' I said. 'I feel sick.'

'I'll have you in the guard-room,' the CSM shouted. 'Sergeant Smithson, get hold of that man. Take him to hell out of here!'

'To the guard-room, sir?'

'No, back to his hut. Anywhere. But get him off the bloody square. Out of my sight.'

'Very good, sir. Come on, you! Quick march!'

But once off the square Sergeant Smithson said: 'You don't need to look so scared, lad. He won't stick you in the guard-room. He don't mean nothing, not really.'

'I'm not scared, Sergeant,' I said. 'I'm sick. I've got a pain.' I could hardly stand up.

'Where's it get you? In the guts?'

'No, not in the guts. In the side.'

'Take off your belt and lie down, then. If you don't feel no better after breakfast you better go sick.'

I lay down on the bed, and lying down the pain didn't seem so bad.

In fact I thought it'd gone, till I tried to sit up. Then I found out my mistake. So I lay down again.

The other blokes came tumbling in; they'd been dismissed. The corporal said: 'Dodging the column again, eh? You ought to be under arrest by rights, you ought, breaking the ranks like that. I reckon you got off bleeding lucky meself.'

Then they all went off to breakfast, rattling their mess-tins. I didn't feel like anything, so I didn't go. I just lay there until they came back again.

'Ain't you eaten nothing?' the corporal said. 'Cor, you *must* be sick.'

'He *looks* sick,' the other blokes said, examining me. 'He don't arf look yellow.'

I didn't care if I looked green, I only wanted to be left alone. The corporal got concerned and put his hand on my forehead.

'You got a temperacher all right. You better go sick.'

'Oh, f—— off,' I said, 'for Christ's sake.'

'Who're you talking to?'

'You,' I said. 'Anyone. F—— off and leave me in peace.'

'He's sick all right,' the corporal said. 'Better ring up the Reception Station.'

'Get an ambulance.'

'Get an M O.'

I didn't mind who they got, it was all one to me. A runner went off to the Reception Station and the others all stood round the bed talking in hushed voices, as though I were already dead.

Presently an ambulance arrived. Two orderlies came in; one shoved a thermometer in my mouth. Then he took it out and looked at the result. The other orderly looked at it and said, 'Cor.' He was impressed. They both shook their heads.

'You in any pain, mate?' the first orderly asked.

'Yes,' I said.

The orderly nodded; he'd expected that. 'Appendix,' he muttered to himself. 'Obvious case.'

The other orderly thought not. He favoured ptomaine poisoning. 'We'd fish for tea last night, remember,' he said. An argument ensued. I could have stopped it by telling them that I'd had my appendix out long ago and that I hadn't eaten any fish the night before, but I didn't feel like a lot of talk.

The corporal said: 'Well, what I want to know, is he for the sick bay or not?'

'Yes, he's for the sick bay all right,' they said.

'Right. Get his small kit together, someone.'

The orderlies lifted me on to a stretcher. The sky tilted round as they carried me down the steps of the hut. Someone threw a hastily-packed haversack into the ambulance after me. Then there was the road running backwards behind us and the sky tilted again as they lifted me out at the Reception Station.

The medical officer looked down at me. 'Hullo, you again?' he said.

This medical officer didn't like me. I didn't like him either, come to that. It was a reciprocal dislike. He said: 'A pain in your side? Which side? H'm. We'd better keep you in. I'll examine you later. Can you walk upstairs, d'you think?'

'I can try, sir,' I said. I started to struggle up off the stretcher, but the pain caught me again and I fell back.

'Carry him up to the sick bay,' the medical officer told them.

Upstairs in the sick bay the wireless was on and the patients were sitting up in bed. Other patients, wearing hospital blues, were sitting in arm-chairs round the stove. All looked round as I was carried in.

A nurse came up with some pyjamas. Screens were erected round a bed and behind these I managed to get undressed, holding myself upright by hanging on to the bedrail. It took me some time, but I managed to do it in the end. I was damned if I'd let anyone else undress me. Then I got into bed. I could hardly breathe at all by this time. When the Sister brought me a glass of something to drink and I tried to say thank you, only a whisper came out. I thought I was dying for sure, and I should have been frightened, but I wasn't. I felt too weak and too tired to be frightened. I lay back in the cool sheets and went off to sleep almost at once.

I woke up to find the MO standing by my bed. I opened my mouth to speak and the Sister thrust a thermometer into it. The thermometer was withdrawn just at the moment when I felt I must spit it out or choke and the MO said: 'Off with your jacket. Let's have a look at you.'

He put on his stethoscope and listened through it to my chest. 'Say ninety-nine.' 'Ninety-nine.' My voice sounded a little louder since I'd had a sleep. The MO said, 'H'm.'

He applied the stethoscope to my back next. 'Take a deep breath.' I did. It hurt and made me cough, and coughing tore something inside me. I tried to cough as gently as possible, but still it hurt. The MO said, 'H'm' again and commenced to tap my chest with his two fingers. I'll say this for him, I didn't like him, but he could get more sound out of my chest with his two fingers than any M O who's examined me before or since. He got a terrific sound out of it. Through the stethoscope it must have sounded deafening. He took the stethoscope off again and said, 'All right.' Then he walked away out of earshot with the Sister and started to give her some instructions. I hoped he wasn't telling her to have me chucked out. I didn't feel able to move.

I watched him walk out and then two nurses came up and started to raise me from the pillows. I thought I was going to be forcibly ejected, but I was wrong. A third nurse came and banked up a lot more pillows behind me. Between them they strapped me bolt upright to a wooden rest and put a bolster between my legs, like the Dutch wife you read about in books about the east.

'Is that comfortable?' they asked. I nodded. It wasn't comfortable, but I felt too weak to argue. I went to sleep again straightaway. Later I woke up in a sweat and the wireless was on. I'd been hearing it in my sleep; it was playing full blast. The patients were having tea, digging marmalade out of a tin. I didn't want any tea. I'd acquired a distaste for the thought of food and in particular for the thought of chocolate and Horlick's: formerly my staple diet at break-times. But they didn't seem to expect me to eat, so that was all right. I didn't feel like smoking either, which was a minor miracle, because ordinarily not a day passes but I smoke at least thirty cigarettes, excluding a few occasions when for some reason or other I've not had any cigarettes to smoke.

The man in the next bed to me was smoking, and the smoke from his cigarette, blowing across at me, smelt like cabbage soup, and I knew that if I lit one it'd taste like that, too, and I didn't mean to try it. I had a drink of barley water that the Sister brought me, and then they fixed a hot poultice on my chest, that smelt strongly of aniseed.

I went back to sleep, or rather I dozed and once I woke or dreamt that I woke, I don't know which. My eyes were open, I'm certain of that. I could see the patients in blue walking up and down, but they didn't seem to make any sound; it was as though I were not really there, but looking at a silent film of them or seeing them through glass. I wondered if perhaps I'd died without knowing it. I once read a book where a man died in a hospital ward and afterwards he could see the whole of the ward and the people moving about and bending over his own dead body. I wondered dimly if this had happened to me, but on the other hand the man who wrote the book had never died himself, so he couldn't really know how you felt afterwards. Anyhow, it was like that at first; I could see them in front of me, but they seemed simultaneously at a distance, and then bit by bit I could hear the wireless. It kept fading in and out as though someone was fooling with the set, but I could see it and nobody was anywhere near. It faded on and off, IN and OUT, IN and OUT, OUT and IN, and the people I was seeing began also to fade in and out with the sound, like watching a series of lap-dissolves, and then there was a final fade-out and I woke next in the middle of the night, everyone in the ward asleep and the lights turned low, and I couldn't remember where I was at first. I felt terrible.

I looked round and saw something sitting by my bed watching me, a shape with some kind of head-dress on, and I knew at once that this was Death waiting patiently his chance. Or her chance: it seemed to be a woman. Well, why not? Somerset Maugham portrayed Death as a woman, and I couldn't see anything against it. I began to feel a bit frightened then, but I thought perhaps it didn't really matter because if I died then I shouldn't presumably feel so terrible.

By the time I thought that, my eyes had got accustomed to the dark and I saw it wasn't in fact Death watching me, but the night Sister.

'Can't you sleep?' she whispered to me.

'No,' I said. 'I feel awful.'

'Sick?'

'Yes.' I didn't have to keep my voice down as she was doing; it was a natural whisper.

'I've got some tablets for you to take,' she said. With her arm around me I managed to sit up and take the tablets; they were washed down with barley water. She turned the pillows and bunched them up again behind me, but I still couldn't sleep. It was a terrible feeling of nausea that I had, but it wasn't really like wanting to vomit; I can't describe what it was like. Later I began to shiver, although I wasn't cold. I just shivered and I had a cold sweat on me. The night Sister kept smoothing the hair from my forehead, which she couldn't have liked doing because it was damp and clammy and horrible.

'You're awfully good to me,' I whispered when finally I'd stopped shivering.

She said, 'It's nothing.' She smiled and I could see her teeth gleam white against her face in the dark. I still couldn't sleep, and then I could, and when I woke the eight o'clock news was on and they were all having breakfast.

The feeling of nausea had subsided and also the pain, but later when I sat up they were there again and I started to retch. I tried to hold it back because it hurt, but I couldn't and the nurse fetched me a bowl. What I brought up felt like blood, and I looked in the bowl and it was.

It was mostly dark, almost black, but there were some bright scarlet threads mixed with it as well, and it was blood all right.

When I saw the blood I got a little scared, but the nurse said there was no need. 'It's quite usual in cases like yours,' she said. I was relieved by that; I'd have hated to do anything irregular. I was so relieved I coughed up quite a blob more blood without minding at all.

The coughing hurt and exhausted me, but I felt much better afterwards. Then the two nurses sponged my face and hands; they wouldn't let me do a thing myself. They even combed my hair for me. 'You mustn't exert yourself,' they said.

'What about shaving?' I said.

They said: 'You'll have to grow a beard.'

Then the MO came round. He looked at the blood in my sputum bowl without much interest and asked me a string of questions. Had I ever had chest trouble before? Was there any chest trouble in my family? Did I feel any better today? The answer to all these questions was No. I felt too exhausted to add Sir, but the MO didn't seem to mind. Perhaps he wasn't really so bad after all.

When he'd gone they put another poultice on me; it was very hot and seemed to bring the pain out through my back. They gave me two more tablets; I went to sleep. I woke and felt sick again. It was like that all day.

During the afternoon Brailowsky came round. He was a Russian boy naturalized British, but not related, so far as I know, to the pianist called that. I liked him, and we used to argue about the way Russian slang should be translated into English and also, because he was Russian, about the soul. But that afternoon when he came I didn't feel like arguing about the soul. I had one of my lap-dissolve periods on and the face of Brailowsky, seen as if through glass, seemed to recede and advance, dissolving and re-forming, in and out, in and out, out and in. I couldn't talk; he sat by the bed awhile and then tiptoed away. I slept.

Next morning I felt better. The news was all about Hess and how he'd landed by parachute and all the patients were talking about Hess and how the bust-up in Germany was coming for sure and the war'd be over by Christmas, you mark my words.

There were too many patients for me to sort them all out, but I noticed that one of them had his face painted a bright orange. I'd noticed this before, but thought it was part of my delirium. Now I saw it was real; he had some spots on his face and the stuff they put on turned him this peculiar colour. He looked extraordinary; he was a New Zealander, someone told me.

Well, there they were, talking about Hess, and after this the wireless continued to be Hess, and it was also a little Roosevelt and dance tunes, 'Falling Leaves' and 'There I Go' and 'Yes, My Darling Daughter', and when I hear these tunes again I shall remember the Reception Station and the poultice drawing out the pain gradually, the orange-faced New Zealander and the tablets that were known as M and B.

They always made me feel sick and the days were divided up by the times I took them and there were also poultice-changing, temperature-taking, barley water and broth. Then there was sweating and sleeping and coughing, less and less blood by degrees, and the tablets made me feel less sick as time went on.

The nights, when I began sleeping better, were my best time because then the night Sister was on duty. I knew all the Sisters by now: the fair, wispy one who was engaged to a subaltern in the eighth, the spectacled talkative one, the tall, thin, dark one, and the two nurses: the short dour Scotch one and the grey elderly tired one. They were all very sweet and kind to me, but best of all I liked the night Sister.

She was not beautiful; there's a temptation to think of her as beautiful because I was sick and she nursed me, but I like to remain a realist, and she was not beautiful, no. She was a big dark girl with a cloud of dark hair under her coif and she had very white teeth. In the night I sometimes woke and I was frightened. I'd not been frightened at first because I was too weak, but later I was, and seeing her sitting by the bed used to stop me being frightened at once. She had also to wake me during the night to give me two of the tablets and she always did this by stroking my forehead.

'Why do you stroke my forehead to wake me?' I asked her once.

'I want you to think you're at home and wake up happy,' she said.

'No one wakes me like that at home,' I told her.

'Not your girl?'

'No. I haven't a girl.'

'Surely you must have a girl.'

'No, I haven't.'

'You're a poor lonely boy,' she said.

'No,' I said. 'I'm poor, but I'm not lonely. I'm hardly ever lonely.'

'Ssh,' she said. 'We're talking too loud. We'll wake the others.'

Then I'd take the tablets and go off to sleep quite happily. The nights were like that, and in the morning she was gone and there was Bing Crosby and the Morning Star on the radio and afterwards Hess.

Now I was better; I no longer coughed up blood, and one day the Sister showed me the thermometer and it was down to normal. I used to lie there and sometimes read, and I used to think of all the sick leave I'd get when I got out of hospital.

I knew now I'd got pneumonia; at first I didn't care what I'd got, but later I became curious and got the orange-faced man to turn round the chart that hung on the end of my bed and this said PLEURISY AND PNEUMONIA. I remembered the company clerk who'd gone down with German measles and how they gave him seven days, and if you got given seven days for measles what'd you get for pneumonia? My mind soared to dizzy heights of sick leave. Twenty-eight days? Two months? The camp with its dust and heat and the CSM shouting seemed agreeably remote – almost a thing of the past. A month anyway, I thought. They can't give me less than a month. I felt so bucked at the thought of a month that I even felt hungry for the first time and ate a piece of chicken cut up into tiny little squares. Hess was having chicken, too, we heard.

Then one morning I'd been asleep and I woke and there was the colour-sergeant rattling a bag of coins and grinning at me; the company commander was with him. It was Friday; I'd been ill for almost a week.

'Here's a quid for you,' the colour-sergeant said. 'Better take it while you can. They'll only pay you eight and six when you shift to the hospital proper.'

So I took the quid and they went round the ward rattling the bag of money. Everyone woke up when they heard it, even the man who'd been carried in nearly dying of something the day before woke up, and all got paid out.

That afternoon Brailowsky came again. He had some news for me.

'D'you remember Collins? In No. 7 Platoon?'

'The one with glasses?' I remembered Collins; he was a country lad and not too good on drill – he just couldn't seem to grasp it somehow.

'A terrible thing happened this morning,' Brailowsky said. 'He had his eye put out; he was blinded. We were on bayonets and a scabbard slipped. It was the corporal's actually, Corporal Evans. It struck Collins and broke his glasses into his eye. It was awful.'

'I should think it was,' I said. 'Poor devil.'

'If only he hadn't worn glasses he'd have been all right. It was the glass breaking that did it really.'

'How awful,' I said. 'Did he faint?'

'No, he was conscious all the time. The corporal's awfully cut up about it.'

'Where is Collins now?'

'At the town hospital. He's to have an operation.'

'Well, there's one thing,' I said, 'he'll get his ticket.'

'Oh, yes, they'll give him that, I should think. And you, d'you think you'll get yours?'

'No such luck.'

Then we talked about the soul. Tolstoy was mentioned, and Dostoievsky. We both got a little exalted and in the end Brailowsky was asked to leave by the Sister in charge. He said he'd be back. I felt a little less exalted when he'd gone and I thought a bit about Collins; I thought principally poor bastard. Anyway, he'd be out of the army, that was one good thing, but was it worth losing an eye for? I decided not.

On the Sunday after that I was moved. There was no warning; the MO suddenly came round about midday and said I was to go to the town hospital that morning. Immediately I was carried out to the ambulance on a stretcher. It was lovely weather and the sun felt good on my face, but I was worried because I hadn't said good-bye to the night Sister. Later, though, she came round to the town hospital, and I saw her there, and when I came out finally I went to look her up, but she'd been transferred and I never saw her again.

At the town hospital they had huts adjoining it for the military, and I was in one of these. When they carried me in there was lunch going on, and I was hungry. I asked for something to eat.

'Bread and milk,' the nurse told me. 'You can have some bread and milk if you like.'

'They're eating stew. Why can't I have some of that?'

'Not until the doctor's seen you.'

'But I'm eating normally now, nurse. I've had no lunch. I'm hungry.'

'Well, you can't have anything till the doctor comes.'

'When will that be?'

'About three o'clock.'

'Oh Christ.'

The nurse was a little shocked. She went away and I watched them eat the stew. Later the nurse returned with some junket. I didn't like junket; I told her so. She said I ought to be glad of anything I could get these days.

Then there was an altercation when she took down my particulars. She wanted my mother sent for. I said I don't want her worried and it all ended in this nurse not liking me. I was surprised at the difference in atmosphere. Of course, these were not VADs; they were trained nurses, and there's the difference between amateur and professional; it's something like that, and there were also more regulations and less food, as I found out later.

The doctor came round about half-past three, and it was a woman doctor. The first thing she did was to knock off the tablets. She said I was progressing satisfactorily. I said could I have something to eat; she said of course. So I ate bread and jam for tea and later stew.

The hut was a long one and stretched down a perspective of beds to long french windows leading on to a lawn. The end beds by the french windows were not filled except one that had a man who had fits in it. We were always waiting for him to have one, but he didn't; we thought he was a washout. Most of the patients were up and about; they used to get free passes to go to the cinema in the afternoons, but at mealtimes they always reappeared and there was a scramble to sit down at the long table that ran down the middle of the room, and the bed patients sat agitatedly up and made desperate signals to the nurses to make sure they didn't get overlooked.

Everyone was always hungry because, although the hospital took military patients, they still had civilian rations and food was scarce. One day we had a major who shouted at us that we were under military discipline and any man misbehaving himself'd damn soon find it out. But we were not interested in discipline; we were interested in food. The food remained unmilitary and we were hungry all the time.

The food we got was mainly vegetable stew with a few shreds of meat in it and beans abounding. The beans had an effect on us that was embarrassing when the matron came round at night; it was like crackers going off all the way down the ward. At each explosion the matron would give a little start as if stung. From the beds behind would come giggles smothered by blankets and a fresh salvo burst out in front, so the matron was caught between two fires, so to speak; it was amusing but embarrassing for everybody.

That was in the evenings; in the mornings there was the wireless, which was now altogether Roosevelt and sometimes Bing Crosby; Hess had fizzled out. Roosevelt made a rousing speech; it was terrific, and the patients all said the war'd be over by October, but some still stuck to Christmas; they were pessimists. With the wireless went washing, and now that I was stronger, shaving, and there was also Yes or No.

At the Reception Station Yes or No had been considered a rhetorical question, but here the nurses began to ask it with increasing urgency, and one came round with potions and pills and various kinds of purges on a trolley. I took a yellow-coloured medicine and several pills without result and they began talking about dynamite.

When I did at last get going it was quite an adventure. The lavatory was just outside the ward, and to get to it you had to pass eight beds. This took me fully five minutes; it was the first time I'd been up. My body felt as light as a blown feather and my legs as though the laws of gravity had altered. I had to look down to make sure that my feet were in fact touching terra firma. I refused the offer of a stick and a nurse's arm. I set off to float down the ward on my own, the other patients cheering me on. As my head seemed also independent and a separate entity, it was an exhausting experience and tired me out for the rest of the day.

The afternoon was merely an interlude between dinner and tea, and during it there was a blanket bath, which I did myself, and rubbing methylated spirit on my body, which was done by a nurse. I was always embarrassed by this, especially since the nurse who did it was a good-looking one. She was a well-set-up girl, and I used to watch her walking down the ward with detachment, and then one day it was no longer with detachment, and I knew then that I was getting definitely better.

Every day after that I got steadily better, and now that the pain had entirely gone and the doctor said the lung was almost healed, I had great pleasure in breathing; every time I breathed my whole body seemed to expand, and it was very pleasant. I could feel my blood circulating freely and I felt very strong; it was always astonishing that when my feet touched the floor I felt dizzy and so weak I could hardly stand.

Sometimes I was allowed to get up and sit in a chair by the stove, which was not lit now as it was the middle of May and warm weather. I used to send out all the time for food; one of the up-patients got it for me. The colour-sergeant's quid soon went, and I ate always with tremendous appetite.

The orange-faced man turned up, but now you couldn't see his face because the new treatment he had caused it to be swathed in bandages, and he looked like the Invisible Man in the film before he actually became invisible.

And then Collins turned up. He didn't see me at first, but I saw him; he had a black patch over his eye and looked really none the worse. I heard what was said when his doctor came round. We each had separate doctors, and his was a doctor who considered it his duty to demobilize the army, or at any rate such part of it as came under his care. I heard him tell Collins that he'd been recommended for discharge and Collins mutter something in his slow country voice, but he didn't seem pleased about it; he seemed just indifferent. Later he saw me and we had a talk.

'How'll you like getting your ticket?' I asked him.

'Oh, I dunno. I ain't so keen. I dunno as I want it really.'

'You don't want it!'

'I ain't all that keen. 'Course I wouldn't mind getting home for the harvest, but still.'

I was astounded. I knew that if I'd been blinded in the army I'd expect my ticket and probably a pension as well. I looked at him and thought he took it so calmly he must have more guts than I had. But then I knew it wasn't guts; it was just that he hadn't the imagination – if something happened to you and you didn't imagine it had not really happened and even the tangible loss of an eye did not entirely happen until it'd been fully imagined. Well, in his case he was better off like that – and who wants imagination, anyway?

I looked at Collins standing there with his black patch and in his hospital blues that were rather too big for him; the sleeves hung down over his hands.

'Well,' I said, 'it looks as though you'll get your ticket whether you want it or not.'

'Ar,' he said. 'Well, I don't mind much either way.'

I watched him walk back to his bed, and later Corporal Evans came, the one who'd done it to him by accident, and I watched the corporal come walking down the ward with a look on his face as though he were going into action; he was Welsh and emotional, and you could see he was all worked up about it.

Collins was sitting on his bed and he stood up and slowly grinned.

'Hullo, Corp,' he said.

I couldn't hear what Corporal Evans said, but I could see Collins wince at the grip his hand got; it must have nearly cracked the bones. Then they sat down and talked. Corporal Evans gesticulated a lot, and I could see Collins shaking his head slowly from time to time. They talked for quite a while, and when Corporal Evans got up to go he seemed tremendously relieved. He left the ward with a shout of laughter and at the door he turned back to wave a hand at Collins. 'So long, lad!'

'So long, Corp,' Collins said, and he sat there on the edge of his bed for some time afterwards smiling to himself, and I couldn't tell what he was thinking about; perhaps he wasn't really thinking at all.

That afternoon, too, Brailowsky came, but Collins was out by that time; he'd gone to the cinema; it was 'All This and Heaven Too'. Brailowsky said I'd been Y listed; it was on orders, twenty-one days in hospital; but as I wasn't an NCO it made no difference to me, I had no stripes for them to strip.

Brailowsky had brought a book by Turgenev, and he'd brought with him also the same book in Russian. He was showing me how the translation differed from the original Russian when a sudden blood-curdling yell from the end of the ward made us both start round.

The yell proceeded from a bed occupied by an Irishman who had some kind of stomach trouble. I'd never spoken to him, but I'd never thought that he was really very ill. We looked round and he was sitting up in bed, gaunt and unshaven, with a wild look on his face.

'I want my wife!' he yelled out.

Two of the nurses came running in and immediately went to his bedside, but he waved them away.

'I don't want you; I want my wife. I'm a dying man. I want my wife.'

The nurses said something; he wouldn't listen. He started to beat on the bedrail with his hand and to shout over and over again, 'I want my wife, I want my wife, I want my wife.'

Brailowsky had turned pale. 'What's wrong with him?' he whispered. I said I didn't know. I was watching the Irishman. Everyone in the ward was watching him; the patients from their beds and some of the patients who'd got back from the cinema stood watching him and the nurses. The Irishman glared back at them with his eyes starting out of his head.

'I'm dying, I tell ye!' he howled. 'I'm dying, and ye can't tell me no different, I know it! I want my wife!'

Suddenly there was a commotion at the other end of the ward. It was the man who had fits; he was having one. The Irishman had evidently upset him. Now attention was divided; our heads kept turning from side to side, and all the nurses made in a body for the man with fits. Screens went up round his bed in no time, but the Irishman, on the other hand, feeling himself abandoned, began to shriek at the top of his voice; it wasn't pleasant.

'I'm dying, I tell ye, I'm dying! I want my wife! I'm dying, I'm dying! I want my wife, I tell ye! I'm dying! I want my wife! I'm dying, I'm dying! The Mother of God have mercy! I'm dying!'

Brailowsky stood up; he'd gone green in the face. You'd have thought that being Russian he'd have been used to this kind of thing, but evidently the naturalized part of his nature asserted itself suddenly and he couldn't take it. He muttered, 'So long,' and left the ward promptly and with expedition.

The Irishman was on to a new tack now. He pointed a furious finger at the patients who stood gaping round his bedside.

'Aye, ye can stare, all of ye, ye can stare. Take a good look; I ain't afraid to die. The Lord God strike ye where ye stand. May he strike all of ye dead!' He added: 'And may a dying man's curse be on ye all!'

More patients came in, attracted by the noise from another ward, and two more nurses; they all stood staring. The Irishman included all these new-comers in his malediction.

'Die, all of ye, die!' he shrieked. 'Ye're dead! Why don't ye die?'

He leant forward and waited for them to die. They didn't; they just stood there. The Irishman cast his eyes to heaven and again called on God to strike them dead.

The bed patients further up now began to call angrily down the ward.

'He's loopy! Lock him up!'

'Fetch a strait-jacket!'

'Fetch the doctor!'

'Fetch a priest!' this evidently from a fellow Catholic, but delivered in a Scots accent.

The Irishman paid no attention to these exhortations. He was watching the group round his bedside, waiting for them to fall.

'Nothing happens,' he muttered after a moment. 'Nothing happens.' He said this hopelessly, his faith was shattered. He dropped his head in his hands and began to sob.

A doctor now rushed in with a stethoscope dangling round his neck and took instant command of the situation. Up went the screens, and from behind them we could hear the Irishman sobbing brokenly.

'Is he really dying?' I asked one of the nurses, who'd halted by my bed on her way down from the man with fits.

'No,' she said, 'of course not. He won't die.'

'What about his wife?'

'She's in Ireland. Besides, he's separated from her.'

The Irishman quietened down after a while, and later he apologized to all of us. It'd been a mistake, he said, the devil had entered into him. We accepted the apology and also the theory of demonical possession, but that night the Irishman had a relapse, and this time he kicked over the screens and hit someone, a sergeant, I think. In the morning when we woke he'd been removed, and I don't know what happened to him because shortly afterwards I was moved myself.

I went to a convalescent home, where I remained for three weeks. And I never got any sick leave after all. An ACI had just come out saying that if you went to a convalescent home you couldn't have sick leave; the MO at the camp took great pleasure in explaining it to me.

I did get my seven days' privilege leave, which was, anyway, six weeks overdue, and they said I was lucky to get even that, because being on light duties I wasn't entitled to any kind of leave without the MO's okay.

When I came back to the camp I saw Collins. He hadn't got his ticket; they'd graded him B2 and given him a job in the company stores. They gave him also a brand-new glass eye, which he's very proud of; he can even move it about in its socket. The boys all call him Nelson, but he doesn't mind that; he doesn't seem to mind anything at all.

[PNW 15, 1942]

JIŘÍ MUCHA

ALEXEY THE COOK

Translated from the Czech by Ewald Osers

'Stand at attention when I speak to you!' shouted Lieut. Knap, peering into the twilight between two big cauldrons under which a cringing fire was smoking.

'Yessir!' sulkily replied a grimy figure, straightening up over the grill.

'Is that the way for a soldier to behave?' Lieut. Knap planted his hands on his hips and leaned slightly forward. 'Man, you're a civilian in disguise. Report to the Orderly Room.'

'Yessir!' came the growl from behind the cauldron.

Lieut. Knap carried on with his tour. He was in a bad mood. In the morning he had drunk cold coffee and from that moment onwards he had been walking about the sleeping town, from sentry to sentry, from cookhouse to cookhouse, encountering everywhere the rancorous and sulky gaze of sleepy soldiers who acted as if their orderly officer was their chief enemy. Alexey wasn't a bad soldier, but soldiers always complain that cooks are stingy and cheeky. Also Alexey had forgotten what a rifle looked like; he thought the whole company existed to suffer his caprices. Instead of the coffee being ready only a few chips of wood burned under the pot. When Lieut. Knap had called him he hadn't even answered. Only at the second shout did a voice come from the shed: 'What's the matter?' 'What a way for a soldier to report!' Lieut. Knap shouted again, but to his amazement he heard, 'Got no time.' He would have liked to look into what was going on in the shed, had it not meant squeezing in among the sooty cauldrons. He therefore wavered indecisively and waited. After a while Alexey's grimy form detached itself from the shed, but then made straight for the grill, knelt down and rummaged among the cinders.

'Why isn't the coffee made?' asked Knap.

''Cause the wood's wet.'

'And why didn't you come straight away?'

''Cause I was chopping wood. I won't have my fire go out because of you.'

This peeved Lieut. Knap so much that he ordered Alexey to report to the Orderly Room. It was all a very unpleasant affair. Anyway, the soldiers were having a rotten time, so why make their lives worse?

Knap returned to his billet by a roundabout way. The sky was already transparently clear like a glass of water held against the light, and the cool scent of the flowering gardens hung over the green meadows and vineyards. In a little while the sun would rise and another hot day would begin, with dust on the roads, with sweaty and smeary faces of soldiers and with bickering with the French until nightfall. Not that one was bound to bicker with the French, but they were so terribly slow about everything. For every trifle one had to run from one to another and so much paper got scribbled on that there was no place to store it all. Still, things down here, at Pezenas, were a lot better than at Agde, even though the soldiers were living in disused cowsheds spacious as baronial halls, with a permanent haze of dust in the air, and, if it was raining, a stream of water pouring in.

Pezenas was an old-fashioned little town in the middle of green Provence, dead and crumbling as if time had stopped there three hundred years ago when war devastated the castle and swept away the ramparts. Since then no one ever thought of building himself a new house or repairing an old one or of making the slightest change in that past which prevailed over all future. And so Pezenas lived on memories, on the vineyards and on inertia; and just as, year after year, the stones came loose and fell from the old walls, men, too, died, leaving behind them gaps which no one came to fill.

The arrival of a Czechoslovak regiment had stirred for a while the calm surface of the life down here. Slim, black-eyed girls, who spoke with a Spanish accent, donned their Sunday dresses of transparent black lace, buxom women leaned from the windows and butchers and bakers planted themselves in front of their shops with their arms folded, and watched the bustling soldiers, who, at first sight, resembled theirs, but who did not understand a word that was said to them. Soon the first notices in Czech appeared in the windows: Washing done here. Fresh Ham. Beer. And, in the shops, they learnt to count up to ten.

Spring was capricious in Pezenas. The gardens in the few little squares which, in March, had looked drab and deserted, suddenly blossomed forth with roses, jasmine, and the countless slender candlesticks of the chestnut trees. And every garden had, clinging close to its whitewashed house, an arbour of vines under which stood a shaky table with a few glasses and a carafe of wine. It was heavy, rough wine, which went quickly to the head, and the wretched quarters of the soldiers were turned every evening into a noisy, restless beehive from which snatches of songs, broken by hisses and requests for quiet, could be heard until late at night.

The roomy shed which housed the First and Second Companies stood close to an uncertain stream of water which now swelled and now dried up according to the fickleness of the spring weather. There the soldiers scrubbed their shirts on an old piece of board, standing knee deep in the stream and splashing at each other to catch the attention of the three sisters who lived on the other bank behind a high farm wall. Often the girls stood there for hours on end, watching the antics of the soldiers, who from time to time walked across to joke with them, laughing at them over the wall. 'Won't you come out for a walk with us?' they would ask. The sisters found a different excuse every time, although their eyes clearly betrayed their desire to break out, along the path into the vineyards, to the flowery hollows of wild thyme and lavender and perhaps up to the thick copse of hawthorn and prickly acacias.

Later they learned that the girls' legs had been paralysed since childhood. There was nothing left to them but to watch motionless the life of another world, a world of laughter and movement which was for ever barred to them.

When the first Czechoslovak regiment was transferred from Agde to Pezenas, Lieut. Knap found himself a room in the Rue Jean Jaurès, on the first floor of a dark house with a multitude of passages and abandoned rooms, a spacious room, equipped with old-fashioned furniture, and with a high french window opening on to the daily evening parade of the townspeople. Occasionally a wandering organ grinder would stop before the house and sing in a high tenor to the accompaniment of his instrument on which a monkey, dressed in a scarlet coat, jumped up and down. Sometimes the monkey would turn round and gnaw the long chain by which it was tied, and when its master stopped singing it would run up to the sauntering crowd with a cap, hopping on its hind legs. Once even a man with a bear appeared under the window. He was beating a drum and poking the bear with a long stick until the animal got up and clumsily stamped its feet. The people laughed and threw the gipsy coppers, which rang on the pavement and rolled under the bear's paws.

From the window one could also see the building of the Town Hall, and the headquarters of the French garrison from which the wizened Town Commander would come out in the blue uniform of the Chasseurs Alpins. If the weather was fine he would stroll twice up and down the main street and then stop for a glass of wine at the entrance to Marcel Bâtiste's, from where gay singing was often heard as early as eleven in the morning.

There were no French soldiers in the garrison. Only those who now and then came home for their leave made an appearance. Once a company of French riflemen passed through with their rifles on strings and without pouches. It was a disquieting sight. The poison had already taken hold, creeping like blight from the northern and eastern frontiers. Throughout France, just as here at Pezenas, millions of equally shabby and wretched soldiers lay down at nine o'clock on their straw, without a wash and without money, without action and without aim, but with a growing hot, sensual desire for a woman and for home. Individually and in groups they talked of peace at any price. The general disgust spread eventually even to those who had come of their own will from Bohemia, Moravia and Slovakia; it gnawed at them and sometimes it showed itself in stubborn, rebellious looks. That was just why Lieut. Knap insisted on discipline. He fought against disintegration, he wanted to uproot it like a weed, but at the same time he couldn't help seeing the misery which crept from the soldiers' pockets to their souls.

The sun had just sprung up over the hills. Colours which till now had seemed vivid paled against the wealth of light and shade which filled the whole scene. The river shone like a black mirror, the meadows were spangled with red and white flowers, the dark filigree of the trees contrasted with the chalk-white stones which bordered the road and the sky arched overhead, saturated with deep blue. On all sides gleamed the yellow and white walls of the vineyards and of the steep little towns with red and green roofs in between the silver of the olive trees and the earthy ochre of the hillsides. A little further to the south one could even see from a slight hill the narrow, pale ribbon where the sea began.

From the distance Lieut. Knap heard the sound of the first bugle. At first it stuttered a little, then its voice rang out, and at last it blared forth far and wide. One after the other the soldiers opened their eyes. For a while they lay in a torpor. Then someone got up, cleared his throat and struggled with the blankets. His neighbour watched him silently. Eventually someone else got up and ran out. The orderly came in and yelled 'Get up!' Some of the soldiers crept grudgingly from their blankets; others quickly shut their eyes again, shamming sleep. The orderly began to grab at their legs. The tempo of life was slow and sluggish. Then some splashing was heard and the clash of tin against tin. Black coffee and bread were brought in. As though at the lash of a whip a hum of life filled the great cowshed and concentrated gradually at the entrance around the pots with the breakfast. After a while the shouting and the humming died down, the soldiers took their mugs to their piles of straw and there, in sacred privacy, they drank hot, insufficiently sweetened coffee.

When Lieut. Knap had finished his tour and had returned to the Second Company, the men were already out, and the orderly, together with a man on fatigue, was sweeping the dust out of the barn-door.

Alexey was sitting in front of the cauldron and finishing his bread.

'Did the men get their breakfast in time?' Knap asked the orderly.

'They did,' said the soldier with the broom, glancing sideways at Alexey.

'Right.' Lieut. Knap then stood in front of the cook. 'Were you in the army in Czechoslovakia?'

'I was,' said Alexey, and got up.

'And yet you don't know the proper way for a soldier to behave?'

'I do.'

'Then why don't you do it?'

Alexey was silent.

'When did you leave home?'

'In the autumn of 1938.'

'After the mobilization?'

'Yes.'

'Aren't you ashamed of yourself? You should set an example to the rest and not behave like a recruit.'

But Alexey merely shrugged his shoulders.

The same day Lieut. Knap went round to see Intelligence Officer Koula. He found him in his office sitting at a table covered with mountains of files. He was just concluding a discussion about French literature with Private Holecek of the Auxiliary Service.

'It doesn't matter at all what you think about it, Holecek,' he was declaring. 'The Christian name doesn't mean much. If someone is called Daudet he goes on the black list, whether he is Alphonse or Léon. Such a thing runs in a family.'

Private Holecek, in civilian life Professor of French literature, did not agree, but held his peace. On the list of prohibited books he entered *Lettres de mon Moulin*, by Alphonse Daudet, confiscated after a personal search from Private Stern, and thought to himself that after all a little too much caution was better than not enough.

The affair of Daudet was finished and Intelligence Officer Koula turned to Knap.

'I've come to ask you about a soldier,' said Knap, planting himself on the edge of the table. 'His name is Alexey, and he is a cook with the Second Company.'

'Alexey? What's he been up to?' Koula automatically stretched his hand to a fat folder of papers. 'I think I know him, but we'll make sure. Adamec . . . Adamek . . . Oh, yes, here he is, Alexey. This is him all right. What would you like to know?'

'It is quite unofficial. Alexey hasn't been up to anything, but just out of curiosity I would like to know what his record is. I told him to report to the Orderly Room.' Lieut. Knap gazed through the window on to the street, where a harnessed mule was resting with drooping ears in the shade of some plane trees.

'He has got a good record,' said Koula. 'No convictions, no excuses, and grumpy, like every cook.'

'He told me that he left home after the mobilization. Didn't he have some trouble there?' It was to ask this question that Knap had come. Soldiers didn't simply leave the army and go abroad.

'Well, there you are. He did have trouble. Something with the Germans.'

Intelligence Officer Koula satisfied himself at a glance that his clerk was discreetly burying his head in some papers.

'After the mobilization he was near the frontier. I think it was in Cheb. Damned hot spot, if you remember. You know what the situation was then. The Germans had a free hand to shoot and we had to keep quiet. But until they bungled it up in Munich there was still a lot that could be done.'

Lieut. Knap fidgeted impatiently.

'I am coming to it in a moment,' Koula continued. 'When the Germans began the occupation our people hurriedly cleared out of their headquarters and armed German "ordners" were snooping around all the time, trying to make trouble.

'Alexey was on guard duty in front of a building watching material being loaded into cars. Suddenly he saw one of those ordners approaching the car from behind and making straight for the tyres with a knife. They say Alexey hardly even stirred. He just raised his rifle slightly and fired. The ordner collapsed and Alexey jumped back into the house. He ran up the stairs and reported to the commanding officer what had happened. In the meantime the Germans were crowding into the streets and shouting that they'd come and fetch the culprit. Lieut.-Colonel Jurek, who had seen everything, didn't hesitate long. He threw a curtain over Alexey and called two chaps, who carried him out like a parcel and dumped him in the car. Five minutes later Alexey was on his way to Plzen.'

'What a story!' remarked Lieut. Knap.

'That's not everything. The Germans might have demanded Alexey's extradition at any moment, and so our authorities gave him a passport to go somewhere abroad. Before he could get away, however, the Germans occupied his home town as well, so that his exit permit was no longer valid. And because Alexey had bad luck they didn't tell him this until he reached the frontier, and then they seized him and sent him straight to a Labour Camp. First to the north, then after three months to Bavaria, and so on for a whole year, until he got to the Rhine, where they were just building fortifications at the Swiss frontier.

'There Alexey fixed it up with two other Czechs that they would swim across the Rhine at night. It was in the middle of winter, but those three made up their minds that they would run away, and one night they actually managed to lose themselves. But they had to return because there were guards on the Rhine, and it took them another fortnight to spy out a spot where the bank was unguarded. So again they set out in the middle of winter. When they had crawled up to the brink of the water and were about to jump in the third man probably got the wind up and left them to swim alone.'

'And did they get across?'

'They did.'

'Thank you. That'll do,' said Lieut. Knap softly, and slid off the table.

'So long, Knap,' Intelligence Officer Koula called after him as he put away his files. 'At your service any time you like.'

In the streets it was beginning to get hot. Between the windows of the narrow streets washing was hung out to dry and haggard dogs with their tongues hanging out ran between the legs of passers-by. Lieut. Knap made for the Market Place, where the Field Post Office was housed. The postmaster, a sergeant with a thick black beard, was usually in session at the wine-shop next door. And so it was today. The door of the post office was locked and the venerable figure of the postmaster was wedged in behind the many-cornered table of the Café Univers, surrounded by several soldiers and clouds of tobacco smoke. Just as Lieut. Knap entered Captain Korba appeared in the doorway beside him.

'Having a quick one?' he asked, blinking his eyes curiously.

'Just seeing if there are any letters for me,' replied Knap, whom the bearded sergeant had by now noticed, and, with a negative movement of his hand, indicated that nothing had come in today.

'Let's have a drink, then,' decided Captain Korba, who welcomed any occasion for a drink. He pushed Knap behind the table and fetched a bottle of rosé.

'Something is worrying you,' he remarked confidentially when they had emptied the first glass.

Knap shrugged his shoulders. 'Do you know much about people?'

'Never worry about them.' Captain Korba kept hold of the bottle. 'It's not worth while.'

'Have you ever met a hero?' Knap asked again.

Korba turned round and cast a suspicious glance at Knap. 'Why do you ask me that?'

'I'd like to know whether you'd recognize at first sight that someone was a hero. Or, if you'd rather put it this way, can a man be a born hero as he can be a born mathematician or a born pianist, or does his heroism waken in him for a moment and then die down again?'

'That's a very difficult thing to decide,' admitted Korba, who would never have dreamed of asking himself such a question.

'I'll tell you what made me think of it. This morning I told a cook to report to the Orderly Room and scolded him for having no discipline – in short, for being a bad soldier. But when I made inquiries they told me the sort of things which will one day be described in school books. And now, you see, it has suddenly occurred to me that we are rather prone to tell a man what we think of him without ever asking what he thinks of us.'

'That's none of his business,' Captain Korba remarked.

'It isn't. As long as he doesn't realize it. I, for instance, feel rather a fool today.'

'Because of what a cook thinks of you?'

'That's just it. You say "a cook", but in my mind his past, which is quite different, keeps coming up.'

'And you don't know how to put the two things together,' Captain Korba laughed. 'When I was a young man like yourself I fell in love with a girl. Nice girl, she was; nothing was sacred enough to me for that girl. The others were beginning to pull my leg about her, and one evening they caught me and dragged me into a pub. They roared with laughter like beasts, and one by one they began to tell me to visualize my girl doing one thing and another. After half an hour of it I had had enough and ran away. But it was the end of my ideal. Not that I had stopped being fond of her. But somehow I had become more careful. She was no longer such a lily. And, believe me, I felt better for it. But the point is that whenever I can't account for something in a man I remember the girl. An angel's face on a perfectly human body. The same goes for famous people or heroes. That's all there is to it.'

Lieut. Knap was not satisfied with the explanation.

'It's not that at all. In such a man there must be something which switches over strangely, and instead of, say, fear of death, as his main instinct, something quite new must appear. Look at the bearded postmaster over there. Is he a hero, or isn't he?'

'And what about yourself?' Captain Korba asked aggressively. 'Are you a hero? Have you ever in your life been in a tight corner?'

'I don't know. I don't think so. Anyhow, today I feel like a coward.'

'Look here, Knap, don't worry about such things. In war there is no time for philosophizing. Keep your men in order. Keep them on the hop so that they will sleep at night and not brawl around the town; look after their boots and their shirts and leave their souls alone. You won't win a war with souls.' Captain Korba finished his drink, said good-bye and left.

Knap remained sitting and looking after him with a feeling of envy. Out of that simple relation of an officer to his men of which Korba had spoken and in which he had been living himself up to this morning, he suddenly saw himself surrounded by hundreds of unfamiliar figures who hid in themselves remarkable pasts which determined their way of thinking. And also their opinion of him, Knap, who up to now had felt safe in his own superiority and whose every word was law. Maybe while he was speaking or giving orders he was being watched by several pairs of eyes of whose presence he had not been aware before, eyes of men like Alexey, who were judging and weighing his every movement. Just as an experienced dancer watches a beginner. All right. Let's see what you do. I've got it all behind me. Right in the middle of Cheb I shot a German. I swam across the Rhine in December. You want to see what a real soldier is? Come along with me, out there to the enemy. I'll show you.

Who, then, was the commander? Knap or those shining eyes under thick eyebrows, those pairs of eyes among the soldiers lined up in the barrack courtyard? Captain Korba escapes all this. He looks after pants and boots and keeps the soldiers on the hop at their exercise, and lets them see to their souls themselves. That's how it should be.

He got up, left the wine-shop and made for the barracks of the Second Company. When he realized where he was going it seemed quite natural to him that he should go to the cook Alexey.

Alexey was sitting on an old crate in front of the cookhouse and playing with a small white dog which came every day to lick out a pan into which the soldiers threw bones for him. Lieut. Knap walked up to the cauldron and lifted the lid.

'What is it you are cooking, then?'

'Goulash, sir,' replied Alexey, standing to attention.

'Right. And don't report to the Orderly Room, Alexey, as the coffee was on time.'

'Thank you, sir.'

'How is it you left home as early as 1938?' Knap put his question as casually as possible.

'They took me away to work in Germany.'

'And from there you ran away?'

'Yes.'

'How did you manage that, Alexey?'

Knap bent down to the little white dog which lay on its back in the dust, waiting patiently for someone to scratch his belly.

'We just did a bunk across the Rhine into Switzerland.'

'But surely that was dangerous, wasn't it?'

'Main thing was that it came off, sir.'

'True. But for such things they ought to give you the War Cross. Don't you think so?'

'Well, sir, there was nothing out of the way about it. If a man knows how to swim he can get across even the Rhine. And if it comes to a War Cross, then it really should belong to the chap we had to leave behind. He worked with us in Germany, and it was with him that I and another man fixed up our get-away. He went with us to the very edge of the water, and only when we were taking off our boots did I notice that he was just sitting and watching us. I said: "Aren't you going to take off your boots?" and he said, "Boys, you'll have to forgive me. I can't come with you. I don't know how to swim, so you just leave me here." Of course we asked him why he had come with us when he knew that it meant crossing the river. But he said we would have been afraid of his giving us away if he had backed out at the beginning. And so he led us to the water, and, believe me, sir, he must have known what was coming to him when they found out in the camp. As a matter of fact the Gestapo did finish him off. You see, sir, chaps like him are rare enough here. Such a man doesn't get a War Cross.'

'You think there aren't many such people here?' Lieut. Knap asked, and he felt as if a burden had slid from his shoulders.

Alexey pondered. 'Maybe. But today it is so difficult to tell the difference between a straight chap and a rascal.'

From the path between the fields came the singing of the marching company as they returned from exercise, and Lieut. Knap went out to the road. The smoke from the tall cookhouse chimney, borne down by a light breeze, spread between the buildings and stung his eyes. Noon was drawing near. In a quarter of an hour it would strike twelve from the nearby tower.

[*PNW 16*, 1943]

DENIS GLOVER

CONVOY CONVERSATION

It was cold at the four-inch gun. They had been closed up at action stations since the early Arctic dawn, and they had watched the great convoy change from a black smudge against the darkened sea to the high, clear shape of ships. And it was at dawn they had beaten off the usual submarine attack.

Now they were awaiting the first wave of planes.

The gun crew was dressed, as destroyer crews do dress at sea, in anything that would keep out the cold – balaclavas, bulky oilskins, duffle-coats, leather jerkins. They were unshaven, and very dirty. Some were stamping round the gun platform to warm their feet, some were slapping their arms against their coats; some smoked with unconcern, and others with a cat-like nervousness kept glancing at the sea and sky and at the herd of freighters moving slowly, oh, so slowly, towards its dangerous destination.

The ready-use lockers were open, and the beautiful bronze-tipped shells lay stacked near the breech of the gun, where the communication number sat with the telepads over his ears drumming with gloved fingers on a gaudily decorated tin hat, and listening with his eyes to the chatter of his mates.

Geordie was spinning a yarn. 'So I says to this party, I says, "Well, ain't you glad to see me?" And she says, "Why, George, where did you come from?" and she starts to wrap herself round my neck. "Wait a minute," I says, "what's all this here? What about that bloody pongo what's been loafing round since I come ashore last?" By Jeez, I was chocker, I was, from what I hears from a townie up north, which is why I never told her I was goin' up the line. Just walked in, see, like that – thought the bastard might be there, and I was goin' to vittle him up.'

There was noisy appreciation of this sentiment, because Geordie was like that. He used to let his feelings run away with him, and puzzle things out afterwards.

'And she says all sweet like, "Why, Gee-orge, you know I wouldn't go out with nobody while you was away."' Geordie pantomimed expressively, and those who were listening laughed again, because sailors are always as worried as hell about what the girl friend is getting up to while they're away.

'Not bloody much she wouldn't!' suggested someone.

'"Not suckin' much you wouldn't," I says, "but what's to stop him comin' here? What d'ya fancy I am, bloody wet?"' And Geordie laughed sardonically, the joke being on him in this piece of deduction.

'Plane out there, man,' interrupted Taffy excitedly, pointing to the horizon.

'Only Charlie loafin' round,' commented Big Scouse. Charlie the Barman was Jerry reconnaissance, and there he was, artlessly cruising round the horizon below the cloudbank. 'Better report him, Bill.'

'Where?' said Wacker Pine, the captain of the gun, anxiously peering round the sky. But the communication number was already making his report.

'Four-inch TS, four-inch TS. Aircraft bearing green one six o, angle of sight o five, goin' right to left. What's that? Lookout reported it five minutes ago? How the hell are we to know that?'

At the news that the plane was somebody else's business, no one took any further notice of it, except that every now and then someone would glance up to see if it was still there, the first evil warning of what was to come.

But no sense of impending danger was going to put Geordie off his narrative. '"Ally," I says, Ally bein' her name like, "Ally, you must fancy I'm bloody wet." And I puts me cap on, and she says "Where you goin', George?" So I says, "I'm goin' to find that bastard pongo and flake him out."'

There was a pause while they turned over this highly satisfying prospect in their minds. 'How d'ja know where he was, Geordie?'

'I never,' said Geordie. 'In fact, I never knew there was no bastard for certain, only what that townie tells me, so how the hell was I goin' to find him?' Big Scouse, who had been idly tossing a fuze key into the air, shook with laughter at this statement. 'Go on,' he said, retrieving the key with a flood of obscenity from under a locker. 'What did she say?'

'Not a bloody thing.' Geordie spoke with disgust. 'Just turned on the tap and snivelled to herself a bit. And after a bit she says, "You better have some supper first if you're goin' out." Of course I never goes much for the big eats when I'm up the line – gimme a couple of pints and a bit of the old doughmaker's and I'm set.' He thumbed with suggestive enjoyment, and grinned. 'But on account of I never et in the train at all, I says, "What've you got?" Christ, boys, and in less time than that I was woofin' down eggs and chips and a big lump of steak, and there was afters, too, but I forget what it was –'

'Four-inch TS!' roared the com. number. This contact with the transmitting station, the nerve centre of the ship, always hushed all talk. 'Aircraft reported thirty miles away. What's that? Repeat. Large group, comin' in.'

There was a startled pause. So this was it, at last?

'Better stand by,' said Wacker with sudden resolution.

'Jesus Christ, man,' said Taffy, and started to unbutton his coat with nervous haste. He hadn't been in air action before this trip, and he was jumpy. Not that everyone didn't show some signs of strain, waiting for it like that. But the convoy and its escort continued to move imperturbably onward.

'You're for it now,' said Scouse, watching maliciously and hooting with laughter. Just as if he wasn't in it, too. But Scouse had survived so many dive-bombings he never seemed to mind another one or two.

'Plenty of time,' put in Geordie with annoyance. He very firmly put down the shell someone had passed him. 'Let me finish what I'm tellin' yer, for suck sake.'

'Are you all ready, Pine?' It was the first lieutenant from the after conning position just for'ard of the gun.

'All ready, sir, yessir.' Pine had been moodily staring out to sea, looking with dislike at the lumbering and vulnerable freighters huddled together like a mob of sheep for the butcher. 'Better close up, boys. Come on now, get cracking!'

The crew moved to their action positions, trainer and layer at their platforms, the fuze-setters each clasping a shell beside their receiver, supply numbers near the magazine hoist. Pine, by the breech lever, examined the interceptor contacts with worried concentration. He looked up suddenly. 'I wish we was back in harbour.' The candour of this admission made everyone grin, and Pine felt it necessary to exert his authority as captain of the gun. 'Now you follow them pointers, Gorman, see? It'll be barrage at first, and they'll be comin' in faster than that. Everyone do what I tell you and you'll be all right, see? Hey, you quit skylarkin' there, Drennan; pay attention to what I'm telling you –'

'Ah wusna skylarking, Wacker,' protested Drennan in voluble indignation. 'A'm juist keeping ma honds warrm.'

'You do what I tell you!' roared Wacker. 'I'm the captain of this gun, and if anything goes wrong it's me takes the can back, not you, see? And when I says you was skylarkin' you was skylarkin', see?'

'Ah wusna –' This altercation broke the tension of waiting, and there were suppressed catcalls and a great simulation of choking laughter just to relieve the feelings and show Wacker it was sink or swim this time, and no gunnery school flannel either.

'Orright,' said Wacker ominously. 'Someone might go on the quarter deck over this. I'm the captain of this gun, and I'll do all the funny stuff round here, see?' Then coaxingly, 'We gotta get these prodgies up the spout, orright? and get 'em away quick as Christ'll let us. You do what –'

'Four-inch TS.' There was strained silence again. 'Forty aircraft approaching right ahead. Follow director. Barrage, barrage, barrage!'

The ship woke to life with a shuddering blast as the for'ard guns opened up, and all the way to the horizon ship after ship took up the tune till the noise of the battle rolled over the empty acres of the sea.

'Four-inch won't bear,' shouted Wacker as the fire buzzer rang for the second salvo.

'Four-inch TS. Four-inch will not bear.' Standing ready for the moment it would bear, the crew searched for the as yet unseen enemy. 'Bombs!' shouted someone as a great explosion rent the sea a mile away. It was followed by others, and looking up they could see the sinister black eggs sailing down here and there from the low cloud. But the bombers above were not the target for the moment.

'There they are!' Strung out in line the torpedo planes swept in from ahead, skimming the surface of the water, undulating as they poised for attack.

'Gun bearing,' yelled the trainer, and with a roar and a blast the long barrel spat flame, and the after guns followed, and the for'ard guns bore round on the beam, till the whole ship heeled and flamed in the shock. The pompom opened up like the rapid hammerblows of a giant, the deadly Oerlikons joined in, and through the sharp ginger smoke of the burnt cordite they could see the cherry-coloured tracer playing like a hose of fire along the bodies of the swooping planes.

The air seemed full of falling bombs, and tinfish like carelessly dropped cigarettes splashed among the crowded ships. Guns of all calibres punched and coughed and boomed. The clouds were pitted with shell-bursts. There were explosions everywhere, and a tremendous roar as an ammunition ship disintegrated into flame. There were planes screaming past in a dive or spinning down to the sea. And in the middle of all this the gun crew toiled and sweated like busy coordinated ants to keep their weapon bearing and firing.

'Got him!' A plane roaring past not three hundred yards away broke into flame as the tracer caught it. The flame streamed in the wind, went out, blazed up again, and wearing a plume of smoke like a shroud the machine plunged into the water.

'Four-inch!' The first lieutenant's voice was urgent. 'Train starboard. Green three oh. Come *on*, get that gun *round*!' A lone Junkers came skimming in to attack from an unexpected quarter. It sang at the ship like an arrow, and two tinfish fell lazily from its belly. The destroyer heeled heavily as she swung bows on to avoid their foaming course.

'Layer on.'

'Trainer on.'

The gun flicked back with a roar.

'Reload. Come *on*!'

Another shell in the breech, a snap as it slid shut. 'Fire!' The gun smashed a great hole of flame in the air. The shell seemed to burst just behind the plane as it fled astern. It rocked, spun over once, and fell like a diving gull.

The gun crew danced and cheered crazily, like drunk men. 'Good work, good work!' shouted the first lieutenant. The barrel, charged again with death, moved sensitively through the arc of the sky, seeking another target.

But there was no more. Down the lanes of the convoy the firing died away. The last of the attackers were astern, heading for home. Several flew crazily, leaving behind them the black stain of a fatal smoke. A last two high-level bombs smashed harmlessly on the sea; and the convoy moved quietly on. But not all of it. There, already falling astern, were drunken ships, some staggering nose in air, some burning, some heeling with slow finality as the ocean reached upward for their decks. The little rescue ships hunted fussily around them among the wreckage and the rafts. There were heads bobbing in that icy water, little figures clinging to a raft, or a battered boat, sometimes a solitary hand waving. The morse lamps winked and flickered busily from one destroyer to another.

'All right, relax,' called down the first lieutenant. 'Tea interval.'

'Jesus,' grumbled Geordie, 'gimme a smoke, someone.' The officer was grinning like a schoolboy, and from his position above them executed a couple of jubilant steps to show his satisfaction. They grinned back at him, grateful in some undefinable way, and they looked at one another appreciatively, in a new and surprising fashion, for they had suddenly become real to one another, working together in the noise and smoke of battle.

'What time is stumps drawn, sir?' inquired Pine, translating himself with petty officer's subservience into the first lieutenant's cricket idiom.

The first lieutenant surveyed the sky with critical concern. 'That depends on the light, Pine,' he replied pleasantly.

'We got that bastard middle stump,' announced Scouse, exploding with greasy mirth.

'Yes.' The first lieutenant turned away to show that this familiarity had now gone as far as the circumstances warranted.

A stoker emerged slowly from below, dragging deeply at a cigarette. 'H'are you, Stokes?'

'What was all them big bangs?' asked the stoker. 'Bombs or depth charges?'

'Both bastards, Stokes, both bastards.' And Scouse rocked with malicious mirth to think of the uncertainty and dread of the stokers below.

'I said there was depth charges,' announced the stoker sourly. 'The boys reckoned they was just bombs. Didn't half make the works rattle, not suckin' much they didn't.'

'How did yer make out, Taff?' inquired Geordie affably.

'Fine, man,' exulted Taffy. 'Jesus bloody Christ it was fine.'

'Yus,' stated Drennan, 'but we dunna want too much o' it, do we, Scouse?'

'What happened about you and the party, Geordie – you know?'

'Aw,' said Geordie carelessly. 'Nothing much.' It was clear he still harboured some sort of grievance for the interruption of his story. 'Matter of fact, she's a good kid, so I takes her down to the boozer after supper a bit and things is all right. But, suck me! I gets that suckin' boozed up I hardly knows what to do with her when I gets her home.'

'Not suckin' much you never,' commented Scouse with profound disbelief. And everyone shouted with rich enjoyment.

'Four-inch TS. Repeat. No more planes reported. Port watch to tea, starboard watch close up to AA defence stations. Stand fast, anti-submarine party.'

Those of the port watch leisurely hung up their tin hats, took off their anti-flash gear and moved off for'ard to the mess. From other stations the starboard watch arrived in ones and twos to replace them, and lounged about, swapping yarns of the attack.

The pale northern night began to fall. Miles astern now, in the wide desert of the ocean, an abandoned ship burned brightly. Nothing else might have happened. The convoy still moved steadily and changelessly on, and the wilderness of air and water imposed for a short time again its oppressive silence.

[*PNW 16*, 1943]

Alun Lewis

Ward 'O' 3 (b)

Ward 'O' 3 (b) was, and doubtless still is, a small room at the end of
the Officers' Convalescent Ward which occupies one wing of the
rectangle of one-storeyed sheds that enclose the 'lily-pond garden' of
No. X British General Hospital, Southern Army, India. The other
three wings contain the administrative offices, the Officers' Surgical
Ward and the Officers' Medical Ward. An outer ring of buildings
consist of the various ancillary institutions, the kitchens, the laboratory of tropical diseases, the mortuary, the operating theatres and the
X-ray theatre. They are all connected by roofed passageways; the
inner rectangle of wards has a roofed verandah opening on the garden
whose flagstones have a claustral and enduring aura. The garden is
kept in perpetual flower by six black, almost naked Mahratti gar-
deners who drench it with water during the dry season and prune and
weed it incessantly during the rains. It has tall flowering jacquarandas,
beds of hollyhock and carnation and stock, rose trellises and sticks
swarming with sweet peas; and in the arid months of burning heat the
geraniums bud with fire in red earthenware pots. It is, by 1943
standards, a good place to be in.

At the time of which I am writing, autumn 1942, Ward 'O' 3 (b),
which has four beds, was occupied by Captain A. G. Brownlow-
Grace, Lieut.-Quartermaster Withers, Lieut. Giles Moncrieff and
Lieut. Anthony Weston. The last-named was an R A C man who had
arrived in India from home four months previously and had been
seriously injured by an anti-tank mine during training. The other three
were infantrymen. Brownlow-Grace had lost an arm in Burma six
months earlier, Moncrieff had multiple leg injuries there and infantile
paralysis as well. 'Dad' Withers was the only man over twenty-five. He
was forty-four, a regular soldier with twenty-five years in the ranks
and three in commission; during this period he had the distinction of
never having been in action. He had spent all but two years abroad; he
had been home five times and had five children. He was suffering from
chronic malaria, sciatica and rheumatism. They were all awaiting a
medical board, at which it is decided whether a man should be

regraded to a lower medical category, whether he is fit for active or other service, whether he be sent home, or on leave, or discharged the service with a pension. They were the special charge of Sister Normanby, a regular QAIMNS nurse with a professional impersonality that controlled completely the undoubted flair and 'it' which distinguished her during an evening off at the Turf Club dances. She was the operating theatre sister; the surgeons considered her a perfect assistant. On duty or off everybody was pleased about her and aware of her; even the old matron whose puritan and sexless maturity abhorred prettiness and romantics had actually asked Sister Normanby to go on leave with her, Sister deftly refusing.

II

The floor is red parquet, burnished as a windless lake, the coverlets of the four beds are plum red, the blankets cherry red. Moncrieff hates red, Brownlow-Grace has no emotions about colours, any more than about music or aesthetics; but he hates Moncrieff. This is not unnatural. Moncrieff is a University student, Oxford or some bloody place, as far as Brownlow-Grace knows. He whistles classical music, wears his hair long, which is impermissible in a civilian officer and tolerated only in a cavalry officer with at least five years service in India behind him. Brownlow-Grace has done eight. Moncrieff says a thing is too wearing, dreadfully tedious, simply marvellous, wizard. He indulges in moods and casts himself on his bed in ecstasies of despair. He sleeps in a gauzy veil, parades the ward in the morning in chaplies and veil, swinging his wasted hips and boil-scarred shoulders from wash-place to bed; and he is vain. He has thirty photographs of himself, mounted enlargements, in S D and service cap, which he is sending off gradually to a network of young ladies in Greater London, Cape Town where he stayed on the way out, and the chain of hospitals he passed through on his return from Burma. His sickness has deformed him; that also Brownlow-Grace finds himself unable to stomach.

Moncrieff made several attempts to affiliate himself to Brownlow-Grace; came and looked over his shoulder at his album of photographs the second day they were together, asked him questions about hunting, fishing and shooting on the third day, talked to him about Burma on the third day and asked him if he'd been afraid to die. What a shocker, Brownlow-Grace thought. Now when he saw the man looking at his mounted self-portraits for the umpteenth time he closes his eyes and tries to sleep himself out of it. But his sleep was liverish and full of curses. He wanted to look at his watch but refused to open his eyes because the day was so long and it must be still short of nine. In his enormous tedium he prays Sister Normanby to come at eleven with a glass of iced nimbo pani for him. He doesn't know how he stands with her; he used to find women easy before Burma, he knew his slim and elegant figure could wear his numerous and expensive uniforms perfectly and he never had to exert himself in a dance or reception from the Savoy in the Strand through Shepheards in Cairo to the Taj in Bombay or the Turf Club in Poona. But now he wasn't sure; he wasn't sure whether his face had sagged and aged, his hair thinned, his decapitated arm in bad taste. He had sent an airgraph to his parents and his fiancée in Shropshire telling them he'd had his arm off. Peggy sounded as if she were thrilled by it in her reply. Maybe she was being kind. He didn't care so much nowadays what she happened to be feeling. Sister Normanby however could excite him obviously. He wanted to ask her to go to a dinner dance with him at the Club as soon as he felt strong enough. But he was feeling lonely; nobody came to see him; how could they, anyway? He was the only officer to come out alive. He felt ashamed of that sometimes. He hadn't thought about getting away until the butchery was over and the Japs were mopping up with the bayonet. He'd tried like the devil then, though; didn't realize he had so much cunning and desperation in him. And that little shocker asking him if he'd been afraid to die. He hadn't given death two thoughts.

There was Mostyn Turner. He used to think about Death a lot. Poor old Mostyn. Maybe it was just fancy but looking at some of Mostyn's photographs in the album, when the pair of them were on shikari tiger-hunting in Belgaum or that fortnight they had together in Kashmir, you could see by his face that he would die. He always attracted the serious type of girl; and like as not he'd take it too far. On the troopship to Rangoon he'd wanted Mostyn to play poker after the bar closed; looked for him everywhere, couldn't find him below-decks, nor in the men's mess deck where he sometimes spent an hour or two yarning; their cabin was empty. He found him on the boat deck eventually, hunched up by a lifeboat under the stars. Something stopped him calling him, or even approaching him; he'd turned away and waited by the rails at the companionway head till Mostyn had finished. Yes, finished crying. Incredible, really. He knew what was coming to him, God knows how; and it wasn't a dry hunch, it was something very moving, meant a lot to him somehow. And by God he'd gone looking for it, Mostyn had. He had his own ideas about fighting. Didn't believe in right and left boundaries, fronts, flanks, rears. He had the guerrilla platoon under his command and they went off into the blue the night before the pukka battle with a roving commission to make a diversion in the Jap rear. That was all. He'd gone off at dusk as casually as if they were on training. No funny business about Death then. He knew it had come, so he wasn't worrying. Life must have been more interesting to Mostyn than it was to himself, being made that way, having these thoughts and things. What he'd seen of Death that day, it was just a bloody beastly filthy horrible business, so forget it.

His hands were as long and thin and elegant as his body and his elongated narrow head with the Roman nose and the eyes whose colour nobody could have stated because nobody could stare back at him. His hands crumpled the pillow he was clutching. He was in a way a very fastidious man. He would have had exquisite taste if he hadn't lacked the faculty of taste.

'Messing up your new sheets again,' Sister Normanby said happily, coming into the room like a drop of Scotch. 'You ought to be playing the piano with those hands of yours, you know.'

He didn't remind her that he only had one left. He was pleased to think she didn't notice it.

'Hallo, Sister,' he said, bucking up at once. 'You're looking very young and fresh considering it was your night out last night.'

'I took it very quietly,' she said. 'Didn't dance much. Sat in the back of a car all the time.'

'For shame, my dear Celia,' Moncrieff butted in. 'Men are deceivers ever was said before the invention of the internal combustion engine and they're much worse in every way since that happened.'

'What is my little monkey jabbering about now,' she replied, offended at his freedom with her Christian name.

'Have you heard of Gipsy Rose Lee?' Moncrieff replied inconsequentially. 'She has a song which says "I can't strip to Brahms! Can you?"'

'Course she can,' said Dad Withers, unobtrusive at the door, a wry old buck, 'so long as she's got a mosquito net, isn't it, Sister?'

'Why do you boys always make me feel I haven't got a skirt on when I come in here?' she said.

'Because you can't marry all of us,' said Dad.

'Deep, isn't he?' she said.

She had a bunch of newly-cut antirrhinums and dahlias, the petals beaded with water, which she put in the bowl, arranging them quietly as she twitted the men. Moncrieff looked at her quizzically as though she had aroused conjecture in the psychoanalytical department of his brain.

'Get on with your letter-writing, Moncrieff,' she said without having looked up. He flushed.

'There's such a thing as knowing too much,' Dad said to her paternally. 'I knew a girl in Singapore once, moved there from Shanghai wiv the regiment, she did. She liked us all, the same as nurses say they do. And when she found she liked one more than all the others put together, it come as a terrible shock to her and she had to start again. Took some doing, it did.'

'Dad, you're crazy,' she said, laughing hard. 'A man with all your complaints ought to be too busy counting them to tell all these stories.' And then, as she was about to go, she turned and dropped the momentous news she'd been holding out to them.

'You're all four having your medical board next Thursday,' she said. 'So you'd better make yourselves ill again if you want to go back home.'

'I don't want to go back "home",' Brownlow-Grace said, laying sardonic stress on the last word.

'I don't know,' Dad said. 'They tell me it's a good country to get into, this 'ere England. Why, I was only reading in the *Bombay Times* this morning there's a man Beaverage or something, made a report, they even give you money to bury yourself with there now. Suits me.'

'You won't die, Dad,' Brownlow-Grace said kindly. 'You'll simply fade away.'

'Well,' said Sister Normanby. 'There are your fresh flowers. I must go and help to remove a clot from a man's brain now. Good-bye.'

'Good-bye,' they all said, following her calves and swift heels as she went.

'I didn't know a dog had sweat glands in his paws before,' Brownlow-Grace said, looking at his copy of *The Field*.

The others didn't answer. They were thinking of their medical board. It was more interesting really than Sister Normanby.

III

Weston preferred to spend the earlier hours in a deck chair in the garden, by the upraised circular stone pool, among the ferns; here he would watch the lizards run like quicksilver and as quickly freeze into an immobility so lifeless as to be macabre, and the striped tree rats playing among the jacquaranda branches; and he would look in vain for the mocking bird whose monotony gave a timeless quality to the place and the mood. He was slow in recovering his strength; his three operations and the sulphanilamide tablets he was taking had exhausted the blood in his veins; most of it was somebody else's blood, anyway, an insipid blood that for two days had dripped from a bottle suspended over his bed, while they waited for him to die. His jaw and shoulderbone had been shattered, a great clod of flesh torn out of his neck and thigh, baring his windpipe and epiglottis and exposing his lung and femoral artery; and although he had recovered very rapidly, his living self seemed overshadowed by the death trauma through which he had passed. There had been an annihilation, a complete obscuring; into which light had gradually dawned. And this light grew unbearably white, the glare of the sun on a vast expanse of snow, and in its unbounded voids he had moved without identity, a pillar of salt in a white desert as pocked and cratered as the dead face of the moon. And then some mutation had taken place and he became aware of pain. A pain that was not pure like the primal purity, but polluted, infected, with racking thirsts and suffocations and writhings, and black eruptions disturbed the whiteness, and coloured dots sifted the intense sun glare, areas of intolerable activities appeared in those passive and limitless oceans. And gradually these manifestations became the simple suppurations of his destroyed inarticulate flesh, and the bandaging and swabbing and probing of his wounds and the grunts of his throat. From it he desired wildly to return to the timeless void where the act of being was no more than a fall of snow or the throw of a rainblow; and these regions became a nostalgia to his pain and soothed his hurt and parched spirit. The two succeeding operations had been conscious experiences, and he had been frightened of them. The preliminaries got on his nerves, the starving, the aperients, the trolley, the prick of morphia, and its false peace. The spotless theatre with its walls of glass and massive lamps of burnished chrome, the anaesthetist who stuttered like a worn gramophone record, Sister Normanby clattering the knives in trays of lysol, the soft irresistible waves of wool that surged up darkly through the interstices of life like water through a boat; and the choking final surrender to the void his heart feared.

And now, two and a half months later, with his wounds mere puckers dribbling the last dregs of pus, his jaw no longer wired up and splinted, his arm no longer inflamed with the jab of the needle, he sat in the garden with his hands idle in a pool of sunlight, fretting and fretting at himself. He was costive, his stockings had holes in the heel that got wider every day and he hadn't the initiative to ask Sister for a needle and wool; his pen had no ink, his razor blade was blunt, he had shaved badly, he hadn't replied to the airmail letter that lay crumpled in his hand. He had carried that letter about with him for four days, everywhere he went, ever since he'd received it.

'You look thrillingly pale and Byronic this morning, Weston,' Moncrieff said, sitting in the deck chair opposite him with his writing pad and a sheaf of received letters tied in silk tape. 'D'you mind me sharing your gloom?'

Weston snorted.

'You can do what you bloody well like,' he said, with suppressed irritation.

'Oh dear, have I gone and hurt you again? I'm always hurting people I like,' Moncrieff said. 'But I can't help it. Honestly I can't. You believe me, Weston, don't you?'

Disturbed by the sudden nakedness of his voice Weston looked up at the waspish intense face, the dark eyebrows and malignant eyes.

'Of course I believe you, monkey,' he said. 'If you say so.'

'It's important that you should believe me,' Moncrieff said moodily. 'I must find somebody who believes me wherever I happen to be. I'm afraid otherwise. It's too lonely. Of course I hurt some people purposely. That dolt Brownlow-Grace for example. I enjoy making him wince. He's been brought up to think life should be considerate to him. His mother, his bank manager, his batman, his bearer – always somebody to mollycoddle him and see to his wants. Christ, the fellow's incapable of wanting anything really. You know, he even resents Sister Normanby having to look after other people beside himself. He only considered the war as an opportunity for promotion; I bet he was delighted when Hitler attacked Poland. And there are other people in this world going about with their brains hanging out, their minds half lynched – a fat lot he understands.' He paused, and seeming to catch himself in the middle of his tirade, he laughed softly. 'I was going to write a letter-card to my wife,' he said. 'Still, I haven't got any news. No new love. Next Thursday we'll have some news for them, won't we? I get terribly worked up about this medical board, I can't sleep. You don't think they'll keep me out in India, Weston, do you? It's so lonely out here. I couldn't stay here any longer. I just couldn't.'

'You are in a state, monkey,' Weston said, perturbed and yet laughing, as one cheers a child badly injured. 'Sit quiet a bit, you're speaking loudly. Brownlow'll hear you if you don't take care.'

'Did he?' Moncrieff said suddenly apprehensive. 'He didn't hear me, did he? I don't want to sound as crude as that, even to him.'

'Oh, I don't know. He's not a bad stick,' Weston said. 'He's very sincere and he takes things in good part, even losing his arm, and his career.'

'Oh, I know you can preach a sermon on him easily. I don't think in terms of sermons, that's all,' Moncrieff said. 'But I've been through Burma the same as he has. Why does he sneer at me?' He was silent. Then he said again, 'It's lonely out here.' He sighed. 'I wish I hadn't come out of Burma. I needn't have, I could have let myself go. One night when my leg was gangrenous, the orderly gave me a shot of morphia and I felt myself nodding and smiling. And there was no more jungle, no Japs, no screams, no difficulties at home, no nothing. The orderly would have given me a second shot if I'd asked him. I don't know why I didn't. It would have finished me off nicely. Say, Weston, have you ever been afraid of Death?'

'I don't think it's as simple as that,' Weston said. 'When I was as good as dead, the first three days here, and for a fortnight afterwards too, I was almost enamoured of death. I'd lost my fear of it. But then I'd lost my will, and my emotions were all dead. I hadn't got any relationships left. It isn't really fair then, is it?'

'I think it's better to fear death,' Moncrieff said slowly. 'Otherwise you grow spiritually proud. With most people it's not so much fear of death as love of life that keeps them sensible. I don't love life, personally. Only I'm a bit of a coward and I don't want to die again. I loathe Burma, I can't tell you how terribly. I hope they send me home. If you go home, you ought to tell them you got wounded in Burma, you know.'

'Good God, no,' Weston said, outraged. 'Why should I lie?'

'That's all they deserve,' Moncrieff said. 'I wonder what they're doing there now? Talking about reconstruction, I suppose. Even the cinemas will have reconstruction films. Well, maybe I'll get a job in some racket or other. Cramming Sandhurst cadets or something. What will you do when you get home?'

'Moncrieff, my good friend,' Weston said. 'We're soldiers, you know. And it isn't etiquette to talk about going home like that. I'm going in where you left off. I want to have a look at Burma. *And I don't want to see England.*'

'Don't you?' Moncrieff said, ignoring the slow emphasis of

Weston's last words and twirling the tassel of his writing-pad slowly. 'Neither do I, very much,' he said with an indifference that ended the conversation.

IV

The sick have their own slightly different world, their jokes are as necessary and peculiar to them as their medicines; they can't afford to be morbid like the healthy, nor to be indifferent to their environment like the Arab. The outside world has been washed out; between them and the encircling mysteries there is only the spotlight of their obsessions holding the small backcloth of ward and garden before them. Anyone appearing before this backcloth has the heightened emphasis and significance of a character upon the stage. The Sikh fortune tellers who offered them promotion and a fortune and England as sibilantly as panders, the mongoose-fight-snake walas with their wailing sweet pipes and devitalized cobras, the little native cobblers and peddlers who had customary right to enter the precincts entered as travellers from an unknown land. So did the visitors from the Anglo-Indian community and brother officers passing on leave. And each visitor was greedily absorbed and examined by every patient, with the intenser acumen of disease.

Brownlow-Grace had a visitor. This increased his prestige, like having a lot of mail. It appeared she had only just discovered he was here, for during the last four days before his medical board she came every day after lunch and stayed sitting on his bed until dusk had conferred upon them an intimacy that evoked in the others a green nostalgia.

She was by any standards a beautiful woman. One afternoon a young unsophisticated English Miss in a fresh little frock and long hair; the next day French and exotic with the pallor of an undertaker's lily and hair like statuary; the third day, exquisitely Japanese, carmined and beringed with huge green amber stones, her hair in a high bun that only a great lover would dare unloose. When she left each evening Sister Normanby came in with a great bustle of fresh air and practicality to tidy his bed and put up his mosquito net. And he seemed equally capable of entertaining and being entertained by both ladies.

On the morning of the medical board Brownlow-Grace came and sat by Anthony among the ferns beside the lily pool; and this being a gesture of unusual amiability in one whom training had made rigid, Weston was unreasonably pleased.

'Well, Weston,' he said. 'Sweating on the top line over this medical board?'

'What d'you mean?' Weston asked.

'Well, d'you think everything's a wangle to get you home or keep you here like that little squirt Moncrieff?'

'I don't think along those lines, personally,' Weston said. He looked at the long languid soldier sprawled in the deck chair. 'The only thing I'm frightened of is that they'll keep me *here*, or give me some horrible office job where I'll never see a Valentine lift her belly over a bund and go grunting like a wild boar at – well, whoever happens to be there. I got used to the idea of the Germans. I suppose the Japs will do.'

'You're like me; no enemy,' Brownlow-Grace said. 'I didn't think twice about it – till it happened. You're lucky, though. You're the only one of us four who'll ever see action. I could kill some more. What do I want to go home for? They hacked my arm off, those bastards; I blew the fellow's guts out that did it, had the muzzle of my Colt rammed into his belly, I could feel his breath, he was like a frog, the swine. You, I suppose you want to go home, haven't been away long, have you?'

'Six months.'

'Six months without a woman, eh?' Brownlow-Grace laughed, yet kindly.

'Yes.'

'I'm the sort who'll take somebody else's,' Brownlow-Grace said. 'I don't harm them.'

Weston didn't reply.

'You've got a hell of a lot on your mind, haven't you, Weston? Any fool can see something's eating you up.' Still no reply. 'Look here, I may be a fool, but come out with me tonight, let's have a party together. Eh?' Surprisingly, Weston wasn't embarrassed at this extreme gesture of kindness. It was so ingenuously made. Instead he felt an enormous relief, and for the first time the capacity to speak. Not, he told himself, to ask for advice. Brownlow-Grace wasn't a clergyman with a healing gift; but it was possible to tell him the thing simply, to shift the weight of it a bit. 'I'm all tied up,' he said. 'A party wouldn't be any use, nor a woman.'

'Wouldn't it?' Brownlow-Grace said drily, standing up. Weston had a feeling he was about to go. It would have excruciated him. Instead he half turned, as if to disembarrass him, and said, 'The flowers want watering.'

'You know, if you're soldiering, there are some things you've got to put out of bounds to your thoughts,' Weston said. 'Some things you don't let yourself doubt.'

'Your wife, you mean?' Brownlow-Grace said holding a breath of his cigarette in his lungs and studying the ants on the wall.

'Not only her,' Weston said. 'Look. I didn't start with the same things as you. You had a pram and a private school and you saw the sea, maybe. My father was a collier and he worked in a wet pit. He got rheumatism and nystagmus and then the dole and then parish relief. I'm not telling you a sob story. It's just I was used to different sounds. I used to watch the wheel of the pit spin round year after year, after school and Saturdays and Sundays; and then from 1926 on I watched it not turning round at all, and I can't ever get that wheel out of my mind. It still spins and idles, and there's money and nystagmus coming into the house or no work and worse than nystagmus. I just missed the wheel sucking me down the shaft. I got a scholarship to the county school. I don't know when I started rebelling. Against that wheel in my head. I didn't get along very well. Worked in a grocer's, and a printer's, and no job was good enough for me, I had a bug. Plenty of friends too, plenty of chaps thinking the same as me. Used to read books in those days, get passionate about politics, Russia was like a woman to me. Then I did get a job I wanted, in a bookshop in Holborn. A French woman came in one day. I usually talked to customers, mostly politics; but not to her. She came in several times, once with a trade union man I knew. She was short, she had freckles, a straight nose, chestnut hair, she looked about eighteen; she bought books about Beethoven, Schopenhauer, the Renaissance, biology – I read every book she bought, after she'd gone back to France. I asked this chap about her. He said she was a big name, you know the way revolutionary movements toss up a woman sometimes. She was a Communist, a big speaker in the industrial towns in North France, she'd been to Russia too. And, well, I just wanted her, more and more and more as the months passed. Not her politics, but her fire. If I could hear her addressing a crowd, never mind about wanting her in those dreams you get.

'And then the war came and most of my friends said it was a phoney war, but I was afraid from the beginning that something would happen to France and I wanted to hear her speaking first. I joined up in November and I made myself such a bloody pest that they posted me to France to reinforcements. I got my war all right. And I met her, too. The trade unionist I told you about gave me a letter to introduce myself. She lived in Lille. She knew me as soon as the door opened.

And I was just frightened. But after two nights there was no need to be frightened. You get to think for years that life is just a fight, with a flirt thrown in sometimes, a flirt with death or sex or whatever happens to be passing, but mostly a fight all the way along. And then you soften up, you're no use, you haven't got any wheel whirring in your head any more. Only flowers on the table and a piano she plays sometimes, when she wants to, when she wants to love.'

'I've never been to France,' Brownlow-Grace said. 'Hated it at school, French I mean. Communists, of course – I thought they were all Bolshies, you know, won't obey an order. What happened after Dunkirk?'

'It was such burning sunny weather,' Weston said. 'It was funny, having fine weather. I couldn't get her out of my mind. The sun seemed to expand inside the lining of my brain and the whole fortnight after we made that last stand with Martel at Cambrai I didn't know whether I was looking for her or Dunkirk. When I was most exhausted it was worst, she came to me once by the side of the road, there were several dead Belgian women lying there, and she said "Look, Anthony, I have been raped. They raped me, the Boche." And the world was crashing and whirring, or it was doped, wouldn't lift a finger to stop it, and the Germans crossing the Seine. A year before I'd have said to the world Serve you right. But not now, with Cecile somewhere inside the armies. She'd tried.'

'And that was the end?' Brownlow-Grace said.

'Yes,' said Weston. 'Just about. Only it wasn't a beautiful end, the way it turned out. I had eight months in England, and I never found out a thing. The Free French didn't know. One of them knew her well, knew her as a lover, he told me; boasted about it; I didn't tell him; I wanted to find her, I didn't care about anything else. And then something started in me. I used to mooch about London. A French girl touched me on the street one night. I went with her. I went with a lot of women. Then we embarked for overseas. I had a girl at Durban, and in Bombay; sometimes they were French, if possible they were French. God, it was foul.'

He got up and sat on the edge of the pool; under the green strata of mosses the scaled goldfish moved slowly in their palaces of burning gold. He wiped his face which was sweating.

'Five days ago I got this letter from America,' he said. 'From her.'

Brownlow-Grace said, 'That was a bit of luck.' Weston laughed.

'Yes,' he said. 'Yes. It was nice of her to write. She put it very nicely, too. Would you like to read it?'

'No,' said Brownlow-Grace. 'I don't want to read it.'

'She said it often entered her mind to write to me, because I had been so sweet to her, in Lille, that time. She hoped I was well. To enter America there had been certain formalities, she said; she'd married an American, a country which has all types, she said. There is a Life, she said, but not mine, and a war also, but not mine. Now it is the Japanese. That's all she said.'

'She remembered you,' Brownlow-Grace said.

'Some things stick in a woman's mind,' Weston said. 'She darned my socks for me in bed. Why didn't she say she remembered darning my socks?'

Brownlow-Grace pressed his hand, fingers extended, upon the surface of the water, not breaking its resistance, quite.

'I don't use the word,' he said. 'But I guess it's because she loved you.'

Weston looked up, searching and somehow naïve.

'I don't mind about the Japanese,' he said, 'if that were so.'

V

Dad Withers had his medical board first; he wasn't in the board room long; in fact he was back on the verandah outside 'O' 3 (b) when Weston returned from sending a cable at the camp post office.

'Did it go all right, Dad?' Weston asked.

'Sure, sure,' Dad said, purring as if at his own cleverness. 'Three colonels and two majors there, and the full colonel he said to me, "Well, Withers, what's your trouble? Lieutenant Quartermaster, weren't you?" And I said "Correct, sir, and now I'm putting my own body in for exchange, sir. It don't keep the rain out no more, sir." So he said, "You're not much use to us, Withers, by the look of you." And I said, "Not a bit of use, sir, sorry to report." And the end of it was they give me a free berth on the next ship home wiv full military honours and a disability pension and all. Good going, isn't it now?'

'Very good, Dad. I'm very pleased.'

'Thank you,' Dad said, his face wrinkled and benign as a tortoise. 'Now go and get your own ticket and don't keep the gentlemen waiting . . .'

Dad lay half sleeping in the deck chair, thinking that it was all buttoned up now, all laid on, all made good. It had been a long time, a life time, more than twenty hot seasons, more than twenty rains. Not many could say that. Not many had stuck it like him. Five years in

Jhansi with his body red as lobster from head to toe with prickly heat, squirting a water pistol down his back for enjoyment and scratching his shoulders with a long fork from the bazaar. Two big wars there'd been, and most of the boys had been glad to go into them, excited to be posted to France, or embark for Egypt. But he'd stuck it out. Still here, still good for a game of nap, and them all dead, the boys that wanted to get away. And now it was finished with him, too.

He didn't know. Maybe he wasn't going home the way he'd figured it out after all. Maybe there was something else, something he hadn't counted on. This tiredness, this emptiness, this grey blank wall of mist, this not caring. What would it be like in the small Council house with five youngsters and his missus? She'd changed a lot, the last photo she sent she was like his mother, spectacles and fat legs, full of plainness. Maybe the kids would play with him, though, the two young ones?

He pulled himself slowly out of his seat, took out his wallet, counted his money; ninety chips he had. Enough to see India just once again. Poor old India. He dressed hurriedly, combed his thin hair, wiped his spectacles, dusted his shoes, and left before the others came back. He picked up a tonga at the stand outside the main gates of the hospital cantonment, just past the MD lines, and named a certain hotel down town. And off he cantered, the skinny old horse clattering and letting off great puffs of bad air under the tongawala's whip, and Dad shouting 'Jillo, jillo,' impatient to be drunk.

Brownlow-Grace came in and went straight to the little bed table where he kept his papers in an untidy heap. He went there in a leisurely way, avoiding the inquiring silences of Weston and Moncrieff and Sister Normanby, who were all apparently doing something. He fished out an airgraph form and his fountain-pen and sat quietly on the edge of his bed.

'Oh damn and blast it,' he said angrily. 'My pen's dry.'

Weston gave him an inkbottle.

He sat down again.

'What's the date?' he said after a minute.

'12th,' Moncrieff said.

'What month?' he asked.

'December.'

'Thanks.'

He wrote slowly, laboriously, long pauses between sentences. When he'd finished he put his pen away and looked for a stamp.

'What stamp d'you put on an airgraph?' he said.

'Three annas,' Moncrieff said patiently.

Sister Normanby decided to abolish the embarrassing reticence with which this odd man was concealing his board result. She had no room for broody hens.

'Well,' she said, gently enough. 'What happened at the board?'

He looked up at her and neither smiled nor showed any sign of recognition. Then he stood up, took up his cane and peaked service cap, and brushed a speck of down off his long and well fitting trousers.

'They discharged me,' he said. 'Will you post this airgraph for me, please?'

'Yes,' she said, and for some odd reason she found herself unable to deal with the situation and took it from him and went on with her work.

'I'm going out,' he said.

Weston followed him into the garden and caught him up by the lily pool.

'Is that invitation still open?' he asked.

'What invitation?' Brownlow-Grace said.

'To go on the spree with you tonight?' Weston said.

Brownlow-Grace looked at him thoughtfully.

'I've changed my mind, Anthony,' he said – Weston was pleasurably aware of this first use of his Christian name – 'I don't think I'd be any use to you tonight. Matter of fact, I phoned Rita just now, you know the woman who comes to see me, and she's calling for me in five minutes.'

'I see,' Weston said. 'O K by me.'

'You don't mind, do you?' he said. 'I don't think you need Rita's company, do you? Besides, she usually prefers one man at a time. She's the widow of a friend of mine, Mostyn Turner; he was killed in Burma, too.'

Weston came back into the ward to meet Sister Normanby's white face. 'Where's he gone?' she said.

Weston looked at her, surprised at the emotion and stress this normally imperturbable woman was showing.

He didn't answer her.

'He's gone to that woman,' she said, white and virulent. 'Hasn't he?'

'Yes, he has,' he said quietly.

'She always has them when they're convalescent,' she said, flashing with venom. She picked up her medicine book and the jar with her thermometer in it. 'I have them when they're sick.'

She left the ward, biting her white lips.

'I didn't know she felt that way about him,' Weston said.

'Neither did she,' said Moncrieff. 'She never knows till it's too late. That's the beauty about her. She's virginal.'

'You're very cruel, Moncrieff.'

Moncrieff turned on him like an animal.

'Cruel?' he said. 'Cruel? Well, I don't lick Lazarus's sores, Weston. I take the world the way it is. Nobody cares about you out here. Nobody. What have I done to anybody? Why should they keep me here? What's the use of keeping a man with infantile paralysis and six inches of bone missing from his leg? Why didn't the board let me go home?'

'You'll go home, monkey, you'll go home,' Weston said gently. 'You know the Army. You can help them out here. You're bound to go home when the war ends.'

'Do you think so?' Moncrieff said. 'Do you?' He thought of this for a minute at least. Then he said, 'No, I shall never go home. I know it.'

'Don't be silly, monkey. You're a bit run down, that's all.' Weston soothed him. 'Let's go and sit by the pool for a while.'

'I like the pool,' Moncrieff said. They strolled out together and sat on the circular ledge. The curving bright branches held their leaves peacefully above the water. Under the mosses they could see the old toad of the pond sleeping, his back rusty with jewels. Weston put his hand in the water; minnows rose in small flocks and nibbled at his fingers. Circles of water lapped softly outwards, outwards, till they touched the edge of the pool, and cast a gentle wetness on the stone, and lapped again inwards, inwards. And as they lapped inwards he felt the ripples surging against the most withdrawn and inmost ledges of his being, like a series of temptations in the wilderness. And he felt glad tonight, feeling some small salient gained when for many reasons the men whom he was with were losing ground along the whole front to the darkness that there is.

'No,' said Moncrieff at last. 'Talking is no good. But perhaps you will write to me sometimes, will you, just to let me know.'

'Yes, I'll write to you, monkey,' Weston said, looking up.

And then he looked away again, not willing to consider those empty inarticulate eyes.

'The mosquitoes are starting to bite,' he said. 'We'd better go now.'

[*PNW 18*, 1943]

Louis Clamorgan

The Midshipman

Translated from the French by Marjorie Mack

[Throughout the winter months, four motor launches of the Fighting French Navy plied up and down the Channel alongside the ships of the Royal Navy. Under their guardianship, a large number of merchant vessels passed through the Straits of Dover without the loss of a single ship.

In the absence of their seniors, many young Frenchmen hardly more than boys underwent their sea apprenticeship in those hazardous waters, during the long hours of darkness, and in a battle zone of almost continuous activity.

Louis Clamorgan tells the story of these young apprentices of life in a novel from which the following extract is taken.]

The flotilla in formation steamed out to meet the convoy that it was to take under escort – a convoy of thirty ships coming down from the north-east coast of England.

In line, two by two, the merchantmen made their weekly trip under the chaperonage of their superintendent, a destroyer. It was a slow procession, each unit of which dawdled a little. Its members were scattered over several miles.

Whilst this procession bore no resemblance to a school crocodile, it had a certain look of one of those Sunday outings of the Bicêtre veterans, the more so as it was neither the smartest nor the newest ships that had been chosen to run the gauntlet of the German batteries within sight of the French coast.

But it was not of the convoy that Jean Compagnon, midshipman on board the *Saint Briac,* was thinking. He was looking out over the sea and amusing himself trying to guess what sort of a night it would be.

The short waves were no stronger than usual, but they seemed made of some steely metal, and the vicious force of their impact as they broke against the vessel's side could be felt from truck to keel. It was not blowing hard, but the wind caught up the spindrift from the surface of the sea and flung it, invisible as spadefuls of sand, full in his face.

Jean took out a cigarette and bent to light it. The flame of the cigarette lighter seemed to shine out with surprising brilliance, and he straightened himself to look around him.

It was daylight still, but a dying day from which the colours had already faded. Jean looked at the sea with the eyes of a doctor who alone can read the secret certain signs of approaching death.

The signalman close beside him could no longer distinguish the colours of the flags which should have given him the merchantmen's numbers. His binoculars, he said, were bad. 'He hasn't noticed,' thought Jean, 'it's the daylight that's dying.'

'It's easy to make out Number Twenty-three, Sir,' he said to the Captain. 'She's the *Baron*. We had her in the last convoy but one.'

'That old collier with the ridiculously long thin funnel aft?'

'That's the one, Sir.'

And presently, in fact, the *Baron* appeared. She was one of those ships that are the curse of all commodores of convoys – an old collier, dirty and broken-winded, making the barest attempt to keep her place in the line, and carrying out signals only when it suited her to do so. And yet somehow she kept going, laden always to capacity, and, if she had something of the gait of a shapeless old slut dancing a jig on a pair of crutches, she always managed to arrive in port along with the others.

The *Saint Briac* took up her position and altered speed and course to that of the convoy. The Captain handed over the watch to the midshipman, saying as he did so: 'Try to leave me in peace tonight, Snotty. I'm tired. I'd give a lot to exchange that settee in the deck house for my own cabin bunk.'

Each time that Jean took the watch he had the impression that this was some totally new game that he was called on to play – that he was having at least to set down an old toy in a new environment. Or as though he were seeking in a new room for some predestined niche in which to place an old and familiar piece of furniture.

It was a game the rules of which changed with every time of playing. And you had to know those rules uncommonly well before the game started.

Jean looked at the map, studied the currents, turned up the Nautical Almanac, calculated distances, logged the revolutions, made sure that the recognition signals were ready.

Then he pulled on his fur gloves, tied a towel round his neck, buttoned up his watch coat and set himself to follow by compass the route he had fixed on.

Then, and not till then, did the game begin. And it was not without a certain measure of anxiety that Jean started to play it. For the whole of his nautical experience was comprised in six months at the Naval School, and it's a far cry between rules hastily conned by heart and the reality, particularly when that reality begins to assume complications, and at times such extremely odd ones.

'It's not going to be a very cheerful convoy,' remarked the signal-man.

'Oh, shut up!' said Jean. 'Don't start worrying before you need.'

The signalman regarded the midshipman with astonishment. 'Who's worrying? And if I was, it's my inside that would do the worrying.'

Jean didn't answer. He looked straight ahead, making the most of these last few moments of peace before the fall of total darkness and their arrival off the Downs. The wind was blowing from the south-west, bringing with it a heavy swell and dense black clouds. The night would be dark indeed.

'It will be all right,' Jean told himself, 'if only I can manage to keep cool.' For he was well aware of his tendency to get worked up. But it isn't easy to keep cool when you are only nineteen; when the masts of a wreck, a mine, or a reef is looming up ahead out of the darkness within fifty yards of where you stand, and when a vast collier is on the point of cutting you in half. When you have to recall theoretic rules and give definite orders in the face of immediate reality.

Jean considered.

'Tonight there'll barely be visibility at a hundred yards. At nine knots, I'm doing five yards a second. So that as soon as I sight anything I shall have just twenty seconds between us and disaster.'

'And that isn't much,' he finished out aloud.

'What isn't much?'

'Those two days C.B. I've a good mind to give you for not warning me of that buoy ahead,' replied the midshipman coolly.

Jean had to use a shaded torch to be able to see to write down the hour at which this buoy was passed in his notebook. The falling night unfolded an opaque screen before his eyes, still filled with the day — still refusing to believe in the night. He had to gaze long at the sea before he could make out the silhouette of the *Baron*, the sole member of the convoy now visible.

'The *Baron* is coming up, Sir,' said the signalman.

'How is her head?' Jean asked the helmsman.

'On the course.'

'Steer five degrees to port.'

'Five degrees to port it is.'

'The Commodore has his own views about the strength of the wind and tide,' thought Jean, 'but as he's the Commodore, I suppose he's right.'

The wireless buzzer sounded. Jean bent down to the receiver.

'Yes,' he answered in English.

'From Dover, Sir. Buoy number four. Light extinguished.'

'Thank you.'

Donald at the wireless was the only Englishman on board.

Jean went below into the deck house, where the Captain was asleep on the bench, rolled in a rug.

'If you please, Sir . . .'

'Yes?'

'Buoy number four. Light extinguished, Sir.'

'Oh well, light it again.'

But Jean stuck to his guns. For if the light on the buoy is extinguished, the course has to be constantly checked, to avoid running on the sandbank. And on a night like this, it would be impossible for him to leave the bridge for more than a few moments at a time.

'But, Sir, it's a radio signal from Dover. Buoy number four is the one marking the bank.'

At last a head was thrust out of the rug.

'God blast you, Snotty, can't you leave me in peace just for tonight?'

Jean returned to the bridge. He looked at the compass and noted the course uneasily. Now five degrees – ten degrees off the course. He would have liked to get the look-out to understand that this night of all others he needed his help. But how could he make such an appeal to the feelings of this twenty-seven-year-old sailor who had been at sea for the last ten years, and who had shown nothing but ironic contempt for the little pink-and-white midshipman of the Naval School?

Fifteen degrees off the course.

'For God's sake, keep an eye on the steering!'

'For God's sake, keep an eye on the steering.' Ironically the words came back to him through the receiver from the helmsman.

'If you'd only give the regular orders, you'd have no insolent answers,' remarked the Captain, coming up on to the bridge.

Jean didn't reply. Couldn't they allow him one piece of sarcasm? If he wasn't always up to the level of his job, was it he that was to blame? Was it his fault if the Admiralty turned out fresh officers by the dozen, so as to replace those who were killed, or who had ceased to fight?

'Where is the convoy?' the Captain asked.

'The *Baron* on the starboard bow,' the signalman answered. 'The only ship in sight.'

'What is your course?'

'Five degrees to port of our course,' said Jean. 'The same as the *Baron*.'

'Where are we now?'

'I haven't been able to check up, Sir. We ought to alter course at 20.45 at buoy number four. But its light has gone out, and in this darkness we shan't sight it till we're almost on top of it.'

'Put a second man on look-out. I'll follow the course from below.'

Jean sent for Kerizel the gunner.

Three men – to call them children would be nearer the mark – were now on watch, seated close together on the narrow bench. Whenever a deluge of water poured over them they ducked their heads together, and together, streaming with water, they raised them again to search the night once more.

Kerizel was sixteen. He had succeeded in getting on board by the simple expedient of adding three years to his papers. Once there, he had arranged his days in a manner to suit himself. It was to play – to play for as much of the day as possible, just as he had made a practice of doing in the fishing village from whence he had come. Not much of a hand on watch, yet the midshipman found a certain satisfaction in his company; his assurance seemed to lighten the atmosphere. His mind registered facts without complaining, so natural a part of the day's work had hardship become. Most probably he never experienced fear, not by reason of his courage, but through a complete unawareness of danger. For him every ship was a fine ship, every captain a great leader, and his own gun better than the other ship's. Once these axioms have been laid down, what more is there to worry about?

Kerizel took the rough with the smooth with the same even temper, like the sun and the rain from heaven. His child's mind, his child's hands instantly refashioned them into some new game more or less skilled, more or less violent; but he was always ready to break out into laughter. And it was this laughter that sounded so sweet tonight in the ears of Jean Compagnon.

'Keep a good look-out, you young scamp,' said Jean.

And he proceeded to explain himself to Kerizel.

'Mark you, to pass through the Downs by night is like walking about without seeing there's a game of skittles going on all round you. The skittles are the rocks and the banks all over the place – ships that have strayed off their course, derelicts. Besides that, it's the deuce of a bad surface you're playing on – frightfully uneven through the action of the currents, the wind and the ground swell. So you've got to be pretty nippy when you throw your ball.'

'It's like a game of skittles, except that it's the other way round,' Kerizel retorted. 'What we have to do is to pass between the skittles without touching them.'

'We shall make the bank in about ten minutes. The tide is low, so it ought to be uncovered. If you see a dark line – something still where everything else is moving, or if you see breakers ahead, sing out at once.'

'If I see surf, I'll holler.'

Jean looked at the time: 20.35.

'Bank! On the port bow!'

'Hard a-starboard . . . Midships . . . Steady.'

Clutching the voice-pipe, Jean shouted the orders. Desperately he stared into the night, masking with his arm the compass, whose pale light now seemed almost blinding.

'There, to port!' Kerizel shouted again, his arm pointing.

Little by little the bank showed dimly – or rather, not so much the bank as a difference between movement and immobility, between the quick and the dead.

The ship rushed straight ahead towards it. It was less than fifty yards away.

'We're going to run on to it,' thought Jean. 'I ought to have reversed engines. I ought to have reversed!'

And yet the Captain, who had sprung on to the bridge at Kerizel's first cry, stood silently beside him, taking no part.

Slowly the vessel's bow began to move to starboard.

'The wind is against us,' thought Jean. 'Every blooming thing!' But at thirty yards distance from the bank, the ship was nearly parallel with it, and the bows were still swinging to starboard. 'Even if I don't run on to it, the propellers will foul it,' thought Jean, on tenterhooks.

'Stop both engines.'

So at least, if the propellers touched, they would not foul the bottom with all their fifteen hundred horse power, there to stick whilst the vessel, carried on by her way, broke both her shafts and raced engines at the risk of jumping them off their beds.

'The propellers are going to foul,' thought Jean, and he held his breath to listen. Well he knew that moan of a grounded ship, the vibration, low and hollow at first, increasing in volume as it runs the whole length of the hull in a long shudder – a tearing groan.

Like a violin that the player feels vibrate beneath his hand, even as he listens to the voice of its lament. Was he to listen thus to the lament of his own ship?

Time stood still. Jean watched wide-eyed whilst the dark bank slipped away astern.

'Full ahead with both. Steer ten degrees to port!' rapped out the Captain from the door of the deck house, and with a sharp movement he uncovered the compass, which was still dimmed.

'Signal the *Baron*, "You are standing into danger",' he cried to the signalman. 'Quick!'

Dragging himself out of his nightmare, Jean turned towards the bows. To starboard appeared the dark mass of the merchantman, rapidly approaching. And the Captain was endeavouring to save the situation by passing across her bows.

'She's going to cut us in two!' somebody shouted.

Under the action of her engines, the *Saint Briac* leapt ahead and plunged into the waves. The Captain, who was getting sheets of water in his face without so much as lowering his head, was steering his ship a little ahead of the course of the merchantman.

'Midships. Steady!'

The signalman kept on sending the signal for danger. The merchantman sent no answer at all, but she was near enough for them to hear any order shouted from her bridge. If she reversed in time, she would save herself from running on to the bank, but would they avert a collision? Her stem, towering higher and higher, came on as menacing, as rigid as a mechanical saw. The motor launch began to gain speed. She seemed to spring forward. Now she was about to cross the merchantman's bows. Now her bows – her engine room, were ahead of that other stem, and at last her stern too, just grazing it.

'We've done it!' cried Kerizel, his voice pitched high with excitement.

Yes, they had done it. The bows of the merchantman had cloven nothing but a white furrow, still foaming. Gradually the *Baron* decreased speed. For a moment she stopped, still pulsating, as if to take breath. Then she turned away slowly whilst the look-out aft was ordered to keep a sharp watch. Then she went ahead.

On board the *Saint Briac* the Captain slackened speed and brought the ship back into position. Then, without a word, he signed to the midshipman to take the watch whilst he remained standing beside him.

'A message from the *Baron*,' announced the signalman. '"Well done. Thank you".'

Peace reigned once more. The ship proceeding slowly on her way mounted the waves rhythmically, effortlessly. The signalman replaced the signalling lamp and stretched his taut muscles, cramped under the nervous strain. Kerizel shook himself like a young dog leaving the water.

Everywhere peace reigned, except in the heart of Jean Compagnon, troubled by an emotion that refused to be dispelled. Scarcely could he find the courage to return to the watch. How was he ever to force himself to give another order, and if he did, who would obey it? Again he weighed the risks he had run and his own responsibility in running them, and the burden weighed heavy upon him. Before his eyes, like some tragic sequence by Epinal, rose a picture of the collision, the *Saint Briac* cut in half, sinking perhaps – no time to rescue anybody – the Inquiry. And then, later on, back in France, the parents of the drowned cursing him who had been responsible for their death. He felt focused upon him the stony gaze of all his judges, and himself, seeking pity and finding not even understanding.

Would he ever have found the words in which to explain what had happened? Can one talk about the darkness of a night in broad daylight? Or of the sea swell in face of a green baize cloth and a lot of inkstands? Or of the sea wind inside a stuffy room? How could he have described those moments of suspense in the night, the light of the buoy extinguished, the five degrees off the course, Kerizel's cry and his own order, and then suddenly the immense void into which he had fallen as he awaited an issue which rested now on fate alone?

Would it have been in his power to defend himself – he who had had no thought to spare for the merchantman, and who could never say how much time had passed waiting, till the Captain's voice, strained and yet deliberate, had recalled him to himself?

Would he even have wished to defend himself?

Jean remembered something else.

The Captain, who had never scrupled to make the most cutting remarks in the presence of the crew, had said nothing at all. Nobody had said anything – not even Kerizel. And suddenly this silence, the sharpest condemnation of all, became intolerable to him. Timidly he turned his head.

'I'm sorry, Sir,' he murmured, and his voice sounded in his own ears like a supplication. But no answer came.

Jean Compagnon, midshipman in the Navy, was almost ready to burst into tears.

He turned then wholly towards his chief and laying a hand on his arm, looked into his face.

The tall body beside him was bowed. The head, dropping forward, swayed slightly in time with the vessel's pitching. The knees sagged, and then straightened themselves immediately. And beneath his hand, the arm was shaking with fever.

'Sir – you are ill!'

Slowly the Captain lifted his head.

'That manoeuvre of yours at the bank – pretty good work, Snotty.'

[*PNW 19*, 1943]

R. D. Marshall

A Wrist-Watch and Some Ants

'Like to buy a wrist-watch?' Robbie had said. 'Cost me six pounds –
let you have it for three.'

And after the deal was settled Robbie went out on patrol, never to
be seen again. A listening post heard the crack of rifle shots and the
banging of grenades and that was all.

Well, it was his watch now. His thumb and forefinger pinched the
smooth metal casing as he experienced all the pride of personal
ownership. He liked the round, black face, the bright numerals and
the white glow of the luminous hands. A fine timekeeper like this was
sure to bring good fortune, and that was where Robbie made a
mistake in giving it away at such a bargain price. Sheer superstition, of
course, but if the watch could bring luck the proof was coming soon.
The time was 0445 hours. In half an hour they would cross the
start-line.

He struggled to his feet within the narrow damp walls of the slit
trench and poked his head above ground level. It was dark, neither
night nor morning, and the chill of the air almost set him sneezing.

Clambering out of the soft lips of the trench that crumbled under his
weight, he stood up to tug off the gas-cape worn to keep out the night
dew.

The outside surface of the cape was wet, and as he lay it out on the
sand to roll it up, he could feel the gritty stuff clinging to it. Sand was a
nuisance. When the wind blew or the shells dropped near, it went
down your neck, into your eyes, nose and everything. The complaint
about sand he had made in a letter home brought back a snooty reply
from father, pointing out he was lucky not to slog in the mud of
Flanders like the last war. There was something in this reminder. At
least sand was clean.

The drumming thunder down the line had died away. Another job
for the Geordies was over.

Now a new attack was starting, and a lot nearer, for he could see the
spluttering gun-flashes winking like devil's eyes, and flares blazing up
and sinking from their zenith, remotely, hanging low in the sky like

stars. Red and green Very lights and coloured anti-aircraft shells spangled the heaven in a crazy pattern.

The men in his platoon slept soundly in their sandpits, undisturbed by the nearness of a fierce battle. You had to snatch sleep when you could. Good luck to whoever was in the show, but it was their business. You had your own worries coming soon.

He hailed the sentry.

'Aye, it's all quiet, sir,' said Dougall.

'Good.'

On the left the guns were booming over the dark desert waste, the sky was shot with coloured tracer, and from above came the sinister organ-drone of the bombers, but there was no trace of paradoxical humour in Dougall's voice.

It struck him as funny, and he smiled.

Sergeant Erskine was asleep when he walked over.

'Time to get ready, Sergeant! Look sharp! Waken the others in platoon headquarters. I'll do the sections myself.'

Late the previous night the battalion had stolen forward and dug in on the start-line taped by the intelligence section. His platoon of three sections lay close to the tape, fifty yards between them. The slit trenches of the sections were laid out in a blunt arrowhead, and the attack developed with the leader at the head of the centre arrow.

In the darkness beyond the white tape were the enemy lines, the attackers crossing a mile of flat open ground until they reached a wadi running diagonally across their front.

Then came the main wadi with a minefield and an anti-tank ditch behind it. After that it was close fighting, and, as the Jocks had it, "every man for hissel"!'

The men were ready now, out of their trenches, and lying on the tape.

In front, over the ground soon to be raped by the soldiers, the milky glare of a flare-light hung in ghost-like suspension. Instinctively they hugged the ground as a shell burst noisily fifty yards in front. It came with an urgent hissing rush, ending in a sudden brevity of flame, red and fierce, and a deafening crash. Thin slivers of metal sang through the air and plopped in the sand around them.

Zwish, zwish, zwish – a fusillade of Spandau bullets whined over their heads.

Crump! Crump! another salvo churned up the vacant space before them.

It was growing lighter. The inky blackness had turned to lilac, and the stars were waning. A faint stir of wind touched their faces. Silver bars oozed from the sun's furnace below the eastern horizon.

He could just discern the navigating party between his company and the right forward company.

His watch told him they had four minutes to go.

This waiting was a bit awkward. You wanted a cigarette badly and there was a 'no smoking' order. You wanted to rush forward wildly in a mad helter-skelter. You wanted the whole show cancelled, and an easy-going cushioned existence back home thousands of miles away.

He felt restless. He rose, and, crouching low, darted back to shake hands with the sergeant. He felt his hand tremble a little.

'Good luck, Sergeant Erskine. Don't think I'm the next to grow jittery. It's only the cold that makes me shiver.'

'Good luck, sir, and don't worry, because I'm thinking the same as you.'

He returned to the tape and lay down. His rifle and bayonet rested on the crook of his arm to keep the sand from clogging the muzzle and the breech. He ran his forefinger down the bayonet blade. It was cold and moist.

The sergeant knew what he was thinking? He wondered. And what should one think about at a time like this?

'My mother, my home, my sweetheart, good times of the past, the way Marion laughed when I tumbled into a mountain torrent in Sutherland, kilt and all? Fear of death, the supernatural, the slender promise of life after this?'

His memory served up broken fragments of the past, but somehow the lingering sentiments wouldn't fit into any prescribed pattern.

I've done this job before. Becomes almost a routine now. It's a cinch I'll be hit again. Infantry subalterns in the first lot that go over haven't much chance of coming through unhurt.

It was like this on the third night in Alamein. Told George I thought it was my turn for an iron ration, and it was.

Wasn't pleasant to hear the air hissing out of my chest, and feeling the blood gurgle in my throat when I tried to breathe. Let's hope it hits me in a safe place this time, like an arm or leg fracture.

Funny, a battlefield would be the most exciting place you could find if you knew you weren't going to be killed or maimed. It would be fun in a way to stride about with hell let loose around you, cutting a heroic figure like Errol Flynn in a movie, with maybe trickles of red-ink blood dribbling down your forehead, and your face mud-daubed by the make-up man, and showing off to the others who are scared, and laughing at death-dealing bullets and flying fragments of metal.

But it doesn't work that way. Nobody can be nonchalant in attack's environment of death and mutilation. It wants every ounce of guts just to keep going and do your duty.

I know that now. I can think coldly and be calculated about it. There's no question of sentiment, self-pity or mock heroism. After you've gone through it once, it all works straight.

Even if this is an attack, it's not a piece of unthinking brutishness. Not simply rushing on and jabbing your bayonet into some poor chap. Often in peace-time you wondered just how stalwart you could be on a battlefield. This is your chance to learn now. Maybe it's worth something to a man to find that out.

As these thoughts flooded his mind and quickly ebbed, it struck him he wasn't a peace-time romancer now, but a trained soldier, conscious of his innate fears and churning them down inside of him, because he had been given orders and must carry them out. This was where military discipline counted. No room in one's head for sentiment or the melancholy burden of self-pity. He was thinking of the plan of the battle, keeping a vigilant eye on the navigating party, wondering if this or that soldier would have the guts to see it through.

It was still growing lighter. The lilac had wasted to a vapourish grey, soon to be brushed aside by the magic touch of a pink desert dawn.

Hundreds of pairs of eyes stared ahead in a vain endeavour to glimpse the evil, unseen world before them.

Suddenly the navigating party on the right rose to their feet. He grasped his rifle, and, quietly calling his men, moved forward.

They crossed the start-line.

There was something weird and unworldly in the half-light about this sectional line of human arrowheads advancing slowly forward. He had seen ants, black ants of the desert, surging on to some mad purpose. He had crushed scores of them under the iron-tipped heel of his ammunition boot, unthinkingly and unfeelingly, when there wasn't much else to do. But men weren't black ants. Flesh and blood of his homeland weren't meant to lie wounded and dying out there in the desolate waste of Southern Tunisia.

Tightly he gripped his rifle, knuckles strained white, and banished the revelation to its proper place.

At the first shock of the Army's artillery barrage the desert sand shuddered beneath their feet. Vicious shells screamed over their heads and beyond. Infernally, everything vibrated to the hellish concussions.

Compass bearing of ten degrees. God, this advance is gallingly slow. One hundred yards in two and a half minutes. Like a funeral march without the hushed silence of reverence, and the music's not so sweet. Be three-quarters of an hour before we get there.

His heart was thumping; his lips were dry.

But we must keep time with the guns.

The left-hand section was straining too far ahead.

'Keep the line on the left!' he shouted above the din, and waved his arm. 'Don't bunch!'

'Keep your dressing!'

His commands seemed woefully inadequate. Surely the puny language of the parade-ground wasn't meant for so momentous an occasion as this.

'Back! Back on the right!'

Sergeant Erskine in the rear was also bawling orders.

Strange we should be yelling at them to go slower. Silly of me to doubt their courage on the start-line. But my men are tired; have been in action for weeks, with daily casualties. I can forgive myself. What men! What a grand battalion!

He glanced round quickly and saw the sergeant, cool and somehow grimly at ease, the only one of them to have the rifle slung on his shoulder, and wanting only a cigarette drooping from his lips to complete a picture of sheer self-control. He felt this man was taking it much better than himself. He waved and they both smiled, as if each was aware of a new sudden upsurge of comradeship.

'That's the stuff, you Highlanders! Come on, keep it up!'

Now the battle was raging furiously.

The battalion were forcing a bridgehead in the enemy lines and holding the breach against fire from left, right and centre. Two more Highland battalions were being thrown in later to enlarge the gap and smash through. Army artillery whammed the strong points, while the brigade on the right were firing all they had from their static positions against the enemy on that flank. Smoke shells screened the attack, confusing the enemy's direct aim. It confounded his automatic fire, for the assaulting troops could hear streams of bullets whistling overhead. Or maybe it was their own machine-guns letting loose. It wasn't easy to tell in the confusion.

But enemy guns and mortars were seeking out victims. They would walk into the hell soon.

Ahead the grey sand and gravel danced madly in incessant eruption, ravished into spouts of flaming sand and dust clouds, overhung by a long, low bank of black smoke. Above, the sky was rent by airburst cracking into snaky black streamers from which jagged metal darted downward. Little more than a hundred yards in front bullets hissed up misty spurts of sand.

I wonder how many of my platoon will survive this racket. Christ! there's three that won't!

He saw them stagger when a shell burst in front. A cloud of smoke engulfed them. He thought the nearest one was Graham. He had dropped his rifle, clutching his chest as he swayed like an axed tree and toppled over face down.

Nobody stopped. He was glad of that. It was hard to pass by wounded men, despite orders. They were all wanted forward, and stretcher-bearers would pick up the wounded later.

He found the sight ugly.

My other attacks have been at night in darkness. A bursting shell or a mine exploding then is only another bang, a flash of flame, and staccato silhouettes. But it's daylight now. You see men dropping, see their actual mutilation.

More men fell as they reached the first wadi: the ant-like figures still kept the line. Down the shallow near slope they tumbled, and climbed up the other side.

They were on ground level again. Superficially, it was quite flat, and its colour a monochrome of yellow; but they found themselves stumbling as they trampled stones, shell-holes and tiny bumps of sand crowned with sparse tufts of scrub and camel-thorn, which in the slanting rays of the morning sun stained the sand in dappled brown shadows.

It was warm in the rising sun, and the strain of the long advance was telling. It didn't seem as if the clash would ever come, this going on and on endlessly to the very dissolution of things. A trickle of sweat ran down from the padding of his steel helmet. Another sweat-drop caught in his eyelash in a tangled shot of iridescent colour.

He swerved to avoid a human leg severed above the knee. It was smooth and unmarked; the boot was there: the puttee and hose-top with a Highlander's red garter-flash. But there was no sign of the body.

At last the main wadi. As they staggered down the deep face he looked along the line. It was still straight. It was still moving on. But it was a lot thinner. There would be black crêpe hanging in many homes in the shire after this.

They were catching it hard now. All round the earth spat and mushroomed smoke and dust. The din was deafening. The enemy couldn't see what he was firing at, yet he was working accurately from map-deduced ranging. The morning air smelt of smoke and dust and cordite.

They swarmed out of the wadi, and, excitedly, he saw through the haze that they had emerged straight on to one of the gaps cleared by sappers under cover of darkness. There was the white tape leading them through. Great stuff!

He waved wildly and the left-hand section darted for the gap. He followed on, leading the others. They were in a long single file. It was impossible to resist the urge to scurry through for fear of being caught by fire in the narrow defile.

They were through. The first section swung to the left in line again, the centre fanned out and the rear section wheeled to the right.

How splendidly the men are behaving! I'm lucky to have such grand fellows. Infantry is rough stuff, but you're dealing with men, not machines.

A fearful rushing noise like an oncoming express train, instantly followed by the inevitable bang, compelled him to turn round. As he feared, the platoon headquarters had caught it. It was a giant shell. The smoke was dense and he saw nothing in the quick rearward glance. Next it was anti-personnel mines, covered with canvas camouflage, and the men jumping hither and thither to avoid the deadly rows. Then they tumbled into the ten-foot drop of the anti-tank ditch.

He looked at his watch. Three minutes to six. The field-guns were concentrating on the ditch from then until the hour. It was easy to remember the plan now, but not in the hectic rush through the minefield.

'Stay in the ditch!' he yelled. 'Only for three minutes.'

Three minutes was like three years. It was living on the slope of a Vesuvius, a crazy row and spouts of fire spraying the men huddled low in the ditch, half burying them in showers of sand and stones. About half his platoon had come thus far. If one shell landed in the narrow confined walls, well . . . it wasn't a nice thought.

He pulled out a packet of army issue cigarettes from his breast pocket and offered one to Martin, who lay next to him.

'Mine's a Minor, Martin. What's yours?' he shouted in the man's ear.

They puffed nervously at the cigarettes and studied the dial of the wrist-watch.

'Like my watch, Martin?'

'It's got a bonny face, sir, but Ah wish it was six o'clock the nicht.'

'So do I.'

Slowly the hand touched the hour. Although the bombardment of their own gunners had stopped, enemy guns were thundering, too.

'Notice any difference, Martin?'

'No verra much,' the soldier replied. His brown hair dangled askew from the helmet over his forehead. He grinned.

'Can't hear you. Shout louder.'

'Ah said, not much, sir.'

'Time's up – help me.'

They stood half upright. Martin cupped his hands, and he stepped on them, pulling himself up the wall of the ditch.

Shells were dropping thickly, and the view was battle-clouded. He read the compass bearing for direction and turned round to see Bill, the company commander, jumping into the ditch.

'Wait for me!' Bill bawled.

Soon they were together, checking the bearing. The platoon on the left were already scaling the wall.

'O K,' Bill cried. 'By the way, your sergeant's in a bad way.'

He knew, from the way Bill said it, Erskine was dead. He shouted to his men, waited until they were beside him, and rushed forward. Now for them. His bayonet was ready.

A man on the right leapt ahead and lunged down. Another two joined him in the bloody work. Then they were all there, yelling and swearing like mad. Must be the first small post shown in the air photograph. There was a hell of a din with shells and mortar-bombs banging all over the place.

Then it came. An ear-splitting blast about four yards in front of him and he was flung backwards on the sand.

Dazedly he looked up to see Bill passing a few feet away. No good asking him to stop: he was wanted in front. Bill shouted something about 'bad luck' and 'stretcher-bearers', then went out of sight.

He knew it was his arm. There was a burning numbness at the elbow. He was lying on his right side, supported by the haversack on his back. His left arm hung loosely, attached by only a couple of sinews from the elbow downwards. The knuckle end of a bone stuck out starkly and the rest was just a shattered bloody mess. The inside of his left boot was torn, and the foot felt warmly wet inside. His shorts were soaking and dark-stained on his right thigh.

Well, he had made a job of it this time. He lay back to recover from the shock of the concussion and tilted his helmet over his head.

A sudden blow struck the helmet which rolled a yard away. He reached for it with his free hand. The steel was dented at the back.

Oh, stop shelling, for Christ's sake! Give me peace. You've got me once, now leave me alone. I'll be all right if you just leave me alone.

He levered himself up on his right elbow and saw Martin lying grotesquely on his back, dead, eyes staring open, his shock of brown hair messed with blood and sand. The cigarette still stuck between his bared, clenched teeth. Martin had it all right, and the girl back home wouldn't like to see him now, all messed up and twisted weirdly as if it hurt to be dead.

He remembered the blood spurting from his arm must be stopped. Was it the Doc who talked about using a stone to squeeze the artery? Good old Doc, he'd be having a busy time today.

He tucked a round stone, egg-size but flatter, under his armpit, and pressed the truncated limb with his other arm. The blood flow slowed down, and started again when he released the pressure. He squeezed again and held it. The stump was still trickling, but he was saving blood this way.

His mind struggled for articulation as he lay resting, for half an hour, an hour, two hours, he didn't know. You couldn't judge time in what looked a kind of hopeless business. The numbing arm was turning angrily to pain, not so bad as he thought it might be, yet devilish. Wouldn't be so bad if they stopped shelling.

If only I got back to the ditch for shelter – better chance of living there with mere blighty wound – no future lying here in these blasted explosions – but can't drag this silly forearm with me.

He struggled with his jack-knife held in the belt-loop of his shorts, and it was free. Shutting his teeth into the nail-slot, he drew open the blade. It took only a minute to cut the sinews of the shattered arm, and there wasn't much pain over the business.

He bit into his lower lip, gritted his teeth, and dragged himself half upright. The foot pained sharply, and he felt queer and dizzy.

Better wait a little longer until I've more strength.

He sank down again. The sky was a pale misty blue through the film of smoke haze and the sun was bright. It was peaceful up there above the air-burst shells in the great archivault of the heavens, and a lark was twittering near the centre of the battalion front, heedless of the earthly hell. A scurrying column of prisoners headed by a white flag was running the gauntlet of their own fire. The battalion were doing well then.

He began to think about Bill and the others in front, and then about the things he wouldn't be able to do single-handed, like knotting a tie and tying shoelaces, dressing up to go to the local dance at home. Perhaps you could do these things with practice. It would be fine when the war was over and you could gallivant again. Would a girl fall for a chap with one arm?

It was time for a cigarette. His matches would be in his left-hand trouser pocket. His right hand encircled his body, fumbling for the box. He held the box between his knees and lit up at first stroke.

A black ant darted into a little hollow a foot away from his nose. It peered over the edge and looked at him. He saw its mandibles quiver and its legs fidget nervously. Then it was still, as if making up its mind whether to come on and dare a detailed exploration.

He puffed a cloud of smoke straight at it. The ant ran quickly to the right in line with the top of his head, so that he had to raise his eyeballs to keep it in sight. He saw the knotty body start, and the black bulbous posterior rear up suddenly with a jerk of the mobile joints of its body. It looked so timid and scared. Perhaps it was going through the same emotions as he did while crouching on the start-line waiting to go over.

Once, back in the desert somewhere, one of his men had left the platoon's sugar ration on the ground with the bag open. A fine crowd of these little creatures they found there in the late afternoon, hundreds of them helping themselves gluttonously to the sugar, one stream rushing headlong to the booty and another stream poking with agitated fury among the white granules and scuttling back to the nest. It was like a constant two-way traffic of black cars going between the metropolis and a seaside resort on a hot summer's day.

Ants liked sugar all right. There was sugar in blood. Some people suffered from diabetes. He didn't have diabetes, but he had sugar in his blood. Maybe the ant wanted the sugar. Well, he wasn't going to let the little bastard have any sugar, though God knows there was enough blood wetting the sand round him, and it wasn't going to be any use to him now.

The ant quivered again, and raced nearer him and past his head, down level with his abdomen, then stopped just as quickly beside a small, chipped grey stone. Slowly and cunningly he raised his right hand until it hovered over the unsuspecting ant. The hand slapped down. The ant struggled, tickling his palm. He plucked at it with two fingers, held it and a pinch of sand gently, held it, and squeezed it into a sticky mass between finger and thumb. A hot nausea flowed through him. He wiped his fingers on the grey stone and threw it away. Bad luck, ant, all that trouble for nothing.

He looked down at his arm, which lay detached at his side. It was white. He touched it with his right forefinger. It was cold and firm, like touching smooth stone. The hairs, bleached golden by the sun of the long desert campaign, were slightly singed by the blast. The rigid fingers of the hand were bent a little. The thumb and forefinger were ink-stained. He wrote a letter to Helen yesterday and the pen leaked.

Sadly he looked at the watch still round his wrist. The hands – the ones that glowed so whitely in the darkness – had stopped at three minutes past six. The tiny second-hand was missing. The glass was smashed. The round black dial that he and Martin admired was dented.

Well, I guess Robbie got the best of the bargain after all.

[*PNW 21, 1944*]

J. E. MORPURGO

THE PIPES

The Command Post was active with the hushed bustle that seems to be the particular possession of command posts. The flicker of the hurricane-lamp, the haze of cigarette smoke, figures bent over maps, traces and artillery boards, and the hushed whisper of compared calculations.

John Bennett remembered many similar occasions during practice camps at Larkhill, at Forfar, at Budden, and only the distant sound of an exploding mine, or the racketing of a machine-gun, hardly heard in the absorption of the work, gave any indication that this was reality. It was impossible to believe that tomorrow morning, precisely at half-past four, the guns would open up all along the line, dropping death at neat mathematically-prepared intervals. He thought of the times when the results of his command post work had been tested by miserly 'one-round gunfire' from Number One guns, and the even more parsimonious occasions, earlier in the war, when the guns had stayed in camp, and results had been checked theoretically by sarcastic instructors in gunnery, who refused to be persuaded that amateur soldiers could achieve in months the degree of accuracy that they had sought for years.

Maclean, the Number One Surveyor, straightened up from his board.

'It's O K, sir. We've checked and rechecked. Shall we pass it out to the troops?'

John looked over at the long line of figures. He knew that they were right, but habit made him check them once more.

Satisfied, he passed the sheets to the orderly. 'Out to the troops.'

Greer, the Number Two Surveyor, took out a packet of cigarettes and offered one to John.

'I'm afraid they're only V's, sir.'

John took the coarse, dry cigarette out of the white packet.

'Thanks. I can smoke anything.'

He kept puffing hard at the cigarette to keep it alight. If for a moment one let these cigarettes dangle, the tips degenerated into a dry brown powder.

There was something about the relief from the tension of hard work of the last four hours that made them all think of other times that they had worked together.

Greer spoke first. 'It's a long time since we started training for this, sir. Do you remember those schemes we used to have at Tain, in the days when you were first GPO, when we used to drive round to Dornoch so that you could have a look at the cathedral?'

Maclean joined in: 'And Mr Cameron used to arrange morning exercise at Dingwall, so that he could go over to see his girl at Strathpeffer?'

John remembered it well. They had looked at him with some suspicion at first, when he had arrived in his new uniform, the first English officer to join a predominantly Scottish Territorial regiment, but their suspicion had soon changed to tolerance, and their tolerance to friendliness. He, for his part, had hated Scotland, for its continual rain, the cold winds and the greyness of the towns; but as he had begun to feel the companionship and warmth of the battery mess, so he had grown to love the country. Now, looking back through the nostalgia and the long months since he had left, he felt that it must have been even lovelier than he had realized.

'Yes, Maclean, and I remember the arguments that we used to have about the bagpipes.'

'You will agree that you were wrong, sir. You've become a Jock yourself, and must have learnt to know the beauty of the pipes.'

'I do not agree. After eighteen months living amongst you uncivilized creatures, I am only more certain that the pipes are a suitable instrument for you, that their racket is barbaric, ear-splitting and as musical as a braying ass.'

It was an old argument, but still enjoyable. They had expected him to reply as he had. It was part of the game to lure him on to make him argue about pipes, high teas, kilts, marmalade, Scottish girls and Dundee cake.

The phone burred.

'The Adjutant for you, sir.'

'Hullo, John.' The Adjutant's voice came over the wire, distinct and metallic. 'All ready for the fireworks?'

'Yes, all OK.'

'Not much for you to do now, I suppose?'

'No, I'm going to get a little sleep until I can see the results of my logarithmic ability.'

'Sorry, old boy. I'm afraid we want you elsewhere. The CO has been on to your battery commander on the blower. Henderson is coming up to take over from you. Jim Barton bought it, and you'll have to take on his troop. Can you get over here right away? The Colonel wants to speak to you.'

'OK. See you in about ten minutes.'

He put down the receiver. For two years he had been hoping to get a troop. He had had dreams of putting up the extra pip and had planned what he would do with the extra pay, but it was disappointing to be dragged out from being GPO on the night of his first big show. Still, the real work was done now.

'Well, good-bye, chaps. I've got to take over Don Troop. Mr Henderson is coming up to take on the Command Post. You can explain everything to him, can't you, Maclean?'

'Yes, sir. I'm sorry to see you go, sir, but I suppose we should congratulate you.'

'Not quite yet. Perhaps soon.'

'Good luck, sir.'

He buckled on his equipment, stubbed his cigarette, and stumbled out into the dark. Over towards the enemy lines the sky was coming to life. The Germans were betraying their nervousness by shooting Very lights, by an occasional burst of machine-gun fire, and by sudden thudding rounds from their field-guns.

The Colonel looked younger than ever that night. He had just been promoted to command, and he was boyishly thrilled at the chance of taking the regiment into action for the first time.

'Hullo, John. Sorry to drag you away from your higher mathematics, but Don Troop have got an important show, and Blount is too young to take over.'

John wondered about Blount's age. Twenty-five. Twenty-six, perhaps – a little older than himself and only four or five years younger than the CO.

'What happened to Barton, sir? Is he –?'

'Oh, no. Nothing very serious. A few splinters in the legs from some chance strafing. We've just got him into the RAP. The Doc's going to evacuate him immediately. Would you like to see him before you move off? I'll walk over with you, and explain your task on the way.'

A squadron of tanks supported by Don Troop were to make a wide sweep around the southern flank to cut off any small enemy force that might attempt to escape through the passes when the real show started at dawn.

'That's why we kept Don Troop out of the barrage,' the Colonel told him. 'You're in the general picture now. The Squadron Commander will give you more details.' He gave John the map reference of the rendezvous. 'Think you can make it?'

'I think so, sir.'

Captain Barton was lying on a stretcher in the RAP, his face white and miserable with disappointment. It was the first time that John had seen the direct effects of wounds on one of his own personal friends, and he felt sick and helpless, but he tried to be hearty.

'You lucky bastard. Groppis and glamorous QAs. Give my love to the bird who wriggles her belly at Dolls.'

Barton smiled. 'I suppose it's a little morbid to say that you've been enviously waiting for dead men's shoes these last two years, John. Well, they're pretty full of blood at the moment. But congratulations. Don't preen yourself too much. I'm going to kick you back to your artillery boards in a couple of weeks.'

'I always did like figures better than men.'

'Mathematical, and female, eh, John?'

'Yes, both.'

Barton winced as some new pain stabbed at his legs, and then tried to act as if he had not done so. The MO, the Colonel and John joined in the pretence.

'You know the troop pretty well, John. Be careful with Blount. He's a bit jumpy, but he's a good GPO.'

'OK, old boy. See you soon.'

'That Don Troop should do their first show commanded by an Englishman. It hurts my Highland soul, John. Good luck to you, you Sassenach.'

They all shook hands. A sufficiently dramatic touch to satisfy Kipling, John thought, and he went off to join his new troop.

The driver of his carrier and his OP Ack. were old friends of John's; he knew Blount well, and so the transition to troop commanding was not too difficult. He got his orders from the commander of the tanks, and passed on all possible information to his own officers and NCOs. Guns and tanks moved off into the night.

By four o'clock they were some miles from the old positions. The tanks were navigating and the noise inside the carrier made conversation impossible. John sat back in his uncomfortable seat and looked at the sky, calm and bright with stars, the only beauty of the Western Desert.

At four-twenty the barrage would open up. Anxiously he looked at his watch. He hoped that nothing had gone wrong with his own calculations. Nothing could have gone wrong; everything had been checked and rechecked. He tried to think of the dangers and responsibilities of his new job, but he could not make himself believe that they were real. This was no different from training schemes, hardly different from TEWTS – tactical exercises without troops. There were troops everywhere now, and some of them would die from this exercise. Over there were Huns, and he, with range tables and slide rule, had prepared their deaths.

'Four nineteen.' He shouted back to his OP Ack. 'The barrage ought to open up any moment now.' He looked at his watch again. The luminous minute-hand slipped over on to the figure four. 'Surely they won't be late. Have you got signal time?'

The bombardier started to pull a watch from his pocket.

Far off on the right flank there was one solitary thud. Not the snap that one hears from a troop command post, only thirty yards from the guns, nor the all-piercing crack that splits the ear when one sits on the firing seat, but a dull boom like the beat on a bass drum. Then, all along the line, as if that one round had turned a lever that opened the gates of hell, the fury started. Gun linked up with gun, troop with troop, battery with battery. Within seconds whole regiments were firing, so rapidly that, from his distance away, it was impossible for John to distinguish the sounds at the gun end from the explosion when the shells landed.

Flame burst all along the line, miles of it, lighting up the sky, and shutting out the first glimpses of sunrise.

To the west John could see more light, less intense and less continuous. The sound was indistinguishable from the general thundering, and only the direction of the flashes told him that the German guns were shouting their reply.

Dawn came, and with it the sharper, more irritable notes of machine-guns, and the steady beating of aircraft engines.

Four times planes passed overhead, and the column spread out. Three times the planes were friendly. The last wave came from the west, but the German fighters were too preoccupied with the main battle to worry about this insignificant force beneath them, and they flew away to the east.

The column stopped for a hurried breakfast, and John moved up to talk to the O C Squadron. He tried to look as if he were used to action, but the M C ribbon on the cavalry major's bush-shirt made John conscious of his own inexperience, and he felt nervous as a boy on his first day at school.

We'll swing up toward the coast from here.' The major pointed the route out on his map and John marked it up on his own chinagraph. 'We've already outflanked them. From here we'll split, as I arranged. I'll go on leaving your troop a section as escort. You yourself keep up with my lads, but the going may be slow. There are minefields about.'

'Right, sir.'

'Your boys are making a hell of a din back there. It's like the sound track of a film about the Somme. I suppose you must be pretty disappointed not to be adding your share to the racket.'

'Yes, we are, in a way. Still, we'll probably get our turn.'

Not long after they had moved off again the main body was stopped. Scouting tanks sighted the dust of moving transport.

John put on the earphones himself so that he could intercept the messages between the advance tanks and their commander, and so get his troops into action more rapidly, but the enemy trucks contained a few Italians, scared by the horrors of the morning barrage, who were endeavouring to get out as best they could, and did not care which way they escaped. He heard the column commander giving orders to them to be disarmed. 'We can't be bothered with prisoners. Give them the map reference of the nearest P O W cage, and tell them to find their own way there.' John listened to the end of the conversation and gave the earphones back to his signaller.

Ahead the tanks started up. The driver switched on and pressed the starter button. There was the usual whine, but no response from the engine. He tried again, and again, and John began to get impatient. The tanks were already out of sight. 'Hurry up and get the bloody thing moving.'

The driver leapt out, and after a couple of seconds shouted up, 'It's O K, sir. Just a short.'

As they moved off, the Italian trucks came towards them, rocking as they raced across the bumpy sand. They slowed up as they passed his carrier, and John caught a glimpse of scared faces, as white as their waving handkerchiefs. They looked dazed and unbelieving.

The driver turned to him and said, 'That'll teach the sods!' then shouted a few unoriginal blasphemies at the passing Italians.

'Save your breath and catch up the tanks,' John ordered.

They were getting nearer the gunfire again, but the sound seemed to be less continuous, and the rattling obstinacy of small arms fire was predominant . . .

There could be no preparation, only the fierce wrench of shocked steel, and then long after the roar of the explosion, and one piercing shriek.

He was running, blood pouring over his eyes, streaming down and mingling with tears and sweat, running on and on until the pain in his foot was too much and he could run no longer. He dropped, helpless, on to the ground.

His head ached, his right arm hung useless at his side, there were pains in his legs and in his back, but nothing was worse than the awful breathless exhaustion. He lay on the ground and tried to recover his breath.

With his left hand he felt his head. His hair was stiff with dried blood. He looked at his legs. One foot flopped back at a ridiculous angle.

'Going may be slow; there are minefields about.' He remembered the casual tone in which the column commander had said it.

He staggered to his knees and looked around for the remains of the carrier, or for his guns.

Suddenly he realized that the sun was high in the sky. It must have been hours since they had struck the mine. He did not know how long he had been running, nor in what direction. John tried to remember the country, but the desert all looked the same – sand and tufts of miserable green.

He fumbled for his compass and the oil ran out over his fingers.

There was a small hillock fifty yards away. Painfully he crawled towards it, but when he got there he could see nothing but the open monotony of the desert.

John tried to think. Which way had his troops gone? 'Which way were our own lines? Where were the Germans?' He knew that he must find some human being, German or British, he did not care. He only knew that he could not stay to die of hunger and thirst – alone.

He must make someone find him. Essaying all his strength, he shouted, his throat and lungs straining, his body aching with the effort. Anxiously he waited for a reply, but none came.

John tried again; his shouts became screams; and then slowly he dropped his head on to the sand. He knew that he could not hear himself.

He was unable to comprehend that which he knew to be true. Then the full realization dawned on him. There was no hope now; he could never be saved. He did not know where he was, he could not move far, he could not hear. To die bravely among his troops, that would be possible, but to die alone and lost, when his body was not yet ready to die, that he could not face. He started to sob, and then to laugh, and, laughing, fell asleep.

He was cold when he woke up, and very weak. He looked up at the sky. The sun was going down. John cursed the unfairness of a God who would not let him die in peace, but must wake him up so that He could enjoy his sufferings.

There was still a little water in his water-bottle. John reasoned with himself that it was useless adding to his hours of agony by drinking, but he could not resist the temptation and drank all that was left.

He thought that he heard something in the distance, a shell or a bomb falling. He started to sob again. He felt that he was going mad before he died; he who was deaf was going to be tortured by the imaginings of sound.

As well end it now. His revolver was still in its holster. He fumbled for it clumsily and pulled it out.

John struggled to his feet, his throat dry, his left hand over his mouth. It was true. He could hear. Over the hill not far away he could hear the pipes, the cheery, breathless, life-giving sound of a Highland march.

Forgetting his weakness, his weariness and his torn body, he began to stagger towards the sound.

Straining all that remained of his strength to make himself forget the hideous pain, dragging his maimed foot, he started to run, an ugly, torturing run, but as he ran he shouted and cheered.

[PNW 22, 1944]

JOCELYN BROOKE

THE BLANKET

The farmhouse lay by itself at the side of a cart-track, a mile or two from our billets. It was like the other houses in the neighbourhood, but somewhat larger than most.

A flight of steps led up the southern wall to an upper room; there was a small vineyard nearby, and a tall, conical haystack, which had been sliced into at need like a cake, and began to look top-heavy. With its white walls and rust-red pantiled roof, the house looked friendly and welcoming in the spring sunshine.

A small boy, playing in the yard, looked at us curiously. Presently he sidled up to us.

'*Sigaretti? Cioccolata?*' he asked hopefully.

'We go to ask some *vino*,' said Kurt.

There were three of us: Kurt Schlegel, the Austrian Jew enlisted in Palestine, Charlie Dacres, the Cockney, and myself. Kurt was teaching himself Italian, and usually acted as our interpreter.

'*Avete del vino?*' he asked now.

'*Si, si,*' the boy answered with a charming smile.

We followed him round to the doorway on the other side. A woman appeared at the door: tall, broad-bosomed, brown-faced, dressed in nondescript clothes which had once been gaily-coloured, and still hung gracefully upon her straight, stalwart body. On her head was a bright-coloured kerchief.

'*Buon giorno*,' she said, with a curious, dramatic sweep of her arm: a stylized, almost operatic gesture of welcome, at once proud and humble, which seemed to imply that we were free to take possession, if we wished, of the entire farm, such as it was. She accompanied the movement with a broad, delightful smile, revealing two rows of strong, white teeth.

'*Dovè il padrone, Signora, per cortesia?*' asked Kurt.

'The *padrone* was out at work,' she replied. '*Cosa vuole?*'

'*Se avete un mezzo-litro di vino . . . ?*'

'*Si, si,*' she exclaimed, and immediately pushed forward three little wooden chairs for us.

'In moment her husband works in the fields,' Kurt explained to Charlie, whose Italian was almost non-existent. 'But she gives us wine.'

We sat down, and presently the woman returned with a jug of wine and three glasses. I poured out the wine, and we all said '*Saluti.*' The woman watched us as we drank; so did the little boy, still on the look-out for chocolate.

'*E buono?*' she asked.

'*Molto buono,*' we said.

It was true: the wine was a *vino nero* – dark, sour, potent, with a purplish glint when held to the light; much better than most of the local wines, which were light and watery, like alcoholic lemonade.

We sat in the sunshine, drinking it slowly, and talking a little to the woman. Kurt did most of the talking: he spoke ungrammatically, but with the confidence of a Central European. I was shy, being British, and had to think up my phrases more carefully. Charlie contented himself with saying '*molto buono*' and playing with the child.

Presently other children appeared, stealing up like shy birds whom the sight of us had driven away: another little boy, a girl of fifteen strikingly like her mother, and another younger girl, perhaps eleven or twelve, blonde and uncannily beautiful.

We were introduced: the elder girl was called Assunta, the younger Graziella, the two boys Leonardo and Giovanni.

'*Quanti bambini?*' Kurt asked.

'*Cinque,*' the woman replied, holding up the five fingers of one hand; adding that one, the eldest son, was working with his father.

'She is beautiful,' Kurt remarked, of Graziella.

'Like a Botticelli,' I said.

'*Volete ancora?*' the woman asked.

'I think we drink some more,' Kurt said, with decision.

'Too bloody true we will,' said Charlie. 'Best *vino* I've had since we came to this place.'

Kurt asked the woman for more, explaining that we would pay for it.

'*Non fa niente,*' she assured us.

'We give her cigarettes,' Kurt suggested.

We pulled out our cases, and contributed ten each. Kurt handed them to the woman.

'*Per il padrone,*' he said.

'*Eh . . . Lei è molto gentile,*' she said, with a half-protesting gesture, and hurried to bring more wine. This time she brought, in addition, three pieces of bread, some cheese, and some sprouts of fennel.

Did we like *finocchio*? she asked.

We said we liked it.

It was not good to drink without eating, she added apologetically.

We sat over the second jug of wine, relaxed and happy in the warm sun. In front of the house, fields sloped down to a little wooded valley; beyond this, the country stretched away flatly to a range of low hills, capped by small villages. The landscape was like some formal vision of 'Spring' in a medieval missal: smooth, brightly-coloured, with a curious quality of *naïveté* and innocence. Two cypresses, a few yards from the house, divided the picture abruptly into sections, like the divisions of a triptych. In the middle-distance, figures moved across the fields, hoeing – perhaps the *padrone* was among them. The stooping forms of women showed as red and blue blobs, indistinct in the bright sunshine.

Presently the beautiful child, Graziella, who had wandered off, reappeared, carrying a little bunch of field-flowers: grape-hyacinths, narcissi, and small yellow tulips. These she presented to us, gravely smiling, then shyly backed away again.

'I've a feeling we're getting well in here,' Charlie said. 'What say we ask for some parster shooter?'

'She'd do it,' I said. 'Go on, Kurt. You ask her. Not today, though. I'm on at five o'clock, you know.'

'No, I don't ask. Always you want me to talk bloody Italian. You ask yourself.'

Finally Kurt and I together approached the topic with as much delicacy as our Italian allowed.

'*E possibile mangiare qui, alla vostra casa?*' we began, and, antiphonally, pressed our point: *pasta asciutta*, perhaps a salad, some eggs. We were so tired of Army food, we explained: we wanted to eat well, *mangiare bene all'Italiano*.

The woman shrugged her shoulders. They had so little food, now, in Italy; the *tedeschi* had taken everything – cattle, poultry, wine, anything they could carry – *e niente pagato*. It was different in peace-time; but now, *in tempo di guerra* . . .

'Heavy going,' I said to Kurt. 'We'll have to use bribery. Jimmy'll give us a tin of bully out of the store, if we get him a bottle of *vino*.'

Kurt nodded, a glint coming into his eye.

'We make business,' he said.

At mention of *carne*, the *signora* obviously began to weaken. She would ask the *padrone*. I added that I would bring some clothes: I had some old civvy vests and pants in my kit which I never wore. The outlook began to seem more hopeful.

At that moment, the *padrone* himself appeared, with his eldest son. The father was short, with a pleasant, sharp-featured face and beady-black eyes; he wore a battered trilby, and a brightly-coloured handkerchief round his neck. The son, about sixteen, was beautiful. If Graziella was Renaissance, Umberto was something archaic: a faun from a Greek vase-painting.

The father was presented with the cigarettes. He immediately called for more wine, and we all sat down again, inside this time. Charlie came in, and the atmosphere became distinctly festive. I wished I wasn't on duty at five: I began to feel rather drunk, and refused any more wine. The bare, white-washed room was very clean; bunches of drying tomatoes hung from the ceiling-beams, and a few *salami*. In the open stone hearth a fire of olive-wood was blazing, and a vast cauldron over it, waiting for the *pasta*, which lay ready for cooking, in a floury pile, on the scrubbed wooden table.

The *padrone* was very friendly. He wanted to know all about the war: we were soldiers, we should know. We explained that we were medical orderlies, *croce rossa, non combattere*. He looked half-convinced. *Ieri sera molto boom-boom-boom*, he insisted: over there, beyond the mountains – pointing northwards. There was a big battle, we said: beyond Pescara, on the way to Bologna. We were lucky, he said, not to fight. Had we many *feriti* in our hospital? No, we only dealt with medical cases, we said, *ammalati*. Our hospital was in the *Scuola Agricola* across the fields.

Time was getting short, and after a discreet interval we broached the subject of food again. Yes, certainly we must come, he said: next Sunday was Easter – *una grande festa*. It was also a special feast for the family – Leonardo, the second son, was to make his first communion. The cigarettes had done their work. We scraped up a few more for Umberto, and prepared to leave. This we were not allowed to do until we had drunk another glass of wine. We repeated, for the *padrone*'s benefit, our promises to the *signora*: we would bring a tin of bully, some old clothes, some chocolate for the *bambini*. Suddenly made bold by our success with her husband, the *signora* took me aside and half-whispered that if we could see our way to bring a *coperta* as well . . .

'They want a blanket,' I said to Kurt.

'They've had it,' Kurt said. 'I don't go over the wall for two years, that's sure.'

'We've all those buckshee ones from Foggia,' I pointed out. 'They've no check on them.'

'I'm not mad,' said Kurt.

'Plenty of blankets,' said Charlie, who had been putting back a good deal of *vino* on the quiet. 'I'll bring her one.' He turned to the *signora*. '*Si, si,*' he assured her, '*molto* blankets – what the –ing hell are blankets?'

'She understands all right.'

'Certainly she does,' said Kurt. 'Don't you be worried.'

'*Io portare molto* – you know, blankets,' Charlie insisted. 'Compree?'

'*Si, si. Lei è troppo gentile,*' the *signora* exclaimed, rewarding Charlie with one of her broad, maternal smiles. She was like a Demeter, an Earth-Goddess, I thought.

'See, she's taken a fancy to me,' Charlie said proudly. 'I told you we'd get well in.'

We promised to come at two o'clock on Easter Sunday, and with difficulty left the house. At the last minute, Assunta presented us each with a little bunch of violets, and Umberto, no doubt on instructions from the *padrone*, brought up a bottle of wine, which I stuffed into the front of my battle-dress. The family watched us out of sight. Looking back across the fields, we saw them standing in the doorway, waving. The house, with its two dark cypresses, stood out brilliantly against the sun-flooded landscape: it seemed like a symbol of happiness, a vision of the good life.

The problem was to get the blanket out of the billets without being seen.

'It is better if you take it at night,' Kurt advised.

'Is it —— ,' retorted Charlie. 'Looks too bloody suspicious. Much better to take it in daylight.'

'So then, Private Dacres, you go over the wall,' Kurt predicted with morbid relish. 'That is sure.'

'And you –ing come with me, Private –ing Schlegel, R A M C,' said Charlie with gusto. 'It's all right, mate, I wasn't born yesterday.'

We walked out of the billets just before two o'clock on Easter Sunday. Charlie had rolled up the blanket – one of a buckshee issue, unchecked, which we had acquired at Foggia – in a bundle, adequately disguised, to unsuspicious eyes, by several layers of dirty linen. Kurt also carried a bundle: he had compromised with his scruples sufficiently to part with a couple of KD shirts which weren't shown on his 1157. My own bundle, innocent enough to all appearances, contained the cast-off civvy underclothes which I'd bought in Cairo; in the front of my battle-dress was a tin of bully for which I had bargained with Jimmy James, the Ration Corporal.

We stepped jauntily out of the hospital entrance, looking rather consciously innocent, and walked straight into Staff-Sergeant Woolf, Acting Sergeant-Major for the Unit.

'Where're you blokes off to?' he said.

My heart sank like a stone. Just our luck, I thought. If Woolfy was in a bad mood, he might quite easily make things awkward. He flogged too much himself, as we all knew, to regard our bundles without suspicion.

'What's in all them –ing bundles?' he asked.

I mentally decided to unroll my own first, if he pressed the point: there was nothing in mine he could pick on. I hoped he wouldn't ask to see Charlie's.

'We take our laundry to a farm,' Kurt explained.

'That's right,' Charlie agreed. 'The old *biancheria*, you know.'

The Staff grunted.

'Remember,' he said, 'if I find anyone in this unit flogging stuff, I'm coming down heavy on them. Very heavy.'

'Ain't got nothing to flog,' Charlie said, nervousness making him cheeky.

The Staff gave him a nasty look.

'Is anyone on duty in this joint?' he asked. 'Who's in the Clinic, eh?'

'Smudge is relieving me,' Charlie said. 'It's my half-day.'

'Who's in the Lab?'

'Nobby does the Lab in moment,' Kurt replied. 'He has two dark-grounds and one instillation, then finish.'

'What about the office?'

'Mac's there,' I said. 'He's on long-trot today.'

'Well, don't get too pissed. If I had my way, I'd have those bloody casas all put out of bounds. You'd think this was a bloody rest-camp, instead of a pox-joint.'

We escaped.

'Miserable old sod,' Charlie muttered. 'Just 'cos he doesn't like *vino*.'

'He likes *finocchio*,' I said. 'We might bring him some.'

'—— him.'

The day was brilliant and cloudless, hot but with a fresh breeze. We walked through a field breast-deep already with pink clover. In the little copse at the field's edge, nightingales were singing. In the meadow beyond the clover-field the stream-side was fringed with white narcissi, their heavy scent evoking the atmosphere of English drawing-rooms in winter.

'It's a wonderful country,' Charlie said. 'Bloody wonderful. Garden-flowers growing wild, and all.'

Kurt and I laughed.

'Three months ago you were saying how bloody awful it was,' I reminded him.

'I didn't know it then.'

'So now you stay in Italy *dopo la guerra* and marry a nice *signorina*, isn't it?' Kurt suggested.

'I might if I hadn't a wife and kids in Blighty,' Charlie agreed.

We came out on to the track, by a little row of houses. Some of the families were standing outside, wearing their best finery for Easter. They greeted us with smiles and welcoming gestures.

'*Buona Pasqua,*' they said; Christ might have risen, this very morning, for their special benefit; so happy did they seem. It was hard to believe there was a war on – and not so far away either. Even as we passed the houses, a muffled rumble came from over the mountains – away beyond the Maiella, white and austere on the horizon.

A family with whom we were friendly – we had treated the daughter for malaria – refused to let us pass without a glass of wine. Their neighbours followed suit. We were not allowed to go on till we had drunk a glass at each house in the row. When at last we arrived at the farmhouse where we were invited, we were, as Charlie said, 'Well away'.

We had been asked for two o'clock, but time in Italy is elastic, and dinner was far from being ready. The *signora* was busy with pots and pans; Assunta, the eldest daughter, was cutting up the *pasta* into long strips like tapeworms. The other children sat with the *padrone* just inside the door. At the hearth sat an ancient woman whom we had not met before: grey-haired, dressed in drab, ragged clothes, she looked like a benevolent witch. Introduced to us as *la nonna*, she croaked an unintelligible greeting, in dialect, and went on with her task of stoking the fire with olive-wood. Leonardo, who had taken his first communion that morning, was the hero of the occasion: with his face scrubbed, and wearing a little suit of snow-white linen, he looked cherubic and very self-important. With immense pride he showed us his *Ricordo della prima communione* – a three-colour print showing an epicene Christ surrounded by very bourgeois-looking children, all with blond hair.

With many nods, gestures, and whispered thanks (as though the entire Corps of Military Police lay in ambush round the house) the blanket, the bully and the underclothes were secreted in a back-room. A two-litre flask of wine appeared as though by magic: this was not good wine, the *padrone* explained; later we would drink good wine, *del vino tanto buono*.

It was good enough for us. We had had no dinner, and must have already drunk nearly a litre apiece on the way. We distributed cigarettes to the *padrone* and Umberto, and chocolate to the children. Leonardo received six bars all to himself, and Giovanni, who resented his brother's hour of glory, burst into tears. He was consoled with half a glass of wine.

'Wish I'd been brought up like that,' said Charlie.

'It's all for a cock, these bloody Catholic *festas*,' said Kurt, who, being both Jew and Communist, objected to Easter on religious and political grounds.

'Ah, you miserable old bugger,' exclaimed Charlie, and, lifting Giovanni on to his knee, consoled him further with an extra piece of chocolate.

Presently the meal began: the steaming, fragrant tomato-juice was poured over the two enormous bowls of *pasta*, and we sat down round the table.

'*Ancora, ancora,*' the *padrone* insisted, before we had finished our first platefuls. '*Oggi festa – mangiamo molto alla Pasqua.*'

After the *pasta* there was chicken cooked with tomato and *peperoni*. This was followed by *salami* fried with eggs. Then came a dish of pork with young peas. Roast sparrows followed, and afterwards a salad. At about the *salami* stage, after several false alarms, the 'good' wine was produced: two bottles the size of magnums.

It was a Homeric meal. Kurt, who had been a student in Vienna before the war, quoted Homer very appropriately, but in German, which nobody understood. Charlie was trying to sing *Lilli Marlene* in Italian to Graziella, who sat on his knee. Umberto produced an ancient concertina and began to play it. Kurt, forgetting Homer, started to sing a very sad Austrian folk-song. The *padrone*, for my benefit, kept up a running commentary on the proceedings, comparing the occasion unfavourably with Easters before the war.

'*Prima la guerra era bella, bellissima*,' he insisted. Today, everyone was poor. '*E sempre la miseria*.' The Germans had taken everything. It could hardly be called a *festa* at all. He was ashamed: ashamed to offer such an Easter meal to his guests, and mortified, moreover, that Leonardo's first communion should be celebrated so wretchedly. '*Siamo poveri, poveri – noi contadini. Eh, la guerra – quando finirà?*'

I was not only extremely drunk by this time, but I had never eaten so much food in my life. So far as I was concerned, Leonardo's first communion party had been more than adequate.

Presently Umberto struck up a *tarantella*, and the whole family, as though at a given signal, took the floor. We all paired off, indifferent as to sex, and bobbed and jigged in time to the music. Charlie insisted on taking *la nonna* for his partner; I danced with the *signora*. I found to my surprise that I was perfectly steady on my feet. Moreover, it seemed that I had been dancing the *tarantella* all my life. Gravely, wearing her calm Demeter-like smile, the *signora* advanced and retreated, hands on hips, bobbed and circled and bowed, all with a goddess-like dignity. Her brown face, beneath her coloured kerchief, was as calm as though she were at Mass; only a beatific happiness irradiated it, as though Christ indeed were risen. She seemed immensely aware, too, of her own personal fulfilment: she had given pleasure to her man, borne him healthy children and (more recently) cooked a dinner fit for those Gods whose Olympian peer she seemed.

The music became faster, the dancing less restrained. The *padrone* whirled about like a ballet-dancer; Giovanni, still taking a rather disgruntled view of the occasion, did a little dance by himself in the corner. Leonardo didn't dance at all: he stood at the doorway and watched the proceedings with the distant air of one who has, that very morning, eaten the body of Christ for the first time. The two girls, Assunta and Graziella, danced a little apart: separated, it seemed, from the rest by a mysterious barrier, a mutual understanding; it was as though they were priestesses, gravely celebrating the godhead of their mother. Umberto sat in a corner, with his concertina: an archaic, sculptured faun, younger and older than anybody else in the room.

At last we could bear it no longer, and staggered out into the late afternoon sun, to cool off. Charlie's face was scarlet, his battle-dress and shirt gaped open, showing a pink, damp expanse of skin. Kurt's hair had fallen over his square, heavy-browed face: he looked like Beethoven would have looked if he had ever got seriously drunk. I told him so.

'Ach, I could write great symphonies in moment,' he declared. 'I am great *Musiker*. Too bloody true I am, you old sod.'

'You're a fat Austrian c—,' Charlie remarked happily.

'It is pity I am not, my friend,' Kurt replied.

Umberto came out, his concertina still slung over his shoulder. He took my hand.

'*Sei felice?*' he asked, his teeth flashing white in his brown face.

'*Sono felice,*' I said.

Beyond the twin cypresses the country lay flooded in the warm, slanting light. Away on the horizon, hill upon hill lay revealed in the evening radiance, each topped with its fairy-tale village or castle. In the oak copse nearby, a chorus of nightingales shouted. Graziella had run into the field, and was gathering a bunch of white narcissi.

'*Eh, la guerra. Quando finirà?*'

It was the *padrone*. He looked sadly across the fields. '*Siamo poveri, poveri,*' he added, as if to himself.

There was a war, they were poor, the landlords in Naples or Rome ground them underfoot, their children were uneducated, the priests were paid to keep them in ignorance . . . I knew it all: I had heard Kurt, the Communist, expound it all – with conviction, with passion, and at length. Yet I knew also that with these people, on this Easter day, I had felt happier, I had felt a more genuine sense of the joy of living, than ever in my life before.

At last we prepared to leave. Farewells were protracted, and delayed by innumerable afterthoughts in the form of presents and souvenirs: a bottle of wine in case we were thirsty on the way, another for when we got home, one more because it was the 'good' wine, the special wine for Leonardo's first communion. A fourth bottle was added for some further, rather complicated, reason: perhaps it was to drink Leonardo's health tomorrow. A bundle of *finocchio* was produced for the Staff-Sergeant, whose partiality for it we had mentioned. Pieces of Easter-cake were pressed upon us for our friends who had not been to the party. A *salami* was offered by the *signora* in case we were hungry in the night – we had had a poor meal after all, she said. Bunches of narcissi and violets could not be refused. Umberto even offered a loaf of bread, in case we should have none with which to eat the *salami*. A pot of some conserve made of pig's blood was proffered by *la nonna*, because a pig had been killed recently.

Our tunics bulging with bottles, our hands clutching *finocchio* and narcissi, we started out across the fields. Half-way, we were overtaken by Umberto with a dozen new-laid eggs. When at last we reached the hospital and staggered across the yard in front of it, we observed Staff Woolf standing before the entrance exactly where we had left him. He was accompanied by MacDowd, the Corporal Clerk, and Smudger Smith. Their mouths opened, they stared. Then Smudge began to laugh; Mac began to laugh too. Only the Staff kept his countenance: he looked as black as thunder.

''Ere you are, Staff; 'ere's the mustard and –ing cress for you,' Charlie bawled, and advanced towards the Staff-Sergeant proffering the bundle of *finocchio*. Unfortunately for the success of the gesture, he tripped over a stone and fell flat on his face: the bottle of wine secreted in his tunic smashed noisily, and spilt itself, like some sudden haemorrhage, over the gravel.

A quiver which might have been a smile flickered over the Staff's prim grey face.

'You'd better get straight into your –ing billets and get to –ing bed before the old man sees you,' he said.

In the billets that night I said to Kurt:

'You can say what you like, these people know how to enjoy themselves. They may be politically uneducated and down-trodden and priest-ridden and all the rest of it, but they know how to live.'

'Too bloody true,' said Charlie, who was finishing off the bottle of 'good' wine.

Kurt sat up in bed, looking more than ever like Beethoven after a night out.

'So then, have you forgotten?' he asked, with the ominous air of a minor prophet. 'You think they give you all that for nothing? You are –ing stupid, both of you.'

''Course I'm stupid. Who wouldn't be after all that?' Charlie commented, and let a satisfied fart.

'Do you not then realize to what you owe this *festa*?' Kurt pursued. 'Well, what?'

'To *una coperta*, one blanket, GS, property of the –ing British Army. To that you owe your bloody *festa*, isn't it?'

'Too bloody true,' Charlie agreed. 'But it was cheap at the price. Wasn't it?' he appealed to me.

'Yes, it was cheap at the price,' I said: thinking of the *signora* dancing like a goddess, the wine and the sunshine and the flowers, and, beyond the dark cypresses, the sun-flooded country rolling away towards the distant hills.

[*PNW* 29, 1947]

Two

The Poets

JOHN CORNFORD

HUESCA

Heart of the heartless world,
Dear heart, the thought of you
Is the pain at my side,
The shadow that chills my view.

The wind rises in the evening,
Reminds that autumn is near.
I am afraid to lose you,
I am afraid of my fear.

On the last mile to Huesca,
The last fence for our pride,
Think so kindly, dear, that I
Sense you at my side.

And if bad luck should lay my strength
Into the shallow grave,
Remember all the good you can;
Don't forget my love.

[*PNW* 2, 1941]

W. H. Auden

Lay Your Sleeping Head

Lay your sleeping head, my love,
Human on my faithless arm;
Time and fevers burn away
Individual beauty from
Thoughtful children, and the grave
Proves the child ephemeral:
But in my arms till break of day
Let the living creature lie,
Mortal, guilty, but to me
The entirely beautiful.

Soul and body have no bounds:
To lovers as they lie upon
Her tolerant enchanted slope
In their ordinary swoon,
Grave the vision Venus sends
Of supernatural sympathy,
Universal love and hope;
While an abstract insight wakes
Among the glaciers and the rocks
The hermit's sensual ecstasy.

Certainty, fidelity
On the stroke of midnight pass
Like vibrations of a bell,
And fashionable madmen raise
Their pedantic boring cry;
Every farthing of the cost,
All the dreaded cards foretell
Shall be paid, but from this night
Not a whisper, not a thought,
Not a kiss nor look be lost.

Beauty, midnight, vision dies:
Let the winds of dawn that blow
Softly round your dreaming head
Such a day of sweetness show
Eye and knocking heart may bless,
Find the mortal world enough;
Noons of dryness see you fed
By the involuntary powers,
Nights of insult let you pass
Watched by every human love.

[*PNW* 3, 1941]

F. G. Lorca

Song

Translated from the Spanish by J. L. Gili and Stephen Spender

The girl with the beautiful face
is gathering olives.
The wind, that gallant of towers,
takes her by the waist.
Four riders passed
on Andalusian ponies,
with suits of blue and green,
with long dark cloaks.
'Come to Cordoba, lass.'
The girl pays no heed.
Three young bullfighters passed,
slender of waist,
with orange-coloured suits
and swords of antique silver.
'Come to Seville, lass.'
The girl pays no heed.
When the evening became
purple, with diffused light,
a youth passed bringing
roses and myrtle of moon.
'Come to Granada, lass.'
And the girl pays no heed.
The girl with the beautiful face
goes on gathering olives,
with the grey arm of the wind
encircling her waist.

[*PNW* 7, 1941]

DAVID GASCOYNE

THE WRITER'S HAND

What is your want, perpetual invalid
Whose fist is always beating on my breast's
Bone wall, incurable dictator of my house
And breaker of its peace? What is your will,
Obscure uneasy sprite: where must I run,
What must I seize, to win
A brief respite from your repining cries?

Is it a star, the passionate short spark
Produced by friction with another's flesh?
You ache more darkly after. Is it power:
To snap restriction's leash, to leap
Like bloodhounds on the enemy? There is no grip
Can crush the fate you fight. Or is it to escape
Into the dream perspectives maps and speed create?

You never listen, disillusion's dumb
To your unheeding ear. But see my hand,
The only army to enforce your claim
Upon life's hostile land: five pale, effete
Aesthetic-looking fingers, whose chief feat
Is to trace lines like these across a page:
What small relief can they bring to your siege!

[*PNW* 7, 1941]

Georg Anders

Song of the Austrians in Dachau

Translated from the German by John Lehmann

Pitiless the barbed wire dealing
Death, that round our prison runs,
And a sky that knows no feeling
Sends us ice and burning suns;
Lost to us the world of laughter,
Lost our loves, our homes, our all;
Through the dawn our thousands muster,
To their work in silence fall.

> *But the slogan of Dachau is burnt on our brains*
> *And unyielding as steel we shall be;*
> *Are we men, brother? Then we'll be men when they've done,*
> *Work on, we'll go through with the task we've begun,*
> *For work, brother, work makes us free.*

Haunted by the gun-mouths turning
All our days and nights are spent,
Toil is ours – the way we're learning
Harder than we ever dreamt;
Weeks and months we cease to reckon
Pass, and some forget the years,
And so many men are broken
And their faces changed with fears.

> *But the slogan of Dachau is burnt on our brains,* etc.

Heave the stone and drag the truck,
Let no load's oppression show,
In your days of youth and luck
You thought lightly: now you know.
Plunge your spade in earth, and shovel
Pity where heart cannot feel,
Purged in your own sweat and trouble
Be yourself like stone and steel.

For the slogan of Dachau is burnt on our brains, etc.

One day sirens will be shrieking
One more roll-call – but the last.
And the stations we'll be seeking –
Outside, brother, prison past!
Bright the eyes of Freedom burning,
Worlds to build, with joy and zest,
And the work begun that morning,
Yes, that work will be our best!

For the slogan of Dachau is burnt on our brains, etc.

(NOTE. – Over the entrance to Dachau Concentration Camp stand the words:
    ARBEIT MACHT FREI!)

[*PNW 8,* 1941]

W. H. AUDEN

THE NOVELIST

Encased in talent like a uniform,
The rank of every poet is well known;
They can amaze us like a thunderstorm,
Or die so young, or live for years alone;

They can dash forward like hussars: but he
Must struggle out of his boyish gift, and learn
How to be plain and backward, how to be
One after whom none think it worth to turn.

For, to achieve his lightest wish, he must
Become the whole of boredom; subject to
Vulgar complaints like love; among the Just

Be just; among the Filthy filthy too;
And in his own weak person, if he can,
Must suffer dully all the wrongs of man.

                    [*PNW 10*, 1941]

DEMETRIOS CAPETANAKIS

DETECTIVE STORY

The stranger left the house in the small hours;
A neighbour heard his steps between two dreams;
The body was discovered strewn with flowers;
Their evenings were too passionate, it seems.

They used to be together quite a lot;
The friend was dressed in black, distinguished looking
The porter said; his wife had always thought
They were so nice and interested in cooking.

And this was true perhaps. The other night
They made a soup that was a great success,
They drank some lager too and all was right,
The talk, the kisses and at last the chess.

'It was great fun!' they said; yet their true love
Throbbed in their breasts like pus that must be freed.
The porter found the weapon and the glove,
But only our despair can find the creed.

[PNW *13*, 1942]

ROY FULLER

ROYAL NAVAL AIR STATION

The piano, hollow and sentimental, plays,
And outside, falling in a moonlit haze,
The rain is endless as the empty days.

Here in the mess, on beds, on benches, fall
The blue serge limbs in shapes fantastical:
The photographs of girls are on the wall.

And the songs of the minute walk into our ears;
Behind the easy words are difficult tears:
The pain which stabs is dragged out over years.

A ghost has made a cell of every bed.
You are not you without me and *The dead
Only are pleased to be alone* it said.

And hearing it silently the living cry
To be again themselves, or sleeping try
To dream it is impossible to die.

                              [*PNW 13*, 1942]

TERENCE TILLER

SHOP WINDOW

In the confused magnificence of love
is no community, but unsharing crowds
of shuttered faces where no secrets move;
but a perpetual early-closing day.
The tender lust that sanctifies our bloods,
that flowered by companionship, the way
of the moth's mind, they neither feel nor speak,
haunted with flames: our world's a spirit-walk.

Behind the dreaming shutters of our faces
the spider fingers thoughts, and we dissect
with sharp artistic hands our gains and losses;
build the mosaic of a filtered world.
We hang a blinding arras upon the fact,
for wild wild unpardonably wild
the roaring of the outer enmity.
Yet we, being islanded, will draw down that sea.

Never believe us; poets tell you lies:
the burglar breaks the window, and the door
blows inward, and the pictures tatter loose.
The snarler with hooked fingers, or the man
with nooses, throw a shadow on the floor.
Sooner or later we shall weep again.
There is no refuge from the teeming road
and the four walkers waiting to be God.

World was not built for dreams, my dear; the dreamer
cores his unsympathy to a navel of gold;
rides home at evening swathed about with clamour,
he in his inward starlight never seeing
commercial colours, or the nervous mould
that hangs their lightning round him. And so being
rapt from humanity, wakes not till their feet
press down his bones to raise up Regent Street.

So our delight will never be alone,
or straight and safe as the lark's tower of air;
familiar things will break it, strange look on
with the fierce laugh of lynchers; and the sea
speak our end in mountains to the shore.
Oh if that future tears us, it will be
but bridal violence. For he loves you still
who leans and weeps upon the window-sill.

[*PNW 13*, 1942]

DEMETRIOS CAPETANAKIS

ABEL

My brother Cain, the wounded, liked to sit
Brushing my shoulder, by the staring water
Of life, or death, in cinemas half-lit
By scenes of peace that always turned to slaughter.

He liked to talk to me. His eager voice
Whispered the puzzle of his bleeding thirst,
Or prayed me not to make my final choice,
Unless we had a chat about it first.

And then he chose the final pain for me.
I do not blame his nature: he's my brother;
Nor what you call the times: our love was free,
Would be the same at any time; but rather

The ageless ambiguity of things
Which makes our life mean death, our love be hate.
My blood that streams across the bedroom sings:
'I am my brother opening the gate!'

[*PNW 16*, 1943]

LOUIS MacNEICE

TWO WAR POEMS

I

BROTHER FIRE

When our brother Fire was having his dog's day
Jumping the London streets with millions of tin cans
Clanking at his tail, we heard some shadow say
'Give the dog a bone' – and so we gave him ours;
Night after night we watched him slaver and crunch away
The beams of human life, the tops of topless towers.

Which gluttony of his for us was Lenten fare
Who mother-naked, suckled with sparks, were chill
Though dandled on a grill of sizzling air
Striped like a convict – black, yellow and red;
Thus we were weaned to knowledge of the Will
That wills the natural world but wills us dead.

O delicate walker, babbler, dialectician Fire,
O enemy and image of ourselves,
Did we not on those mornings after the All Clear,
When you were looting shops in elemental joy
And singing as you swarmed up city block and spire,
Echo your thought in ours? 'Destroy! Destroy!'

II

THE SPRINGBOARD

He never made the dive – not while I watched.
High above London, naked in the night
Perched on a board. I peered up through the bars
Made by his fear and mine but it was more than fright
That kept him crucified among the budding stars.

Yes, it was unbelief. He knew only too well
That circumstances called for sacrifice
But, shivering there, spreadeagled above the town,
His blood began to haggle over the price
History would pay if he were to throw himself down.

If it would mend the world, that would be worth while
But he, quite rightly, long had ceased to believe
In any Utopia or in Peace-upon-Earth;
His friends would find in his death neither ransom nor reprieve
But only a grain of faith – for what it was worth.

And yet we know he knows what he must do.
There above London where the gargoyles grin
He will dive like a bomber past the broken steeple,
One man wiping out his own original sin
And, like ten million others, dying for the people.

[*PNW 16, 1943*]

ROY FULLER

THE GREEN HILLS OF AFRICA

The green, humped, wrinkled hills: with such a look
Of age (or is it youth?) as to erect the hair.
They crouch above the ports or on the plain,
Under the matchless skies; are like the offered
Shoulders of a girl you only half know.
What covers them so softly, vividly?
They break at the sea in a cliff, a mouth of red:
Upon the plain they are unapproachable,
So massive, furrowed, so dramatically lit.

Can you be much surprised at what the hills
Contain? The girls run up the slope,
Their oiled and shaven heads like caramels.
Behind them is the village, its corrugated
Iron and, like a wicked habit, the store.
The villagers cough, the sacking blows from the naked
Skin of a child, a white scum on his lips.
The youths come down in feathers from the summit.
And over them all a gigantic frescoed sky.

The murder done by infinitesimal doses,
The victim weaker and weaker, but uncomplaining.
Soon they will only dance for money, they'll
Discover more and more things can be sold.
What gods did you expect to find here, with
What healing powers? What subtle ways of life?
No, there is nothing but the forms and colours,
And the emotion brought from a world already
Dying of what starts to infect the hills.

[*PNW 16*, 1943]

NORMAN NICHOLSON

THREE POEMS
SHORTEST DAY, 1942

The damp December light
Settles like fog on roofs
And gable-ends of slate;
The wind blows holes in the sky; the rain
Shines on the road like tin,
And rain-drops hang on the privet, round and white.

Behind a freestone wall,
Between the houses and the street,
In twelve or less square feet
Of tarmac and black soil
Blooms the purple primula
Bright as a lollipop or an aniseed ball.

And so a smile will flower,
A kiss like a child's laugh, or more
Like a friendly terrier's bark,
While the town huddles beneath a dark
Drizzle of misery, and the wind
Flings down sleet from the frozen fells of war.

FOR THE NEW YEAR

The stars wheel past the windows
Like flocks of winter sparrows;
The bell clangs out the hours,
And frost sparkles like stars,
And the wind blows up the dawn
With spring behind it and rain
And the spikes of daffodils
And June on fire in the hills.
The apples crowd the bough
Beneath the frosty Plough,
And autumn snow is blown
White as a harvest moon
On currant and raspberry cane,
And the wild ganders fly
Nightly across the sky.
The seasons flit like linnets,
And years whirl past like planets,
And the earth's orbit mars
The changeless map of stars.
The splintered light which now
Gently probes my eye
Is of a star that burned
When the Scots fired the land,
When the Norsemen robbed the dales
And hacked their names on the fells,
Or when the iceberg lakes
Elbowed among the rocks
And carried the Devil's stone
To the hill above the town,
Where through the dormer bay
Drizzles the Milky Way.

WAITING FOR SPRING, 1943

A grey wind blows
Through the woods, and the birches are bare,
And the hazel crooks its catkins tight as a starling's claws;
But out in the fields where the dyker hacks the branches
Of purple willow and elder and wrenches
The trunks square to the run of the hedge, there
The yellow lamb's-tails dangle in the frosty air.

So also we
On the perimeter and fringe of war,
Open to the sunlight and the wind from the western sea,
Wounded by the knife of winter, still
Feel the bright blood rise to bear
White and daring blossoms, fledged before
The seabirds leave the ploughland or the snow leaves the fell.

Let us not forget
Those in whom autumn dug deep furrows of pain,
Those to whom winter has been the kindliest season yet,
The snow their only eiderdown, the frost
Their only morphia; they will not greet again
The sap that stings in the bone, nor the bird on the nest
That hatches globes of suffering in the probing rain.

Blood flows back
Into the frozen hand with pain,
And children whimper as the wind flogs them again awake.
To those defeated by the winter's cold
Spring is a terrible season, atonement not to be told
To us in our temperate valleys, who scarcely have begun
To feel the anger of love beneath the conquering sun.

[*PNW 17*, 1943]

NO ORPHEUS, NO EURYDICE

Nipples of bullets, precipices,
Ropes, knives, all
Now would seem as gentle
As far the away kisses
Of her these days remove
– To the mad dervish of his mind
Lost to her love.

There where his thoughts alone
At night dance round his walls,
They paint his pale darling
In a piteous attitude standing
Amongst winds of cold space,
Dead, and waiting in sweet grace
For him to follow when she calls.

For how can he believe
Her loss less than his?
'True it is that she did leave
Me for another's kiss;
Yet our lives did so entwine
That the blank space of my heart
Torn from hers apart,
Tore hers too from mine.'

O, but if he started
Upon that long journey
Of the newly departed
Where one and all are born poor
Into death naked,
Like a slum Bank Holiday
Of bathers on a desolate shore;

If, with nerves strung like a harp
He searched amongst the spirits there
Looking and singing for his wife
To follow him back into life
Out of this dull leaden place,
He would never find there
Her cold, starry, wondering face.

For he is no Orpheus,
She no Eurydice.
She has truly packed and gone
To live with someone
Else, in pleasures of the sun,
Far from his kingdoms of despair
Here, there or anywhere.

[*PNW 17*, 1943]

STEPHEN SPENDER

A TRANCE

Her love, enclosed in lineaments of grace,
Which is my care, as my love is her care,
Burns through us when we kiss
— The sapphire in the rose of the embrace.
Her loving virtue witnesses
The love in me, which it saved from despair,
Under the care of her caress.

Sometimes, apart in sleep, by chance,
She falls out of my care alone,
Into the chaos of a trance.
I see a cloud move through the sunset bone
Of her familiar head, and, torn
Across the petals of her mouth, is shown
The slumbering path left by a thorn.

Restless, she turns to me, and presses
Those timid words against my ear
Which thunder at my heart like stones.
'Mercy,' she murmurs, and asks 'Who blesses?'
Or 'I am pursued by time,' she moans.
I watch that precipice of fear
She treads, among her naked distresses.

To that deep care we are committed
Beneath the forests of our flesh
And shuddering scenery of these dreams,
Where unmasked agony is permitted
And bones are bared of flesh that seems;
Our hands, unravelling beauty's mesh,
Meet our real selves, our charms outwitted.

Her pure trance is the oracle
Which speaks no language but the heart.
Our angel with our devil meets,
In the atrocious night, nor do they part,
But each each forgives and greets,
And their mutual terrors heal
Within our love's deep miracle.

[*PNW 18*, 1943]

DEMETRIOS CAPETANAKIS

THE ISLES OF GREECE

The sun is not in love with us,
Nor the corrosive sea;
Yet both will burn our dried-up flesh
In deep intimacy

With stubborn tongues of briny death
And heavy snakes of fire,
Which writhe and hiss and crack the Greek
Myth of the singing lyre.

The dusty fig-tree cries for help,
Two peasants kill one snake,
While in our rocky heart the gods
Of marble hush and break.

After long ages all our love
Became a barren fever,
Which makes us glow in martyrdom
More beautiful than ever.

Yet when the burning horses force
Apollo to dismount
And rest with us at last, he says
That beauty does not count.

[*PNW* 20, 1944]

EDITH SITWELL

GIRL AND BUTTERFLY

('. . . how breezes and butterflies move their four wings.')

I, an old man,
Bent like Ixion on my broken wheel the world,
Stare at the dust and scan
What has been made of it . . . and my companion

Shadow, born with a wolfish pelt –
Grey dress to wear against the invincible cold
Sits at my feet . . . we scan the old
And young, we stare at the old woman
Who bears a stone in her breast
That will not let her rest
Because it once was a world in the grey dawn
When sap and blood were one.

We stare at the young girl chasing a yellow butterfly
On the summer roads that lead from Nothing to Nowhere.

What golden racers, young winds, have gone! For the dust like a
    great wave
Breaks over them – the shade of mortality lying
On the golden hand (the calyx outshining all flowers) –
The hand that drew the chart of the undiscovered,
And the smile for which great golden heroes marched with the pride
And pomp of waves – and like the waves they died.
The words that drew from the shade
A planetary system!
               These are gone——

And the Grey Man that waits on the road from Nothing to Nowhere
Does not care how the breezes and butterflies move their four wings –
And now the old woman who once was a world and my earth
Lies like time upon my heart, or a drift of the grey dust.

But the young girl chases the yellow butterfly.
Happiness . . . what is the dust that lies on its wings?
Is it from far away –
From the distance that lies between lover and lover, their minds
    never meeting
Like the bright continents? . . . Are Asia, Africa, and Cathay,
But golden flowers that shine in the fields of summer
– As quickly dying?

[*PNW 20,* 1944]

JOHN LEHMANN

THE SPHERE OF GLASS

So through the sun-laced woods they went
Where no one walked but two that day,
And they were poets, and content
Sharing the one deep-vistaed way,
Sister and brother, to walk on
Where years like thickets round them lay.

It was the Roman dyke that ran
Between the bluebells and the fern,
The loam so fresh, they half began
To feel the bones deep under turn,
And, listening, dreamed their argument
Something from ancient death would learn.

One bird among the golden-green
Spangle of leaves was poised to sing:
They heard the opening trill, and then
Silence; as if its heart could bring
No note so pure but would disturb
The soundless fountain of the Spring.

Within the wood, within that hour
It seemed a sphere of glass had grown
That glittered round their lives, with power
To link what grief the dyke had known
With voices of their vaster war
The sun-shot bombers' homing drone,

And make one tragic harmony
Where still this theme, their hope, returned,
And still the Spring unchangeably
In fires of its own sap was burned
And poetry, from love and death,
The peace their human contest earned.

It might have been all history
Without the sphere of wonder lay
And just beyond their colloquy
Some truth more pure than they could say,
While through the bluebells and the fern
Sister and brother made their way.

[*PNW* 20, 1944]

DIANA WITHERBY

CASUALTY

Death stretched down two hands,
One on desert sands
Shut his eyes. The other in her head
Opened the third eye of ruin; instead
Of doubt, which veiled it, certainty now gives it sight,
Staring dark and twitching when she sleeps at night,
When she wakes turning her, indifferent, from light.

Sometimes looking through a door into a sunny room, cold,
Full of furniture, but empty except for herself, old
In the mirror. Sometimes resting on fields flowing their green gold
Flowers, giving her an illusion of summer, but her thawing tear
Freezes quickly in the eternal ice of confirmed fear.
Sometimes, drifting along the canal of fatigue, he seems near,
The eye is closing – then suddenly starts in her brain,
Opens – He is gone. She, with walls, iron-coloured rain,
Railings silhouetted either side, is alone again.

We, who for our own comfort, imagined that a grief
Could be smoothed and stroked by time to its relief,
Looking at her face, know now that only their brief
Past stands. The sun has equal entrance there
With mist or wind. We move in talking where
Gates stood – but voices fade,
Transfixed, in her stone shade.

[*PNW* 22, 1944]

NORMAN CAMERON

EL AGHIR

Sprawled on the bags and crates in the rear of the truck,
I was gummy-mouthed from the sun and the dust of the track;
And the two Arab soldiers I'd taken on as hitch-hikers,
At a torrid petrol-dump, had been there on their hunkers
Since early morning. I said, in a kind of French,
'On m'a dit qu'il y a une belle source d'eau fraîche,
Plus loin, à El Aghir.' It was eighty more kilometres
Until round a corner we heard a splashing of waters,
And there, in a green, dark street, was a fountain with two facets,
Discharging both ways, from full-throated faucets
Into basins, then into troughs and then into brooks.
Our negro corporal driver slammed his brakes,
And we yelped and leapt from the truck and went at the double
To fill our bidons and bottles and drink and dabble.
Then, swollen with water, we went to an inn for wine.
The Arabs came, too, though their creed might have stood between;
'After all,' they said, 'it's a boisson,' without contrition.

Green, green is El Aghir. It has a railway station,
And the wealth of its soil has borne many another fruit,
A mairie, a school and an elegant Salle de Fêtes.
Such blessings, as I remarked, in effect, to the waiter,
Are added unto them that have plenty of water.

[*PNW* 22, 1944]

A. S. J. TESSIMOND

TWO POEMS
THE BRITISH

We are a people living in shells and moving
Crablike; reticent, awkward, deeply suspicious;   .
Watching the world from a corner of half-closed eyelids,
Afraid lest someone show that he hates or loves us,
Afraid lest someone weep in the railway train.

We are coiled and clenched like a foetus clad in armour.
We hold our hearts for fear they fly like eagles.
We grasp our tongues for fear they cry like trumpets.
We listen to our own footsteps. We look both ways
Before we cross the silent empty road.

We are a people easily made uneasy,
Especially wary of praise, of passion, of scarlet
Cloaks, of gesturing hands, of the smiling stranger
In the alien hat who talks to all or the other
In the unfamiliar coat who talks to none.

We are afraid of too-cold thought or too-hot
Blood, of the opening of long-shut shafts or cupboards,
Of light in caves, of X-rays, probes, unclothing
Of emotion, intolerable revelation
Of lust in the light, of love in the palm of the hand.

We are afraid of, one day on a sunny morning,
Meeting ourselves or another without the usual
Outer sheath, the comfortable conversation,
And saying all, all, all we did not mean to,
All, all, all we did not know we meant.

THE NEUROTICS

We are the double people, gaoled and gaoler,
Sparrow and hawk in one uneasy body;
We are a battlefield but cannot clearly
Remember why the fight or when it started.

We are the builders of small doorless houses,
Walls to defy the other world which always
Peers in at us through widening cracks that vainly
We cram with mud or paper or our fingers.

Some of us build our secret world by gathering
Fans or old playing cards or Balkan watches
To hoard and pattern, love and list and label:
Kingdom in which we're king and none may enter.

Some of us build our world with pornographic
Postcards or drugs or mistresses or money,
Private religions or a cipher diary
Or great inventions in an attic drawer.

Some of us spend our lives preventing others
From doing what we cannot or we dare not,
And stand in shadow spitting at the sunlight,
And watch at keyholes for the Day of Judgement.

Some of us play at games with blood and nightmares,
Pricking a tender nerve with mental needles,
Twisting a mind as schoolboys twist a forearm,
Pinning the human fly beneath the tumbler.

Some of us populate our days and nights with
Enemies laying plots to trip or maim us,
To make us halt by roofs when tiles are falling
Or lose umbrellas, chances, buses, lovers.

Some of us wander reaching, reaching, reaching
Backwards in time as down into dark water
To find the clockwork mouse that broke, the woolly
Bear that we lost among the tall black fir-trees.

We are the dwellers in the middle limbo,
Land that we hate yet land that holds our landmarks,
Land where we cannot rest yet stay unresting,
Land that we long to leave but fear to start from.

We are the walkers in eternal circles
To whom the circle's better than its breaking,
To whom unhappiness has long grown easier
Than happiness; to whom this twilight's home.

[*PNW 24, 1945*]

ALAN ROSS

NIGHT PATROL

Leaving harbour at dusk, the red moon
rising in a paper lantern, setting fire
to the water, the black headland disappearing
into the shadow of its clenched lion's paw.

The quayside loses itself, screened with dark
distance, cranes like useless arms suspended
over the railway, the silent unloading of coal
starkly silhouetted under the harsh arc-lights.

Turning south, the moon moves like a white face
between the masts, the knotted aerials swing
against the horizon, tilting the world
of sea into a rose of opening darkness.

Night and towards midnight, the stars high
over Europe, cold and frozen, nailed on the sky,
like tinsel above the white flickering lights
of Holland, the flashes of gunfire

licking out over the silent coastline, betraying
the stillness. Taking up position, night falls
like a cloak about us, the cruising wakes
of MTBs lacing the dark with green speed.

From Dunkirk the flames open fanwise
in a hand of light, like the rising moon
setting fire to the sky, the remote
image of death burning on the water.

The slow tick of hours. Clouds grow visible.
Altering course and the moon on a new
bearing. Northwards again, and Europe receding
with the first sharp splinters of dawn.

The orange sky lies over the harbour,
derricks and pylons like scarecrows
black in the early morning light. And minesweepers
passing us, moving out slowly to the North Sea.

[*PNW* 25, 1945]

HENRY REED

CHRYSOTHEMIS*

I cannot follow them into their world of death,
Or their hunted world of life, though through the house,
Death and the hunted bird sing at every nightfall,
I am Chrysothemis: I sailed with dipping sails,
Suffered the winds I would not strive against,
Entered the whirlpools and was flung outside them,
Survived the murders, triumphs and revenges,
Survived; and remain in a falling, decaying mansion,
A house detested and dark in the setting sun,
The furniture covered with sheets, the gardens empty,
A brother and a sister long departed,
A railing mother gone.
It is my house now. I have set myself to protect,
Against the demons that linger inside our walls,
Their saddened, quiet children of darkness and shame:
They lie on inherited beds in their heavy slumbers,
Their faces relaxed to nocturnal innocence.
I will protect them in the decaying palace.

In the dying sun, through slots in the shuttered windows,
I can see the hanging gardens carved on our mountain
Above and below us, terraces, groves and arbours,
The careful rise of the trees to meet the heavens,
The deliberate riot of the wilderness,
The silent arch through which my brother returned,
And again returned.

In the long broad days of summer,
On the great hill the house lay, lost and absorbed and dreaming,
The gardens glittered under the sweeping sun,

---

* In this poem, Chrysothemis is the sister of Orestes and Electra, about whom the
ancients speak so little. The children referred to are the children of Clytemnestra and
Aegisthus, born after the murder of Agamemnon.

The inmates kept to their rooms, and hope
Rose in the silence.
                              And indeed
It seemed the agony must die. But then
The house would seem to sigh, and then again,
A sigh and another silence. Through the slotted shutters
I would see them there, my mother and my sister
Wandering and meeting in the garden's quiet
(And I moved from room to room to see them better).
There seemed a truce between them, as if they had
Called off their troops in order to bury their dead.
I could not hear my sister speak; but clearly,
She spoke with calm and patience, and my mother gave
The answer designed to please, wistful and eager;
And her words would be quietly taken, twisted and turned,
Ropes, that would loose the rivers to flood again;
The fragile dams would burst, indeed constructed
Only for breaking down.

This was the yawn of time while a murder
Awaited another murder. I did not see
My father's murder, but I see it now always around me,
And I see it shapeless: as when we are sometimes told
Of the heroes who walk out into the snow and blizzard
To spare their comrades' care, we always see
A white direction in which the figure goes,
And a vague ravine in which he stumbles and falls.
My father rises thus from a bath of blood,
Groping from table to chair in a dusky room
Through doorways into darkening corridors,
Falling at last in the howling vestibule.

In the years that followed, the winds of time swept round
The anniversaries of the act; and they
Were shouted down: my mother prepared for them
Music and dance, and called them celebrations.
They did not, fever-laden, creep on her unaware.
But did the nights not turn on her? Did she not
Dream music in the false-dawn faltering, phrases
Repeating endlessly, a figure of the dance
Halting and beckoning?

It is my house now, decaying but never dying,
The soul's museum, preserving and embalming
The shuttered rooms, the amulets, the pictures,
The doorways waiting for perennial surprises,
The children sleeping under the heat of summer,
And lastly the great bronze doors of the bridal chamber,
Huge and unspeaking, not to be pressed and opened,
Not to be lingered near, then or thereafter,
Not to be pounded upon by desolate fists,
Mine least of all.
                          I sailed with dipping sails.
I was not guilty of anybody's blood.
I will protect them in the decaying house.

With this resolve, concluded like a prayer,
From the eyes of the window gently stealing away,
As in a ritual I wipe the dust from the mirror
And look through the dark at the dim reflection before me.
The lips draw back from the mouth,
The night draws back from the years,
And there is the family smile in the quivering room.
The sun has gone, and the hunted bird demands:
'*Can the liar guard the truth, the deceiver seek it,*
The murderer preserve, the harlot chasten, or the guilty
Shelter the innocent? And shall you protect?'

[*PNW* 26, 1945]

EARLE BIRNEY

THE ROAD TO NIJMEGEN*

December, my dear, on the road to Nijmegen,
between the stones and the bitter skies was your face.

At first only the gathering of graves
along the lank canals, each with a frosted
billy-tin for motto; the bones of tanks
beside the stoven bridges; old men in the mist
knifing chips from a boulevard of stumps;
or women riding into the wind on the rims of their cycles,
like tattered sailboats tossing over the cobbles.

These at first and the fangs of homes, but more
the clusters of children like flies at the back of mess-huts,
or groping in gravel for knobs of coal,
their legs standing like dead stems out of their clogs.

Numbed on the long road to mangled Nijmegen,
I thought that only the living of others assures us;
we remember the gentle and true as trees walking,
as the men and women whose breath is a garment about us;
that we who are stretched now in this tomb of time
may remount like Lazarus into the light of kindness
by a treasured hold in the hands of the kind.

And so in the sleet as we neared Nijmegen
searching my heart for the hope of our minds,
for the proof in the flesh of the words we wish,
for laughter outrising at last the rockets,
I saw the rainbow answer of you,

* Pronounced Ny-may'-khen.

of you and your seed who, peopling the earth, would distil
our not impossible dreamed horizon,
and who, moving within the nightmare Now,
give us what creed we have for our daily crimes,
for this road that arrives at no future,
for this guilt
in the griefs of the old and the graves of the young.

[*PNW* 26, 1945]

JOHN LEHMANN

THE NIGHTMARE

The nightmare was more vivid than the day —
I had escaped, I dared to hope again —
The nightmare was a house that could not smile
For all its grey-winged eaves and trellis-rose,
The doves, the peacocks, everything was vain
In that secret base of souls who'd lost their way —
But I had escaped, and climbed across the stile
Following the path that wound over the plain
Through fields so full of corn, the corn so ripe
In throbbing Summer's trance — O my blood froze
To hear them snigger at their victims' pain
And shoot again, and laugh, and calmly wipe
Blood from their boots, those souls where devils danced —
But I had escaped, and somewhere in that plain
Knew there was a farm where love would rescue me
Welcoming with guiltless hand as he advanced —
And there were giant statues black as jet
Prone at my feet, and in the ripened grain
Circles of ancient stones I paled to see
That hummed and rocked — and mysteries I forget.

The nightmare seemed as urgent when awake
As when I dreamed; and though we ease our minds
As we might search an ebb-tide-cluttered shore
Tracing each image in the dire event
To drifting sea-wrack of the day before,
And in this flotsam soon elucidate
The patched disguise our exiled cravings take
To trick the coastguards; yet such easing blinds
The searching eye that still may intimate
Some deeper riddle in the dream was meant,

And in those broken reels of drama finds
The symbol of the unapparent fate,
The act we dread but waits not our consent.

[*PNW* 26, 1945]

LAURIE LEE

THISTLE

Thistle, blue bunch of daggers
rattling upon the wind,
saw-tooth that separates
the lips of grasses.

Your wound in childhood was
a savage shock of joy
that set the bees on fire
and the loud larks singing.

Your head enchanted then
smouldering among the flowers
filled the whole sky with smoke
and sparks of seed.

Now from your stabbing bloom's
nostalgic point of pain
ghosts of those summers rise
rustling across my eyes.

Seeding a magic thorn
to prick the memory,
to start in my icy flesh
fevers of long lost fields.

[*PNW 28*, July 1946]

DENYS L. JONES

CAIN IN THE JUNGLE

I have killed my brother in the jungle;
Under the green liana's clammy tangle
I hid, and pressed my trigger, and he died.

Smooth as the spotted panther crept my brother,
Never a creak of his equipment's leather,
Never a leaf dislodged nor bird offended.

With his palaeozoic prototype
My mother shared her own ungainly shape
In caverns on some slow Silurian stream;

And with the cublings played my father's sons,
Shoulder to shoulder chipped their flints and bones
Or scraped a greasy ichthyosaurus hide.

And, when the floods of purple slime receded
My brother's hutments by the apes were raided,
I lay beneath my brother's legs and cried.

Yet I have fought my brother for the planets;
I have never stopped to hear the linnets,
Or watch the cocos grow against the moon.

I have only slain him in the shadows,
I have made his slant-eyed women widows
And inherited his empty meadows.

[*PNW 28, 1946*]

DOUGLAS NEWTON

INVASION WEATHER

Two August voices
The summer flows in golden waves
To wash the trees and clean away
A winter's umber from the leaves

And leave them light as glazer's green.
The valley lakes of gold divide
Before the binders' even pace,

Ebb and abide in lively pools,
Until the labourers come
To labour home the wheaty foam.

Harvest! Harvest! the farmers all
— The Fathers roll their eyeballs underground —
All the young fork-bearing Neptunes — ah!

But now the avid Fathers sit them down
Upon the fresh raw wracks to supervise
The madmen coupled to the squealing swine:

Yet *still* the lovers lie between the sheaves
— Though an enormous head glares through the soil —
Still thigh is whispering to thigh,

And the gold breast rolls on the bronze chest,
An orange softly rolled upon a table;
The little drummer, even 's, allowed his dance;

So summer flows.
       While under Mycenae
The ghost of Agamemnon, like a bee,
Hums in the groining of his vaulted tomb.

[*PNW* 29, 1947]

The Thrushes

Translated from the Russian by George Reavey

A broody lunch-time silence reigns
  About this station so remote.
Close by the railway, in the lanes,
  Greenfinches sing their lifeless note.

Sultry and boundless as desire
  Is this straight village road and space.
A lilac wood looks all on fire
  Beneath a grey cloud's hair-topped face.

Along a leafy road, the trees
  Engage in play a plodding horse.
In hollows, saying take me please,
  Snow and violets, mould and gorse.

It is from hollows such as these
  That thrushes drink, when in exchange,
With ice and fire in their knees,
  Of rumoured day they ring the change.

Here syllables, now short, now long,
  And here the showers, hot and cold;
Thus throats are fashioned like a gong,
  Brass-lined with puddles sheen and mould.

They have allotments on the stumps,
  Their games of peeping Tom, sly looks,
Their long-day fuss and rowdy romps,
  And chattering in airy nooks.

And dashing through their wide-flung chambers
  Enigmas dart in public rhyme.
Theirs is the clock of drowsy quavers
  And branches chanting quarter-time.

Such is the thrushes' shady bower.
    They dwell in woods spared by the rake,
As artists should, tuned to this power.
    Theirs is the way I also take.

[PNW 30, 1947]

ODYSSEUS ELYTIS

THE AGE OF BLUE MEMORY

Translated from the Greek by Nanos Valaoritis

Olive-trees and vines spreading to the sea,
And, beyond, red fishing-boats as far as memory,
The golden sheaths of August over our midday sleep
Full of sea-weed and shells. And this a green vessel
Newly built spelling in the waters' peaceful embrace:
> *Our Lord will provide.*

Like leaves, like pebbles the years went by,
I remember the young sailors leaving
With sails the colour of their hearts
They sang of the four horizons
They carried North winds tattooed on their chests.

What was I looking for when you came in the colour of dawn?
The age of the sea in your eyes
The health of the sun in your body
— What was I looking for
Deep in the sea-caves in those spacious dreams
Where the wind flung his feelings like foam,
A blue stranger carving his sea-emblem on my chest.

With sand on my fingers I clasped my fingers
With sand on my eyes I clasped my fingers
It was the sadness
I remember it was in April when I first felt your human heaviness.
Your human body of clay and sin
As on our first day on earth
The amaryllis were being celebrated — I remember
You suffered from a deep bite on the lips
A deep nail-mark on the skin
Where Time is being eternally traced.

I left you then

The wind thundered and swept the white houses
And scattered the clean white feelings over the sky
The light shining from a smile.

Now I shall have by my side a jug of immortal water
A form of the wind's shattering freedom
And these your hands where love suffers
And this your shell where echoes the Aegean.

[*PNW 31*, 1947]

TERENCE TILLER

DOUBLE WEATHER

Stiff mask of gold, the firelight pressed
like fever on my face: I lay
watching the weather be undressed,
the stormy bridal of the day.

But clouds that streamed with riches were
rocked in the wind's enormous wash:
their only touch was troubled air
– a distant voice, a lightning flash.

The river and the restless tree
lay in each other's eyes, and shone:
the diving boughs untakeably
the wave too far to lean upon.

Passionate on bloodless glass
image and view came fingering
the mirror neither side could pass.
But in the weather's writhe and sting,

bare as the glitter of the pane,
a world of dubious light looked through
the pale surrender of the rain
and the embrace of striding blue.

I wore the heat like armour; she
like the wind's enfolding weight
and let a stream of hair fall free
towards the whispering of its light.

[*PNW 31, 1947*]

Iain Scott-Kilvert

FOUR POEMS FROM CAVAFY

Che Fece il Gran Rifiuto

To some men there befalls a fatal day
Demanding the great Yes or the great No.
He who holds the Yes ready within him
Is instantly revealed, and speaking forth
Stands ranged with honour and his own strong faith.
For him who refuses there is no repentance,
And if again challenged again he would refuse.
And yet that No, however just,
Shall overwhelm him all his life to come.

Desires

As the beautiful bodies of the dead
Which have not grown old,
But are laid away with tears in some shining tomb,
Roses at their head and jasmine at their feet,
Even so are desires that pass without fulfilment,
Those longings which never taste the ecstasy
Even of a single night, a single dazzling morning.

The Afternoon Sun

This room, how well I know it!
Now it is let, this and next door
For business offices.
The whole house has become an office block
For promoters, and merchants, and companies.

Ah! this room, how I know every inch of it.
Close to the door was our sofa,
And in front of it a Turkish carpet,
And nearby the shelf with the two yellow vases.
On the right, no, opposite stood a cupboard with a mirror,

In the centre of the room was the table where he used to write,
And the three big cane chairs,
Next to the window was the bed;
Where we made love so many times.

These wretched things must still be knocking around somewhere!

Next to the window was the bed,
And the afternoon sun would steal halfway up it.

It was at four in the afternoon that we parted,
Just for a week . . .   Alas,
That week became forever.

COLOURED GLASS

There is one detail which greatly moves me
At the coronation, in Vlachernae, of John Cantacuzene
And Irene, daughter of Andronikus Asan.
Since they possessed few gems of any value
(So great was the poverty of our unhappy empire)
They resorted to artificial stones,
And decked themselves in glass jewelry, coloured red and green and
    blue.

And yet I find nothing cheap nor unbecoming
In these scraps of coloured glass
Rather I find them a bitter reproach to fate
Against the undeserved ill fortune of the pair

For these are the symbols of their true estate
Of the magnificence which was after all their due

At the coronation of an Emperor John Cantacuzene
And an Empress Irene, daughter of Andronikus Asan.

[PNW 32, 1947]

BERNARD SPENCER

TWO POEMS

ON A CARVED AXLE-PIECE FROM A SICILIAN CART

The village craftsman stirred his bravest yellow
and (all the carpentry and carving done)
put the last touches to his newest cart,
until no playing-card had brighter panels;
with crested knights in armour, king and crown,
Crusaders slaughtering infidels, and crimson
where the blood laves:
and took his paintpot to that part
around the axle where a Southern memory
harking back out of Christendom, imagined
a chariot of glory
and Aphrodite riding wooden waves.

So some tanned peasant paid his money down
and till the years
put a full-stop to him or his purchase, jaunted
half around Sicily with wood for the fire,
long muscat grapes
or tangerines for the market in the town.
Thus answering, as his fathers' fathers had,
those metaphysical gaps and fears
which drain the blood of the age or drive it mad;
Who is God? Where do I come from? Are we dying?

— With a salty way of speech; with tasselled harness
with a cart to match the sea and all the flowers;
with Roger the Christian and Palermo towers;
and in between the dusty wheels
the Queen of Love in a yellow gown,
featured like a peasant child,
her three red horses rearing from the foam
and their carved manes blown wild.

ON THE ROAD

Our roof was grapes, and the broad hands of the vine
as we two drank in the vine-chinky shade
of harvest France:
and wherever the white road led we could not care;
it had brought us there
to the arbour built on a valley side where Time,
if Time any more existed, was that river
of so profound a current, it at once
both flowed and stayed.

We two. And nothing in the whole world was lacking.
It is later one realizes. I forget
the exact year or what we said. But the place
for a lifetime glows with noon; there are the rustic
table and the benches set; across the river
forests as soft as fallen clouds; and in
our wine and eyes I remember other noons.
It is a lot to say, nothing was lacking.
River, sun and leaves; and I am making
words to say 'grapes' and 'her skin'.

[*PNW 32*, 1947]

ROBERT PAGAN

A RECENT DISCOVERY

(An old bass-viol was lately bought for a few shillings at a farm sale not a thousand miles from Mellstock. Pasted on the inside of it was the following poem in a well-known handwriting. It is regretted that technical difficulties prevent its reproduction in facsimile. R.P.)

A RIGHT-OF-WAY: 186—

Decades behind me
When courting took more time,
In Tuphampton ewe-leaze I mind me
Two trudging aforetime:
A botanist he, in quest of a sought-after fleabane,
Wheedling his leman with 'Do you love *me*, Jane?'

Yestreen with bowed back
(To hike now is irksome),
Hydroptic and sagging the cloud-wrack,
I spied in the murk some
Wayfarer myopic Linnaeus-wise quizzing the quitches
And snooping at simples and worts in the ditches.

Remarked he, 'A path here
I seek to discover,
A right-of-way bang through this garth here,
Where elsewhiles a lover
I prinked with a pocket herbarium, necked I and cuddled:
Now I'm all mud-besprent, bored and be-puddled.

'I'm long past my noon-time.
The Unweeting Planner
Again proffers bale for one's boon-time
By tossing a spanner
Or crowbar into the works without recking the cost, sir.
At eighty,' intoned he, 'life is a frost, sir.

'When erst here I tarried
I knew not my steady
Had coolly, concurrently married
Three husbands already,
Nor learnt I till later, what's more, that all three were brothers,
Though sprung they, it seems, of disparate mothers.

'Well, we two inspected
The flora of Wessex;
More specimens had we collected
Had she pondered less sex;
We botanized little that year . . . But I must be wending;
My analyst hints at amnesia impending.'

[*PNW 33*, 1948]

MICHAEL HAMBURGER

TWO POEMS

FROM THE NOTE-BOOK OF A EUROPEAN TRAMP

I

Even in mid-October there is spring
when after frost from Iceland breezes come
all laden with the basking South to bring
bright life to yellow leaves and kiss the numb
fingers of tramps on sun-forsaken roads;
when the high tide of summer zest rolls back
out of the veins and no swift fever goads
me onwards, onwards to wilder track;
when almost towns like a weird painted girl
hold me with sweetly-sickly-smelling charms,
so that, half cosmopolitan, half churl,
I flirt obscenely with the streets' white arms; —
then the warm winds refuel me: I spit
into the gutter and walk on, a friar
without a mission, horse without a bit,
bound for the perfect Nowhere of desire.

II

'Christmas will break your hearts,' an old hand said,
'such stillness and the churchbells crying out,
and you alone in the cold; — you'll not be glad
you chose to be a lousy gadabout.'
It's Christmas now and all is just the same;
the snow's no deeper than it was last week,
the night's no quieter; why should a name
melt the old fellow's guts and make him meek?
Surely a wretched scribbler gone astray!
To hoard up Christian love the whole year round
and pour it all into a single day,
stale sickly seed into exhausted ground!

In the tramp's calendar Christmas is when
he's one with all things, squirrel, toad and sow,
even the richest of his fellow men,
that is, at any time and anyhow.
As for my heart, it broke some time ago
when, in the towns of Europe, I still tried
to live like other men and not to know
that all we lived for had already died.

[*PNW 34*, 1948]

Norman Nicholson

TWO POEMS

I

FIVE MINUTES

'I'm having five minutes,' he said,
Fitting the shelter of the cobble wall
Over his shoulders like a cape. His head
Was wrapped in a cap as green
As the lichened stone he sat on. The winter wind
Whined in the ashes like a saw,
And thorn and briar shook their red
Badges of hip and haw;
The fields were white with smoke of blowing lime;
Rusty iron brackets of sorrel stood
In grass grey as the whiskers round an old dog's nose.
'Just five minutes,' he said;
And the next day I heard that he was dead,
Having five minutes to the end of time.

II

GATHERING STICKS ON SUNDAY

If the man in the moon
Gazing at the waning earth, watches
How the frayed edge of the sunset catches
Thimbles and nodules of rock,
Hachuring distinct with threads of shadow
All that is hammered flat in the earth's brass noon;
And if he sees,
New in the level light, like pock-
marks on a face, dark craters,
The size of acorn cups, or scars
Vast as his own dried oceans, then
He'll know that soon
The living world of men
Will take a lunar look, as dead as slag,
And moon and earth will stare at one another
Like the cold, yellow skulls of child and mother.

[*PNW 35*, 1948]

JOHN SHORT

DE QUINCEY IN WESTMORLAND

These are the poppy heads,
The mountain peaks whose milk
Comforts the sleepless in their beds.
See how it streams
Out of the ripening hills
And pours away, whiter than cream,
From splitting crag and ghyll!

Green poppy heads!
Your tangy syrups
Lull me to sleep.
The very air
Loosens great petals of ribbed silk
And drops them there
Where the black clappers of the stamens toll
Bourdon across the night and fell
Saying, 'Be satisfied, sleep well'.

And hills are poison pods
Beneficent, whose black
Volcanic seeds can summon Gods
Out of their sagas to my hand.
See how their heads
Burn in this fiery yellow room
And strong about my bed
Strike down the furies of my doom!

[*PNW 36*, 1949]

BERNARD SPENCER

TWO POEMS

I

AT COURMAYEUR

This climbers' valley with its wayside shrines
(the young crowned Mother and her dying flowers)
became our theme for weeks. Do you remember
the letters that we wrote and how we planned
the journey there and chose our hotel; ours
was to be one 'among the pines'?

Guesses went wide; but zig-zag past that ridge
the road climbs from the Roman town; there stand
the glittering peaks, and one, the God, immensely
tossing the clouds around his shoulders; here
are what you asked for, summer pastures and
an air with glaciers in its edge.

Beyond each pause is mountain water falling;
at night, the river seems to draw more closely:
darling, how did you think I could forget you,
you who for ever stayed behind? Your absence
is hard and real as rocks. Just now it was
those hangdown flowers that meant recalling.

II

THE BOATS

Five boats beside the lake,
pulled bows first up the shore; how hard it is
to draw them, from each angle changing, elegant:
their feminine poise, the 'just so' lifting sweep
of the light timbers round the flanks sucked thin
into the thirsty bows;
                      the same or nearly
as makes no difference, since men settled first
near these magnolias, lived the different life
that is always the same; fished, traded, hammered, gossiped,
wanted their food and wine, appeased the Powers,
meditated journeys
or turned and turned in their mind some woman's
image lost or distant.
                Near this bench and the keels
someone has scratched in the dust the name E L S A.

[*PNW 37*, 1949]

E. J. SCOVELL

RETURN FROM THE BEACH

Across the sands burdened with their dark tone,
With heat of honey and with seams of stone-
   blue shade under the day-long azure,
   The holiday-makers turn from pleasure,

Turn from the brilliant west in twos and fours,
In groups dispersed and quiet, with their powers
   Of play before the light failing,
   With trailing child and his spade trailing;

The women bearing their weight, the youths their lightness,
The outriding boys still in a mould of brightness,
   The girl tranced by beatitude,
   The man pleased with his hardihood,

All in their human posture pacing on
As if they carried their lives in the form of a crown.
   Late cricketers, a lingering couple
   With gulls possess the world of opal.

[*PNW 37*, 1949]

JAMES MICHIE

TWO POEMS

I

ARIZONA NATURE MYTH

Up in the heavenly saloon
Sheriff sun and rustler moon
Gamble, stuck in the sheriff's mouth
The fag end of an afternoon.

There in the bad town of the sky
Sheriff, nervy, wonders why
He's let himself wander so far West
On his own; he looks with a smoky eye

At the rustler opposite turning white,
Lays down a king for Law, sits tight
Bluffing. On it that crooked moon
Plays an ace and shoots for the light.

Spurs, badge and uniform red,
(It looks like blood, but he's shamming dead),
Down drops the marshal, and under cover
Crawls out dogwise, ducking his head.

But Law that don't get its man ain't Law.
Next day, faster on the draw,
Sheriff creeping up from the other side,
Blazes his way in through the back door.

But moon's not there. He's ridden out on
A galloping phenomenon,
A wonder horse, quick as light.
Moon's left town. Moon's clean gone.

II

THE ROBIN AND THE LARK

Tail like a painful splinter,
Sham blood running down his chest,
Robin makes the best
Of begging, and with 'Oh sir' 'Please sir' acts
Orphan all winter.

Type of the bumsucker, he thieves
By a trick of doleful pertinacity
Housemaid's pity,
Picturesque bread and water, but does not see
That the world disbelieves.

And feathers his nest better
Than true outcasts, unheard sufferers,
Since man prefers
To miserable thanks in charity
Cheerfulness from the debtor

Yet forfeits by the stratagem
The larger adulthood of larks,
Who set up marks
Too high for themselves, and are frozen flying;
Odes are for them,

Death, like a cold comet,
Falling and failure. Robin, at home
With pram wheel, garden gnome,
Is nursery-rhymed, and, limed with children's praise,
Cannot fly from it.

[*PNW* 40, 1950]

GEORGE BARKER

CHANNEL CROSSING

And just by crossing the short sea
To find the answer sitting there
Combing out its snakey hair
And with a smile regarding me
Because it knows only too well
That I shall never recognize
The verities that I should prize
And the lies that I should tell.

I saw the question in the sky
Ride like a gull to fool me, as
The squat boat butted at the seas
As grossly as through mysteries I
Churn up a frothy wake of verbs
Or stir a muddy residue
Looking for the answer who
Sanctifies as she disturbs.

The horror of the question-mark
Looking back I saw stand over
The white and open page of Dover
Huge as the horn of the scapegoat. Dark
It stood up in the English day
Interrogating Destiny
With the sad lip of the sea:
'What can a dead nation say?'

As these words wailed in the air
I looked at Europe and I saw
The glittering instruments of war
Grow paler but not go from where
Like a livid sunset on
The marble of the horizon
They lay foretelling for tomorrow
Another day of human sorrow.

But when I turned and looked into
The silent chambers of the sea
I saw the displaced fishes flee
From nowhere into nowhere through
Their continent of liberty.
O skipping porpoise of the tide
No longer shall the sailors ride
You cheering out to sea.

I thought of Britain in its cloud
Chained to the economic rocks
Dying behind me; saw the flocks
Of great and grieving omens crowd
About the lion on the stone;
I heard Milton's eagle mewing
Her dereliction in the ruin
Of a great nation alone.

That granite and gigantic sigh
Of the proud man beaten by
Those victories from which we die;
The gentle and defeated grief
Of the gale that moans among
Trees that are a day too strong
And, victorious by a leaf,
Show the winner he was wrong.

The continent of discontent
Rose up before me as I stood
Above the happy fish. Endued
With hotter and unhappier blood,
Contented in my discontent,
I saw that every man's a soul
Caught in a glass wishing bowl:
To live at peace in discontent.

O somewhere in the seven leagues
That separate us from the stricken
Amphitheatre of the spirit,
O somewhere in that baleful sea
The answer to sad Europe lodges,
The clue that causes us to sicken
Because we cannot find and share it,
Or, finding, cannot see.

So in the sky, the monstrous sun
Mocked like a punishment to be,
Extending now to you and me
The vision of what we have done:
And as the boat drew to the quay
I thought, by crossing this short water
I shall not find, in its place,
The answer with the silent face.

[*PNW* 40, 1950]

Three

Stories, Memoirs, Impressions

George Orwell

Shooting an Elephant

In Moulmein, in Lower Burma, I was hated by large numbers of people – the only time in my life that I have been important enough for this to happen to me. I was subdivisional police officer of the town, and in an aimless, petty kind of way anti-European feeling was very bitter. No one had the guts to raise a riot, but if a European woman went through the bazaars alone somebody would probably spit betel juice over her dress. As a police officer I was an obvious target and was baited whenever it seemed safe to do so. When a nimble Burman tripped me up on the football field and the referee (another Burman) looked the other way, the crowd yelled with hideous laughter. This happened more than once. In the end the sneering yellow faces of young men that met me everywhere, the insults hooted after me when I was at a safe distance, got badly on my nerves. The young Buddhist priests were the worst of all. There were several thousands of them in the town and none of them seemed to have anything to do except stand on street corners and jeer at Europeans.

All this was perplexing and upsetting. For at that time I had already made up my mind that imperialism was an evil thing and the sooner I chucked up my job and got out of it the better. Theoretically – and secretly, of course – I was all for the Burmese and all against their oppressors, the British. As for the job I was doing, I hated it more bitterly than I can perhaps make clear. In a job like that you see the dirty work of Empire at close quarters. The wretched prisoners huddling in the stinking cages of the lock-ups, the grey, cowed faces of the long-term convicts, the scarred buttocks of the men who had been flogged with bamboos – all these oppressed me with an intolerable sense of guilt. But I could get nothing into perspective. I was young and ill-educated and I had had to think out my problems in the utter silence that it imposed on every Englishman in the East. I did not even know that the British Empire is dying, still less did I know that it is a great deal better than the younger empires that are going to supplant it. All I knew was that I was stuck between my hatred of the empire I served and my rage against the evil-spirited little beasts who tried to make my job impossible. With one part of my mind I thought of the British Raj as an unbreakable tyranny, as something clamped down, *in saecula saeculorum*, upon the will of prostrate peoples; with another part I thought that the greatest joy in the world would be to drive a bayonet into a Buddhist priest's guts. Feelings like these are the normal by-products of imperialism; ask any Anglo-Indian official, if you can catch him off duty.

One day something happened which in a roundabout way was enlightening. It was a tiny incident in itself, but it gave me a better glimpse than I had had before of the real nature of imperialism – the real motives for which despotic governments act. Early one morning the sub-inspector at a police station the other end of the town rang me up on the 'phone and said that an elephant was ravaging the bazaar. Would I please come and do something about it? I did not know what I could do, but I wanted to see what was happening and I got on to a pony and started out. I took my rifle, an old .44 Winchester and much too small to kill an elephant, but I thought the noise might be useful *in terrorem*. Various Burmans stopped me on the way and told me about the elephant's doings. It was not, of course, a wild elephant, but a tame one which had gone 'must'. It had been chained up as tame elephants always are when their attack of 'must' is due, but on the previous night it had broken its chain and escaped. Its mahout, the only person who could manage it when it was in that state, had set out in pursuit, but he had taken the wrong direction and was now twelve hours' journey away, and in the morning the elephant had suddenly reappeared in the town. The Burmese population had no weapons and were quite helpless against it. It had already destroyed somebody's bamboo hut, killed a cow and raided some fruit-stalls and devoured the stock; also it had met the municipal rubbish van, and, when the driver jumped out and took to his heels, had turned the van over and inflicted violences upon it.

The Burmese sub-inspector and some Indian constables were waiting for me in the quarter where the elephant had been seen. It was a very poor quarter, a labyrinth of squalid bamboo huts, thatched with palm-leaf, winding all over a steep hillside. I remember that it was a cloudy stuffy morning at the beginning of the rains. We began questioning the people as to where the elephant had gone, and, as usual, failed to get any definite information. That is invariably the case in the East; a story always sounds clear enough at a distance, but the nearer you get to the scene of events the vaguer it becomes. Some of the people said that the elephant had gone in one direction, some said that he had gone in another, some professed not even to have heard of any elephant. I had almost made up my mind that the whole story was a pack of lies, when we heard yells a little distance away. There was a loud, scandalized cry of 'Go away, child! Go away this instant!' and an old woman with a switch in her hand came round the corner of a hut, violently shooing away a crowd of naked children. Some more women followed, clicking their tongues and exclaiming; evidently there was something there that the children ought not to have seen. I rounded the hut and saw a man's dead body sprawling in the mud. He was an Indian, a black Dravidian coolie, almost naked, and he could not have been dead many minutes. The people said that the elephant had come suddenly upon him round the corner of the hut, caught him with its trunk, put its foot on his back and ground him into the earth. This was the rainy season and the ground was soft, and his face had scored a trench a foot deep and a couple of yards long. He was lying on his belly with arms crucified and head sharply twisted to one side. His face was coated with mud, the eyes wide open, the teeth bared and grinning with an expression of unendurable agony. (Never tell me, by the way, that the dead look peaceful. Most of the corpses I have seen looked devilish.) The friction of the great beast's foot had stripped the skin from his back as neatly as one skins a rabbit. As soon as I saw the dead man I sent an orderly to a friend's house near by to borrow an elephant rifle. I had already sent back the pony, not wanting it to go mad with fright and throw me if it smelled the elephant.

The orderly came back in a few minutes with a rifle and five cartridges, and meanwhile some Burmans had arrived and told us that the elephant was in the paddy fields below, only a few hundred yards away. As I started forward practically the whole population of the quarter flocked out of the houses and followed me. They had seen the rifle and were all shouting excitedly that I was going to shoot the elephant. They had not shown much interest in the elephant when he was merely ravaging their homes, but it was different now that he was going to be shot. It was a bit of fun to them, as it would be to an English crowd; besides, they wanted the meat. It made me vaguely uneasy. I had no intention of shooting the elephant – I had merely sent for the rifle to defend myself if necessary – and it is always unnerving to have a crowd following you. I marched down the hill, looking and feeling a fool, with the rifle over my shoulder and an ever-growing army of people jostling at my heels. At the bottom, when you got away from the huts, there was a metalled road and beyond that a miry waste of paddy fields a thousand yards across, not yet ploughed but soggy from the first rains and dotted with coarse grass. The elephant was standing eighty yards from the road, his left side towards us. He took not the slightest notice of the crowd's approach. He was tearing up bunches of grass, beating them against his knees to clean them and stuffing them into his mouth.

I had halted on the road. As soon as I saw the elephant I knew with perfect certainty that I ought not to shoot him. It is a serious matter to shoot a working elephant – it is comparable to destroying a huge and costly piece of machinery – and obviously one ought not to do it if it can possibly be avoided. And at that distance, peacefully eating, the elephant looked no more dangerous than a cow. I thought then and I think now that his attack of 'must' was already passing off; in which case he would merely wander harmlessly about until the mahout came back and caught him. Moreover, I did not in the least want to shoot him. I decided that I would watch him for a little while to make sure that he did not turn savage again, and then go home.

But at that moment I glanced round at the crowd that had followed me. It was an immense crowd, two thousand at the least and growing every minute. It blocked the road for a long distance on either side. I looked at the sea of yellow faces above the garish clothes – faces all happy and excited over this bit of fun, all certain that the elephant was going to be shot. They were watching me as they would watch a conjuror about to perform a trick. They did not like me, but with the magical rifle in my hands I was momentarily worth watching. And suddenly I realized that I should have to shoot the elephant after all. The people expected it of me and I had got to do it; I could feel their two thousand wills pressing me forward, irresistibly. And it was at this moment, as I stood there with the rifle in my hands, that I first grasped the hollowness, the futility of the white man's dominion in the East. Here was I, the white man with his gun, standing in front of the unarmed native crowd – seemingly the leading actor of the piece; but in reality I was only an absurd puppet pushed to and fro by the will of those yellow faces behind. I perceived in this moment that when the white man turns tyrant it is his own freedom that he destroys. He becomes a sort of hollow, posing dummy, the conventionalized figure of a sahib. For it is the condition of his rule that he shall spend his life in trying to impress the 'natives', and so in every crisis he has got to do what the 'natives' expect of him. He wears a mask, and his face grows to fit it. I had got to shoot the elephant. I had committed myself to doing it when I sent for the rifle. A sahib has got to act like a sahib; he has got to appear resolute, to know his own mind and do definite things. To come all that way, rifle in hand, with two thousand people marching at my heels, and then to trail feebly away, having done nothing – no, that was impossible. The crowd would laugh at me. And my whole life, every white man's life in the East, was one long struggle not to be laughed at.

But I did not want to shoot the elephant. I watched him beating his bunch of grass against his knees, with that preoccupied grandmotherly air that elephants have. It seemed to me that it would be murder to shoot him. At that age I was not squeamish about killing animals, but I had never shot an elephant and never wanted to. (Somehow it always seems worse to kill a *large* animal.) Besides, there was the beast's owner to be considered. Alive, the elephant was worth at least a hundred pounds; dead, he would only be worth the value of his tusks – five pounds, possibly. But I had got to act quickly. I turned to some experienced-looking Burmans who had been there when we arrived, and asked them how the elephant had been behaving. They all said the same thing: he took no notice of you if you left him alone, but he might charge if you went too close to him.

It was perfectly clear to me what I ought to do. I ought to walk up to within, say, twenty-five yards of the elephant and test his behaviour. If he charged I could shoot, if he took no notice of me it would be safe to leave him until the mahout came back. But also I knew that I was going to do no such thing. I was a poor shot with a rifle and the ground was soft mud into which one would sink at every step. If the elephant charged and I missed him, I should have about as much chance as a toad under a steam-roller. But even then I was not thinking particularly of my own skin, only of the watchful yellow faces behind. For at that moment, with the crowd watching me, I was not afraid in the ordinary sense, as I would have been if I had been alone. A white man musn't be frightened in front of 'natives'; and so, in general, he isn't frightened. The sole thought in my mind was that if anything went wrong those two thousand Burmans would see me pursued, caught, trampled on and reduced to a grinning corpse like that Indian up the hill. And if that happened it was quite probable that some of them would laugh. That would never do. There was only one alternative. I shoved the cartridges into the magazine and lay down on the road to get a better aim.

The crowd grew very still, and a deep, low, happy sigh, as of people who see the theatre curtain go up at last, breathed from innumerable throats. They were going to have their bit of fun after all. The rifle was a beautiful German thing with cross-hair sights. I did not then know that in shooting an elephant one should shoot to cut an imaginary bar running from ear-hole to ear-hole. I ought, therefore, as the elephant was sideways on, to have aimed straight at his ear-hole; actually I aimed several inches in front of this, thinking the brain would be further forward.

When I pulled the trigger I did not hear the bang or feel the kick – one never does when a shot goes home – but I heard the devilish roar of glee that went up from the crowd. In that instant, in too short a time, one would have thought, even for the bullet to get there, a mysterious, terrible change had come over the elephant. He neither stirred nor fell, but every line of his body had altered. He looked suddenly stricken, shrunken, immensely old, as though the frightful impact of the bullet had paralysed him without knocking him down. At last, after what seemed a long time – it might have been five seconds, I dare say – he sagged flabbily to his knees. His mouth slobbered. An enormous senility seemed to have settled upon him. One could have imagined him thousands of years old. I fired again into the same spot. At the second shot he did not collapse but climbed with desperate slowness to his feet and stood weakly upright, with legs sagging and head drooping. I fired a third time. That was the shot that did for him. You could see the agony of it jolt his whole body and knock the last remnant of strength from his legs. But in falling he seemed for a moment to rise, for as his hind legs collapsed beneath him he seemed to tower upwards like a huge rock toppling, his trunk reaching skyward like a tree. He trumpeted, for the first and only time. And then down he came, his belly towards me, with a crash that seemed to shake the ground even where I lay.

I got up. The Burmans were already racing past me across the mud. It was obvious that the elephant would never rise again, but he was not dead. He was breathing very rhythmically with long rattling gasps, his great mound of a side painfully rising and falling. His mouth was wide open – I could see far down into caverns of pale pink throat. I waited a long time for him to die, but his breathing did not weaken. Finally I fired my two remaining shots into the spot where I thought his heart must be. The thick blood welled out of him like red velvet, but still he did not die. His body did not even jerk when the shots hit him, the tortured breathing continued without a pause. He was dying, very slowly and in great agony, but in some world remote from me where not even a bullet could damage him further. I felt that I had got to put an end to that dreadful noise. It seemed dreadful to see the great beast lying there, powerless to move and yet powerless to die, and not even to be able to finish him. I sent back for my small rifle and poured shot after shot into his heart and down his throat. They seemed to make no impression. The tortured gasps continued as steadily as the ticking of a clock.

In the end I could not stand it any longer and went away. I heard later that it took him half an hour to die. Burmans were arriving with dahs and baskets even before I left, and I was told they had stripped his body almost to the bones by the afternoon.

Afterwards, of course, there were endless discussions about the shooting of the elephant. The owner was furious, but he was only an Indian and could do nothing. Besides, legally I had done the right thing, for a mad elephant has to be killed, like a mad dog, if its owner fails to control it. Among the Europeans opinion was divided. The older men said I was right, the younger men said it was a damn shame to shoot an elephant for killing a coolie, because an elephant was worth more than any damn Coringhee coolie. And afterwards I was very glad that the coolie had been killed; it put me legally in the right and it gave me a sufficient pretext for shooting the elephant. I often wondered whether any of the others grasped that I had done it solely to avoid looking a fool.

[PNW 1, 1940]

ANDRÉ CHAMSON

MY ENEMY

Translated from the French by John Rodker

As I came down to the river I saw there was a boy swimming about in the pool. He was naked, save for the handkerchief tied round his waist, as he swam with slow breast strokes, spluttering among the wavelets that receded from his path. Above his hidden face the close cropped hair dripped with tiny drops. He was swimming towards me, with his eyes fixed on the shelving bottom. As he reached the edge he raised himself erect against the perpendicular bank and looked up. It was Maubert. He saw me in the very instant that I realized who it was, and taking a deeper breath, put up his hands to get a hold on the rock.

While he was trying to hoist himself up on the bank I was hurriedly gathering stones. In a second or two I had four in my left hand, and tight in my right, still another, oval, bulging, and heavy like some precious metal. With my arm flung back I shouted at the boy who was trying to drag himself up the rocky walls polished to glassy smoothness by the spring-time spates:

'Stop where you are!'

With one swift look he calculated his chances. Naked, half in the water, precariously balanced, he was in no position to defend himself. Wherever he looked there seemed no way out. I swung my arm above his head. He knew well my aim would be sure. And thereupon he let himself drop into deep water again, and gazed at me while floating on his back.

It was Maubert, my enemy. I trembled with rage and ecstatic joy as I looked at him. My blood, beating violently in my veins, thudded through the hand clenched round my missile, as I thought, 'Got him!' in much the same way as one becomes aware how difficult some action is only when it has successfully been accomplished.

Oh, he looked pretty crestfallen with twelve feet of water under him, and hemmed in by the slippery walls. His eyes, full of tears, fixed themselves intently on me. I could not conjure up the slightest pity for him. Our childish hatred was of too long standing. A dozen times we had fought each other already, without either of us getting the upper hand. There came to my mind that night when he had pounced on me with a couple of his chums. They were pushing a wheelbarrow along. The street had been dark and it was near the bridge. Totally unsuspecting, all I had heard was my name 'Tchamsoun', pronounced in the local way, and the thud of the wheelbarrow's two legs suddenly hitting the ground. And, immediately, I had been blinded with blows. Nevertheless, by wildly kicking out, striking round me and biting whatever met my teeth, I made them give way long enough to enable me to retreat still facing them, like an angry cat pursued by dogs. But it was not the others that mattered, it was Maubert on whom all my hatred fell. When our two schools fought together on Saturdays, for instance, under the chestnut trees of the fair ground, it was always Maubert I aimed at. We would load stones with insults and spit on them at the very moment they were hurled, so as to bewitch them and make them truly strike their goal. And Maubert, too, always aimed at me whenever we had these clashes. Now I had him in my power, one against one, with every advantage on my side. It was as thrilling as ambushing a whole troop of enemies in a ravine.

I sat myself down on the bank. He was just opposite me, but if he so much as let the current begin to carry him away, threateningly I raised my arm. Then paddling a little with his hands, utterly docile and unable to take his eyes off my stone, he would return to the old place.

With all the sternness I could summon up, I gazed at him, as though my glances, too, could have struck. With every moment my rage increased. He was the worst enemy I had. We did not go to the same school. Our parents did not want us to know each other. Mine said, 'They're people you couldn't trust an inch,' and that blind rancour of theirs was unquestioningly accepted by me. His grandfather had denounced the Republicans in the time of the Second Empire, and my own grandfather had had to go before the mixed Commissions. At the age of six we were already hating each other. Everything his family owned seemed horrible to me. They had a tiny vineyard and a little house outside the town, on the road to Elze, and all around seemed like a spot accursed in the midst of our own valley; a spot abhorred by the sun, sodden with unhealthy damp and devoured by insects and decay. Always I avoided the street they lived in in the centre of our town, and the manner in which his parents gained their living seemed both repulsive and suspicious in my eyes. They were folk of a different race. Their only thought was how to do us harm, and we felt our hatred justified because we knew how ready we were to forgive and forget the ancient wrongs. And yet the hatred between our families sprang into being as each new child was born, and from the age of eight we were always fighting each other, backed up by our gangs of good-for-nothings who shared the same hates.

I'd got him. He was a good swimmer, but he was already beginning to show signs of fatigue. At moments his whole head would go under and come up again, spluttering out the water he had swallowed. I looked at him with fury. I had never seen him so close. In fact, I had hardly known what he looked like. He was fourteen, like me. You could not have called him good-looking, with his cropped hair clotted to right and left like wheat-ears after a storm. Whenever he spat the motion made by his lips sent a spasm of disgust through all my body. They were too thick, too pulpy altogether. As I looked at them I thought, 'They look like the lips of a girl.' Round his waist the handkerchief floated like some aquatic plant, while the crystal-clear water foreshortened his small, thin, dark-skinned, shapely body.

I watched him carefully, my missile ready. Suppose, instead, he had caught me in the pool. I'd have had that stone hurled at me long ago. I could read his thoughts in his shifty eyes. If only he could! But just let him try and drift away on the current. If I do aim I'll go for his head. So much the worse for him. And if I kill him? Oh, stones don't kill. He'll manage to get out of the water all right with his head broken open and his face all bloody. They gave me a pretty good gruelling, they did, that night when they had the wheelbarrow, and I was one against three.

'Stop where you are, I tell you . . . You just dare to let the current carry you away . . .'

I had jumped up with my arm flung back. He came nearer again, swimming on his back. He seemed at the last gasp, frozen. His teeth were chattering like a toy. I reseated myself on the rocks, and began looking at his face once more. 'The shifty swine. If one gave in to them . . . they wouldn't take long . . . But I'm on top this time. We'll see if he'll dare flinch.'

The sun sank, the pool fell more and more in shadow, the water turned to ink. Maubert still spat out mouthfuls of water from time to time. But now I was looking at him without disgust, thinking, 'Funny, all the same, I should have caught him here! He comes swimming here in the mountain like me? And he knows about my pool. No! He must have passed by accident and wanted a swim. He hadn't even got his bathing drawers with him . . . What cheek that he should have come up here! And pick on my own pool! Ah, but if he'd been the one to catch me here.'

By now the cold must have penetrated him through and through. In late June the water is still very cold. One can catch one's death of cold by staying too long in our local rivers. He kept on watching me, and seeming to be waiting for something to happen. 'Oh, you're waiting, are you? Well! I'll attend to you. I'll give you a good bang on the head with this stone, or on the arm, or even close to your body and send you under.'

I was standing up, turning the stone about in my fingers, to get a solid grip. I knew how it had to be hurled to keep it straight on the mark. It was a splendid stone, beautifully polished in the water, a shepherd's stone with which I could have brought down a bird thirty feet away. A terrific swing, a sudden release from the arrested arm, and away it would fly as though one single pencil of whistling stone stretched to his forehead from my arm. People like that must be crushed like snakes, before they have time even to strike. He hasn't even the courage to resist. He's stupefied by fear. If it was me, I should have dived and swum under water to the other side of the pool: I too would have gathered my stones on the other bank . . . But he doesn't think of anything. All he does is look at me with that girlish face. Now I see who he reminds me of. It's his sister. That big seventeen-year-older. He's got the same sort of lips.

Maubert was motionless now, waiting for me to strike, keeping himself afloat with slight movements of the forearms. He had the appearance of being knocked senseless already, struck in the temple by my stone, as he lay there on his back. For a moment I looked at him thus, picturing him dead, and suddenly I let the stones fall out of my left hand. Then, from the other, I hurled the stone high over his head, on to the other bank of the mountain torrent, and said, 'Get out of the water . . . Come here.'

I had hardly finished speaking before he was clinging to the bank, shuddering with cold and making a brrr . . . sound with his lips. He dragged himself up the rocky wall, covered his parts with his hands, and ran to the foot of a bush where he had left his clothes. I remained looking at the pool while he dressed. After some moments I looked back over my shoulder, and saw him coming towards me slowly, fastening his belt. He seemed to be thinking. I began looking at the water again, with the thought in my mind, 'Now he's going to throw a stone at my head. He's where the stones are, he has lots more round him than I have.'

When I decided to look round I saw he was now very close. He had turned up his collar, and his cheeks were beginning to glow again as though whipped by the mountain wind. Whereupon I said, 'You're not cold?'

'I've my flannel shirt, luckily.'

A fresh wave of that disgust, which only Maubert could awake, surged through me. The thought of that flannel shirt made me want to vomit. All that family always wore flannel.

He had sat down near me. I stretched out on the rock, and turned towards him.

'What made you come here? Who gave you permission to come to this pool?'

'Who gave me permission? I come here often. It's my special pool.'

'Yours?'

I drew in. I thought, 'His special pool? We'll soon see!' Then suddenly I said:

'Your special pool? I've been coming here for a year now. I found it one day as I was coming down from La Tessonne. It was in May.'

I saw a sudden recrudescence of his hate for me flash from his eyes. His teeth clenched as he looked at me. But we were equally matched. What kept me from leaping at his throat kept him also. We were not afraid of each other, it was a mutual respect. He continued:

'I discovered it by myself too, last year. I come here often. I like it better than the Chaussée or the Pradet. You're alone, and when you're in you can always see the bottom through the water.'

'There's nothing you can dive off. Otherwise it would be the best pool around here. I've often tried to do it from the other side, but that spur of rock's in the way. You'd split your head open if you hit it.'

Maubert smiled. He was looking at the hidden rock that he must himself have been well acquainted with. He went on.

'No, there's not room . . . That doesn't matter though, it's a good pool. The water's good. You can feel the air it's caught up in the waterfalls.'

So the difference between one pool and another mattered to Maubert! He could tell when the water was light or heavy. He loved them then? I could discuss all the secrets of our rivers with him?

'By the time it gets to the Pradet the water's lost all its air. It's as heavy as clay.'

He nodded affirmation, and looked suspiciously at me. I had discovered his secrets too. We fell silent as we stared at the pool. You could see the clouds passing over it, high above our heads, and trooping towards the summit to press onwards to the pass. Suddenly Maubert asked:

'Why didn't you throw it?'

'You were by yourself.'

'You think I'm afraid of you?'

'What about me then? Why, I'll take on three of you, and with a barrow thrown in.'

He flushed slightly. I had not budged, though I was ready to leap up. Even stretched out I could leap to my feet with one bound. I was thinking, 'If he moves, I'll hurl myself head foremost at his face.' He did not move however.

'Why do you hate me?' he said at last.

'It's you . . .' My indignation would not let me proceed. But immediately I resumed . . . 'It's you who's worst . . . Who ever did anything . . . ?'

As if expressing some obvious truth, he answered simply:

'Your lot . . .'

'Our lot . . . ?'

'You're not the same as we are.'

Again disgust overcame me. I hated Maubert, his thick lips, cropped hair and flannel shirt. Everything that came in contact with him seemed to me utterly vile. I thought of the fruit he must eat. An apple bitten by his teeth, chewed in his mouth, and finally swallowed! And now he was afraid. I could see that perfectly well. He raised himself a little on his elbows. He knew I was the stronger.

'I didn't shoot to teach you a lesson. If I wanted to I could smash you altogether, see! But I prefer just to talk. That way you'll realize who you have to deal with. We're not the same as you are . . . Fortunately! Our sort are not shifty brutes like you, or liars either. In our school we learn more than you do. I can ask you questions that prove it. Take French history, for example. Tell me who ruled these parts after the Romans and before the Franks? Oh, yes, rack your brains all right, but that won't help you much.'

Maubert did not know. He felt like crying, but suddenly, as though struck by an inspiration, he cried:

'Well, how many times does 25 go into 375? In your head, in your head, don't try to work it out on your fingers! You just don't know, that's all.'

For the life of me I could not find the answer. The figures danced in front of my eyes. Mental arithmetic was not my strong point, and I answered:

'The Visigoths. Haven't you ever heard of the Visigoths?'

'Fifteen. I say fifteen and I'll prove it in my head. Ten times twenty-five . . .'

We had succeeded in humiliating each other, but instead of increasing, our hatred had only been weakened by it. I lifted my face to the sky, and noting the direction from which the breeze came, said:

'Wind from the sea . . .'

'Means tomorrow wet will be.'

'When Cape Coste puts a cap on . . .'

'The shepherd must put his wrap on.'

Maubert laughed with glee at being able to finish my phrases, at knowing how to complete the local saws.

'When you came across this pool, you must have been coming back from La Tessonne?'

'I had been looking for tulips.'

'Under the big rocks?'

'That's not the only place, you know! Do you know another place? Well . . . La Tessonne . . . It isn't very high. One can get there in an afternoon. I like hereabouts best though.'

He winked one eye, and with a finger began to draw the road that led to Prat-Coustal. I followed its every curve, watching for the least mistake, but he made none. Past the village, the path took him straight through the pasture patches, followed the line of firs, and struck the road to the pass. 'And there you are!' he said.

'Do you go often?'

He nodded yes. When he did that I felt real liking for him. For the first time he seemed a decent, straightforward chap. Of course, he was still far from being a chum like Jean or Maurice. Still, I felt I could have gone off on a trip with him, and if need were, drunk from the same can, shared the same loaf and jampot, slept under the same blanket. He added:

'I know you go up there a lot. My sister's always saying, "What can that skinny fellow know about mountains?"'

The blood rushed suddenly to my face. I had stopped wanting to leap at Maubert's throat, but how I should have liked to hurl myself on that big sister that looked so much like him.

'She must know a fat lot about it! Has she ever been up it even?'

'Why, yes, she's the one I always go with. Just listen, I'll prove it. Once, when we were up La Luzette, we saw you climbing the Cap de Coste. You were with Jean and Maurice. My sister said, "Let's hide in the wood," you know, where the dead firs are, and there we watched you go past. My sister said, "They make good walkers, those little skinny chaps. Just hark at them singing." She meant you, of course. "Why, you'd think the whole mountain belongs to that little warbler there!"'

I had lost all notion of whether we were enemies or not. It was as though we had roamed the mountain side together, and were now reminiscing about it.

'Yes, you see, we were going up to the Aigoual. Was it morning? Had you just been up . . . ? You can tell your sister that I'll give her an hour's start any time she wants to climb up by Cap de Coste. We'll jolly soon see who the mountain belongs to . . . Take it from me, never to a girl.'

Maubert agreed. He felt with me that none of the girls in the valley — not even his sister — could compete with us. A gust of masculine solidarity welded us as one against the girls.

'I'd like to join your lot just once . . . You'd see if I couldn't keep up . . . But Father wouldn't let me . . .'

'Why? Won't he let you talk to us?'

Almost imperceptibly Maubert nodded. He looked as though the prohibition made him feel ashamed. And to justify himself, he added:

'He says that nothing good will ever come of you . . .'

Then, in a whisper, 'Because you haven't got any religion.'

'And what's wrong with your own father, that nothing good ever comes of him, eh? Not the priests, I imagine?'

'We belong to these parts,' said Maubert. 'We're not so well off. But there's no need to insult my father.'

'Well, why does he . . . ? We don't belong to these parts, I know, so what? Are we so well off? And how do you know we haven't any religion?'

'It isn't the true one . . .'

'A lot you know whether it's true or not. You say Protestants have got black throats and ears stuck to their heads . . . Well, look, just take a look. Ah . . . My throat's black isn't it? And what about your own ears, jolly fine aren't they? Well what about your own ears, eh?'

Again we were in the grip of the old hatreds. But talking together thus it was impossible to keep them up. It was the mystery in Maubert that had made an enemy of him. A sort of secret in himself made an antagonist of him. Near neighbours though we were, in the same remote countryside, we loathed each other because we did not know each other.

I said to Maubert:

'Your brother's school turns everyone into dunderheads.'

'The town school turns them into scamps and ragamuffins.'

'We'll soon see . . . What do you want to do when you're a man? Why, you don't even know! As for me, I mean to be somebody. You'll come asking favours when I'm a man. We'll see who are the scamps and ragamuffins then.'

Maubert had risen. I did not budge. I was sure he had no idea of attacking me. He seemed not to have heard the last words I said, or at any rate, did not wish to appear as though he considered them insulting. Instead of staring me out, he gazed at the huge dint of the valley and the way in which the torrent had cut its levels out of the mountain. Meditatively, he took the measure of the rocky bluffs, the long granite slabs that rose obliquely over our heads.

'There would be time to get to the top,' he said at last. 'What do you say about our going up together? I don't mean going round, but up over the rocks. I shouldn't think anyone had ever got that way up. Does it frighten you? You wouldn't dare climb that wall.'

But I was already on my feet. I threw back my head the better to take in the long rampart to which here and there clung tiny patches of grass.

'You're the one who'd never follow up there. It's steeper than it looks. Enough to make a goat turn giddy. You've got to climb over that patch of grass, get by that rock face there and then that gully, and turn left and follow that ledge.'

At last we had found a way to fight each other. I was already scrambling over the stones and gravel fallen from the mountain side, followed by Maubert tucking his trousers up and tightening his belt. I was thinking, 'He'll soon be asking me for help . . . Not much chance of him managing to get through. I've tried a dozen times with Jean. But we've always given in when we've come to the last face. This time I swear I will get through. And he'll have to stay there on the ledge, fifty feet below . . . It took us more than the first time to get up . . . But now I know how it's done. There's a hand-hold just at the turn, that place where the hold is just for one foot . . . Jean was the one who found it out. There he was, hanging in space for five good minutes, not daring to go forward or back.'

Now we had crossed the patch of pasture. Our rope-soled sandals clung to the rock. The first granite outcrop was easy enough. I went first, not bothering much about Maubert. All my attention was fixed on the loose stones. It seemed hardly playing the game, to make things difficult for him with showers of loose stones. I had to get him up to the ledge. That was where the test would begin.

The narrow gully stretched some yards or so. I dragged myself out, one elbow first, got my other arm free, and slid upon my belly to a tiny patch of green. The pasture climbed obliquely up to the narrow ledge, which here overhung the mountain torrent some fifty feet or so. Flat on the grass, I watched Maubert emerge. He was a stranger among these rocks, that was clear enough. He was looking round, groping to find somewhere to place his arms. The slope frightened him. He had not expected it to be so steep. He cast a glance down, his hands trembled a little, he looked at me, and then with a supple movement, slid himself to my side. There was sweat between his nose and thick lips. But the expression on his face was deadly earnest.

'Are you done?' he asked. 'I'm going up to the top of the pasture.'

He began crawling up it on all fours, whereupon I rose, balancing with difficulty on the wet grass.

'Let me pass! The top of the pasture doesn't count. The thing is to get past that ledge.'

'Have you gone crazy?'

We were both in front of the cleft that led to it. The granite face bulged out to meet us at the head of the pasture. A rocky floor, narrow and slippery, continued the pasture as far as the turn. Beyond, there was nothing but the empty void to be seen. I knew that the ledge continued on the other side, that the hand-hold was about shoulder high, and that it could be done if one clung to the rock with one's arm at a right angle. Maubert said to me:

'Impossible to get any further . . . We've got here together.'

'Well, see what your sister can do for you!'

I was already on the ledge. Hugging the rock, I went forward to where the rock face bulged outwards. I tried not to think of the yawning gulf behind me. My knees trembled a little. I gulped great breaths of air to keep my limbs under control. I stretched my hand into space . . . 'About shoulder high . . . A little further though . . . Not quite yet . . . I've got to get more reach by putting my feet together . . . Is my arm still too high?' I lower my hand. Ah, there's the hold. My fingers clutch fiercely on the rock. Like gripping an exercise ring, almost. I turn my head slightly and see Maubert six feet off. He has stood up. The yawning hole no longer frightens him. He is staring at me, keeping back the cry that rises to his lips. Just wait . . . till I've got round to the other side. Now I must put my left leg forward into space. For a moment or two I try for the hold. The ledge is higher on that side

I had forgotten that. Well, I must give one strong pull. My hand grips, my foothold is secure, I let go on Maubert's side, and with a single effort pull myself round to the other face.

Luckily the ledge is wider here. I go on breathing with all my strength to stop the trembling of my knees, and at the top of my voice, still under control, I shout:

'We're waiting, you rock-climber you!'

I can see nothing past the pure line of the granite. Maubert will never come. I begin to sing at the top of my voice, and when I stop, the sound of the water suddenly rises from the maze of waterfalls.

Suddenly I saw a hand wavering in the air. My enemy had crept to the end of the ledge and was groping for a hand-hold. I went nearer, and gazed in silence at that hand. It was no longer Maubert, but a small, sinewy yet powerful hand that somehow conveyed an impression of courage. It felt out the rock face, clung to the slightest protuberances, and made me feel that, on the other side of the ledge, a taut hand was trying to test the measure of its endurance. But the hand slid away, and again sought to find something to cling to in the void. The real hold was just at its side but, unawares, it brushed by without sensing it. Vainly it struck against the rock, the veins swelled up, and, suddenly, a slight trembling began to animate it.

'Maubert . . . You'll never do it . . . Stay on the other side!'

But still the hand went on seeking. It seemed overcome with giddiness and swaying like a person about to fall. I took it in my own hand and led it to the hold. It felt the dint, and clamped itself upon it like some tool . . . Almost at the same instant I saw Maubert's left leg set itself upon the ledge, and the lad come suddenly round my side.

'Here I am!' he said.

'There's harder still to come!'

We were side by side on the ledge, our backs to the rock. Below, the ravine wound easily between the perpendicular walls. Necklaces of white bubbles, woven in the eddies of the falls, drifted slowly away and burst against the banks. Further, the torrent plunged towards the valley, disclosing the rocks and woods that framed our countryside, its apple orchards, farms and villages.

'You've been here before,' said Maubert. 'That doesn't count. I've got my own places too . . .'

'Well, even if I have been as far as here before, I know as much as you do now. I've never been able to get any further. See, up there, is where we have to get. "Bar of wood, bar of iron," I swear I've never been here before.'

In the midst of the granite wall was an almost vertical fissure stretching some thirty feet, the sides lined with greenish mosses swollen with oozing water, while half way up a bush protruded, rooted in some deeper crevice.

'If you've never been able to get through, you won't get through today. Let's go down again.'

But I had already started along the chimney. The first half was easy. Then, with my back wedged well against the wall I looked up at the jutting bush. This was the place where we had finally given up the idea of going further. Even when I stretched full length I could not manage to touch the knotty trunk. I must have been at least three feet short, and there was nothing at all to help me cover the gap. From the trunk I could have crawled up over the edge of the gully. But to get there, I had to venture to work myself a little higher, like a chimney sweep. I lacked the courage to look at Maubert. He would have made me realize the void there was beneath my feet. But it was of him I was thinking. The last time, with Jean, we had given up here, beaten by the rock, yet nevertheless proud of ourselves. Now, if I gave up I should be humiliating myself in front of Maubert.

My feet had left the last morsel of jutting rock. With my knees against one wall and my back against the other, I jerked myself up. Then I relaxed. Relaxing, I felt myself growing less and less solid. I dared not move my legs any more. One of my arms, raised over my head, groped in the void, and suddenly touched the trunk with the tips of its fingers. A moment after I managed to get both my hands well round. Dragging myself up on to it, I found new holds, and cleared the next few yards with ease. Then I was clear of the wall.

My hands were bleeding a bit. Two finger nails were broken. How angry Jean would be that evening, to hear I had conquered the wall. He would want us to do it again so that he could do it too. He could go to the devil if he chose, I should never do it again.

Meanwhile Maubert was climbing also. His eyes had followed each of my gestures. He repeated them with the whole of his taut body. I felt he would rather have rolled down into the torrent than retrace his steps. Flat on my belly, looking down at him, I watched him coming up, terrified he might roll into the void. My own muscles, identical with those which he was using, twitched and contracted to help him on. My back humped as I saw him crawl into the chimney, and my hand opened to seize the trunk as he reached up.

'Go on, Maubert, you're all right now . . .'

He had got himself into an awkward position underneath the bush and could not manage to seize the trunk. I caught his wrist in both my hands and all but made him loose his hold. Then he was at my side, pale as a ghost, with everything whirling round him.

It was then I said:

'I've won, I've won.'

We moved away from the precipice a little. It rejoiced me to have conquered the wall. We should never have done it with Jean. I had done it because Maubert was my enemy, and I would have preferred death rather than say to him as to one of my chums: 'It's crazy. It can't be done.'

Maubert, too, would never have done it without me. We had carried our childish skill and courage beyond what they could have achieved of themselves. So it would be, all through our lives. I should go forward always, not to remain behind Maubert, my enemy.

But anyhow we were friends now. Friends, because deep in us we shared the same loves, the same joy – pitting ourselves against the things of our own countryside. We both talked the local speech, we had both roamed the same mountains, and climbed the same peaks. Lying stretched out among the last thin chestnut trees where the holly and pines thinned out, relaxing after our efforts and proud of having together conquered the same rock face, we began reminiscing in the way only possible to those who have grown up from childhood together.

'Next best to the mountains, I'm happiest among our vines.'

'Where? At Elze?'

'They're the only ones we have. We've an old chap working, helps us make our wine. A wonderfully handy chap, full of stories . . . it's a jolly good place, Elze . . . It only catches the sun in the morning though. Still, it's just as good.'

'We've got the sun all day, we have.'

'At Goulsou?'

'D'you know our vines then? But you've never been there, have you?'

'You've got a magnolia and a cypress in front of the house . . . And fig trees against the top wall.'

'You've been there then?'

'I've seen it from the turn in the new road . . . I even climbed the wall once, just under the plum tree . . . I know the sort of spot you like.'

So we went on talking about things and people. Together we made the tour of our domains, conscious that the same waters bathed them and that the same odours, rich with the same fruits, enveloped them both. Speaking together thus, we plunged into a similar past, peopled with wiry peasants, muscular and taciturn, and men of the uplands, worn to the same pattern by toil and exposure to the elements. Looking at each other, we could see obvious traces of the same blood mingling in each of us. Maubert, smaller than myself, was solid and broad-shouldered, with a round head and blue eyes under the line of bristly hair. He looked like my mother's grandfather whose portrait we still possessed. I, on the other hand, thin and tall, with prominent chin and narrow face, too strongly resembled our shepherds and herdsmen for there to be any doubt as to the race to which I belonged. The homogeneity of our race derived from all its many minglings, and among us, in each family line, distant and remote types would suddenly reappear in an inextricable fraternity of the flesh, the bones, the pigmentation, and the profound urges of the whole being.

What could turn us into enemies now? We had no longer any secrets from each other. Everything we loved we could now possess in common. No longer was there any need to keep each to his own side of the mountain.

Meanwhile, by the open passes to the north, evening began to descend, urging its shadows forward to meet the clouds that rushed to climb the heavens from the sea. It was time to think of getting back. Through pasturage and woods, and between the rocky bluffs, we rushed downwards to the town. Already we had passed two children returning to their farm in the valley, who turned to gaze in astonishment at seeing us together. Sitting on a wall of dry stones, an old man seemed to gaze after us with a derisive smile. It embarrassed us to be walking together, and as we had slowed down to a walk to catch our breaths again, Maubert said, though without looking at me,

'You'd better leave me before we get to Rochebelle.'

'So you're ashamed to be seen with me? I'll tell everybody we aren't together, if you like.'

'I'm not with you!' said Maubert with an obstinate expression.

He began to run again, and when he had got about a hundred yards ahead dropped to a walk, looking about leisurely on every side, like someone out walking by himself. I followed without bothering about him, but also without taking any precaution to observe our distances. Insensibly I drew nearer. On this, after glancing behind him several times, Maubert turned, and I saw him shouting something at me, though I could not hear the words, while his face appeared distorted with rage. I began gathering stones and started running to get somewhat nearer to him.

'Oh, you want to go in front, do you? See if this will help you then . . .'

Maubert fled, but even while he did so, flung a couple of stones at me that whistled round my head. I met them by jumping right and left and then stopped to hurl them in my turn. Bent double in the act, and before even the stone had touched the ground, I shouted at him like a threat, in which perhaps, too, was something of regret:

'I'll get you yet . . . I'll get you yet some day.'

[*PNW 1*, 1940]

CHRISTOPHER ISHERWOOD

A BERLIN DIARY (Autumn 1930)

From my window, the deep solemn massive street. Cellar-shops where the lamps burn all day, under the shadow of top-heavy balconied façades, dirty plaster frontages embossed with scrollwork and heraldic devices. The whole district is like this: street leading into street of houses like shabby monumental safes crammed with the tarnished valuables and second-hand furniture of a bankrupt middle class.

I am a camera with its shutter open, quite passive, recording, not thinking. Recording the man shaving at the window opposite and the woman in the kimono washing her hair. Some day, all this will have to be developed, carefully printed, fixed.

At eight o'clock in the evening the house-doors will be locked. The children are having supper. The shops are shut. The electric-sign is switched on over the night-bell of the little hotel on the corner, where you can hire a room by the hour. And soon the whistling will begin. Young men are calling their girls. Standing down there in the cold, they whistle up at the lighted windows of warm rooms where the beds are already turned down for the night. They want to be let in. Their signals echo down the deep hollow street, lascivious and private and sad. Because of the whistling, I do not care to stay here in the evenings. It reminds me that I am in a foreign city, alone, far from home. Sometimes I determine not to listen to it, pick up a book, try to read. But soon a call is sure to sound, so piercing, so insistent, so despairingly human, that at last I have to get up and peep through the slats of the venetian blind to make quite sure that it is not – as I know very well it could not possibly be – for me.

The extraordinary smell in this room when the stove is lighted and the window shut; not altogether unpleasant, a mixture of incense and stale buns. The tall tiled stove, gorgeously coloured, like an altar. The washstand like a Gothic shrine. The cupboard also is Gothic, with carved cathedral windows: Bismarck faces the King of Prussia in stained glass. My best chair would do for a bishop's throne. In the corner, three sham medieval halberds (from a theatrical touring company?) are fastened together to form a hatstand. Frl. Schroeder unscrews the heads of the halberds and polishes them from time to time. They are heavy and sharp enough to kill.

Everything in the room is like that: unnecessarily solid, abnormally heavy and dangerously sharp. Here, at the writing-table, I am confronted by a phalanx of metal objects – a pair of candlesticks shaped like entwined serpents, an ashtray from which emerges the head of a crocodile, a paper-knife copied from a Florentine dagger, a brass dolphin holding on the end of its tail a small broken clock. What becomes of such things? How could they ever be destroyed? They will probably remain intact for thousands of years: people will treasure them in museums. Or perhaps they will merely be melted down for munitions in a war. Every morning, Frl. Schroeder arranges them very carefully in certain unvarying positions: there they stand, like an uncompromising statement of her views on Capital and Society, Religion and Sex.

All day long, she goes padding about the large dingy flat. Shapeless but alert, she waddles from room to room, in carpet slippers and a flowered dressing-gown pinned ingeniously together, so that not an inch of petticoat or bodice is to be seen, flicking with her duster, peeping, spying, poking her short pointed nose into the cupboards and luggage of her lodgers. She has dark, bright, inquisitive eyes and pretty waved brown hair of which she is proud. She must be about fifty-five years old.

Long ago, before the War and the Inflation, she used to be comparatively well off. She went to the Baltic for her summer holidays and kept a maid to do the housework. For the last thirty years she has lived here and taken in lodgers. She started doing it because she liked to have company.

'"Lina," my friends used to say to me, "however can you? How can you bear to have strange people living in your rooms and spoiling your furniture, especially when you've got the money to be independent?" And I'd always give them the same answer. "My lodgers aren't lodgers," I used to say. "They're my guests."

'You see, Herr Issyvoo, in those days I could afford to be very particular about the sort of people who came to live here. I could pick and choose. I only took them really well connected and well educated – proper gentlefolk (like yourself, Herr Issyvoo). I had a Freiherr once, and a Rittmeister and a Professor. They often gave me presents – a bottle of cognac or a box of chocolates or some flowers. And when one of them went away for his holidays he'd always send me a card – from

London, it might be, or Paris, or Baden-Baden. Ever such pretty cards I used to get . . .'

And now Frl. Schroeder has not even got a room of her own. She has to sleep in the living-room, behind a screen, on a small sofa with broken springs. As in so many of the older Berlin flats, our living-room connects the front part of the house with the back. The lodgers who live on the front have to pass through the living-room on their way to the bathroom, so that Frl. Schroeder is often disturbed during the night. 'But I drop off again at once. It doesn't worry me. I'm much too tired.' She has to do all the housework herself and it takes up most of her day. 'Twenty years ago, if anybody had told me to scrub my own floors, I'd have slapped his face for him. But you get used to it. You can get used to anything. Why, I remember the time when I'd have sooner cut off my right hand than empty this chamber . . . And now,' says Frl. Schroeder, suiting the action to the word, 'my goodness! it's no more to me than pouring out a cup of tea!'

She is fond of pointing out to me the various marks and stains left by lodgers who have inhabited this room:

'Yes, Herr Issyvoo, I've got something to remember each of them by . . . Look there, on the rug – I've sent it to the cleaners I don't know how often but nothing will get it out – that's where Herr Noeske was sick after his birthday party. What in the world can he have been eating, to make a mess like that? He'd come to Berlin to study, you know. His parents lived in Brandenburg – a first-class family; oh, I assure you! They had pots of money! His Herr Papa was a surgeon, and of course he wanted his boy to follow in his footsteps . . . What a charming young man! "Herr Noeske," I used to say to him, "excuse me, but you really must work harder – you with all your brains! Think of your Herr Papa and your Frau Mama; it isn't fair to them to waste their good money like that. Why, if you were to drop it in the Spree it would be better – at least it'd make a splash!" I was like a mother to him. And always, when he'd got himself into some scrape – he was terribly thoughtless – he'd come straight to me: "Schroederschen," he used to say, "please don't be angry with me . . . We were playing cards last night and I lost the whole of this month's allowance. I daren't tell Father . . ." And then he'd look at me with those great big eyes of his. I knew exactly what he was after, the scamp! But I hadn't the heart to refuse. So I'd sit down and write a letter to his Frau Mama and beg her to forgive him just that once and send some more money. And she always would . . . Of course, as a woman, I knew how to appeal to a

mother's feelings, although I've never had any children of my own . . .
What are you smiling at, Herr Issyvoo? Well, well! Mistakes will
happen, you know!

'And that's where the Herr Rittmeister always upset his coffee over
the wall-paper. He used to sit there on the couch with his fiancée.
"Herr Rittmeister," I used to say to him, "do please drink your coffee
at the table. If you'll excuse my saying so, there's plenty of time for the
other thing afterwards . . ." But no, he always would sit on the couch.
And then, sure enough, when he began to get a bit excited in his
feelings, over went the coffee-cups . . . Such a handsome gentleman!
His Frau Mama and his sister came to visit us sometimes. They liked
coming up to Berlin. "Fräulein Schroeder," they used to tell me, "you
don't know how lucky you are to be living here, right in the middle of
things. We're only country cousins – we envy you! And now tell us all
the latest Court scandals!" Of course, they were only joking. They had
the sweetest little house, not far from Halberstadt, in the Harz. They
used to show me pictures of it. A perfect dream!

'You see those ink-stains on the carpet? That's where Herr Professor Koch used to shake his fountain-pen. I told him of it a hundred
times. In the end, I even laid sheets of blotting-paper on the floor
around his chair. He was so absent-minded . . . Such a dear old
gentleman! And so simple. I was very fond of him. If I mended a shirt
for him or darned his socks, he'd thank me with the tears in his eyes.
He liked a bit of fun, too. Sometimes, when he heard me coming, he'd
turn out the light and hide behind the door; and then he'd roar like a
lion to frighten me. Just like a child . . .'

Frl. Schroeder can go on like this, without repeating herself, by the
hour. When I have been listening to her for some time, I find myself
relapsing into a curious trance-like state of depression. I begin to feel
profoundly unhappy. Where are all those lodgers now? Where, in
another ten years, shall I be, myself? Certainly not here. How many
seas and frontiers shall I have to cross to reach that distant day; how
far shall I have to travel, on foot, on horseback, by car, push-bike,
aeroplane, steamer, train, lift, moving-staircase and tram? How much
money shall I need for that enormous journey? How much food must I
gradually, wearily consume on my way? How many pairs of shoes
shall I wear out? How many thousands of cigarettes shall I smoke?
How many cups of tea shall I drink and how many glasses of beer?
What an awful, tasteless prospect! And yet – to have to die . . . A
sudden vague pang of apprehension grips my bowels and I have to
excuse myself in order to go to the lavatory.

*

Hearing that I was once a medical student, she confides to me that she is very unhappy because of the size of her bosom. She suffers from palpitations and is sure that these must be caused by the strain on her heart. She wonders if she should have an operation. Some of her acquaintances advise her to, others are against it:

'Oh dear, it's such a weight to have to carry about with you! And just think – Herr Issyvoo: I used to be as slim as you are!'

'I suppose you had a great many admirers, Frl. Schroeder?'

Yes, she has had dozens. But only one Friend. He was a married man, living apart from his wife, who would not divorce him.

'We were together eleven years. Then he died of pneumonia. Sometimes I wake up in the night when it's cold and wish he was there. You never seem to get really warm, sleeping alone.'

There are four other lodgers in this flat. Next door to me, in the big front-room, is Frl. Kost. In the room opposite, overlooking the courtyard, is Frl. Mayr. At the back, beyond the living-room, is Bobby. And behind Bobby's room, over the bathroom, at the top of a ladder, is a tiny attic which Frl. Schroeder refers to, for some occult reason, as 'The Swedish Pavilion'. This she lets, at twenty marks a month, to a commercial traveller who is out all day and most of the night. I occasionally come upon him on Sunday mornings, in the kitchen, shuffling about in his vest and trousers, apologetically hunting for a box of matches.

Bobby is a mixer at a west-end bar called the Troika. I don't know his real name. He has adopted this one because English Christian names are fashionable just now in the Berlin demi-monde. He is a pale worried-looking smartly dressed young man with thin sleek black hair. During the early afternoon, just after he has got out of bed, he walks about the flat in shirt-sleeves, wearing a hair-net.

Frl. Schroeder and Bobby are on intimate terms. He tickles her and slaps her bottom; she hits him over the head with a frying-pan or a mop. The first time I surprised them scuffling like this, they were both rather embarrassed. Now they take my presence as a matter of course.

Frl. Kost is a blonde florid girl with large silly blue eyes. When we meet, coming to and from the bathroom in our dressing-gowns, she modestly avoids my glance. She is plump but has a good figure.

One day I asked Frl. Schroeder straight out: 'What was Frl. Kost's profession?'

'Profession? Ha, ha, that's good! That's just the word for it! Oh, yes, she's got a fine profession. Like this –'

And with the air of doing something extremely comic, she began waddling across the kitchen like a duck, mincingly holding a duster between her finger and thumb. Just by the door, she twirled triumphantly round, flourishing the duster as though it were a silk handkerchief, and kissed her hand to me mockingly:

'Ja, ja, Herr Issyvoo! That's how they do it!'

'I don't quite understand, Frl. Schroeder. Do you mean that she's a tight-rope walker?'

'He, he, he! Very good indeed, Herr Issyvoo! Yes, that's right! That's it! She walks along the line for her living. That just describes her!'

One evening, soon after this, I met Frl. Kost on the stairs, with a Japanese. Frl. Schroeder explained to me later that he is one of Frl. Kost's best customers. She asked Frl. Kost how they spent the time together when not actually in bed, for the Japanese can speak hardly any German.

'Oh, well,' said Frl. Kost, 'we play the gramophone, you know, and eat chocolates, and then we laugh a lot. He's very fond of laughing . . .'

Frl. Schroeder really quite likes Frl. Kost and certainly hasn't any moral objections to her trade: nevertheless, when she is angry because Frl. Kost has broken the spout of the teapot or omitted to make crosses for her telephone-calls on the slate in the living-room, then invariably she exclaims:

'But after all, what else can you expect from a woman of that sort, a common prostitute! Why, Herr Issyvoo, do you know what she used to be? A servant girl! And then she got to be on intimate terms with her employer and one fine day, of course, she found herself in certain circumstances . . . And when that little difficulty was removed, she had to go trot-trot . . .'

Frl. Mayr is a music-hall *jodlerin* – one of the best, so Frl. Schroeder reverently assures me, in the whole of Germany. Frl. Schroeder doesn't altogether like Frl. Mayr, but she stands in great awe of her; as well she may. Frl. Mayr has a bull-dog jaw, enormous arms and coarse string-coloured hair. She speaks a Bavarian dialect with peculiarly aggressive emphasis. When at home, she sits up like a war-horse at the living-room table, helping Frl. Schroeder to lay cards. They are both adept fortune-tellers and neither would dream of beginning the day without consulting the omens. The chief thing they both want to know at present is: when will Frl. Mayr get another engagement? This question interests Frl. Schroeder quite as much as Frl. Mayr, because Frl. Mayr is behind-hand with the rent.

At the corner of the Motzstrasse, when the weather is fine, there stands a shabby pop-eyed man beside a portable canvas booth. On the sides of the booth are pinned astrological diagrams and autographed letters of recommendation from satisfied clients. Frl. Schroeder goes to consult him whenever she can afford the mark for his fee. In fact, he plays a most important part in her life. Her behaviour towards him is a mixture of cajolery and threats. If the good things he promises her come true she will kiss him, she says, invite him to dinner, buy him a gold watch: if they don't, she will throttle him, box his ears, report him to the police. Among other prophecies, the astrologer has told her that she will win some money in the Prussian State Lottery. So far, she has had no luck. But she is always discussing what she will do with her winnings. We are all to have presents, of course. I am to get a hat, because Frl. Schroeder thinks it very improper that a gentleman of my education should go about without one.

When not engaged in laying cards, Frl. Mayr drinks tea and lectures Frl. Schroeder in her past theatrical triumphs:

'And the Manager said to me: "Fritzi, Heaven must have sent you here! My leading lady's fallen ill. You're to leave for Copenhagen tonight." And what's more, he wouldn't take no for an answer. "Fritzi," he said (he always called me that), "Fritzi, you aren't going to let an old friend down?" And so I went . . .' Frl. Mayr sips her tea reminiscently: 'A charming man. And so well-bred.' She smiles: 'Familiar . . . but he always knew how to behave himself.'

Frl. Schroeder nods eagerly, drinking in every word, revelling in it:

'I suppose some of those managers must be cheeky devils? (Have some more sausage, Frl. Mayr?)'

'(Thank you, Frl. Schroeder; just a little morsel.) Yes, some of them . . . you wouldn't believe! But I could always take care of myself. Even when I was quite a slip of a girl . . .'

The muscles of Frl. Mayr's nude fleshy arms ripple unappetizingly. She sticks out her chin:

'I'm a Bavarian; and a Bavarian never forgets an injury.'

Coming into the living-room yesterday evening, I found Frl. Schroeder and Frl. Mayr lying flat on their stomachs with their ears pressed to the carpet. At intervals, they exchanged grins of delight or joyfully pinched each other, with simultaneous exclamations of *Ssh!*

'Hark!' whispered Frl. Schroeder, 'he's smashing all the furniture!'

'He's beating her black and blue!' exclaimed Frl. Mayr, in raptures. 'Bang! Just listen to that!'

'Ssh! Ssh!'

'Ssh!'

Frl. Schroeder was quite beside herself. When I asked what was the matter, she clambered to her feet, waddled forward and, taking me round the waist, danced a little waltz with me: 'Herr Issyvoo! Herr Issyvoo! Herr Issyvoo!' until she was breathless.

'But whatever has happened?' I asked.

'Ssh!' commanded Frl. Mayr from the floor. 'Ssh! They've started again!'

In the flat directly beneath ours lives a certain Frau Glanterneck. She is a Galician Jewess, in itself a reason why Frl. Mayr should be her enemy: for Frl. Mayr, needless to say, is an ardent Nazi. And, quite apart from this, it seems that Frau Glanterneck and Frl. Mayr once had words on the stairs about Frl. Mayr's yodelling. Frau Glanterneck, perhaps because she is a non-Aryan, said that she preferred the noises made by cats. Thereby, she insulted not merely Frl. Mayr, but all Bavarian, all German women: and it was Frl. Mayr's pleasant duty to avenge them.

About a fortnight ago, it became known among the neighbours that Frau Glanterneck, who is sixty years old and as ugly as a witch, had been advertising in the newspaper for a husband. What was more, an applicant had already appeared: a widowed butcher from Halle. He had seen Frau Glanterneck and was nevertheless prepared to marry her. Here was Frl. Mayr's chance. By roundabout inquiries, she discovered the butcher's name and address and wrote him an anonymous letter. Was he aware that Frau Glanterneck had (a) bugs in her flat, (b) been arrested for fraud and released on the ground that she was insane, (c) leased out her own bedroom for immoral purposes, and (d) slept in the bed afterwards without changing the sheets? And now the butcher had arrived to confront Frau Glanterneck with the letter. One could hear both of them quite distinctly: the growling of the enraged Prussian and the shrill screaming of the Jewess. Now and then came the thud of a fist against wood and, occasionally, the crash of glass. The row lasted over an hour.

This morning we hear that the neighbours have complained to the portress of the disturbance and that Frau Glanterneck is to be seen with a black eye. The marriage is off.

The inhabitants of this street know me by sight already. At the grocer's, people no longer turn their heads on hearing my English accent as I order a pound of butter. At the street corner, after dark, the three whores no longer whisper throatily: 'Komm, Süsser!' as I pass.

The three whores are all plainly over fifty years old. They do not attempt to conceal their age. They are not noticeably rouged or powdered. They wear baggy old fur coats and longish skirts and matronly hats. I happened to mention them to Bobby and he explained to me that there is a recognized demand for the comfortable type of woman. Many middle-aged men prefer them to girls. They even attract boys in their 'teens. A boy, explained Bobby, feels shy with a girl of his own age but not with a woman old enough to be his mother. Like most barmen, Bobby is a great expert on sexual questions.

The other evening, I went to call on him during business hours.

It was still very early, about nine o'clock, when I arrived at the Troika. The place was much larger and grander than I had expected. A commissionaire braided like an archduke regarded my hatless head with suspicion until I spoke to him in English. A smart cloak-room girl insisted on taking my overcoat, which hides the worst stains on my baggy flannel trousers. A page-boy, seated on the counter, didn't rise to open the inner door. Bobby, to my relief, was at his place behind a blue and silver bar. I made towards him as towards an old friend. He greeted me most amiably:

'Good evening, Mr Isherwood. Very glad to see you here.'

I ordered a beer and settled myself on a stool in the corner. With my back to the wall, I could survey the whole room.

'How's business?' I asked.

Bobby's care-worn, powdered, night-dweller's face became grave. He inclined his head towards me, over the bar, with confidential flattering seriousness:

'Not much good, Mr Isherwood. The kind of public we have nowadays . . . you wouldn't believe it! Why, a year ago, we'd have turned them away at the door. They order a beer and think they've got the right to sit here the whole evening.'

Bobby spoke with extreme bitterness. I began to feel uncomfortable:

'What'll you drink?' I asked, guiltily gulping down my beer; and added, lest there should be any misunderstanding: 'I'd like a whisky and soda.'

Bobby said he'd have one, too.

The room was nearly empty. I looked the few guests over, trying to

see them through Bobby's disillusioned eyes. There were three attractive, well-dressed girls sitting at the bar: the one nearest to me was
particularly elegant, she had quite a cosmopolitan air. But during a lull
in the conversation, I caught fragments of her talk with the other
barman. She spoke broad Berlin dialect. She was tired and bored; her
mouth drooped. A young man approached her and joined in the
discussion; a handsome broad-shouldered boy in a well-cut dinner-
jacket, who might well have been an English public-school prefect on
holiday.

'Nee, nee,' I heard him say. 'Bei mir nicht!' He grinned and made a
curt, brutal gesture of the streets.

Over in the corner sat a page-boy, talking to the little old lavatory
attendant in his white jacket. The boy said something, laughed and
broke off suddenly into a huge yawn. The three musicians on their
platform were chatting, evidently unwilling to begin until they had an
audience worth playing to. At one of the tables, I thought I saw a
genuine guest, a stout man with a moustache. After a moment,
however, I caught his eye, he made me a little bow and I knew that he
must be the manager.

The door opened. Two men and two women came in. The women
were elderly, had thick legs, cropped hair and costly evening-gowns.
The men were lethargic, pale, probably Dutch. Here, unmistakably,
was Money. In an instant, the Troika was transformed. The manager,
the cigarette-boy and the lavatory attendant rose simultaneously to
their feet. The lavatory attendant disappeared. The manager said
something in a furious undertone to the cigarette-boy, who also
disappeared. He then advanced, bowing and smiling, to the guests'
table and shook hands with the two men. The cigarette-boy reappeared with his tray, followed by a waiter who hurried forward with
the wine-list. Meanwhile, the three-man orchestra struck up briskly.
The girls at the bar turned on their stools, smiling a not-too-direct
invitation. The gigolos advanced to them as if to complete strangers,
bowed formally and asked, in cultured tones, for the pleasure of a
dance. The page-boy, spruce, discreetly grinning, swaying from the
waist like a flower, crossed the room with his tray of cigarettes:
'Zigarren! Zigaretten!' His voice was mocking, clear-pitched like an
actor's. And in the same tone, yet more loudly, mockingly, joyfully, so
that we could all hear, the waiter ordered from Bobby: 'Heidsieck
Monopol!'

With absurd, solicitous gravity, the dancers performed their intricate evolutions, showing in their every movement a consciousness of

the part they were playing. And the saxophonist, letting his instrument swing loose from the ribbon around his neck, advanced to the edge of the platform with his little megaphone:

'Sie werden lachen,
Ich lieb'
Meine eigene Frau . . .'

He sang with a knowing leer, including us all in the conspiracy, charging his voice with innuendo, rolling his eyes in an epileptic pantomime of extreme joy. Bobby, suave, sleek, five years younger, handled the bottle. And meanwhile the two flaccid gentlemen chatted to each other, probably about business, without a glance at the night-life they had called into being; while their women sat silent, looking neglected, puzzled, uncomfortable and very bored.

Frl. Hippi Bernstein, my first pupil, lives in the Grünewald, in a house built almost entirely of glass. Most of the richest Berlin families inhabit the Grünewald. It is difficult to understand why. Their villas, in all known styles of expensive ugliness, ranging from the eccentric-rococo folly to the cubist flat-roofed steel-and-glass box, are crowded together in this dank, dreary pinewood. Few of them can afford large gardens, for the ground is fabulously dear: their only view is of their neighbour's back-yard, each one protected by a wire fence and a savage dog. Terror of burglary and revolution has reduced these miserable people to a state of siege. They have neither privacy nor sunshine. The district is really a millionaires' slum.

When I rang the bell at the garden gate, a young footman came out with a key from the house, followed by a large growling Alsatian.

'He won't bite you while I'm here,' the footman reassured me, grinning.

The hall of the Bernsteins' house has metal-studded doors and a steamer clock fastened to the wall with bolt-heads. There are modernist lamps, designed to look like pressure-gauges, thermometers and switchboard dials. But the furniture doesn't match the house and its fittings. The place is like a power-station which the engineers have tried to make comfortable with chairs and tables from an old-fashioned, highly respectable boarding-house. On the austere metal walls, hang highly varnished nineteenth-century landscapes in massive gold frames. Herr Bernstein probably ordered the villa from a popular *avant-garde* architect in a moment of recklessness; was

horrified at the result and tried to cover it up as much as possible with
the family belongings.

Frl. Hippi is a fat pretty girl, about nineteen years old, with glossy
chestnut hair, good teeth and big cow-eyes. She has a lazy, jolly,
self-indulgent laugh and a well-formed bust. She speaks schoolgirl
English with a slight American accent, quite nicely, to her own
complete satisfaction. She has clearly no intention of doing any work.
When I tried weakly to suggest a plan for our lessons, she kept
interrupting to offer me chocolates, coffee, cigarettes: 'Excuse me a
minute, there isn't some fruit,' she smiled, picking up the receiver of
the house-telephone: 'Anna, please bring some oranges.'

When the maid arrived with the oranges, I was forced, despite my
protests, to make a regular meal, with a plate, knife and fork. This
destroyed the last pretence of the teacher-pupil relationship. I felt like
a policeman being given a meal in the kitchen by an attractive cook.
Frl. Hippi sat watching me eat, with her good-natured, lazy smile:

'Tell me, please, why you come to Germany?'

She is inquisitive about me, but only like a cow idly poking with its
head between the bars of a gate. She doesn't particularly want the gate
to open. I said that I found Germany very interesting:

'The political and economic situation,' I improvised authorit-
atively, in my schoolmaster voice, 'is more interesting in Germany than
in any other European country.'

'Except Russia, of course,' I added experimentally.

But Frl. Hippi didn't react. She just blandly smiled:

'I think it shall be dull for you here? You do not have many friends
in Berlin, no?'

'No. Not many.'

This seemed to please and amuse her:

'You don't know some nice girls?'

Here the buzzer of the house-telephone sounded. Lazily smiling, she
picked up the receiver of the house-telephone but appeared not to
listen to the tinny voice which issued from it. I could hear quite
distinctly the real voice of Frau Bernstein, Hippi's mother, speaking
from the next room.

'Have you left your *red* book in here?' repeated Frl. Hippi mockingly and smiling at me as though this were a joke which I must share:
'No, I don't see it. It must be down in the study. Ring up Daddy. Yes,
he's working there.' In dumb show, she offered me another orange. I
shook my head politely. We both smiled: 'Mummy, what have we got
for lunch today? Yes? Really? Splendid!'

She hung up the receiver and returned to her cross-examination:

'Do you not know no nice girls?'

'*Any* nice girls . . .' I corrected evasively. But Frl. Hippi merely smiled, waiting for the answer to her question.

'Yes. One,' I had at length to add, thinking of Frl. Kost.

'Only one?' She raised her eyebrows in comic surprise. 'And tell me, please, do you find German girls different than English girls?'

I blushed. 'Do you find German girls . . .' I began to correct her and stopped, realizing just in time that I wasn't absolutely sure whether one says *different from* or *different to*.

'Do you find German girls different than English girls?' she repeated, with smiling persistence.

I blushed deeper than ever. 'Yes. Very different,' I said boldly.

'How are they different?'

Mercifully the telephone buzzed again. This was somebody from the kitchen, to say that lunch would be an hour earlier than usual. Herr Bernstein was going to the city that afternoon.

'I am so sorry,' said Frl. Hippi, rising, 'but for today we must finish. And we shall see us again on Friday? Then good-bye Mr Isherwood. And I thank you very much.'

She fished in her bag and handed me an envelope which I stuck awkwardly into my pocket and tore open only when I was out of sight of the Bernsteins' house. It contained a five-mark piece. I threw it into the air, missed it, found it after five minutes' hunt, buried in sand, and ran all the way to the tram-stop, singing and kicking stones about the road. I felt extraordinarily guilty and elated, as though I'd successfully committed a small theft.

It is a mere waste of time even pretending to teach Frl. Hippi anything. If she doesn't know a word, she says it in German. If I correct her, she repeats it in German. I am glad, of course, that she's so lazy and only afraid that Frau Bernstein may discover how little progress her daughter is making. But this is very unlikely. Most rich people, once they have decided to trust you at all, can be imposed upon to almost any extent. The only real problem for the private tutor is to get inside the front-door.

As for Hippi, she seems to enjoy my visits. From something she said the other day, I gather she boasts to her school friends that she has got a genuine English teacher. We understand each other very well. I am bribed with fruit not to be tiresome about the English language: she, for her part, tells her parents that I am the best teacher she ever had.

We gossip in German about the things which interest her. And every three or four minutes, we are interrupted while she plays her part in the family game of exchanging entirely unimportant messages over the house-telephone.

Hippi never worries about the future. Like everyone else in Berlin, she refers continually to the political situation, but only briefly, with a conventional melancholy, as when one speaks of religion. It is quite unreal to her. She means to go to the university, travel about, have a jolly good time and eventually, of course, marry. She already has a great many boy friends. We spend a lot of time talking about them. One has a wonderful car. Another has an aeroplane. Another has fought seven duels. Another has discovered a knack of putting out street-lamps by giving them a smart kick in a certain spot. One night, on the way back from a dance, Hippi and he put out all the street-lamps in the neighbourhood.

Today, lunch was early at the Bernsteins'; so I was invited to it, instead of giving my 'lesson'. The whole family was present: Frau Bernstein, stout and placid; Herr Bernstein, small and shaky and sly. There was also a younger sister, a schoolgirl of twelve, very fat. She ate and ate, quite unmoved by Hippi's jokes and warnings that she'd burst. They all seem very fond of each other, in their cosy, stuffy way. There was a little domestic argument, because Herr Bernstein didn't want his wife to go shopping in the car that afternoon. During the last few days, there has been a lot of Nazi rioting in the city.

'You can go in the tram,' said Herr Bernstein. 'I will not have them throwing stones at my beautiful car.'

'And suppose they throw stones at me?' asked Frau Bernstein good-humouredly.

'Ach, what does that matter? If they throw stones at you, I will buy you a sticking-plaster for your head. It will cost me only five groschen. But if they throw stones at my car, it will cost me perhaps five hundred marks.'

And so the matter was settled. Herr Bernstein then turned his attention to me:

'You can't complain that we treat you badly here, young man, eh? Not only do we give you a nice dinner, but we pay you for eating it!'

I saw from Hippi's expression that this was going a bit far, even for the Bernstein sense of humour; so I laughed and said:

'Will you pay me a mark extra for every helping I eat?'

This amused Herr Bernstein very much; but he was careful to show that he knew I hadn't meant it seriously.

During the last week, our household has been plunged into a terrific row.

It began when Frl. Kost came to Frl. Schroeder and announced that fifty marks had been stolen from her room. She was very much upset; especially, she explained, as this was the money she'd put aside towards the rent and the telephone bill. The fifty-mark note had been lying in the drawer of the cupboard, just inside the door of Frl. Kost's room.

Frl. Schroeder's immediate suggestion was, not unnaturally, that the money had been stolen by one of Frl. Kost's customers. Frl. Kost said that this was quite impossible, as none of them had visited her during the last three days. Moreover, she added, *her* friends were all absolutely above suspicion. They were well-to-do gentlemen, to whom a miserable fifty-mark note was a mere bagatelle. This annoyed Frl. Schroeder very much indeed:

'I suppose she's trying to make out that one of *us* did it! Of all the cheek! Why, Herr Issyvoo, will you believe me, I could have chopped her into little pieces!'

'Yes, Frl. Schroeder. I'm sure you could.'

Frl. Schroeder then developed the theory that the money hadn't been stolen at all and that this was just a trick of Frl. Kost's to avoid paying the rent. She hinted as much to Frl. Kost, who was furious. Frl. Kost said that, in any case, she'd raise the money in a few days: which she already has. She also gave notice to leave her room at the end of the month.

Meanwhile, I have discovered, quite by accident, that Frl. Kost has been having an affair with Bobby. As I came in, one evening, I happened to notice that there was no light in Frl. Kost's room. You can always see this, because there is a frosted glass pane in her door to light the hall of the flat. Later, as I lay in bed reading, I heard Frl. Kost's door open and Bobby's voice, laughing and whispering. After much creaking of boards and muffled laughter, Bobby tiptoed out of the flat, shutting the door as quietly as possible behind him. A moment later, he re-entered with a great deal of noise and went straight through into the living-room, where I heard him wishing Frl. Schroeder good night.

If Frl. Schroeder doesn't actually know of this, she at least suspects it. This explains her fury against Frl. Kost: for the truth is, she is terribly jealous. The most grotesque and embarrassing incidents have been taking place. One morning, when I wanted to visit the bathroom, Frl. Kost was using it already. Frl. Schroeder rushed to the door before I could stop her and ordered Frl. Kost to come out at once: and when Frl. Kost naturally didn't obey, Frl. Schroeder began, despite my protests, hammering on the door with her fists. 'Come out of my bathroom!' she screamed. 'Come out this minute, or I'll call the police to fetch you out!'

After this she burst into tears. The crying brought on palpitations. Bobby had to carry her to the sofa, gasping and sobbing. While we were all standing round, rather helpless, Frl. Mayr appeared in the doorway with a face like a hangman and said, in a terrible voice, to Frl. Kost: 'Think yourself lucky, my girl, if you haven't murdered her!' She then took complete charge of the situation, ordered us all out of the room and sent me down to the grocer's for a bottle of Baldrian Drops. When I returned, she was seated beside the sofa, stroking Frl. Schroeder's hand and murmuring, in her most tragic tones: 'Lina, my poor little child . . . what have they done to you?'

[*PNW 1*, 1940]

V. S. PRITCHETT

SENSE OF HUMOUR

It started one week-end. I was working new ground and I decided I'd stay at the hotel the week-end and put in an appearance at church.

'All alone?' asked the girl in the cash desk.

It had been raining since ten o'clock.

'Mr Good has gone,' she said. 'And Mr Straker. He usually stays with us. But he's gone.'

'That's where they make their mistake,' I said. 'They think they know everything because they've been on the road all their lives.'

'You're a stranger here, aren't you?' she said.

'I am,' I said. 'And so are you.'

'How do you know that?'

'Obvious,' I said. 'Way you speak.'

'Let's have a light,' she said.

'So's I can see you,' I said.

That was how it started. The rain was pouring down on to the glass roof of the office.

She'd a cup of tea steaming on the register. I said I'd have one, too. What's it going to be and I'll tell them, she said, but I said just a cup of tea.

'I'm TT,' I said. 'Too many soakers on the road as it is.'

I was staying there the week-end so as to be sharp on the job Monday morning. What's more it pays in these small towns to turn up at church on Sundays, Presbyterians in the morning, Methodists in the evening. Say 'Good morning' and 'Good evening' to them. 'Ah!' they say. 'Church goer! Pleased to see that! TT, too.' Makes them have a second look at your lines in the morning. 'Did you like our service, Mister — er — er?' 'Humphrey's my name.' 'Mr Humphrey?' See? It pays.

'Come into the office, Mr Humphrey,' she said, bringing me a cup. 'Listen to that rain.'

I went inside.

'Sugar,' she said.

'Three,' I said. We settled to a very pleasant chat. She told me all about herself, and we got on next to families.

'My father was on the railway,' she said.

'The engine gave a squeal,' I said. 'The driver took his pocket knife and scraped him off the wheel.'

'That's it,' she said. 'And what is your father's business? You said he had a business.'

'Undertaker,' I said.

'Undertaker?' she said.

'Why not?' I said. 'Good business. Seasonable like everything else. High class undertaker,' I said.

She was looking at me all the time wondering what to say and suddenly she went into fits of laughter.

'Undertaker!' she said, covering her face with her hands and went on laughing.

'Here,' I said. 'What's up?'

'Undertaker!' she laughed and laughed. Struck me as being a pretty thin joke.

'Don't mind me,' she said. 'I'm Irish.'

'Oh I see,' I said. 'That's it, is it? Got a sense of humour.'

Then the bell rang and a woman called out, 'Muriel! Muriel!' and there was a motor bike making a row at the front door.

'All right,' the girl called out. 'Excuse me a moment, Mr Humphrey,' she said. 'Don't think me rude. That's my boy friend. He wants the bird, turning up like this.'

She went out but there was her boy friend looking over the window ledge into the office. He had come in. He had a cape on, soaked with rain and the rain was in beads in his hair. It was fair hair. It stood up on end. He'd been economizing on the brilliantine. He didn't wear a hat. He gave me a look and I gave him a look. I didn't like the look of him. And he didn't like the look of me. A smell of oil and petrol and rain and mackintosh came off him. He had a big mouth with thick lips. They were very red. I recognized him at once as the son of the man who ran the Kounty garage. I saw this chap when I put my car away. The firm's car. A lock-up, because of the samples. Took me ten minutes to ram the idea into his head. He looked as though he'd never heard of samples. Slow – you know the way they are in the provinces. Slow on the job.

'Oh, Colin,' says she. 'What do you want?'

'Nothing,' the chap said. 'I came in to see you.'

'To see me?'

'Just to see you.'

'You came in this morning.'

'That's right,' he said. He went red. 'You was busy,' he said.

'Well, I'm busy now,' she said.

He bit his tongue, and licked his big lips over and took a look at me. Then he started grinning.

'I've got the new bike, Muriel,' he said. 'I've got it outside.'

'It's just come down from the works,' he said.

'The laddie wants you to look at his bike,' I said. So she went out and had a look at it.

When she came back she had got rid of him.

'Listen to that rain,' she said.

'Lord, I'm fed up with this line,' she said.

'What line?' I said. 'The hotel line?'

'Yes,' she said. 'I'm fed right up to the back teeth with it.'

'And you've got good teeth,' I said.

'There's not the class of person there used to be in it,' she said. 'All our family have got good teeth.'

'Not the class?'

'I've been in it five years and there's not the same class at all. You never meet any fellows.'

'Well,' says I, 'if they're like that half wit at the garage they're nothing to be struck on. And you've met me.'

I said it to her like that.

'Oh,' says she. 'It isn't as bad as that yet.'

It was cold in the office. She used to sit all day in her overcoat. She was a smart girl with a big friendly chin and a second one coming and her forehead and nose were covered with freckles. She had copper-coloured hair too. She got her shoes through the trade from Duke's traveller and her clothes too off the Hollenborough mantle man. I told her I could do her better stockings than the ones she'd got on. She got a good reduction on everything. Twenty-five or thirty-three and a third. She had her expenses cut right back. I took her to the pictures that night in the car. I made Colin get the car out for me.

'That boy wanted me to go on the back of his bike. On a night like this,' she said.

'Oh,' she said when we got to the pictures. 'Two shillings's too much. Let's go into the one and sixes at the side and we can nip across into the two shillings when the lights go down.'

'Fancy your father being an undertaker,' she said in the middle of the show. And she started laughing as she laughed before.

She had her head screwed on all right. She said:

'Some girls have no pride once the lights go down.'

Every time I went to that town I took a box of something. Samples, mostly, they didn't cost me anything.

'Don't thank me,' I said. 'Thank the firm.'

Every time I took her out I pulled down the blinds in the back seat of the car to hide the samples. That chap Colin used to give us oil and petrol. He used to give me a funny look. Fishy sort of small eyes he'd got. Always looking miserable. Then we would go off. Sunday was her free day. Not that driving's any holiday for me. And, of course, the firm paid. She used to take me down to see her family for the day. Start in the morning and taking it you had dinner and tea there, a day's outing cost us nothing. Her father was something on the railway retired. He had a long stocking somewhere, but her sister, the one that was married, had had her share already.

He had a tumour after his wife died and they just played upon the old man's feelings. It wasn't right. She wouldn't go near her sister and I don't blame her, taking the money like that. Just played upon the old man's feelings.

Every time I was up there Colin used to come in looking for her.

'Oh, Colin,' I used to say. 'Done my car yet?' He knew where he got off with me.

'No, now I can't, Colin. I tell you I'm going out with Mr Humphrey,' she used to say to him. I heard her.

'He keeps on badgering me,' she said to me.

'You leave him to me,' I said.

'No, he's all right,' she said.

'You let me know if there's any trouble with Colin,' I said. 'Seems to be a harum scarum sort of half wit to me,' I said.

'And he spends every penny he makes,' she said.

Well, we know that sort of thing is all right while it lasts, I told her, but the trouble is that it doesn't last.

We were always meeting Colin on the road. I took no notice of it first of all and then I grew suspicious and awkward at always meeting him. He had a new motor bicycle. It was an Indian, a scarlet thing that he used to fly over the moor with, flat out. Muriel and I used to go out over the moor to Ingley Wood in the firm's Morris – I had a customer out that way.

'May as well do a bit of business while you're about it,' I said.

'About what,' she said.

'Ah ha!' I said.

'That's what Colin wants to know,' I said.

Sure enough, coming back we'd hear him popping and back-firing close behind us, and I put out my hand to stop him and keep him following us, biting our dirt.

'I see his little game,' I said. 'Following us.'

So I saw to it that he did follow. We could hear him banging away behind us and the traffic is thick on the Ingley road in the afternoon.

'Oh let him pass,' Muriel said. 'I can't stand those dirty things banging in my ears.'

I waved him on and past he flew with his scarf flying out, blazing red into the traffic. 'We're doing fifty-eight ourselves,' she said, leaning across to look.

'Powerful buses those,' I said. 'Any fool can do it if he's got the power. Watch me step on it.'

But we did not catch Colin. Half an hour later he passed us coming back. Cut right in between us and a lorry – I had to brake hard. I damn nearly killed him. His ears were red with the wind. He didn't wear a hat. I got after him as soon as I could but I couldn't touch him.

Nearly every week-end I was in that town seeing my girl, that fellow was hanging around. He came into the bar on Saturday nights, he poked his head into the office on Sunday mornings. It was a sure bet that if we went out in the car he would pass us on the road. Every time we would hear that scarlet thing roar by like a horse-stinger. It didn't matter where we were. He passed us on the main road, he met us down the side roads. There was a little cliff under oak trees at May Ponds, she said, where the view was pretty. And there, soon after we got there, was Colin on the other side of the water, watching us. Once we found him sitting on his bike, just as though he were waiting for us.

'You been here in a car?' I said.

'No, motor bike,' she said and blushed. 'Cars can't follow in these tracks.'

She knew a lot of places in that country. Some of the roads weren't roads at all and were bad for tyres and I didn't want the firm's car scratched by bushes, but you would have thought Colin could read what was in her mind. For nine times out of ten he was there. It got on my nerves. It was a red, roaring powerful thing and he opened it full out.

'I'm going to speak to Colin,' I said. 'I won't have him annoying you.'

'He's not annoying me,' she said. 'I've got a sense of humour.'

'Here Colin,' I said one evening when I put the car away. 'What's the idea?'

He was taking off his overalls. He pretended he did not know what I was talking about. He had a way of rolling his eyeballs, as if they had got wet and loose in his head, while he was speaking to me and you never knew if it was sweat or oil on his face. It was always pale, with high colour on his cheeks and he had very red lips like a consumptive's.

'Miss MacFarlane doesn't like being followed,' I said.

He dropped his jaw and gaped at me. I could not tell whether he was being very surprised or very sly. I used to call him 'Marbles' because when he spoke he seemed to have a lot of marbles in his mouth.

Then he said he never went to the places we went to, except by accident. He wasn't following us, he said, but we were following him. We never let him alone, he said. Everywhere he went, he said, we were there. Take last Saturday, he said, we were following him for miles down the by-pass, he said. But you passed us first and then sat down in front, I said. I went to Ingley Wood, he said. And you followed me there. No, we didn't, I said, Miss MacFarlane decided to go there.

He said he did not want to complain but fair was fair. I suppose you know, he said, that you have taken my girl off me? Well you can leave *me* alone, can't you?

'Here,' I said. 'One minute! Not so fast! You said I've taken Miss MacFarlane from you. Well, she was never your girl. She only knew you in a friendly way.'

'She was my girl,' was all he said.

He was pouring oil into my engine. He had some cotton-wool in one hand and the can in the other. He wiped up the green oil that had overflowed, screwed on the cap, pulled down the bonnet and whistled to himself.

I went back to Muriel and told her what Colin had said.

'I don't like trouble,' I said.

'Don't you worry,' she said. 'I had to have someone to go to all these places with before you came. Couldn't stick in here all day Sunday.'

'Ah,' I said. 'That's it, is it. You've been to all these places with him.'

'Yes,' she said. 'And he keeps on going to them. He's sloppy about me.'

'Good God,' I said. 'Sentimental memories, eh?'

I felt sorry for that fellow. He knew it was hopeless but he loved her. I suppose he couldn't help himself. Well, it takes all sorts to make a world, as my old mother used to say. If we were all alike it wouldn't do. Some men can't save money. It just runs through their fingers. He couldn't save money so he lost her. I suppose all he thought of was love.

I could have been friends with that fellow. As it was I put a lot of business his way. I didn't want him to get the wrong idea about me. We're all human after all.

We didn't have any more trouble with Colin after this until Bank Holiday. I was going to take her down to see my family. The old man's getting a bit past it now and has given up living over the shop. He's living out on the Barnum Road, beyond the tram stop. We were going down in the firm's car as per usual, but something went wrong with the mag. and Colin had not got it right for the holiday. I was wild about this. What's the use of a garage who can't do a rush job for the holidays! What's the use of being an old customer if they're going to let you down! I went for Colin bald-headed.

'You knew I wanted it,' I said. 'It's no use trying to put me off with a tale about the stuff not coming down from the works. I've heard that one before.'

I told him he'd got to let me have another car, because he'd let me down. I told him I wouldn't pay his account. I said I'd take my business away from him. But there wasn't a car to be had in the town because of the holiday. I could have knocked the fellow down. After the way I'd sent business to him.

Then I saw through his little game. He knew Muriel and I were going to my people and he had done this to stop it. The moment I saw this I let him know that it would take more than him to stop me doing what I wanted.

I said:

'Right. I shall take the amount of Miss MacFarlane's train fare and my own from the account at the end of the month.'

I said:

'You may run a garage, but you don't run the railway service.'

I was damned angry going by train. I felt quite lost on the railway after having a car. It was crowded with trippers too. It was slow – stopping at all the stations. The people come in, they tread all over your feet, they make you squeeze up till you're crammed against the window, and the women stick out their elbows and fidget. And then, the expense! A return for two runs you into just over a couple of quid. I could have murdered Colin.

We got there at last. We walked up from the tram stop. Mother was at the window and let us in.

'This is Miss MacFarlane,' I said.

And mother said:

'Oh, pleased to meet you. We've heard a lot about you.'

'Oh,' mother said to me giving me a kiss, 'are you tired? You haven't had your tea, have you? Sit down. Have this chair, dear. It's more comfortable.'

'Well, my boy,' my father said.

'Want a wash?' my father said. 'We've got a wash basin downstairs,' he said. 'I used not to mind about washing upstairs before. Now I couldn't do without it. Funny how your ideas change as you get older.'

'How's business?' he said.

'Mustn't grumble,' I said. 'How's yours?'

'You knew,' he said, 'we took off the horses: except for one or two of the older families, we have got motors now?'

But he'd told me that the last time I was there. 'You've forgotten I used to drive them for you,' I said. I'd been at him for years about motor hearses.

'Bless me, so you did,' he said.

He took me up to my room. He showed me everything he had had done to the house. 'Your mother likes it,' he said. 'The traffic's company for her. You know what your mother is for company.'

Then he gives me a funny look.

'Who's the girl?' he says.

My mother came in then and said,

'She's pretty, Arthur.'

'Of course she's pretty,' I said. 'She's Irish.'

'Oh,' said the old man. 'Irish! Got a sense of humour, eh?'

'She couldn't be marrying me if she hadn't,' I said. And then I gave *them* a look.

'Marrying her, did you say!' exclaimed my father.

'Any objection?' I said.

'Now Ernest dear,' said my mother. 'Leave the boy alone. Come down while I pop the kettle on.'

She was terribly excited.

'Miss MacFarlane,' the old man said.

'No sugar, thank you, Mrs Humphrey. I beg your pardon, Mr Humphrey?'

'The Glen Hotel at Swansea, I don't suppose you know that?' my father said.

'I wondered if you did being in the catering line.'

'It doesn't follow she knows every hotel,' my mother said.

'Forty years ago,' the old man said. 'I was staying at the Glen in Swansea and the head waiter . . .'

'Oh no, not that one. I'm sure Miss MacFarlane doesn't want to hear that one,' my mother said.

'How's business with you, Mr Humphrey?' said Muriel. 'We passed a large cemetery near the station.'

'Dad's Ledger,' I said.

'The whole business has changed so that you wouldn't know it in my life time,' said my father. 'Silver fittings have gone clean out. Everyone wants simplicity these days. Restraint. Dignity,' my father said.

'Prices did it,' my father said.

'The war,' he said.

'You couldn't get the wood,' he said.

'Take ordinary mahogany, just an ordinary piece of mahogany. Or teak,' he said. 'Take teak. Or walnut.'

'You can certainly see the world go by in this room,' I said to my mother.

'It never stops,' she said.

Now it was all bicycles over the new concrete road from the gun factory. Then traction engines and cars. They came up over the hill where the A A man stands and choked up round the tram stop. It was mostly holiday traffic. Everything with a wheel on it was out.

'On this stretch,' my father told me, 'they get three accidents a week.' There was an ambulance station at the crossroads.

We had hardly finished talking about this, in fact the old man was still saying that something ought to be done when the telephone rang.

'Name of MacFarlane?' the voice said on the wire.

'No! Humphrey,' my father said. 'There is a Miss MacFarlane here.'

'There's a man named Colin Mitchell lying seriously injured in an accident at the Cottage Hospital, gave the name of MacFarlane as his nearest relative.'

That was the Police. On to it at once. That fellow Colin had followed us down by road.

Cry, I never heard a girl cry, as Muriel cried, when we came back from the hospital. He had died in the ambulance. Cutting in, the old game he used to play on me. Clean off the saddle and under the Birmingham bus. The blood was everywhere, they said. People were still looking at it when we went by. What a mess! Don't let's talk about it.

She wanted to see him but they said 'No.' There wasn't anything recognizable to see. She put her arms round my neck and cried 'Colin, Colin,' as if I were Colin, and clung to me. I was feeling sick myself. I held her tight and I kissed her and I thought, 'Holiday ruined.'

'Damn fool man,' I thought. 'Poor devil,' I thought.

'I knew he'd do something like this.'

'There, there,' I said to her. 'Don't think about Colin.'

Didn't she love me, I said, and not Colin? Hadn't she got me? She said, Yes, she had. And she loved me. But 'Oh Colin! Oh Colin!' she cried. 'And Colin's mother,' she cried. 'Oh it's terrible.' She was crying her heart out.

We put her to bed and I sat with her and my mother kept coming in. 'Leave her to me,' I said. 'I understand her.'

Before they went to bed they both came in and looked at her. She lay sobbing with her head in the pillow.

I could quite understand her being upset. Colin was a decent fellow. He was always doing things for her. He mended her electric lamp and he riveted the stem of a wine glass so that you couldn't see the break. He used to make things for her. He was very good with his hands.

She lay on her side with her face burning and feverish with misery and crying, scalded by the salt, and her lips shrivelled up. I put my arm under her neck and I stroked her forehead. She groaned. Sometimes she shivered and sometimes she clung to me crying, 'Oh Colin! Colin.'

My arm ached with the cramp and I had a crick in my back, sitting in the awkward way I was on the bed. It was late. There was nothing to do but to ache and sit watching her and thinking. It is funny the way your mind drifts. When I was kissing her and watching her I was thinking out who I'd show our new Autumn range to first. Her hand held my wrist tight and when I kissed her I got her tears on my lips. They burned and stung. Her neck and shoulders were soft and I could feel her breath hot out of her nostrils on the back of my hand. Ever noticed how hot a woman's breath gets when she's crying? I drew out my hand and lay down beside her and 'Oh Colin, Colin,' she sobbed, turning over and clinging to me. And so I lay there, listening to the traffic, staring at the ceiling, and shivering whenever the picture of Colin, shooting white off that damned red thing into the bus, came into my mind – until I did not hear the traffic any more, or see the ceiling any more, or think any more, but a change happened – I don't know when. This Colin thing seemed to have knocked the bottom out of everything and I had a funny feeling we were going down and down and down in a lift. And the further we went the hotter and softer she got. Perhaps it was when I found with my hands that she had very big breasts. But it was like being on the mail steamer and feeling the engines start under your feet, thumping louder and louder. You can feel it in every vein of your body. Her mouth opened and her tears dried. Her breath came through her open mouth and her voice was sort of blind and husky. Colin, Colin, Colin, she said and her fingers were hooked into me. I got out and turned the key in the door.

In the morning I left her sleeping. It did not matter to me what my father might have heard in the night, but still I wondered. I don't think to this day they know anything about it. She would hardly let me touch her before that. I told her I was sorry but she shut me up. I was afraid of her. I was afraid of mentioning Colin. I wanted to go out of the house there and then and tell someone everything. Did she love Colin all the time? Did she think I was Colin? And every time I thought of that poor bastard covered over with a white sheet in the hospital mortuary, a kind of picture of her and me under the sheets with love came into my mind. I couldn't separate the two things. Just as though it had all come from Colin.

I'd rather not talk any more about that. I never talked to Muriel about it. I waited for her to say something but she didn't. She didn't say a word.

The next day was a bad day. It was grey and hot and the air smelled of oil fumes from the road. There's always a mess to clear up when things like this happen. I had to see to it. I had the job of ringing up the boy's mother. But I got round that, thank God, by ringing up the garage and getting them to go round and see the old lady. My father is useless when things are like this. I was the whole morning on the phone: to the hospital, the police, the coroner – and he stood fussing beside me, jerking up and down like a fat india rubber ball. I found my mother washing up at the sink and she said:

'That poor boy's mother! I can't stop thinking of her.' Then my father comes in and says – just as though I was a customer:

'Of course if Mrs Mitchell desires it we can have the remains of the deceased conveyed to his house by one of our new specially sprung motor hearses and can, if necessary, make all the funeral arrangements.'

I could have hit him because Muriel came into the room when he was saying this. But she stood there as if nothing had happened.

'It's the least we can do for poor Mrs Mitchell,' she said. There were small creases of shadow under her eyes which shone with a soft light I had never seen before. She walked as if she were really still in that room with me asleep. God, I loved that girl! God, I wanted to get all this over, this damned business that had come right into the middle of everything like this, and I wanted to get married right away. I wanted to be alone with her. That's what Colin did for me.

'Yes,' I said. 'We must do the right thing by Colin.'

'We are sometimes asked for long distance estimates,' said my father.

'It would be a little something,' my mother said.

'Dad and I will talk it over,' I said.

'Come into my office,' said my father. 'It occurred to me that it would be nice to do the right thing by this friend of yours.'

We talked it over. We went into the cost of it. There was the return journey to reckon.

We worked it out that it would come no dearer to old Mrs Mitchell, than if she took the train and buried the boy here. That is to say, my father said, if I drove it.

'It would look nice,' my father said.

'Saves money and it would look a bit friendly,' my father said. 'You've done it before.'

'Well,' I said. 'I suppose I can get a refund on my return ticket from the railway.'

But it was not as simple as it looked because Muriel wanted to come. She wanted to drive back with me and the hearse. My mother was very worried about this. It might upset Muriel, she thought. Father thought it might not look nice to see a young girl sitting by the coffin of a grown man.

'It must be dignified,' my father said. 'You see, if she was there it might look as though she were just doing it for the ride -- like these young women on baker's vans.'

My father took me out into the hall to tell me this because he did not want her to hear. But she would not have it. She wanted to come back with Colin.

'Colin loved me. It is my duty to him,' she said. 'Besides,' she said, suddenly, in her full open voice – it had seemed to be closed and carved and broken and small – 'I've never been in a hearse before.'

'And it will save her fare too,' I said to my father.

That night I went again to her room. She was awake. I said I was sorry to disturb her but I would go at once, I only wanted to see if she was all right. She said, in the closed voice again, that she was all right.

'Are you sure?' I said.

She did not answer. I was worried. I went over to the bed.

'What is the matter? Tell me what is the matter?' I said.

For a long time she was silent. I held her hand, I stroked her head. She was lying stiff in the bed. She would not answer. I dropped my hand to her small white shoulder. She stirred and drew up her legs and half turned and said, 'I was thinking of Colin.'

'Where is he?' she asked.

'They've brought him round. He's lying downstairs.'

'In the front room?'

'Yes, ready for the morning. Now be a sensible girl and you go back by train.'

'No, No!' she said. 'I want to go with Colin. Poor Colin. He loved me and I didn't love him!' And she drew my hands down to her breasts.

'Colin loved me,' she whispered.

'Not like this,' I whispered.

It was a warm grey morning like all the others when we took Colin back. They had fixed the coffin in before Muriel came out. She came down wearing the bright blue hat she had got off Dormer's millinery man and she kissed my mother and father good-bye. They were very sorry for her. 'Look after her, Arthur,' my mother said. Muriel got in beside me without a glance behind her at the coffin. I started the engine. They smiled at us. My father raised his hat, but whether it was to Muriel and me or to Colin, or the three of us, I do not know. He was not, you see, wearing his top hat. I'll say this for the old boy, thirty years in the trade have taught him tact.

After leaving my father's house you have to go down to the tram terminus before you get on to the by-pass. There were always one or two drivers, conductors or inspectors there, doing up their tickets, or changing over the trolley arms. When we passed I saw two of them drop their jaws, stick their pencils in their ears and raise their hats. I was so surprised by this that I nearly raised mine in acknowledgement, forgetting that we had the coffin behind. I had not driven one of my father's hearses for years.

Hearses are funny things to drive. They are well-sprung, smooth running cars, with quiet engines and, if you are used to driving a smaller car, before you know where you are, you are speeding. You know you ought to go slow, say 25 to 30 maximum, and it's hard to keep it down. You can return empty at 70 if you like. It's like driving a fire engine. Go fast out and come back slow – only the other way round. Open out in the country but slow down past houses. That's what it means. My father was very particular about this.

Muriel and I didn't speak very much at first. We sat listening to the engine and the occasional jerk of the coffin behind when we went over a pot hole. We passed the place where poor Colin — but I didn't say anything to Muriel and she, if she noticed — which I doubt — did not say anything to me. We went through Cox Hill, Wammering and Yodley Mount, flat country, don't care for it myself. 'There's a wonderful lot of building going on,' Muriel said at last.

'You won't know these places in five years,' I said.

But my mind kept drifting away from the road and the green fields and the dullness and back to Colin — five days before he had come down this way. I expected to see that Indian coming flying straight out of every corner. But it was all bent and bust up properly now. I saw the damned thing.

He had been up to his old game, following us, and that had put the end to following. But not quite; he was following us now, behind us in the coffin. Then my mind drifted off that and I thought of those nights, at my parents' house, and Muriel. You never know what a woman is going to be like. I thought, too, that it had put my calculations out. I mean, supposing she had a baby. You see I had reckoned on waiting eighteen months or so. I would have eight hundred then. But if we had to get married at once we should have to cut right down. Then I kept thinking it was funny her saying 'Colin!' like that in the night; it was funny it made her feel that way with me, and how it made me feel when she called me 'Colin'. I'd never thought of her in that way, in what you might call the 'Colin' way.

I looked at her and she looked at me and she smiled but still we did not say very much, but the smiles kept coming to both of us. The light railway bridge at Dootheby took me by surprise and I thought the coffin gave a jump as we took it.

'Colin's still watching us,' I damn nearly said.

There were tears in her eyes.

'What was the matter with Colin?' I said. 'Nice chap, I thought. Why didn't you marry him?'

'Yes,' she said. 'He was a nice boy. But he'd no sense of humour.'

'And I wanted to get out of that town,' she said.

'I'm not going to stay there at that hotel,' she said.

'I want to get away,' she said. 'I've had enough.'

She has a way of getting angry with the air, like that. 'You've got to take me away,' she said. We were passing slowly into Muster, there was a tram ahead and people thick on the narrow pavements, dodging out into the road. But when we got into the Market Square where they were standing around, they saw the coffin. They began to raise their hats. Suddenly she laughed. 'It's like being the King and Queen,' she said.

'They're raising their hats,' she said.

'Not all of them,' I said.

She squeezed my hand and I had to keep her from jumping about on the seat as we went through, like a child.

'There they go.'

'Boys always do,' I said.

'And another.'

'Let's see what the policeman does.'

She started to laugh but I shut her up. 'Keep your sense of humour to yourself,' I said.

Through all those towns that run into one another as you might say, we caught it. We went through, as she said, like royalty. So many years since I drove a hearse I'd forgotten what it was like.

I was proud of her, I was proud of Colin and I was proud of myself. And, after what had happened, I mean on the last two nights, it was like a wedding. And although we knew it was for Colin, it was for us too, because Colin was with both of us. It was like this all the way.

'Look at that man there. Why doesn't he raise his hat? People ought to show respect for the dead,' she said.

[*PNW 1*, 1940]

H. T. HOPKINSON

I HAVE BEEN DROWNED

(To Antonia White)

When I was a boy my mother took me to a gipsy. She was a dirty old woman in a tent. My mother hoped, I suppose, that she would foretell me fame and fortune. I was hoping she would foretell me a pony for my birthday.

The gipsy looked for a long time into a crystal. Then she spoke, and in a clear voice quite unlike the gruff dialect in which she bargained, lied and quarrelled, the gipsy said, 'The boy will meet death by drowning.' Then she added, rather oddly, 'I see him drown; at least I think I do.'

Even at my age I realized that her hesitation set the stamp of truth on what she said. If she had wanted to invent a tale she would have made up a high-sounding one, full of the good fortune and grand events for which my mother longed.

Though I accepted death by drowning as my fate from that day on, I was never in the least haunted by the thought of it. I have always felt in my heart I should prefer to die that way, and now it is clear to me I never shall, I feel almost as though I had been cheated of a promised honour, degraded from my own peculiar destiny to be as other men.

Anyone who remembers being a child will recall the overwhelming desire which seized one for an object, not beautiful nor useful, which could only be a nuisance to one when one had it. I have been kept awake at night by a craving for a white mouse belonging to a friend. I stole the mouse, and was awake next night with the excitement of the theft and the mad joy of possession.

Something of the sort must have happened to me, I suppose, on the hot June afternoon when I saw *Stella*.

Stella, I could see straightway, was almost everything a boat ought not to be. She was too fine forward, so that she would thrust her nose into the waves instead of lifting to them. She was too square aft, so that a following sea would smash her from side to side with constant danger of a jibe. She had a long deep keel, making it impossible to run for shelter into the small muddy inlets of the coast where I should sail her.

I went into the builder's yard above which I had seen her much too tall mast tower, and looked her over inch by inch. When I had done I hated the very sight of her, hated her with the hatred one can only feel for something to which one is inextricably married, married not by force of circumstances which may change or weaken, but by an unchanging thing implanted in the substance of one's self.

There were some few points in *Stella*'s favour. I had hoped as I looked at her to find her rotten, and so to be given excuse for never seeing her again. She was as dry as a barrel and tough as a concrete pavement, built of teak.

'She don't make a cupful of water in two years,' said the builder, kicking angrily at her side – I could see he hated the boat as much as I did, and would gladly have scored off her by leaving her in his yard to rot unsold – adding in explanation, 'She've got two skins.'

Her enormous keel was of lead – worth money in itself – and she had a prodigious variety of sails, ranging from a tiny trysail and storm-jib to a towering mainsail and pot-bellied spinnaker. At the worst, I thought, I could ride out bad weather with two of the smallest pocket-handkerchiefs. Then I looked at the steeping mast and loaded keel and saw that without a stitch of sail the thresh and strain in any wind and sea would be terrific.

I bought *Stella*, as I had known all along I should. I paid £120 for her. It was nothing for a boat of her size and condition. From the point of view of anyone wanting a pleasant sail, it was money thrown down the drain. Sailing her could only be a nightmare.

As I went out of the yard I looked at the builder. 'She's a maniac's boat,' I said. 'Built by a lunatic, to be sailed by idiots. She ought to be broken up now, before someone injures themselves in her. If I had any sense, I'd pay you twice the money not to let me have her.'

The dealer looked at me under his wedged-down bowler hat. The deal was finished. I should not back out. 'She's a drowning boat,' he said.

I took *Stella* away from the yard a fortnight later. She scarcely needed touching. I had her painted black with varnished decks. She was copper-fastened all through and her fittings were brass.

I sailed her down the Medway and across to the Essex coast – where I lived aboard, and got to know her. But 'got to know' are not the words to use of *Stella*. I had known everything about her long before. She played no trick which I had not foreseen and dreaded. Her good qualities I had counted on without even proving they were there.

She buried her bows instead of lifting them, as I had known she would. When running before a wind, I had to be 'steering' all the time, spinning the wheel as a following wave crashed against her counter, spinning it back before the boom could fly over and snap the mast off like a hemlock stalk. A good boat steers herself. A good helmsman scarcely uses the wheel; he thinks instead. It was no good thinking at *Stella*. You had to take two hands to her and use all the strength of arms and planted legs and lever body.

As against that, she would sail almost into the wind's eye in defiance of all nature, and with her monstrous spread of canvas would go driving on, as if towed by an unseen army of porpoises, when other boats were tossing helplessly up and down, their crews playing nap for occupation.

At first I sailed *Stella* with a paid hand. That was all right for a week or two. But before long I began to find fault with everything he did. He could never set a sail just right. He left specks on the brass-work. At the wheel he let her fall away, shipped more seas than he need. I sacked him. When he went off he looked not at all angrily at me, but sympathetically, as a man might look at another he must leave for the winter in the frozen North.

From that time I ministered to all *Stella*'s wants myself. I would let no one so much as splice a rope for her. By the end of the summer I would not even let other people come aboard. If, in an access of friendship or desire I asked someone to stay on her for the week-end, I would be certain the day before to send a wire and put them off. My friends all gave me up.

I did not mind. During August and September I won seven firsts and two second prizes with *Stella* in ten races, sailing her with a young fisherman whom I paid for every race and packed off as soon as it was over. He hated the sea, and said so, and he hated me and my boat more than ever he could find words to say.

The day on which I was to drown was the day of the Yantlet Regatta. It was a dirty day, and a falling glass showed worse to follow. There was talk of calling the regatta off. All the competitors in my class – we had to sail an eighteen-mile course out of the estuary and back – agreed that if our race were to be held they would refuse to sail it.

I found a note in the rules of the Club saying that if one member of a class wished to sail the course he could do so and claim the race. I declared that I would sail and claim. The others held together and refused. 'It's a game for lunatics,' they said.

I found my fisherman and offered him double money for the race. 'You know what you can do with that,' he said. I offered him £20 – double the prize money – for himself. He looked down at his boots, round at the sky, and went to get his oilskins.

There was nobody except the officials of the Club to see us start. The race had been banned by the members. They were watching the dinghies race behind a breakwater.

We tacked out to the buoy, six miles in all, with four of open sea, *Stella* sailing as she had never sailed before. If the other boats had come out they would have looked like cart-horses. After that we had to beat to windward – five further miles of open water, as 'open' as any water I ever sailed above and through – then we rounded a lightship and set off for home, doing ten knots and the boat half lost in spray.

We had covered perhaps a quarter of the way on this last leg when mist came down, not a nice gentle mist, but a foul blinding mist; not a mist that is laid round you like a blanket, but a mist that is flung at you like rough-cast. At the same time the tide turned.

The sea was now running out and the wind blowing in. The waves got bigger every minute. *Stella* began to plunge her nose. Great slews of water flushed along the deck. I had been soaked two hours before. Now the water was battering me solid. It was as much as I could do to stand. 'Better take in sail,' said the fisherman; they called him Jack.

'You'll take in nothing,' I shouted at him through the wind. Jack did not answer. He went forward and began to reef the foresail.

'Blast him,' I thought. 'I'll show him.'

We were running then over a sand-bar, a spit that would be dried out at low water. Now there was two or three fathoms over it. The waves were pounding and threshing, half breaking, instead of lifting and then sliding away beneath her keel. There was a big one just ahead and as we came to it, instead of turning *Stella*'s bows away so that she met it slightly on her quarter, I drove them in. She took it solid. A great belch of water burst along the deck, splitting over every obstacle, re-uniting again the second it was past.

It took Jack waist-high, knocked him off his feet. I thought for a second he was gone. But it takes more than a wave to drown a fisherman, and as he swept down the scuppers he grabbed hold of one of the stays and clung till the burst of water had gone by. That happened in one second.

In the next there was a crack, a painful crack like the sound of a living body broken, then an outbreak of smaller cracks, wires and ropes whipped through the air or sank coiling by my feet, all of the decks forward and yards of sea on either side were suddenly over-spread with canvas, through which the water welled and over which it spread.

The weight and shock of that sea smashing her nose down, while a gust was bursting and lifting into her sails behind, had snapped the mainmast short.

I had thought very often of what I should do if *Stella* went down at sea, and she was going to go down now. Without way on her she would not steer. The next two or three waves would hammer her counter round and broach her to. Once broadside on, a couple of waves would fill her, and the tons of valuable lead on her bottom would do the rest.

I slithered and bolted forward to where a lifebelt was fixed on top of a skylight, tore it off, thrust head and arms inside, and went overboard in a patch of sea clear of sail and cordage. Two minutes later she was gone.

As soon as I found myself in the sea I knew what I must do. I never wore sea-boots on *Stella*. I did not trust her well enough. I could keep afloat with my lifebelt for several hours if I did not exhaust myself in swimming. A fool would have tried to make the coast against the tide. But to make those four or five miles – an hour's quick walking – I would have needed to swim twenty. I could not even hold my place and hope to be washed back when the tide turned in six hours' time. All I could do was to keep afloat and save my strength.

Having a lifebelt, I know, is not everything. Plenty of drowned bodies are washed up with lifebelts underneath their arms. You have got to keep your face out of the water, not easy when the waves are running high, and you have got to keep yourself from dying of exhaustion, though normally you feel cold after a five-minutes bathe.

I reckoned I had two chances of life. One was to drift down to the lightship we had rounded, and hope to grab one of her chains or rouse her men by shouting. The other was that some of the men at the Yacht Club would set out to look for me.

They would not do that for several hours, because we had been making much faster time than ever they'd expect, and when we did not turn up they'd only think we had run into a creek for shelter, and would telephone round for a while to see if there was news of us. There was a chance of a stray steamer catching sight of me, but it was just as likely in the mist she would cut me down.

I decided to swim gently to keep the blood flowing, first on my breast, then on my back, shifting the lifebelt slightly as I turned from one position to the other. Once as I was swimming forward it slipped back and caught for a moment on my hips, lifting my body and pressing my face into the water. I rolled over on my back and worked it free. Once as I changed position my arm got pinned inside the belt. With muscles weakening, I had a horror that I could not get it back. I got it back quite easily and went on swimming.

I swam as I had been taught to swim, in long slow sweeping strokes, driving with my legs, which are strong and slow to tire, using my arms for direction and support, drawing great breaths of air upon the upward stroke, blowing it out from my mouth before me through the water as my arms came in and forward. I took as much care with my style as though I had been in for a competition, and there were judges pacing beside me in a bath, for in the swim I had embarked on, just one more stroke, or ten or twenty might serve, I knew, to keep me in the world.

At first, while I was over the bar where the waves were breaking, I thought I should be choked. Water beat up my nose, into my mouth. My throat was full of water and I thought my lungs must be filling too. A man must breathe to live, and every time I took in air I took in sea. Then I drifted into deep water where there was swell instead of breakers, and breath came more easily. I felt for a moment as glad as if I had been rescued. I looked round, and swam on almost gaily through the mist and swell.

I had been in the water for perhaps half an hour when I happened to catch sight of my fingers. Two of the fingers of my left hand and the little finger of my right hand were pale green. I have never been much at home in water, and after a short bathe it takes me half an hour to get my blood flowing properly through my limbs. There was no chance to get it flowing again now.

It was not long before my other fingers had gone dead. I imagined the paralysis moving up like the mercury in a thermometer, from wrist to elbow, elbow to shoulder, and then running on down inside my body. It became necessary for me to know if my toes were dead as well, to see if the paralysis were coming from both ends, or only one. I did actually raise my feet in the water and tried to take one of my shoes off to find out, but my dead fingers would no longer work.

I cannot say how long I had been in the sea before I saw the lightship. I was conscious one moment of something dark seen out of the corner of my eye. The next instant there she was, not as I had pictured her, a comfortable and friendly presence with men waiting ready to haul me out and take me in, but a great heaving mass rolling her iron belly up with every surge, then crashing back with showers of spray into the swell, a dreadful heap of metal uncontrolled, terrifying to a thing of flesh.

Her cables, which I had pictured as so firm and steady, almost like life-chains in a swimming-bath, whipped through the waves as though themselves alive, the links grinding and crashing like goods-trucks in a siding – but goods-trucks crashing and grinding of their own volition and capriciously, escaped from reason and control. I kicked away from her with all the strength I had, and as I kicked I shouted.

I shouted once, a high-pitched shriek. There came no sign or answer. I thought the thin sound might seem too like a sea-gull's cries. I gathered up air into my lungs, and burst it all out again in roars. In the wild clatter and grind of everything on board, in the explosions all round me of the bursting seas, I could scarcely hear the sound myself.

As the lightship passed away out of sight I began to expect death. It would not be possible for me much longer to keep my face out of the waves. It was already impossible to keep it from the crests, and I drew breath in deep gulps in the quiet troughs. Soon whether crests or troughs would be alike to me, my face would lie helplessly forward on the surge and water would make its way into my lungs, driving the last air out in bubbles from my nose.

My weary arms were becoming with every stroke more difficult to lift. I had to force them to serve my purpose, almost shouting my orders to them with my mouth, as they began to disregard the messages sent along sinews from my brain.

I was becoming a prey to bodily fancies that would have stopped me swimming altogether had I heeded them. It was not my arms that weighed so much and were so difficult to move, it was the burden of my clothing on my arms which had now grown weightier than I could lift. It was the thickness of the clothing on my body which prevented me dividing the waters like a fish.

So conscious was I of my painful arms that I forgot the existence of my legs, and when for some reason they came into my mind, I could not feel their presence for the cold. I imagined I had swum away from them entirely or else that they had kicked loose from their joints, and was urgent in myself to get them back, feeling I could never make land without their help.

Inside my body I endured a feeling of extreme and painful cold, as though my entrails had been taken out and ice sewn in. The sole remaining patch of warmth, it seemed to me, was around my heart, and in the upper part of my chest, between my ribs and shoulder-blades.

As I swam on, these various pains lifted and moved away from my outlying parts, becoming centred on my controlling, guiding, head. The driving rain, the flung spume lashing from the waves against my face, the constant muscular effort to peer my eyes out of their sockets and lose no chance of sighting ship or boat, combined with the opposite effort to draw them right in beneath their brows for shelter, had caused inside my head a deadly pain, as though the metal of my forehead were on fire.

At the time these things were happening to me in the body, quite other things were happening in my mind.

I had no experience at all of that delightful coloured-cinema phenomenon in which the whole of one's past life is said to unroll progressively before one's eyes, and at the same time, to be presented to one in a flash. Yet certain moments in my life, or as it were, pictures from my story, resurged before me with a more than natural vividness, rising and falling, growing sharper in image or receding in time to the rising and falling of the waves.

I had, first, a picture of myself as infant, bundled together within my mother's womb, drawing life in through a tube as a diver draws air down from the surface.

I watched myself grow from a small swimming fish into a dwarf, enormous-headed, sightless-eyed, his useless limbs tucked round him for convenience, the whole creature shaken and quivering from the pulsing of his own determined heart.

This, the first vision that I saw, was curiously without colour. It had rather the grey appearance of a photograph, the nebulous vagueness of an X-ray picture.

Then, with no intervening stages, I was become a small boy of seven or eight, constructing for myself a house of packing-cases in the garden. No house, it seemed to me, is complete without store of food, and I was scratching with a trowel a hole in the turf floor, in order to let in a biscuit-tin larder for odd crusts and cakes, a green apple and a bottle which had once held lemonade.

And now, a few years older, I was making of my bicycle a sort of moving home, covering the handle-bars and frame with fittings, lashing a tiny tent against the saddle, delighting to show myself independent of the world on those two travelling wheels.

At seventeen, a senior boy at school, I owned a study. It had no door, consisted of no more than a slab of wood for desk, a seat close up against the slab, a bookshelf running round the sides. No bride ever lavished more care on her first home of love than I on that small wooden stall. Its sides I draped with flowered cloth, hung or pinned pictures over that, bargained with other boys for ornaments that caught my fancy.

My study and my youth washed by me on a wave.

Now, a young man, I walked through a town where I once lived. It was a seaport, whose tall, gabled warehouses darkened the street through which I passed.

Suddenly from a doorway ran a cat, a small and common tabby. At the sight I was filled with such a passion of tenderness I stopped still where I was, to follow with clenched hands its progress up the street. The cat turned off the road, crept low with flattened paunch beneath a warehouse door. My breath ran slowly out in a long sigh. The cat was safe. No wheel would break its back, no boot its belly.

I stopped there in the street to marvel at myself. What was the cat to me – that I should be its loving lord and father? And even as I stopped and asked, I saw the answer. The cat was pregnant. Two days before my love had told me there was a child of mine inside her body.

Over all these pictures as they dawned and faded, I experienced no emotion of regret. There was nothing I wished to bring back of what was gone, no untried course I wished that I had rather followed. I did not even wish or unwish the experience of seeing what I saw. The visions simply came before my eyes and glowed and died.

In between the vanishing of one and the appearance of the next were some few moments of absolute torment when I thought, not that my soul was being withdrawn from my body, but that my body was being wrenched by violence from my living soul.

Illusions of size and shape obsessed me. Now I traced all my sufferings to the batterings of the waves which had compressed my frame to the substance of a tiny pellet, so that all I was bearing had been concentrated and rendered more intense by the small space in me available for suffering.

Now, now, it was the dreadful opposite. My racked and elongated body sprawled over so vast an acreage of water, that not one only, but a thousand waves attacked it from all sides. The tides both ebbed and flowed along its length. A million screaming gulls let fall their fishy droppings on my freezing back.

Again I was suffering, not from my size but from my shape. I had become a sponge. A hundred broad and narrow inlets carried the coldness of the sea into the very centre of my being.

'If only,' I shouted, 'I were smooth. If I were smooth and solid, then I should keep out the water as a house keeps out the rain. My skin would defend the secrets of my body. But now I am all spread out upon the sea. Salt water runs in all my vitals. It crystallizes in my heart and veins.' And I seemed in the darkness of the water under me to discern the flowing away from me of all my precious blood.

Throughout this time, as a man may feel in a limb which he has lost, so I swam on with strength that was long since spent. I had not died, and till I died my legs and arms, however in revolt, could not refuse their work. But what an hour ago was a smooth sweeping stroke had become the convulsive kick of a frog touched by a forceps on its nerve. I had no plan, no hope. I did not know if I was moving towards, or from, the shore, or whether perhaps there was no shore at all.

When I first entered the sea the world had withdrawn into two elements. There was the water upon which I rose and fell, and there was the mist that drove above me and from which I sucked in the dry air needed by my human lungs. But now the distinction between these elements was vanishing away. It seemed to me that the world as I swam had somehow been turned over. The water was now on the top, the needed air beneath. The breaths I was drawing from above had become too thick and watery to feed my lungs. I should do better, I saw, to draw breath from below.

With this discovery, that I could draw breath from the sea, there succeeded a strangely happy mood. I had done the most that could be expected of me. I had swum quite truly all I could. Exhausted but not terrified, I should swim now straight on from this life to the next. The dead would see me swimming as I entered upon the tideways of their world. I should come upon my new life, not drifting like a coward or amoeba, but swimming like a man. The thought gave comfort to me.

In life I had always loved and admired sailors above other men. Many sailors, I thought, must have passed from one life to the other in this way, upon cold bellies and with working arms and legs. I was proud and glad of the company I kept. I took a deep breath of water to sustain me, and swam on.

Of my sad, slow return to life one thing alone remains – a feeling of pain, compared to which all that I had gone through till now was only prelude.

The reason for this pain was clear. I had become caught between the elements. The sky, that had supported itself above the world for centuries, was fallen. It lay heavy upon the tossing waters of the sea. I alone among men had been trapped between the two.

Each cloud, collapsed upon the water, trailed its full weight across my chest, for I was held lying on my back. The surge and heaving of each wave forced my crushed body up, up, against the broken sky.

Clenching my teeth until they cracked, I lay waiting for the pain-storm to pass over, thinking in torment, but quite lucidly, 'This is the worst. This is the most. There can come no further pain than this.'

There could. One scorch of fire flared through me, and I sat up, shaking, crying, coughing, chattering. There were no angels by my side, but ordinary men. Their voices came to me from far away like the voices of men calling across an estuary at evening for a ferry.

'You have been drowned,' they said.

[PNW 2, 1941]

Robert Pagan

Happy Days

My Aunt Jobiska recently had the commonplace experience of being bombed out of house and home, and among the oddments salvaged from what was left of her belongings were two or three old newspapers, dating from the years 1905 to 1907. When I asked her why she had kept them, she said she couldn't for the life of her remember. Then she said that that was a very happy period of her life, and she thought perhaps that on days when she had been particularly happy she had kept the daily paper as a kind of souvenir. Turning over these relics, she chuckled reminiscently over goodness knows what un-auntlike frolics, and then, thrusting them into my hands, said, 'There! I don't care what anybody says, those *were* better days than these. Have a look for yourself. You won't find anything in them about air raids, at any rate.'

I have been having a look, and true enough, there was nothing about air raids. But the *Daily Telegraph* for November 1, 1905, had some ructions in Russia to record. The Tsar had issued a manifesto promising constitutional reforms, but the general situation remained one of undiminished gravity. 'Revolution is not only possible in Russia,' the leading article began, 'the Revolution has happened.' And it ended with a hint to Russian patriots that 'all constructive politics are based upon compromise'. There had certainly not been much compromise at Odessa the day before, where Cossacks had charged a crowd, many were killed, and 'a terrible panic spread through the whole town'.

In London there was no panic, there were no Cossacks. Owing to constructive politics based upon compromise, there was music all day at the Criterion Restaurant, where luncheon cost half a crown. Ibsen and Shakespeare and opera were to be seen and heard, and the light tripe of the period, plays with titles like *On the Love Path* and *Lady Madcap*. At Maskelyne and Devant's, where part of the magic consisted of 'animated photographs' (sandwiched among the usual turns in music halls as 'the bioscope'), Mr David Devant, in full glare of the footlights, and without aid of covers, grasped a living woman, representing a moth, who shrivelled into nothingness in less than one second. What a massacre of living women, representing moths, there must have been!

A couple of weeks later, on the 16th to be precise, there was still a 'grave situation' in Russia. From Constantinople came less obvious news: 'News has been received of the arrival of Mr Wills at Monastir, minus an ear. There are no further details.' Could anything be more tantalizing? Does history record – and if not, why not? – how Mr Wills lost his ear? The rubbish-loving British public was lending its own ear to a new comedy with music, *Mr Popple*. 'The ladies of the chorus', said a critic, 'looked "quite too lovely" in their white motor-coats'; and another observed that 'the audience shouted itself hoarse with delight at it all'. Nine months later the Russians were still at their tricks, and the English at *theirs*. A general strike had begun on a large scale in St Petersburg, and it 'showed unmistakably the temper of the people,' said the *Daily Telegraph*, while 'the story of the *Potemkin*'s aimless cruise under the red flag in the Black Sea was an excellent exemplification of the difficulties which beset successful mutiny in these days'. *Aimless* seems not quite the word, as we look back. Aimlessness was rather to be found at the Hippodrome or the London Pavilion. At the former was an 'enormous rush of 300,000 gallons of water,' garnished with 'plunging bulls, diving horses, sheep, goats, dogs, etc.' accompanied by 'torrents of real rain'. At the Pavilion a lady called La Milo, the Fin de Siècle Venus, was proving the fascination of simplicity for nearly the hundredth time – 'Nature casts the gauntlet to the Fashion Plate Girl!'

Nature casts the gauntlet, and time mooches on. Russia seems to have simmered down into compromise, but disorderly incidents, according to the *Evening Standard* of October 26, 1907, had marked a meeting in Poplar Town Hall the night before. 'A number of the militant section of the Suffragists were present, and were responsible for a scene of uproar which lasted fully three-quarters of an hour.' Those animated pictures had come to stay; at the Polytechnic they depicted 'Our Navy' and the wonderful resources of British Guiana. But the news of the day was an accident on the Metropolitan Railway at West Hampstead. There were 'appalling scenes' and a 'tremendous crash even louder than a peal of thunder'. 'Wild reports gained currency as to the number of killed and injured' – who were, in fact, few – and the leading article stated that 'this dreadful business at West Hampstead will have the effect of a positive bombshell'. (Those of us who have grown accustomed to positive bombshells would call the dreadful business at West Hampstead a negative bombshell, or mere fleabite.)

So far there was no particular clue to Aunt Jobiska's happiness, but perhaps the women's page is a clue. There are some drawings of women dressed up like a dog's dinner, and there is an account of a wedding dress, worn by a Miss Bainbridge, which is almost too good to be true. There was a pearl corsage 'showered with daisy-head motifs composed of pear-shaped pearls to give variety to the scheme'. On one side 'this lovely broderie' was caught up with a thick rope of pearls, tied in a bow and hung with heavy pearl tassels. 'Pearl-sewn bretelles' (braces to you) bordered 'the huge armholes' and the 'jupe' (skirt to you) had only one 'hint of elaboration' – 'two giant motifs of pearls finished with a pendant pearl lattice-work edged with heavy tassels, which suggest the termination of an immensely wide stole'. The train was 'carried out' – carried out, mark you, not simply *made* – 'in soft satin partially veiled with centuries-old point d'Angleterre, and lined with foamy bouillonnées of chiffon, while a tulle veil surmounted by a Russian tiara of orange blossom completes the scheme'. You are spared an account of what the bridesmaids wore, and of the ex-Miss Bainbridge's going-away gown, of which the bodice was 'showered with huge pois as large as sixpenny bits' and the skirt adorned with 'giant castellations' of satin. Suffice it to say that she left for her honeymoon under 'a huge Gainsborough hat of stretched black satin lined with velvet, and smothered under an all-enveloping panache of blue-grey ostrich plumes'.

Women like walking drapers' shops, Cossacks charging, theatres full of nonsense, music all day, railway accidents as big as revolutions, politics based on compromise – these, then, were some of the phenomena of the days when Aunt Jobiska was happy. Good luck to the old girl and her sunny memories, but the fact remains that, so far as England was concerned, the two decades preceding the war of 1914 were of an extraordinary spiritual sterility. Poets like Kipling, novelists like Wells, Bennett and Galsworthy, painting like – no, let's forget it. A fantastic efflorescence of material comfort, a vulgar extravagance, for those who could afford it, and poverty gnawing like a gaunt rat at the base of a wedding-cake: nationalism boiling up, *laissez faire* boiling over, and 'the Revolution has happened'. But had it? No, it had only just begun, and it was the very Revolution we are living through now – for everybody who has thought twice about it knows that the present war is part of a revolution. One side is fighting to upset a more or less established order, and the other side, if it has any sense, is not fighting to re-establish it. The fighting itself is a kind of re-volution, for mechanized total war is something entirely revolutionary.

Now all revolutions have their prophets, and in the days when Aunt Jobiska was happy, and the audience at *Mr Popple* was shouting itself hoarse with delight, and a battleship was cruising under the red flag in the Black Sea, the prophet of Fascism, of Hitler, of total war, had already appeared on the scene. His name was Marinetti, and even before 1914 he had become notorious as a 'futurist' poet. Futurist, indeed, and something of a buffoon, as you would expect of a man who paved the way for buffoons like Mussolini and Goering and Antonescu. Turning from my Aunt Jobiska's old newspapers, I find one from New York, dated December 3, 1940, and in it I find a report by its Rome correspondent of a lecture given the day before by this very same Marinetti, 'a member of the Italian Academy, friend of Mussolini, and inventor of the air-cooled hat'. 'I am sorry,' he said, 'that I can only speak instead of shoot, but I will give you some important moral projectiles. The aesthetic beauty of war was foretold thirty years ago by futurist poets and painters who wanted to clear away the rubbish of old ideas.' At the lecture, his poems were recited by his disciple Farfa. They included one about machine-guns, with the refrain *Tapatapatapa*, and another called *Aerosong of Petrol*, which runs, 'Thousands desire thee, O pipe-line, but to me alone thou givest thy gasoline kisses.' Another poem proclaims that 'Women do not love silent gentle little aeroplanes that do not know how to bomb.' The lecture included a proposal for the formation of a limited liability company for the exportation of Italian love. When Marinetti began to recite a poem which included imitations of the sound of falling bombs ('Zoom! Bong!') some women in the audience called out, 'We have had enough!'

An interesting thing about all this is the confusion of the ideas of loving and killing. There is nothing futuristic about that. It is an old idea that the act of love is a kind of death, and in many languages the idea of virility is associated with the soldier, whose weapon signifies not only the power to kill but power in a more general sense. So, in fact, this 'futurist' has got hold of an old, primitive idea, and in a sense he is not a revolutionary at all. He stands for savagery, death, and destruction, not for life and liberty. He is as old-fashioned as Aunt Jobiska. He dates, like a cart-wheel hat loaded with ostrich feathers. The real futurists at that lecture were the women who cried, 'We have had enough!'

[*PNW* 3, 1941]

ROSAMOND LEHMANN

WHEN THE WATERS CAME

Very long ago, during the first winter of the present war, it was still possible to preserve enough disbelief in the necessity for disaster to waver on with only a few minor additions and subtractions in the old way. The first quota of evacuated children had meant a tough problem for the local ladies; but most of them, including her own, had gone back to London. Nothing very disturbing was likely to happen for the present. One thought, of course, of sailors freezing in unimaginable wastes of water, perhaps to be plunged beneath them between one violent moment and the next; of soldiers numb in the black-and-white nights on sentry duty, crammed, fireless, uncomforted on the floors of empty barns and disused warehouses. In her soft bed, she thought of them with pity – masses of young men, betrayed, helpless, and so much colder, more uncomfortable than human beings should be. But they remained unreal, as objects of pity must remain. The war sprawled everywhere inert: like a child too big to get born it would die in the womb and be shovelled underground, disgracefully, as monsters are, and after a while, with returning health and a change of scene, we would forget that we conceived it. Lovers went on looking on the bright side, stitching cosy linings, hopeful of saving and fattening all the private promises. The persisting cold, the catastrophes of British plumbing, took precedence of the war as everybody's topic and experience. It became the political situation. Much worse for the Germans, of course. Transport had broken down, there was no coal in Berlin. They'd crack – quite likely – morale being so low already.

The climax came one morning when the wind changed, the grey sky let out rain instead of snow. Then, within an hour, the wind veered round again to the north, the rain froze as it fell. When she went into the kitchen to order the day's meals, the first of the aesthetic phenomena greeted her. The basket of vegetables had come in folded in a crust of ice. Sprouts, each crinkled knob of green brilliance cased in a clear bell, looked like tiny Victorian paperweights.

The gardener scratched his head.

'Never seen nothink like it in fifty years. Better be careful walking out 'M. There'll be some broken legs on the 'ill. It's a skating rink. I slipped up a matter of five times coming along. Young Bert's still trying to get up to the sheep at the top. He ain't done it yet.' He chuckled. 'It's a proper pantomime. The old Tabbies'll have to mind their dignities if they steps out today.'

The children ran in with handfuls of things from the garden. Every natural object had become a toy: twigs, stones, blades of grass cased in tubes of ice. They broke up the moulds, and inside were the smooth grooved prints of stems and leaves: a miracle.

Later she put on nailed shoes and walked with difficulty over the snowy field path to the post office. The wind was a steel attack; sharp knobs of ice came whirling off the elms and struck her in the face. She listened by what was once a bush of dogwood, now a primeval growth of long ice pipes that jangled and clashed together, giving out a hollow musical ring, like a ghostly xylophone.

At the post office, the customary group of villagers was gathered, discussing the portents, their slow, toneless, deprecating voices made almost lively by shocked excitement. The sheep in the top field had been found frozen to the ground. Old Mrs Luke had slipped up on her doorstep and broken her thigh. The ambulance sent to take her to hospital had gone backwards into the ditch and overturned. Pigeons were stuck dead by their claws on branches. The peacock at the farm had been brought in sheathed totally in ice: that was the most impressive item.

'I *wish* I'd seen it!'

Stiff in its crystal case, with a gemmed crest, and all the blue iridescence gleaming through: a device for the birthday of the Empress of China.

That night was the end of the world. She heard the branches in the garden snapping and crashing down with a brittle rasp. It seemed as if the inside of the earth with all its roots and foundations had become separated from the outside by an impenetrable bed of iron; so that everything that grew above the surface must inevitably break off like matchwood, crumble and fall down.

Towards dawn the wind dropped and snow began to fall again.

The thaw came in February, not gradually but with violence, overnight. Torrents of brown snow-water poured down from the hills into the valley. By the afternoon, the village street was gone, and in its stead a turbulent flood raced between the cottages. The farm was almost beleaguered: water ran through the back door, out the front door. The ducks were cruising under the apple trees in the orchard. Springs bubbled up in the banks and ditches, gushed out among roots and ivy. Wherever you looked, living waters spouted, trickled, leaped with intricate overlapping voices into the dance. Such sound and movement on every hand after so many weeks of silence and paralysis made you feel light-headed, dizzy; as if you, too, must be swept off and dissolved.

'Oh, children! We shall never see the village looking like this again.'

She stood with them at the lower garden gate, by the edge of the main stream. There was nobody in sight.

'Why not?' said John, poking with the toe of his Wellington at the fringe of drifted rubbish. 'We might see it next year. No reason why not if we get the same amount of snow.'

Where were all the other children? Gathered by parents indoors for fear of the water? The cottages looked dumb.

'It's like a village in a fairy story.'

'Is it?' said Jane, colouring deeply. 'Yes, it is.' She looked around, near and far. 'Is it safe?'

'Of course it's safe, mutt,' said her brother, wading in. 'Unless you want to lie down in the middle of it and get drowned.'

'Has anything got drowned, Mum?'

'No. The cows and horses are all safe indoor. Only all the old dead winter sticks and leaves are going away. Look at them whirling past.'

The water ran so fast and feverish, carrying winter away. The earth off the ploughed fields made a reddish stain in it, like blood, and stalks of last year's dead corn were mixed and tumbled in it. She remembered *The Golden Bough*, the legend of Adonis, from whose blood the spring should blossom; the women carrying pots of dead wheat and barley to the water, flinging them in with his images. Sowing the spring.

The children ran along the top of the bank, following the stream, pulling sticks from the hedge and setting them to sail.

'Let's race them!'

But they were lost almost at once.

'Mum, will they go to the sea?'

'Perhaps. In time.'

Jane missed her footing and slithered down into the ditch, clutching at John, pulling him after her.

'It's quite safe!' he yelled. 'It only comes half-way up her boots. Can't we wade to the cross-roads and see what happens?'

'Well, be terribly careful. It may get deep suddenly. The gravel must be washing away. Hold her hand.'

She watched them begin to wade slowly down away from her, chattering, laughing to feel the push and pull of the current at their legs.

'It's *icy*, Mum! It's lovely. Bend down and feel it.'

Moving farther away, they loosed hands and wandered in opposite directions, gathering up the piles of yellow foam-whip airily toppling and bouncing against every obstruction. She saw Jane rub her face in a great handful of it.

Oh, they're beginning to look very far away, with water all round them. It can't be dangerous, I mustn't shout. They were tiny, and separated.

'Stay together!'

She began to run along the bank, seeing what would happen; or causing it to happen. It did happen, a moment before she got there. Jane, rushing forward to seize a branch, went down. Perfectly silent, her astonished face framed in its scarlet bonnet fixed on her brother, her Wellingtons waterlogged, she started to sink, to sway and turn with the current and be carried away.

'How could you . . . John, why didn't you? . . . No, it wasn't your fault. It was mine. It wasn't anybody's fault. It's all right, Jane! What a joke! Look, I'll wrap you in my fleecy coat, like a little sheep. I'll carry you. We'll hurry home over the field. We'll be in hot baths in ten minutes. I'm wet to my knees, I've got ice stockings – and all of Jane's wet. How much of John is wet?'

'None of me, of course,' said John, pale and bitter. 'Have *I* got to have a bath?'

An adventure, not a disaster, she told herself unhopefully, stumbling and splashing up towards the garden over the ploughed field, weighed into the earth with the weight of the child, and of her ever more enormous clogged mud-shoes that almost would not move; and with the weight of her own guilt and Jane's and John's, struggling together without words in lugubrious triangular reproach and anxiety.

But by the end of the day it was all right. Disaster had vanished into the boothole with the appalling lumps of mud, into the clothes-basket with sopping bloomers and stockings, down the plug with the last of the mustard-clouded bath water. Jane lay wrapped in blankets by the nursery fire, unchilled, serene and rosy. John toasted the bread and put on his two yodelling records for a celebration. Adventure recollected in tranquillity made them all feel cheerful.

'I thought I was done for that time,' said Jane complacently.

'It'll take more than that to finish you – worse luck,' said John, without venom. 'We haven't had a moment's peace, any of us, since you were born. Tomorrow I'm going to make a raft and see how far I can get.'

'I'm afraid by tomorrow it'll all be dry land again.'

She looked out of the window and saw that the water in the fields had almost disappeared already. After countless white weeks, the landscape lay exposed again in tender greens and browns, caressing the eye, the imagination, with a promise of mysterious blessing. The air was luminous, soft as milk, blooming in the west with pigeon's breast colours. In the garden the last of the snow lay on the flower-beds in greyish wreaths and patches. The snowman stood up at the edge of the lawn, a bit crumpled but solid still, smoking his pipe.

What will the spring bring? Shall we be saved?

'But you were wrong about one thing, Mum,' said Jane, from the sofa. 'You know what you said about . . . you know.'

'About what?'

'Go *on*. Cough it up.'

'About nothing being . . . you know,' said Jane with an effort. 'Drowned.'

'Oh, dear, was I wrong?'

'Yes, you were wrong. I sor a chicking. At least, I think so.'

[*PNW* 3, 1941]

FRANK SARGESON

A GREAT DAY

It was beginning to get light when Ken knocked on the door of Fred's bach.

'Are you up?' he said.

Fred called out that he was, and in a moment he opened the door.

'Just finished my breakfast,' he said. 'We'd better get moving.'

It didn't take long. The bach was right on the edge of the beach, and they got the dinghy on to Ken's back and he carried it down the beach, and Fred followed with the gear. Ken was big enough to make light work of the dinghy, but it was all Fred could do to manage the gear. There wasn't much of him and he goddamned the gear every few yards he went.

The tide was well over half-way out, and the sea was absolutely flat without even a ripple breaking on the sand. Except for some seagulls that walked on the sand and made broad-arrow marks where they walked there wasn't a single thing moving. It was so still it wasn't natural. Except for the seagulls you'd have thought the world had died in the night.

Ken eased the dinghy off his shoulders and turned it the right way up, and Fred dropped the anchor and the oars on the sand, and heaved the sugar bag of fishing gear into the dinghy.

'I wouldn't mind if I was a big, hefty bloke like you,' he said.

Well, Ken didn't say anything to that. He sat on the stern of the dinghy and rolled himself a cigarette, and Fred got busy and fixed the oars and rowlocks and tied on the anchor.

'Come on,' he said, 'we'll shove off.' And with his trousers rolled up he went and tugged at the bow, and with Ken shoving at the stern the dinghy began to float, so Fred hopped in and took the oars, and then Ken hopped in and they were off.

'It's going to be a great day,' Fred said.

It certainly looked like it. The sun was coming up behind the island they were heading for, and there wasn't a cloud in the sky.

'We'll make for the same place as last time,' Fred said. 'You tell me if I don't keep straight.' And for a time he rowed hard without sending the dinghy along very fast. The trouble was his short legs, he couldn't get them properly braced against the stern seat. And Ken, busy rolling a supply of cigarettes, didn't watch out where he was going, so when Fred took a look ahead he was heading for the wrong end of the island.

'Hey,' he said, 'you take a turn and I'll tell you where to head for.'

So they changed places and Ken pulled wonderfully well. For a time it was more a mental shock you got with each jerk of the dinghy. You realized how strong he was. He had only a shirt and a pair of shorts on, and his big body, hard with muscle, must have been over six feet long.

'Gee, I wish I had your body,' Fred said. 'It's no wonder the girls chase you. But look at the sort of joker I am.'

Well, he wasn't much to look at. There was so little of him. And the old clothes he wore had belonged to someone considerably bigger than he was. And he had on an old hat that came down too far, and would have come down farther if it hadn't bent his ears over and sat on them as if they were brackets.

'How about a smoke?' Fred said.

'Sure! Sorry!'

And to save him from leaving off rowing Fred reached over and took the tin out of his shirt pocket.

'That's the curse of this sustenance,' Fred said. 'A man's liable to be out of smokes before pay-day.'

'Yes, I suppose he is,' Ken said.

'It's rotten being out of work,' Fred said. 'Thank the Lord I've got this dinghy. D'you know last year I made over thirty pounds out of fishing?'

'And how've you done this year?'

'Not so good. You're the first bloke I've had go out with me this year that hasn't wanted me to go shares. Gee, you're lucky to be able to go fishing for fun.'

'It's about time I landed a position,' Ken said. 'I've had over a month's holiday.'

'Yes, I know. But you've got money saved up, and it doesn't cost you anything to live when you can live with your auntie. How'd you like to live in that damn bach of mine and pay five bob a week rent? And another thing, you've got education.'

'It doesn't count for much these days. A man has to take any position he can get.'

'Yes, but if a man's been to one of those High Schools it makes him different. Not any better, mind you. I'm all for the working-class because I'm a worker myself, but an educated bloke has the advantage over a bloke like me. The girls chase him just to mention one thing, specially if he happens to be a big he-man as well.'

Ken didn't say anything to that. He just went on pulling, and he got Fred to stick a cigarette in his mouth and light it at the same time as he lit his own. And then Fred lolled back in his seat and watched him, and you could tell that about the only thing they had in common was that they both had cigarettes dangling out of their mouths.

'Pull her round a bit with your left,' Fred said. 'And there's no need to bust your boiler.'

'It's O K,' Ken said.

'You've got the strength,' Fred said.

'I'm certainly no infant.'

'What good's a man's strength anyway? Say he goes and works in an office?'

'I hadn't thought of that.'

'Another thing, he gets old. Fancy you getting old and losing your strength. Wouldn't it be a shame?'

'Sure,' Ken said. 'Why talk about it?'

'It sort of fascinates me. You'll die some day, and where'll that big frame of yours be then?'

'That's an easy one. Pushing up the daisies.'

'It might as well be now as any time, mightn't it?'

'Good Lord, I don't see that!'

'A man'd forget for good. It'd be just the same as it is out here on a day like this. Only better.'

Ken stopped rowing to throw away his cigarette.

'My God,' he said, 'you're a queer customer. Am I heading right?'

'Pull with your left,' Fred said. 'But I'll give you a spell.'

'It's O K,' Ken said.

And he went on rowing and after a bit Fred emptied the lines out of the sugar bag and began cutting up the bait. And after a bit longer when they were about half-way over to the island he said they'd gone far enough, so Ken shipped his oars and threw the anchor overboard, and they got their lines ready and began to fish.

And by that time it was certainly turning out a great day. The sun was getting hot, but there still wasn't any wind, and as the tide had just about stopped running out down the Gulf the dinghy hardly knew which way to pull on the anchor rope. They'd pulled out less than two miles from the shore, but with the sea as it was it might have been anything from none at all up to an infinite number. You couldn't hear a sound or see anything moving. It was another world. The houses on the shore didn't belong. Nor the people either.

'Wouldn't you like to stay out here for good?' Fred said.

'Ring off,' Ken said. 'I got a bite.'

'So did I, but it was only a nibble. Anyhow, it's not a good day for fish. It wants to be cloudy.'

'So I've heard.'

'I've been thinking;' Fred said, 'it's funny you never learnt to swim.'

'Oh, I don't know. Up to now I've always lived in country towns.'

'Doesn't it make you feel a bit windy?'

'On a day like this! Anyhow, you couldn't swim that distance yourself.'

'Oh, couldn't I? You'd be surprised . . . get a bite?'

'Yes, I did.'

'Same here . . . you'll be settling down here, won't you, Ken?'

'It depends if I can get a position.'

'I suppose you'll go on living with your auntie?'

'That depends, too. If I got a good position I might be thinking of getting married.'

'Gee, that'd be great, wouldn't it?'

'I got another bite,' Ken said.

'Same here. I reckon our lines are crossed.'

So they pulled in their lines and they were crossed sure enough, but Ken had hooked the smallest snapper you ever saw.

'He's no good,' Fred said. And he worked the fish off the hook and held it in his hand. 'They're pretty little chaps, aren't they?' he said. 'Look at his colours.'

'Let him go,' Ken said.

'Poor little beggar,' Fred said. 'I bet he wonders what's struck him. He's trying to get his breath. Funny, isn't it, when there's plenty of air about? It's like Douglas credit.'

'Oh, for God's sake,' Ken said.

'I bet in less than five minutes he forgets about how he was nearly suffocated,' Fred said, and he threw the fish back. And it lay bewildered for a second on the surface, then it flipped its tail and was gone. It was comical in its way and they both laughed.

'They always do that,' Fred said. 'But don't you wish you could swim like him?'

Ken didn't say anything to that, and they put fresh bait on their hooks and tried again, but there were only nibbles. They could bring nothing to the surface.

'I'll tell you what,' Fred said, 'those nibbles might be old men snapper only they won't take a decent bite at bait like this.'

And he explained that off the end of the island there was a reef where they could get plenty of big mussels. It would be just nice with the tide out as it was. The reef wouldn't be uncovered, it never was, but you could stand on it in water up to your knees and pull up the mussels. And if you cut the inside out of a big mussel you only had to hang it on your hook for an old man snapper to go for it with one big bite.

'It's a fair way,' Ken said.

'It doesn't matter,' Fred said. 'We've got oceans of time.' And he climbed past Ken to pull up the anchor, and Ken pulled in the lines, and then Fred insisted on rowing and they started for the end of the island.

And by that time the tide had begun to run in up the Gulf, and there was a light wind blowing up against the tide, so that the sea, almost without your noticing it, was showing signs of coming up a bit rough. And the queer thing was that with the movement the effect of another world was destroyed. You seemed a part of the real world of houses and people once more. Yet with the sea beginning to get choppy the land looked a long way off.

'Going back,' Ken said, 'we'll be pulling against the wind.'

'Yes,' Fred said, 'but the tide'll be a help. Anyhow, what's it matter when a man's out with a big, hefty bloke like you?'

Nor did he seem to be in too much of a hurry to get to his reef. He kept resting on his oars to roll cigarettes, and when Ken said something about it he said they had oceans of time.

'You're in no hurry to get back,' he said, 'Mary'll keep.'

Well, Ken didn't say anything to that.

'Mary's a great kid,' Fred said.

'Sure,' Ken said. 'Mary's one of the best.'

'I've known Mary for years,' Fred said.

'Yes,' Ken said. 'So I've gathered.'

'I suppose you have. Up to a while ago Mary and I used to be great cobbers.'

'I'll give you a spell,' Ken said.

But Fred said it was OK.

'Mary's got a bit of education, too,' he said. 'Only when her old man died the family was hard up so she had to go into service. It was lucky she got a good place at your auntie's. Gee, I've been round there and had tea sometimes when your auntie's been out, and, oh, boy, is the tucker any good!'

'Look here,' Ken said, 'at this rate we'll never get to that reef.'

'Oh, yes we will,' Fred said, and he pulled a bit harder. 'If only a man hadn't lost his job,' he said.

'I admit it must be tough,' Ken said.

And then Fred stood up and took a look back at the shore.

'I thought there might be somebody else coming out,' he said, 'but there isn't. So thank God for that.' And he said that he couldn't stand anybody hanging around when he was fishing. 'By the way,' he said, 'I forgot to do this before.' And he stuffed pieces of cotton-wool into his ears. 'If the spray gets in my ears it gives me the earache,' he said.

Then he really did settle down to his rowing, and with the sea more or less following them it wasn't long before they were off the end of the island.

Nobody lived on the island. There were a few holiday baches, but they were empty now that it was well on into the autumn. Nor from this end could you see any landing-places, and with the wind blowing up more and more it wasn't too pleasant to watch the sea running up the rocks. And Fred had to spend a bit of time manoeuvring around before he found his reef.

It was several hundred yards out with deep water all round, and it seemed to be quite flat. If the sea had been calm it might have been covered to a depth of about a foot with the tide as it was. But with the sea chopping across it wasn't exactly an easy matter to stand there. At one moment the water was down past your knees, and the next moment you had to steady yourself while it came up round your thighs. And it was uncanny to stand there, because with the deep water all round you seemed to have discovered a way of standing up out in the sea.

Anyhow, Fred took off his coat and rolled up his sleeves and his trousers as far as they'd go, and then he hopped out and got Ken to do the same and keep hold of the dinghy. Then he steadied himself and began dipping his hands down and pulling up mussels and throwing them back into the dinghy, and he worked at a mad pace as though he hadn't a moment to lose. It seemed only a minute or so before he was quite out of breath.

'It's tough work,' he said. 'You can see what a weak joker I am.'

'I'll give you a spell,' Ken said, 'only keep hold of the boat.'

Well, Fred held the dinghy, and by the way he was breathing and the look of his face you'd have thought he was going to die. But Ken had other matters to think about, he was steadying himself and dipping his hands down more than a yard away, and Fred managed to pull himself together and shove off the dinghy and hop in. And if you'd been sitting in the stern as he pulled away you'd have seen that he had his eyes shut. Nor did he open them except when he took a look ahead to see where he was going, and with the cotton-wool in his ears it was difficult for him to hear.

So for a long time he rowed like that against seas that were getting bigger and bigger, but about half-way back to the shore he took a spell. He changed over to the other side of the seat, so he didn't have to sit facing the island, and he just sat there keeping the dinghy straight on. Then when he felt that he had collected all his strength he stood up and capsized the dinghy. It took a bit of doing, but he did it.

And after that, taking it easy, he started on his long swim for the shore.

[*PNW 5, 1941*]

Rosamond Lehmann

For Virginia Woolf

Her biography will be written; many articles about her will go on pouring out. There are unpublished works of hers which, when published, will enlarge or re-balance the portrait of her life. Those who knew her well will speak and write of her as the woman she was in daily domestic life – a life outwardly uneventful, devoid of publicity, blessed by a few close friendships and by a love that cared for and supported her from first to last. But for those, such as myself, whose meetings with her were infrequent, she was bound to preserve intact a quality of poetic significance which colours, sharpens, perhaps distorts her figure in memory.

Everything one can say about her at this moment seems too soon or too late; and to try to tell the truth about a person so unusual and of such integrity is so important one scarcely dares to make the attempt. One fears to plant lilies: she would have disliked that. Even to write poems about her – in a sense the most suitable kind of elegy for her – seems too much like wrapping her in a lullaby and singing her to rest.

Many good poets have been prose figures, with their genius locked away in a separate compartment; but she was in herself, in her person, a perfectly poetic creature. There was no process of readjustment to go through on seeing her, no disappointment to overcome. The only surprise was to find a human being so all of a piece without and within: one who so clearly expressed her spirit in her body. She was extremely beautiful, with an austere intellectual beauty of bone and outline, with large melancholy eyes under carved lids, and the nose and lips, the long narrow cheek of a Gothic Madonna. Her voice, light, musical, with a throaty note in it, was one of her great charms. She was tall and thin, and her hands were astonishingly exquisite. She used to spread them out to the fire, and they were so transparent one fancied one saw the long fragile bones through the fine skin. She dressed like an aesthetic don. There was something about her that made one think of William Morris and the New Age and the Emancipation of Women.

Her conversation was a brilliant mixture of reminiscence, gossip, extravagantly fanciful speculation and serious critical discussion of books and pictures. She was malicious, and she liked to tease. Now and then her tongue had a corrosive edge, and one suspected that she enjoyed the embarrassment and discomfiture of a victim. She delighted to draw people out, plying them with questions, riotously embroidering upon what they told her, and generally suggesting to them a conception of themselves as leading lives of superlative interest and originality. To her friends she was the soul of sympathy and understanding.

She was very quiet, rather slow, not graceful, in her movements, economical in her gestures; yet she gave an impression of quivering nervous excitement, of a spirit balanced at a pitch of intensity impossible to sustain without collapse. One felt that she had to guard herself against the attack of humanity; that the pressure of other people upon her might at any moment become too painful and shatter her in pieces. She loved jokes, cracked them herself without decorum, and laughed at those of others. She enjoyed praise and was terribly sensitive to misunderstanding or adverse criticism; but fundamentally she had complete artistic humility and sincerity, and was never satisfied with what she had accomplished. Nobody was ever less arrogant, spoilt or vulgar.

She had her share of griefs and bore them with courage and unselfishness. It is important to say this in view of the distasteful myths which will arise – have already arisen – around her death: the conception of her as a morbid invalid, one who 'couldn't face life', and put an end to it out of hysterical self-pity. No. She lived under the shadow of the fear of madness; but her sanity was exquisite.

She never grew accustomed, she never dried up. It is impossible to imagine her ceasing to be able to make poetry out of experience. One epitaph might be that there was something better than she had ever done which she could still, even in old age, have done. There was never an end to the meanings within meanings that memories and characters and any ordinary event or spectacle contained for her. A family meal, a walk by the seashore, the crowds passing in the street, a young man returning to his college rooms at night, a woman carrying a baby, the flying arc cut by a bird's wing, a fin turning in a waste of waters – all are seen, not as objects in themselves alone, but lit in all directions by flashes of symbolic and spiritual meaning. What human beings did, their everyday material occupations and professions, the surface means by which they communicated, had for her less reality than the under side of them – their mysteriousness, their bewildering and inapprehensible destiny: 'as if time and eternity showed through skirts and waistcoats, and she saw people passing tragically to destruction'.

Although she never used a difficult or an obscurantist expression, though her dialogue is so simple as almost to seem written for a child, and the total impression is of something said or sung in a voice of piercing lucidity, the underlying structure of her novels defies a strict analysis. Visions of the passage of time run through them, visions of perpetual change and flux, of chaos cohering suddenly into a centre of order and stability, an abstract shape of peace. She was intensely aware of the spiritual reality of human beings. All we can see of them, she seems to say, is the luminous and iridescent haze surrounding the dark core. Then all at once she causes this haze to become incandescent; and there, over and over again, darkly burning within their haloes, appear Jacob, Mrs Dalloway, Mrs Ramsay, Percival, fixed in lasting moments of youth and age, of beauty and love, of happiness and pathos; focusing and embodying the continuity of life and its inscrutable meaning.

What is life? What is its meaning? Her work is a perpetual exploration with this question like a lamp held up above the theme. Unwaveringly vigilant, she bends the lamp here and there upon complexity and paradox; suggesting, so it seems, precisely this, her method, as a clue to the proper function of human consciousness: saying it is experiment and search, is a preparation for the unexpected, the unknown; a leap any day, in any place, at any age, from a pinnacle into the elements of darkness. Offering no promise of final consolation or ultimate truth revealed, still less does she imply negativity, defeat or resignation. Her voice is both austere and ecstatic; a voice that cries, always, without self-indulgence or escapism, life! – not death.

Perhaps it is impossible to attempt to build a bridge between Virginia Woolf and the 'average man'. Certainly when he asserts that normal people don't go on and on asking what is the meaning of life and shying off from any definite conclusion, that such an attitude is unwholesome, absurd, that it gets you nowhere, one can only reply: 'Yes, she was far from normal, and what she had to say helps nobody to get on in the world. She wasn't at all tough, she quite lacks the cheery commonsense point of view, and there's no plot or story in her novels.'

But there is another attack, equally truculent and self-righteous, and more dogmatic, which descends already upon her; and against criticism of this type it is a duty to protest, because it is an attack upon culture in the name of culture. In a recent number of a new publication of the Left, in the course of an article consigning to wholesale perdition or oblivion most of the better-known English writers of our time on the grounds that they have 'consistently rejected history' I read: 'Virginia Woolf, the outstanding prose writer of the English Twilight of individual subconsciousness, has accepted the judgment of history and taken the logical step.' Leaving aside the questionable taste, at such a moment, of this bland obituary, one is obliged to ask: Whose history? Is one political party alone to identify itself with history and pronounce verdicts against which there can be no appeal? Are the values of art henceforth to be rigidly geared to the development of the class war, and imaginative sensibility to be assessed exclusively in terms of 'political consciousness'? Surely the hand that so arbitrarily and complacently sweeps away 'outworn' culture in the name of 'history' bears a disquieting resemblance to the hand that reaches for its revolver at the very mention of culture. And surely, not to speak out upon this issue, for her sake, for her art's sake, and in the name of that very 'idea of change which is the beginning of revolution' – an idea to which she was as receptive and sympathetic as any poet of her generation – would indeed be the descent of the English Twilight.

It is true that there was much which she lacked, much which was outside the scope of her powers. She was not equipped for a broad grasp of humanity, she had not the kind of richness and sanity, the rooted quality which comes from living a completely fulfilled life as a woman and a mother. She had a romantic view of charwomen and prostitutes; and her conception of the governing classes, of rank, fashion, titles, society – all that – was perhaps a shade glamorous and reverential. Then, as regards her technique: she had two styles, one clear, logical and concise, an admirable instrument for her admirable critical prose; the other for her imaginative work, a poetic style, full of light flexible expanded rhythms; and this, in spite of its brilliance and beauty, has moments when it irritates, when one detects tricks, when it seems too airy, giddy almost; a trifle archly hesitant. In spite of the extraordinary loveliness of her images, there are moments when the quivering antennae of her senses seem too receptive, and almost stifle one with minute impressions. Blinds sway, brooms tap, chairs creak too frequently. Also there are moments, particularly in *The Waves*, when her sense of the duality in human consciousness – the I forever watching the I – gives one an uneasy feeling of a neurotic split in personality.

But when all this is said, to re-read *Jacob's Room*, *Mrs Dalloway*,

To The Lighthouse, *The Waves* is to recapture a vision of life of enchanting freshness, of deepening poignancy and profundity. To my mind, it is in *To The Lighthouse* that she grasped and expressed it with the greatest sweep and lyrical ecstasy, the most moving imagery. There is not one paragraph that flags or falters; and it contains more human love, grief and happiness than do any other of her books.

In another sphere, her last published work, the biography of Roger Fry, is her masterpiece. The best powers of her intellect and her emotions went to the making of it; and it is remarkable no less for its solid sense of form than for its background of an age and a way of life, and for the roundness, warmth and depth of its central portrait. Here, in this life of her friend, we see, unshadowed by hesitations and withdrawals, the firm values by which she lived: the values of art, of learning and of personal relationships.

[*PNW* 7, 1947]

Yuri Olyesha

Love

Translated from the Russian by Anthony Wolfe

Shuvalov was waiting for Lelia in the park. It was warm, midday. A lizard crept on a stone. He thought: a lizard on a stone is quite defenceless; you can see it at once. 'Mimicry,' he thought. And the thought of mimicry made him think about chameleons.

'Good morning,' said Shuvalov. But not one single chameleon appeared.

The lizard crept away.

Shuvalov was angry. He left the bench and walked quickly along the path. He was bitterly angry. He had a sudden impulse to attack someone, anyone. He stood quite still and shouted at the top of his voice:

'Oh, to hell with it all! Why should I be thinking of mimicry and chameleons. Really, they are quite useless – these thoughts.'

He crossed the grass and sat down on the stump of a tree. Insects flew all round him. The grass rustled gently. The architectural flight of the birds, of the gnats, of the winged beetles seemed curiously unreal; but he discerned the shapes they made in their flight, arches, bridges, towers, terraces – a whole city quickly changing, every second altering its shape.

'They are beginning to have power over me,' he thought. 'The sphere of my vision is becoming choked by them. I am becoming an eclectic. What is this which has power over me? I am beginning to see things which don't exist.'

Lelia did not come. He remained longer than he had intended in the garden. He went for a stroll. He became convinced of the existence of many different species of insects. A small insect climbed a blade of grass. He seized it and placed it in the palm of his hand. Suddenly its little stomach glittered brilliantly. He was still angry.

'Hell! In another half-hour I shall become a naturalist!'

The blades of grass were of many kinds; leaves, stems; he saw grasses jointed like bamboo-canes. And he was surprised at the variety of colours on the flower called the 'Grassy Shroud', and many colours of the soil seemed entirely unexpected.

'I don't want to be a naturalist,' he cried out. There was a note of an anguish in his voice. 'There is no need for me to make these fortuitous observations.'

But Lelia did not come. Already he had made some statistical deductions and drawn up a list of classifications. Already he was in a position to affirm that the majority of the trees in the park had broad leaves shaped like trefoils. He recognized the vibrations of the insects. And his vision, contrary to his desires, was filled with a number of things which had no interest for him.

But Lelia did not come. He sighed for her; he was angry. Instead of Lelia an unknown stranger appeared, a stranger in a black hat. He sat opposite Shuvalov on the green grass. His head hung down a little. On each of his knees lay a white hand. He was young, silent. Later it appeared that this singular young man was suffering from colour-blindness. They began to talk.

'I envy you,' said the young man. 'People say the leaves are green. But I have never seen a green leaf. On the other hand, I have occasionally seen blue pears.'

'You can't eat blue,' thought Shuvalov. 'If you had blue pears, you would be starving in no time.'

'But I do eat blue pears,' said the man who was colour-blind, sorrowfully.

Shuvalov shuddered.

'Tell me,' he said. 'Have you noticed, when birds fly all round you, you get an impression of a town, of imaginary lines.'

'No, I haven't noticed it,' said the man who was colour-blind.

'You mean – you see everything just as other people see it?'

'Everything, except a few colours,' he replied, turning his pale face in the direction of Shuvalov. 'Are you in love?' he asked a moment later.

'Yes,' said Shuvalov truthfully.

'Some of the colours, of course, seem a little confused. But otherwise I see everything just as other people see it,' said the man who was colour-blind, happily. Thereupon he made a patronizing gesture at Shuvalov.

'But blue pears! That's – terrible!' said Shuvalov. He was smiling.

In the distance Lelia could be seen coming towards them. Shuvalov jumped up. The man who was colour-blind raised his hat and began to move away.

'Do you play the violin?' asked Shuvalov. He was relentless.

'You can see that I don't exist. It's quite obvious,' he replied.

Shuvalov cried out in a loud voice:

'But you look exactly like a violinist!'

The man who was colour-blind was still speaking as he moved away and Shuvalov thought he heard him saying: 'You're taking a dangerous course –'

Lelia was walking quickly. He moved towards her, made a few steps towards her. The boughs, which were covered with leaves shaped like trefoils, stirred gently in the wind. Shuvalov stood in the middle of the pathway. The branches roared. She walked on, receiving an ovation from the leaves. The man who was colour-blind was thinking as he moved away to the right: 'There's windy weather coming.' He looked up at the leaves. A leaf, like all the other leaves, was stirring in the wind. He saw the blue tree swinging from side to side. Shuvalov saw a green tree; and all the time he was making preposterous theories about them. He thought: 'The trees are greeting her and she is receiving an ovation.' The man who was colour-blind was making a mistake, but Shuvalov was making a still greater mistake.

'I see what is not,' said Shuvalov.

Lelia came up to him. In one hand she held a small bag filled with apricots. The other was outstretched towards him. The whole world made a violent *volte-face*.

'Why are you making such a face?' she asked.

'I must be blind,' he replied.

Lelia took an apricot out of the bag, broke it across its tiny rump and threw the stone away. The stone fell on the grass. He watched it, fascinated. He watched it and saw that the stone which had fallen there was now a tree, a thin glittering sapling, a miraculous umbrella. Then Shuvalov turned to Lelia.

'This is absurd. I am beginning to think in images. For me the laws of nature have ceased to exist. Here, in five years' time, there will be an apricot-tree. Of course, it is quite possible, quite possible. It is something quite according to the laws of nature. But in defiance of all natural laws, I have seen the tree five years before its appointed time. Absurd! I am becoming an idealist.'

'It's because you're in love,' she replied, bleeding with apricot juice.

She sat up on the pillows, waiting for him. The bed had been moved into a corner. Over their heads golden haloes glowed. He went up to her and she embraced him. She was so young, so light, that when she was undressed, wearing only her dressing-gown, it seemed absurd to think that she could be naked. Their first embrace was tempestuous. The childhood locket leapt from her breast and caught in her hair: like a golden almond. Shuvalov bent his head towards her slowly, while she sank down into the pillows, as though she was dying.

The lamp was burning.

'I'll blow it out,' she said.

Shuvalov lay under the wall. The corner of the room drew near. Shuvalov traced the pattern of the wall-paper, with his fingers. He thought: 'That part of the pattern of the wall-paper, that part of the wall under which he was sleeping, led a double existence — by day no one would notice it, it was too ordinary, a number of haloes; but at night it led an altogether different existence, one which one could know only five minutes before falling asleep. If you watched closely, you would see the pattern suddenly growing, becoming more detailed, continually changing.' On the verge of falling asleep, when he was almost living among sensations which came from his childhood, he refused to cry out against the changes taking place among familiar shapes bound together according to definite laws; and there was all the more reason for his refusal because these movements stirred him to the quick and instead of the old curls and flourishes, he saw live goats and kitchen-maids.

'And there's the key of your violin,' said Lelia, throwing her arms round him.

'And there's the chameleon,' he whispered as he fell asleep.

He woke up early in the morning. Too early. He woke up and looked from side to side and screamed. A powerful note of music issued from his throat. After that night the transformation which had taken place in the world when first they had come to know each other became complete. He awoke into a new world. The brilliant morning-light filled the room. He saw the window-sill and on the window-sill he saw a flowerpot filled with many coloured flowers. Lelia was still asleep, her back turned towards him. She lay curled up, her back arched, and through her skin he could pick out the lines of her spine, the thin bamboo-cane. 'A fishing-rod,' he thought. 'Or a bamboo-cane.' In this new world everything moved him deeply and everything was absurd. Voices flew through the open window. Men in the street below remarked on the bowl of flowers which stood in her window.

He got up, dressed, with difficulty held himself to the earth. Gravitation no longer had any existence for him. He did not yet understand the laws of this new world and therefore he behaved carefully, cautiously, afraid that the least careless movement on his part would precipitate a clap of thunder. He felt that it was dangerous even to think, even to touch anything. Had he developed during the night the faculty of being able to materialize his dreams? He had every reason to imagine that he had. For example, buttons fastened themselves. For example, the moment he decided to moisten his hairbrush – he wanted to plaster his hair – he heard the sound of water dripping. He looked round. Against the wall, where the sun was shining, a bundle of Lelia's clothes were burning like a fire-balloon.

'Here I am!' said the voice of the tap out of the pile of clothes.

Under the pile of clothes he found the sink and the tap. A piece of pink soap lay quite close to them. Then Shuvalov began to be afraid of thinking of anything terrible. 'Into the room came a tiger.' He was prepared to fight against this desire of his: but all he could do was to turn away from his thought. Once, in a terrible fear, he looked towards the door. Something did materialize, but his thought was not complete enough and the materialization was only approximate, not at all perfect. Through the window flew a wasp, strippled, bloodthirsty.

'Lelia! The tiger!' he screamed.

Lelia woke up. The wasp hung suspended over a plate. It was droning like a gyroscope. Lelia jumped out of bed: the wasp flew at her. She brushed it aside and soon both the wasp and the trinket were flying all round her. Shuvalov killed the trinket with the palm of his hand. Then they started to massacre the wasp. Lelia covered it with her straw hat.

Shuvalov left her. They bade farewell to each other in a draught which seemed curiously real and loud-voiced for the world they were living in. The draught opened a door downstairs. It sang like a washerwoman. It wrapped itself round the flowers in the window-sill, lifted Lelia's straw hat, let free the wasp, hurled it among the lettuce. It made her hair stand on end. It whistled.

It lifted her dressing-gown above her head.

They said farewell to each other and Shuvalov rushed down the stairs so happily that he could not feel the stairs and even when he reached the door he did not notice the doorstep and even when he reached the porch he did not feel the steps leading down into the road. And it was there, in the roadway, that he discovered that it was not a mirage and that it was all so real that his legs were hanging suspended in the air and he was flying.

'To fly on the wings of love,' they were saying, as he passed an open window.

He shot up while his shirt revolved like a crinoline, a fever on his lips, flying in the air, snapping his fingers at everyone.

At two o'clock he went to the park. Tired out with joy and love for Lelia he fell asleep on a green bench. He slept; and sweat from the sun seethed from his face. He slept; and his collarbone protruded from his unbuttoned shirt.

Slowly, along the road, his hands behind his back, as demure as a Roman Catholic priest, wearing clothes which at once suggested a *soutane*, in a black hat and powerful blue spectacles, stooping, his head perched high above his body, came the stranger.

He came to the bench and sat opposite Shuvalov.

'I am Isaac Newton,' said the stranger as he removed his hat. Through his spectacles the world seemed blue, photographical.

'Good morning,' said Shuvalov.

The venerable scientist sat straight up, alert, on pins and needles. He listened intently, his ears jerked, one of the fingers of his left hand waved in the air, accurately following the music of an invisible choir which was ready to burst into song at a sign from his fingers. Everything in nature seemed to be holding its breath. Stealthily, Shuvalov hid himself behind the bench. Once the gravel under his heels screamed out aloud. The famous scientist was listening to the deep silence of nature. Far in the distance above a cluster of green, like an eclipse of the sun, a star appeared. It grew cold.

'Over there!' shouted Newton. 'Can you hear it?'

Without looking towards him, Newton stretched out his hand and drew Shuvalov towards him, raising his body and pulling him away from his hiding-place. They moved across the grass. As Newton's huge boots tripped gently across the grass, they left a white trace. In front of them, often looking over its shoulder, ran a lizard. They passed through a thicket while swan's down and ladybirds decorated the iron rim of his spectacles. A clearing opened to their gaze. Shuvalov recognized the sapling he had seen the day before.

'An apricot tree?' he asked.

'No,' replied the scientist in a tone of exasperation. 'An apple-tree.'

The pattern of the tree, the close-cropped outline of the branches, light and fragile like a fire-balloon, stood there with a sparse covering of leaves. Nothing stirred, everywhere there was silence.

'Well,' said the scientist, bending his body backwards. Through bending back too much, his voice rose to a shout. He held an apple in his hands. 'What do you think it means?' he asked.

It was obvious that he did not often bend his back like that. Stiffening his body, he shook himself several times, easing his spine,

the old bamboo-cane of his spine. An apple which he held in three
fingers remained perfectly still.

'What does it all mean?' he asked. The sound of his words mingled
with a sigh. 'Why did the apple fall down? Tell me that.'

Like William Tell Shuvalov regarded the apple.

He murmured: 'The laws of gravitation.'

After a short pause the venerable scientist turned to him again:

'Young man, they tell me you made a flight today.' His eyebrows
flew up above his glasses.

'You're a young Marxist, aren't you, and today you made a flight?'

A ladybird crept from his finger on to the apple. His eyes narrowed.
In his eyes the ladybird was a dazzling blue. He made a wry face. The
ladybird jumped off the highest point of the apple and flew away,
spreading wings which she had drawn from some place behind her
body, just as a man draws his handkerchief from the swallow-tail of
his morning coat.

'So you went for a flight today?'

Shuvalov was silent.

'Swine!' said Isaac Newton.

Shuvalov woke up.

'You swine!' said Lelia who was standing near. 'You little swine!
What do you mean by going to sleep while you are waiting for me?'

She flicked the ladybird off his forehead, smiling gently as she
thought that the belly of the insect was like iron.

'Hell!' he shouted. 'I hate you! Once I thought of it as a ladybird and
I knew nothing else about it, except that it was a ladybird. I might even
have come to the conclusion that its name was somehow anti-
religious. Since the day we first met, something has happened to my
eyes. I see blue pears and fly-agaric the colour of a ladybird.'

She wanted to embrace him.

'Leave me alone! Leave me alone!' he shouted. 'I'm tired of you! I'm
ashamed!'

And still crying out, he ran away: he was like a stag. Laughing and
with wild leaps he ran, trying to escape from his own shadow, his eyes
squinting. When he was out of breath he stopped short. Lelia
vanished. He decided to forget everything. The world which he had
lost had to be restored again.

'Good-bye,' he whispered. 'We shall never see each other again.'

He sat down at last on a slope, on a tuft of earth; from there he could
see far in the distance, a wide view studded with little country villas.
He sat on the tip of a prism, his legs dangling down the sides. Below

him spun the sunshade of an ice-cream merchant and all the trappings of the ice-cream merchant at that moment seemed to suggest a negro village.

'I am living in Paradise,' said the young Marxist softly.

'Are you really a Marxist?' said the voice at his side.

It was the young man in the black hat, his friend, the man who was colour-blind. He sat quite close to Shuvalov.

'Yes – I am a Marxist,' said Shuvalov.

'Then you can't possibly live in Paradise,' said the man.

He was playing with a twig. Shuvalov sighed.

'What am I to do? The world has turned into a Paradise,' he sighed.

The man who was colour-blind whistled. He was scratching his ear with the twig.

'Do you know,' Shuvalov continued, whimpering. 'Do you know what I have been doing? Well, today I flew.'

Obliquely, like the lines of a postmark, a kite appeared in the sky.

'Do you want me to show you. I'll fly over there if you like.' (He pointed with his hand.)

'Thank you, no. I have no intention of watching you reduced to infamy.'

'Yes, it *is* terrible,' said Shuvalov in a soft voice. 'I know exactly how terrible it is.' Then he continued: 'You know how much I envy you?'

'No.'

'I can easily tell you. Your world, except for a few colours, is correctly defined. But you never live in Paradise. The world does not escape from *you*. Everything is in its accustomed place. And what about me? You think I am just a healthy materialist. But sometimes my eyes see suddenly illegal, unscientific deformations in things.'

'Terrible,' said the man who was colour-blind. 'But then, it is because you are in love.'

With unexpected warmth Shuvalov seized the stranger by the hand.

'Listen,' he shouted. 'Yes, that's true. I agree with you! Give me your rainbow-coloured world and take away from me my love.'

The man who was colour-blind slipped down the slope.

'I'm sorry,' he said. 'I'm in a terrible hurry. Good-bye. Live in Paradise.'

He moved with difficulty down the slope. As he fell, his legs wide apart, he lost his resemblance to men and assumed a resemblance to a man's reflection in water. At last he reached level ground. He moved away, joyful. He threw the twig away and blew a kiss to Shuvalov. Then he shouted: 'My kind regards to Paradise!'

*

But Lelia was asleep. An hour after he had met the man who was colour-blind Shuvalov went in search for her, into the depths, into the heart of the park. He was not a naturalist and he could no longer distinguish among the things which surrounded him, hazel-nut, hawthorn, elderberry, eglantine. On all sides branches, shrubbery, pressed upon him and he walked like a tramp, weighed down and dispirited as he sought to make a pathway through the timid interlacing of the branches – and they became still more entangled towards the centre. He brought a basket with him, and filled it with leaves, petals, thorns, berries, birds.

Lelia lay on her back in her red dressing-gown, her breast uncovered. She was asleep. He heard the gentle crackling of the film in her nose. He lay by her side.

Then he placed his head on her breast and with his fingers felt the calico of the cloth and his head lay on her clammy breast and he saw the nipple, rose-tinted, with soft wrinkles, like the wrinkles on the scum over milk. He heard neither the rustle of her dress nor her groans nor the sound of her movements.

The man who was colour-blind leapt from the shrubbery on to the transom. But he fell down again.

'Listen,' said the man who was colour-blind.

Shuvalov lifted his head from her sweet face.

'Don't come near me, you little fool!' said Shuvalov.

'Listen, Shuvalov. Oh, I agree with you now. Take away from me my rainbow-coloured world and give me your love instead!'

'Go and eat blue pears,' said Shuvalov.

[*PNW* 9, 1941]

WILLIAM SANSOM

THROUGH THE QUINQUINA GLASS

Although we shared the same table, Jean sat in the shade whereas I was able to enjoy the sunlight. Between us the crenellated shadow of the café awning drew a sharp division across the table. Cigarette tips burned like white gold in the light and in the shade the siphons made from blue glass glinted evilly.

Over on the quai a sailor in a striped sweater trundelled a barrel of oil through the hot sunlight. Three curiously tall boys played a game of bowls with some small wooden balls. In the very middle of the road a lean honey-coloured dog with degenerate pale blue eyes stretched itself lazily for the flies. An old woman sat knitting beneath a dusty plane tree. This was the only life on an empty stage. From the campanile back in the town came the slow tolling of a funeral bell. It was three o'clock, the hour for siesta, and no time for men to be abroad. And yet . . . here was a man in a severe black coat just arrived and taking his place in the long row of empty café tables! The man was a stranger to us. We watched him lazily. He looked like an office worker from the town, an advocate perhaps.

Jean was saying, 'Damn that waiter! Why must he bring me quinquina instead of pastis? Why must he be insolent into the bargain?'

'Because he's a man,' I said. 'Because he has a private life beneath his dicky. Because his wife may be delivering and he just can't stand being a waiter this afternoon. How can you know the facts?'

Jean mumbled, 'Nevertheless he's a waiter – and on duty.'

'But I can't agree. You are influenced in advance by the dicky. You deny the man. If you had seen the man first, you would deny the waiter. We see a man cleaning a car – and we say to ourselves, "There is a man cleaning a car." But perhaps that man is really wondering whether he should propose marriage to his girl. That, of course, is of more moment than cleaning a car. So what we are seeing is in truth a man wondering about a proposal – not a man cleaning a car. We should be more humble in our judgements: we should say, at the most, "There is a man."'

I raised my glass and drank the quinquina. Then, holding the glass to the light, I looked through it. In that café, they serve quinquina in green glasses. Framed in the green glass I found the stranger who had recently arrived.

'Take our new arrival,' I said. 'There he sits, a man. By some accident of taste, he chooses to wear a black coat. Let us reconstruct his story. He is not only a man in a black coat. His name, let us say, is . . . Aristide Fougeres. He is forty years old, he is an advocate in this small Corsican town, he discovered six months ago that his wife had deceived him. Let us see what might be the story of Aristide.'

Through the quinquina glass the scene was sunless. The life had left it. It had taken on the quality of a picture in oils when the pigments have faded with age. Or it seemed that a mysterious storm had drifted from nowhere, that sudden clouds shrouded our world with gloom. I lowered the glass. I was just beginning to speak when I realized that something was wrong. Something unearthly had happened. I had lowered the glass – yet the scene retained its lurid quality. There was no sun – yet the green gloom persisted. The air was leaden. I could not believe it. I knew there was no real storm. The fact was simply that the quinquina glass had left its imprint on the world. I refused to admit this. I imagined it to be a momentary hallucination. So that I went on talking – consciously avoiding my fearful impression.

'Well, this M. Fougeres discovered that his wife had spent the night with a commercial traveller from Auxerres. Let us return through six months to that occasion. The circumstances of the discovery are unimportant. Perhaps it was a letter, a word from an unkind neighbour, or a sock found at the bottom of his bed. However it went, the evidence was confirmed. What is more important is the action taken by M. Fougeres on his discovery. For he neither sought out the man, nor accused his wife. M. Fougeres remained silent upon the matter. He contained his misery within himself, never breathing a word upon the matter to a living soul.

'The shock of the discovery affected M. Fougeres in two ways. First, his vanity was wounded. Secondly, he found himself in possession of a secret which he soon discovered he was using as a weapon. Mme Fougeres was a woman whose forceful character dominated husband and household. Now M. Fougeres found that he held a trump card with which he could annihilate his wife's ascendant at any moment of his choosing. On the production of such an accusation her composure would crumble, a sense of guilt would sweep the certainty from her eyes, her voice would tremble with a refreshing note of appeal. Thus he felt a sudden secret sensation of power. Yet this was not the only effect the discovery had on M. Fougeres.'

(This story was coming to my lips with a peculiar fluency. Ordinarily I would have hesitated. I would have paused before the choice of alternatives to the story. Now, it was as if I repeated a story already known to me. I would not say that I felt actually *impelled* to speak. But I was curiously *sure* of my words. The dull light of the quinquina glass alone illumined the scene. The air was breathless.)

'They lived in a narrow house just off the market square. M. Fougeres occupied the ground floor with his offices, while the two upper floors served as dwelling quarters. M. Fougeres had managed to maintain the privacy of his own personal office. This was his holy of holies upon the door of which even Madame must knock and await his leisured "*Entrez*". In this room stood the big desk. It was a heavy mahogany piece with a sturdy roll-top that could drop a reassuring curtain over his private affairs. One day, two weeks after the discovery, M. Fougeres cleared out one-half of this desk. All the old papers he crammed away into a strong box – and there lay eight empty pigeonholes and three clean drawers! This clearance was to be part of a new system. Its purpose was to house evidence of the guilt of Madame and the collection of evidence relating to any future misdemeanour. For M. Fougeres had decided to employ a detective.

'M. Fougeres wanted more information for a variety of reasons. I have said that his vanity had suffered. In addition to this, the memory of his courting days had been sullied. He had not treasured his wife's body for some years now. She was still a handsome woman, but the perfection he himself had once known was fading. Yet he still treasured the memory of her young loveliness. And for this he felt a fierce jealousy. This memory lived somewhere within the frame of his wife in her present form. That another man should know intimately even the ghost of his young love brought a thrill of horror to the stomach. At night in bed, in the privacy of darkness, with his wife asleep and unseeing beside him, he would torment himself with deliberate images of the commercial traveller's caresses. The torture was voluntary, and it was he who exerted every imaginative effort to devise new and ingenious refinements. His first, and understandable, sense of injury changed to a deliberate masochistic delight. And that was why M. Fougeres had commissioned a detective. He told himself that he must be sure that her infidelity had been no more than a passing "one night" *affaire*. He deprecated that this was "wishful thinking": yet excused himself on these same grounds. Actually, it was "wishful thinking" – of another sort. Perversely, he really wished to discover a new infidelity. He did not yet admit this to himself. But soon he realized that he was *disappointed* when the detective brought him no news of an incriminating nature.

'As the weeks went by, he developed new and exciting methods of detection. First, he took great trouble to obtain a duplicate key to his wife's bureau. There he found and read her private letters. From these he gleaned nothing – except for one short note from the commercial traveller himself. This referred to the first and so far the sole visit. M. Fougeres removed this letter to his own desk. He read it many times. It rested in the pigeonhole devoted to the personal details of the commercial traveller himself, alongside a photograph of that gentleman. With these trophies M. Fougeres would amuse himself for hours on end. He would choose an hour when there could be no fear of disturbance. Nevertheless he would lock the door behind him with precise care. As he walked from the door to the desk, he would experience a delightful sense of anticipation. He was like a child who stores up a secret moment for the inspection of some very special treasure – a bird's nest, a hidden cupboard in a doll's house, the hour when the candle is snuffed and the nursery fire flickers strangely on the ceiling, the hour reserved for delicious speculation on fine times to come.

'M. Fougeres would unroll his desk and spend some time selecting his first subject. Then he would sit for perhaps two hours, sometimes reading a detective's report, sometimes studying the photograph, sometimes the letter. He would invent new interconnections, new possibilities. At times his temples would throb with the hot blood of indignation, at times he would sink into an apathy of self-pity. There were occasions when he granted himself the luxury of striding the length of his office – right on the point of a stern decision to go and "have it out" with the commercial traveller. Again, he would engineer periods of "clear thinking", when his was the generous, logical mind that could honestly admit a sympathy with the commercial traveller; after all, they were surely men of similar taste? And then he would dream of the day when he would reveal his knowledge to his wife. But most of all he would sit and wonder at the absolute irrevocability of what had been done. Nothing could undo this terrible wrong. And the tears would well in his eyes as he exaggerated the importance of the injury done to him. Each one of these different sensations was a lasting pleasure. And to refine his torment still further, M. Fougeres would constantly accuse himself for his whole attitude over the matter.

Normally he was a balanced man. Up to this point he realized that he, too, was committing an underhand action. Two wrongs do not make a right. In deceiving the deceiver, he was acting in a mean and ungenerous manner. M. Fougeres accused himself.

'Added to these pleasures was a more elementary thrill. It was the thrill of adventure. He took risks, he gambled at "Not being found out". When, for instance, he would quickly run through his wife's bag while she was in the very next room, while he could actually hear the rustle of her skirts! How quickly his fingers worked on such occasions! How alert was his brain!

'But as the weeks passed into months, such little perverted pleasures developed into a dangerous mania. This happened because no new evidence of infidelity presented itself. M. Fougeres sensed that the importance of the matter was fading. Perhaps the moment for taking some dramatic advantage of his secret had slipped by. Time dulls the finer edges of resentment. Gradually he could only think of the episode in minuscule – much as though he regarded some grand object through the wrong end of a telescope. As its importance eluded him, so he redoubled his efforts to discover something new.

'On returning from any period of absence – even an afternoon's business in some neighbouring town – he would examine immediately and in detail every ash-tray in the house. Perhaps one day he would find a cigar stub, the end of an unfamiliar brand of cigarette! He took great care to smell the cushions and the curtains for the aroma of a strange pomade or the stale breath of tobacco. He interrupted for a period his usual custom of shaving in the wash-basin: he endured the discomfort of shaving over the bath, some yards from his mirror, because he wished to leave the wash-basin plughole free from the trace of his own shaved whiskers. Thus, returning from some overnight absence he would make his way immediately to the bathroom, lock the door, and scrape out the film of soap and dirt that clung to the dark sides of the hole. He would spread this film over a shaving paper and inspect it thoroughly. One day he might discover a bristle shaved off by his own razor! His own razor callously lent by his wife to her visitor of the night!

'The mania developed and M. Fougeres endured greater discomforts, went to greater lengths to achieve his object. He would arrange fake visits to fictitious friends in the country. During these periods he would watch for hours outside the house, sitting in the darkness of a workman's café or pressed self-consciously into the shade of a small alley. Then he would have to sleep at an hotel in the town. The money he spent! And the valuable hours of business wasted! For sometimes, having previously arranged to be absent for the night, he would interrupt negotiations in a distant town to catch the last bus home so that he might appear unexpectedly. On these occasions, his excitement rose to great heights. For on his entrance, he would imagine that the man might still be secreted somewhere in the house. He delighted to scrutinize his wife's face for a revealing embarrassment. He loved to search every room and every closet, watching her during these operations and at the same time making subtle excuses that he was looking for this thing or that thing. Sometimes he would make some casual reference to a fictitious acquaintance bearing the same name as the commercial traveller. Once, even, he hinted that he had run into the fellow on a fictitious visit to Auxerres. On this occasion his wife's eyes had brightened and she had looked away. So she still remembered! In addition he would engineer long conversations with his wife on the subject of infidelity.

'Some two months ago M. Fougeres tried another tack. In a moment of delirious misery he visited a brothel. He parted the bead curtains of a brothel and accompanied a girl up the stairs. Every night for a week he continued to visit this place. His pleasure was vicarious. He bathed in the squalor of this medical experience. He delighted in the clinical efficiency of the beds and the bathrooms. He prolonged the money bargain, enjoying its indignity. He always chose the ugliest and oldest woman in the house.

'But these visits were soon to cease. In the first place, they had been a gesture and became tedious on reiteration. In the second place, Fougeres became terrified that his wife would by chance find him out—and in her turn remain silent. Thus she would again be in the ascendant. So M. Fougeres cast around for some other plan. And he found one. It was the finest plan of all. He hit upon it only last week. It was so ingenious that he shuddered to imagine that perhaps it might never have entered his mind. Perhaps he would have died without thinking of it! It was so simple a plan as to be elusive: it was so far-reaching a plan that it might never have occurred to him. It was this. It was that he should go to Auxerres, meet the commercial traveller, and make of him a bosom friend. In this way he would always have the man near him — a far more satisfactory instrument of torture than a photograph. And, in a certain sense, the situation would make up a deficiency in his wife's guilt. For his wife's liaison of one night might have been but a passionate lapse, duly regretted, which a generous husband might even forgive. But now, in a roundabout way, she would have deceived him with his best friend. Oh, the injustice of it! And, to make matters worse, she might even be tempted to offer herself to this man again!

'Well . . . M. Fougeres has just returned from Auxerres. After four days of inquiries at the hotels – and later at the Town Hall – he has discovered that the commercial traveller has died from a tubercular kidney five months before. So that all this time he has been jealous of a dead man! Death can turn the tables completely on life. Dead men tell no tales, dead men feel no pride in the past possession of women. In a sense, his wife is a widow – and in some artificial manner suddenly rendered blameless. M. Fougeres has just left the station. He is sitting down to a glass of coffee. Dressed in his fusty black coat, he sits there bereft in a moment of his exclusive interest in life – his secret. Now just what is M. Fougeres to do?'

I paused. I did not quite know how to finish the story.

Just then the sunlight snapped on. The green of the quinquina glass vanished as queerly as it had arrived. Suddenly the air was fresh.

At that identical moment, the man in the black coat rose from his chair. He stood for a few seconds staring at the ground just in front of his table. Then he raised his hand quickly to his ear. A shot rang out. I saw the black revolver fall from his hand before he himself toppled stupidly over the table, off the table, and down on to the ground.

[*PNW 14*, 1942]

JEAN-PAUL SARTRE

THE ROOM

Translated from the French by John Rodker

There was a piece of Turkish Delight in Madame Darbédat's fingers. Carefully she bore it to her lips, holding her breath lest she should scatter the fine dust with which it was coated. 'It's a pink one,' she thought. Suddenly she bit into the glassy flesh, and a perfume of stagnation filled her mouth. 'It's odd how being ill intensifies one's sensations.' And she began to think of mosques, obsequious Orientals (she had spent her honeymoon in Algiers), and a faint smile parted her pale lips. There was something obsequious about Turkish Delight.

Yet, in spite of her care, she had to rub her palm over the pages of her book, because the fine powder now sprinkled them, the tiny specks rolling, gritting and sliding over the smooth paper as she rubbed them with her hands. 'They remind me of Arcachon, reading on the beach.' It was there she had spent the summer in 1907. In those days she wore a large straw hat trimmed with green ribbon. She used to ensconce herself near the pier with a novel by Gyp or Colette Yver. The wind sent cascades of sand showering over her knees, and now and again she would shake her book as she held it by the corners. It was the very same feeling, but the grains of sand had been dry, whereas these specks of sugar stuck slightly to her fingers. Again she saw a strip of pearly sky over a dark sea. 'Eve hadn't been born then.' She felt heavy with memories, precious as a sandal-wood box. Suddenly, she remembered the name of the book she had been reading. *The Little Madam* it was called: it was a bit boring really! Now since this nameless illness had kept her to her room, Madame Darbédat preferred Memoirs or books on history. She hoped that her suffering, serious reading, an unremitting attention to her loveliest memories, plus those sensations from which she derived the acutest pleasure, would make her ripen like some fine hot-house fruit.

Then, somewhat irritably, she thought that her husband would soon knock at the door. On other days of the week, he only appeared towards night, silently kissed her brow and sat in the arm-chair reading *Le Temps*. But Thursday was his 'day': when he spent an hour at his daughter's, usually from three to four. Before he left he looked in on his wife, and they would talk bitterly of their son-in-law. These Thursday talks, predictable to their minutest details, wore her out. The quiet room became filled with his presence. He never sat down, stalked to and fro, swung suddenly round. Every outburst pierced her like a glass splinter. This Thursday, it was worse than usual: the thought that she would soon have to recount what Eve had confessed to her, see his large terrifying body bound in fury, made her break out in a sweat. She took a lump of Turkish Delight from the saucer, gazed at it dubiously for a moment, then sadly laid it aside: she did not like her husband to see her eating Turkish Delight.

She started when the knock came, and in a weak voice said, 'Come in.'

M. Darbédat walked in on tip-toe.

'I'm going to see Eve,' he said, as he did every Thursday.

Mme Darbédat smiled at him.

'Kiss her for me.'

M. Darbédat did not reply, and an anxious wrinkle lined his brow. Every Thursday at about this time, the same deep-seated irritation seemed to add to the weight inside his stomach.

'I'll drop in on Franchot after I've seen her. I'd like him to have a serious talk with her; do his best to convince her.'

He frequently visited Dr Franchot. But vainly. Mme Darbédat raised her brows. In the past, when she had been well, she had quite liked shrugging her shoulders. But since this illness had thickened her body, such gestures, which would have tired her too much, were now replaced by facial expressions, and she would say 'Yes' with her eyes or the corners of her lips: now she raised her brows instead of her shoulders.

'It ought to be possible to remove him by force.'

'I've already told you that it's impossible. Besides, the law's such a muddle. Franchot was telling me the other day that they've incredible bothers with the families: people who can't make their minds up: who insist on keeping their sick ones at home. The doctors have their hands tied. They can give their advice, but that's all. He'd have to get into some trouble in public, or else she herself would have to apply to have him shut up.'

'And that,' said Mme Darbédat, 'isn't happening tomorrow.'

'No.'

Turning to the mirror, he began combing his beard through his fingers. There was no affection in the glance that rested on the powerful red neck of her husband.

'If she goes on,' said M. Darbédat, 'she'll get crazier than he is; it's horribly unhealthy. She won't let him out of her sight for a moment, she never goes anywhere except to see you, nobody visits them. The air in their room is simply unbreathable. She never opens the window because Pierre won't have it. As if a sick man ought to be asked! They must burn incense, I imagine; some sort of filth in an incense burner: it's like being in church. 'Pon my honour, I sometimes wonder . . . there's such an expression at times in her eyes . . .'

'I haven't noticed,' said Mme Darbédat, 'she seems all right to me. She looks depressed, naturally . . .'

'She looks half dead to me. Is she sleeping? Eating? You can't ask her a thing. But with a chap like Pierre there all the time, I don't suppose she sleeps a wink.' He shrugged his shoulders. 'But what seems so incredible to me, is that we, her parents, haven't the right to protect her from herself. Not to mention that Pierre would be better off at Franchot's. There's a huge garden. Besides, it seems to me,' he added, smiling slightly, 'that he'd get on better with his own sort. Those sort of people are like kids, they ought to be kept together, like freemasons, as you might say. That's where he should have gone from the beginning, and in my opinion, for his own sake. For his own sake, absolutely!'

And after a moment he added: 'Yes, I must say I don't like the idea of her being alone with him, especially at night. I'm always fancying something will happen. He looks so horribly sly.'

'I don't know,' said Mme Darbédat, 'if you're justified in feeling so upset, seeing that he's always looked so. He always seemed to be poking fun at us all. Poor fellow,' she went on, sighing, 'to have been as proud as he was, and to have come to this. He thought he was cleverer than us all. He had a way of saying "You're right," that shut one up immediately . . . It's a blessing for him he can't see the state he's in . . .'

Sourly, she remembered that long sarcastic face of his, the head always a little bent to one side. In the early days of Eve's marriage, Mme Darbédat would have asked nothing better than to be friendly with him. But he had discouraged her efforts, hardly spoke, and always agreed in a hurry with a distant look in his eyes.

M. Darbédat went on with his thoughts.

'Franchot showed me over his place,' he said. 'It's magnificent. The patients have separate rooms, each with a leather arm-chair, if you please, and divan beds. There's a tennis court, you know, and they're going to make a swimming pool.'

He had planted himself in front of the window, and gazed through the panes, as he swayed slightly on braced legs. Suddenly, he pirouetted on his heels, with his shoulders hunched and his hands in his pockets as though ready to spring. Mme Darbédat felt she was going to break out in a sweat. It was always the same: now he would begin stalking to and fro like a caged bear, his shoes creaking at every step.

'My dear,' she said, 'I implore you, sit down: you wear me out.' And hesitatingly, she added, 'I've something serious to say to you.'

M. Darbédat sat down in the arm-chair, and placed his hands on his knees: a slight shudder ran down Mme Darbédat's spine: the moment had come, she would have to say it.

'You know,' she said, with an embarrassed cough, 'that Tuesday I saw Eve.'

'Yes?'

'We gossiped about all sorts of things, she was very sweet: it must be ages since she was so open with me. Well, I began asking her this and that, made her talk about Pierre. And do you know,' she added, with fresh embarrassment, 'I discovered that he meant *everything* to her.'

'Well, don't I damn well know it!' said M. Darbédat.

Really, he was beginning to exasperate her a little. One always had to explain everything so carefully to him, dot all the *i*'s. Mme Darbédat dreamt of a life spent among subtle, sensitive beings, who would have understood her at a nod.

'But I mean,' she went on, 'in another way than the one we imagine.'

M. Darbédat's eyes rolled in his head with anxiety and fury, as always whenever he could not grasp some reference or bit of news.

'What do you mean by that?'

'Charles,' said Mme Darbédat, 'don't wear me out. You ought to know that a mother may find it painful to say certain things.'

'I don't understand a blessed word of all you're saying,' said M. Darbédat angrily. 'Still, you don't mean to say . . .'

'Well, yes! I do!' she said.

'They still . . . even now?'

'Yes, yes, yes!' she answered irritably, with three short, sharp nods.

M. Darbédat spread wide his arms, lowered his head, and said nothing.

'Charles,' she said, disquieted, 'I shouldn't have told you. But I couldn't keep silent about a thing like that.'

'Our child . . .' he said slowly, 'with that madman? He doesn't even recognize her any more, he calls her Agatha. She must have lost all sense of pride.' He raised his head and looked sternly at his wife.

'You're sure you've got it right?'

'I couldn't have made a mistake. I was like you,' she added quickly. 'I could hardly believe my ears: still I don't understand what she can be about. Why, the very idea of being touched by that poor wretch . . . well,' she sighed, 'I suppose that's how he's got his hold over her . . .'

'Alas!' said M. Darbédat. 'You remember what I told you when he came to ask for her hand? I said then, "I believe he's too pleasing to Eve," but you wouldn't believe me.'

Suddenly he struck the table with his hand and flushed purple.

'It's pure perversion, that's what it is. He hugs her and kisses her and calls her Agatha, while he trots out all his tomfoolery about flying statues, and God knows what all else! And she puts up with it. But what keeps them together like this? She might be as sorry for him as she likes, or have him sent to a home where she could visit him every day: that would be all right. But I could never have imagined . . . I thought of her as a widow . . . Listen, Jeannette,' he said gravely, 'I'm going to talk frankly to you. Well, if she needs that sort of thing, I would even rather she had a lover!'

'Charles, you mustn't!' cried Mme Darbédat.

M. Darbédat, with an air of discouragement, took from the stand the hat and stick he had laid down on entering.

'After what you've just told me,' he concluded, 'I haven't much hope left. Anyway, I'll talk to her just the same, it's my duty.'

Mme Darbédat anxiously awaited his departure.

'You know,' she said, to cheer him up, 'I think that, whatever we may say, there's more obstinacy in Eve . . . than the other thing. She knows he's incurable, but she's determined not to give way: she won't admit she's been wrong.'

M. Darbédat was stroking his beard dreamily.

'Obstinacy? Yes, perhaps! Well, if you're right, she'll end by getting tired of it. He isn't always very easy to get on with, and besides, he's nothing to talk about. When I say "Hullo" to him, he sticks out a limp hand and says not a word. When they're alone, I imagine he sinks back into his obsessions: she tells me he sometimes starts yelling like a lunatic because of the hallucinations he has. Statues! They fill him with fear, because of the humming they make. He says they fly all around, showing the whites of their eyes.' He pulled on his gloves, and went on: 'She'll get tired of it, I don't deny. But if she goes off the rails first herself? I wish she'd go out a bit, see people: she might meet some nice young man – ah, someone perhaps like that Shroeder, the engineer at Simpson's, someone with a future in front of him: she'd see him a bit here, a bit there, and gradually get used to the idea of remaking her life.'

Madame Darbédat did not reply for fear of starting up a new conversation. Her husband bent over her.

'Well, well!' he said, 'I've got to be going.'

'Good-bye, Daddy,' said Mme Darbédat, putting up her brow. 'Give her a good hug, and tell her from me she's a poor darling.'

When her husband had gone, Mme Darbédat let herself sink back into her arm-chair, and shut her eyes, exhausted. 'What vitality,' she thought with reproach. When she felt a little stronger, still with shut eyes, her pallid hand groped gently out to the saucer, and picked up a piece of Turkish Delight.

Eve and her husband lived on the fifth floor of an old building in the rue du Bac. Lightly, M. Darbédat climbed up the hundred and twelve stairs. When he pressed the door-bell, he was not even breathless. With satisfaction, he reminded himself of what Mlle Dormoy had once said to him: 'For your age, Charles, you're simply miraculous.' He never felt as strong, as well, as on Thursdays, especially after darting up these stairs.

It was Eve who opened the door to him. Of course, they haven't a maid. They simply *can't* keep them, and I don't wonder. He kissed her:

'Hullo, my poor one!'

She greeted him with a certain coldness.

'You look a little off-colour,' said M. Darbédat, touching her cheek: 'You don't take enough exercise.'

A silence followed.

'Is Mamma all right?' asked Eve.

'So so! You saw her Tuesday? Well, that's how she always is. Your Aunt Louise was visiting her yesterday, she was glad of the visit. She likes seeing people, but she gets quickly tired. Aunt Louise came up about those mortgages, I think I mentioned it to you before. She brought the children. It's a funny business. She came to the office to ask my advice. I told her she'd practically no alternative, that she'd have to sell. Anyway, she's found a buyer: Bretonnel. You remember him, don't you? He's retired now.'

He stopped suddenly. Eve was barely listening to him. Sadly he thought 'Nothing interests her now! Like books! Once he had had to drag her away from them. Now she did not read any more.'

'How's Pierre?'

'Well!' said Eve. 'Would you like to see him?'

'Why, of course,' said M. Darbédat gaily. 'I'll pop in for a minute.'

He was full of pity for the *wretched* young man, but he could not see him without repulsion. 'I detest ill people.' Of course, it wasn't Pierre's fault, he had a frightfully bad heredity. M. Darbédat sighed. 'In spite of all one's precautions, one always gets to know things too late. No, it wasn't Pierre's fault. Still, the seeds had always been in him, it was the fundamental thing about him. It wasn't like cancer or TB: those you could always set aside in judging a man. But that vivid charm, that swift response, which had so taken Eve when they were courting, had in fact been the flowers of madness. He was mad already when they were married, but then it wasn't perceptible.

'You can't help wondering,' thought M. Darbédat, 'where the responsibility begins – or rather where it ends. Whichever way, he was too much given to self-analysis. All the time turned in on himself. But is that the cause or effect of his disease?' He followed his daughter through a long dark passage.

'This flat is too big for you,' he said, 'you ought to move.'

'You always tell me that, Daddy,' answered Eve, 'but I've already told you that Pierre doesn't want to give up his room.'

She was really incredible! One wondered at times whether she realized her husband's condition. He was raving mad, and yet she respected his wishes and opinions, as though he still had his sanity.

'But what I'm saying's meant for you,' went on M. Darbédat, in some irritation. 'It seems to me that if I were a woman, I should feel afraid in these old badly-lit rooms. What I should like to see you in is one of those bright new flats they've been building out at Auteuil: three small airy rooms. They've begun reducing the rents, because of the difficulty of finding tenants: this is just the moment for you.'

Eve turned the door handle softly, and they went into the room. A heavy odour of incense caught him by the throat. The curtains were drawn. In the darkness he became aware of a thin neck rising from the back of an arm-chair. Pierre's back was turned, and he was eating.

'Hullo, Pierre,' said M. Darbédat, raising his voice. 'Well! And how are we today?'

M. Darbédat went closer: the invalid was sitting up to a little table: there was a sly expression on his face.

'Ah, we've been eating boiled eggs,' said M. Darbédat, raising his voice. 'Was it good, eh?'

'I'm not deaf,' said Pierre softly.

M. Darbédat, annoyed, turned to Eve, to call her to witness. But Eve looked at him sternly and said nothing. M. Darbédat realized he had pained her. 'Well, so much the worse for her.' It was impossible to hit the right note with the wretched creature: he hadn't the intelligence of a child of four, and yet Eve wanted one to treat him like a grown-up. M. Darbédat could not prevent himself impatiently wishing the moment would come when all these idiotic precautions would no longer be necessary. Invalids always irritated him somewhat – and especially madmen, because they were wrong. Poor Pierre, for instance, was wrong all along the line: he never spoke without talking nonsense, and yet one couldn't expect even the humblest apology, not even the least admission he was wrong.

Eve took away the egg-shells and egg-cup, then put down a knife and fork.

'And what's he going to eat now?' said M. Darbédat jovially.

'A steak.'

Pierre had picked up the fork, and was holding it in his long, pale finger-tips. Minutely he inspected it, then lightly laughed.

'It won't be this time,' he murmured, replacing it, 'I had a warning.'

Eve moved over, and gazed at the fork with an intense scrutiny.

'Agatha,' said Pierre, 'give me another.'

Eve obeyed, and Pierre began eating. She had taken the suspect fork, and was holding it, clenched in her hand, her eyes still fixed on it. She seemed as though making a violent effort. 'How shady everything they do; and everything about them seems,' thought M. Darbédat. He felt very uncomfortable.

'Look out,' said Pierre, 'you must hold it by the middle, because of the claws!'

Eve sighed, and laid the fork on the sideboard. M. Darbédat felt his anger beginning to get the better of him. He did not think it a good thing to humour all the fantasies of this poor wretch; even for Pierre's sake it was a bad thing to do. Hadn't Franchot himself said:

'One should never humour a madman's illusions.' Instead of giving him another fork, it would have been better to reason gently with him, and make him see that the first was exactly like the others. He went up to the sideboard, ostentatiously picked up the fork, and ran a finger lightly over the prongs. Then he turned to Pierre. But the latter was peacefully cutting his meat, and looked at his father-in-law calmly and without expression.

'I should like to have a little chat with you,' said M. Darbédat to Eve.

Eve followed him docilely into the drawing-room. As he sat on the sofa, M. Darbédat saw that the fork was still in his hand, and threw it ill-humouredly down on a table.

'It's better here,' he said.

'I'm never in it!'

'May I smoke?'

'Of course, Daddy,' she said eagerly. 'Would you like a cigar?'

M. Darbédat preferred making himself a cigarette. He thought, not unpleasurably, of the talk they were going to have. In talking about Pierre, he felt embarrassed by his reason, as a giant might be of his strength in play with a child. Clear-sighted, direct and meticulous as he was, these things were now against him. 'With my poor Jeannette, I must confess, it's something of the same thing.' Of course, Madame Darbédat wasn't mad, but her illness had . . . dulled her. Eve, on the other hand, took after her father; her nature was forthright and logical: discussion with her became a pleasure. 'That's why I don't want her ruined for me.' M. Darbédat raised his eyes: he wanted to see his daughter's clever, subtle features again. But he was disappointed: the face that was once so rational, so open, now in some way seemed clouded and shut. Eve had always been very beautiful, and M. Darbédat noticed that she had made herself up with infinite care, ceremonially even. She had put blue on her lids, and blacked her long lashes. The elaborate care of this make-up made a painful impression on her father.

'You're green under your make-up,' he said to her. 'I'm afraid you'll make yourself ill. And how you lay it on nowadays, when you always used such a little.'

Eve made no reply, and M. Darbédat gazed for a moment with embarrassment at the striking worn face, under its masses of dark hair. He thought she looked like an actress. 'Yes, that's exactly what she does resemble. That woman, that Rumanian who acted in *Phedra* in the arena at Orange.' He regretted having made such an unpleasant remark. 'It escaped me. Better not upset her about such little things.'

'I'm sorry,' he said, smiling. 'You know I'm an old simple-lifer. I don't much care for all those greases that women nowadays stick on their faces. But I know I'm wrong. We must go with the times.'

Eve smiled at him amiably. M. Darbédat lit his cigarette and took a few puffs.

'My child,' he began, 'I was going to say, let's have a chat, we two, like old times. Come, sit down, and listen to me nicely. You just trust your old Daddy.'

'I'd rather stay standing,' said Eve. 'What was it you wanted to say?'

'I want to ask you a simple question,' said M. Darbédat, a little more dryly. 'Where's all this leading you to?'

'All this?' repeated Eve in astonishment.

'Well, yes, all, all this life you've made for yourself. Listen,' he went on, 'you mustn't think I don't understand you' (a sudden inspiration had come to him). 'But what you're trying to do is beyond human powers. You're trying to live in a purely imaginary world, aren't you? You won't admit he's ill, you refuse to see Pierre as he is today, isn't that so? All you can see is the Pierre you used to know. My darling child, my little one, it's a wager that no one could keep,' went on M. Darbédat. 'Here, I'll tell you a story that perhaps you don't know. When we were at Sables d'Olonne, you were three at the time, your mother struck up a friendship with a charming young woman who had a magnificent little boy. You used to play on the beach with this little chap, you were both of you as high as sixpenn'orth of ha'pence, you were sweethearts together. Some time after, in Paris, your mother thought she would like to meet this young woman again, and that was how she got to know that something frightful had happened; her lovely baby boy had had his head cut off by the front wing of a motor. Your mother was told she might visit her, but above all, she was not to refer to the death of her child, for the woman refused to believe he was dead. Your mother went along to see her, and found a half-crazed creature living as though the baby was still alive: she used to talk to him, lay his place at the table. Well, she was in such a state of nervous tension all the time, that six months later they had to remove her forcibly to a Home, and there she remained for three years. No, my child,' said M. Darbédat, shaking his head, 'these things are not possible. It would have been better for her to have admitted the truth to herself courageously. She would have suffered frightfully, of course, but then time would have done its healing work. There's nothing like looking things in the face, take my word for it!'

'You're mistaken,' said Eve, with difficulty. 'I know very well that Pierre is . . .'

The word remained unspoken. She stood rigid, resting her hands on the back of an arm-chair. There was something parched and ugly in the lower part of her face.

'Well, what?' asked M. Darbédat in astonishment.

'What?'

'You . . . ?'

'I love him as he is,' said Eve quickly, and with an air of embarrassment.

'It isn't true,' M. Darbédat said violently. 'It isn't true. You don't love him, you can't love him. One can only have such feelings for someone who is normal, sane. What you feel for Pierre is pity, I'm sure, and no doubt there's the memory of the three years' happiness you owe him. But don't tell me you love him, for I won't believe you.'

Eve remained silent, gazing absently at the carpet.

'You might at least reply,' said M. Darbédat coldly. 'Don't think this conversation is any less painful to me, than it must be to you.'

'But you wouldn't believe me anyway!'

'Well, then, if you love him,' he cried out in exasperation, 'it's a great misfortune for you, for me, and for your poor mother, because I'm going to tell you something I'd rather have kept hidden: in three years from now Pierre will have become completely demented. He'll be no better than a brute.'

He looked at his daughter with hard eyes, full of resentment because she had forced him, by her obstinacy, to make a revelation so painful to her.

Eve did not flinch: she did not even raise her eyes.

'I know.'

'Who told you?' he asked in stupefaction.

'Franchot. I've known it for six months.'

'And I, who begged him not to alarm you,' said M. Darbédat bitterly. 'Still, perhaps it's better this way. But, given the situation, you must realize that it would be unpardonable to keep Pierre here. The struggle you've embarked on is doomed to fail: his illness must take its course. If there were anything to be done, if you could save him by your efforts, I don't say. But think! You were pretty, intelligent, gay: and you're destroying yourself to please yourself and help no one. Well, of course, you've been wonderful, but there you are, it's over, you've done your duty, more than your duty: and now, as things are, it would be immoral to persist. One also has one's duties towards oneself, my child. Besides, you give no thought to us. The thing to do,' he went on, hammering out the words, 'is for you to put Pierre in Dr Franchot's Home. You'll give up this flat, where you've never been anything but wretched, and come back home. If you feel you want to be useful, relieve the sufferings of others, well, there's your mother. The poor woman has nothing but nurses to care for her, she could well do with a little affection. And *she*,' he added, 'she could appreciate what you did for her, and be grateful.'

There was a long silence. M. Darbédat heard Pierre singing in the adjoining room, though it could hardly be said to be singing, but rather a sort of shrill hurried chant. M. Darbédat raised his eyes to his daughter.

'So it's no!'

'Pierre will stay here,' she said softly, 'we get on well together.'

'So long as you mess about all day . . .'

Eve smiled and shot a strange, mocking, almost cheerful glance at her father. 'It's true,' M. Darbédat thought furiously, 'that's all they do together . . . in bed.'

'You're as mad as can be!' he said, rising.

Eve smiled sadly and murmured, as though to herself:

'Not enough!'

'Not enough! There's only one thing I can tell you, my child; you frighten me.' He kissed her hastily and went out. Going downstairs he was thinking: 'They ought to send along a couple of burly fellows to drag that poor dish-clout off by force, and stick him under a shower without even asking his leave.'

It was a fine autumn day, without mystery, and sunlight gilded the faces of those who passed by. M. Darbédat was struck by the simple expression on people's faces. Some were tanned, others pale, but all reflected the joys, the preoccupations with which he was familiar.

'I know just what it is I complain of in her,' he thought, turning into the Boulevard Saint Germain. 'I reproach her for living out of touch with humanity. Pierre's no longer a human being: all the nursing, all the love she bestows on him, she robs in some degree from all those here. One hasn't the right to hold oneself off from mankind. Be it as it may, we're all members of society.'

With sympathy, he gazed into the passing faces; serious open expressions filled him with love. There, in these sunny streets, among men, one felt secure, as though in the midst of one huge family.

Hatless, a woman stood in front of a stall, holding a little girl by the hand.

'What is it?' the little girl asked, pointing to a wireless set.

'Don't touch!' her mother said. 'It's wireless, and it makes music.'

For a while they remained there entranced and silent. M. Darbédat was moved. He nodded towards the little girl and smiled.

II

'He's gone!' The flat door had given a sharp click. Eve was alone in the room. 'I wish he'd die.'

She clenched her fingers on the back of the arm-chair at the sudden reminiscence of her father's eyes. M. Darbédat had bent over Pierre with a professional air; he had said, 'Was it good, eh?' like someone accustomed to talking to the sick. He had gazed down, and Pierre's face had mirrored itself deep in those big terrible eyes. I hate him when he looks at Pierre, when I think *he sees*.

Eve's hands slid down the back of the chair, and she turned to the window. It dazzled her. Sunlight filled the room, it was everywhere: in circular patches on the carpet: like blinding dust in the air. She had grown unaccustomed to the prying diligent light which ferreted all through the room, and scoured out every corner: which rubbed the furniture and made it glitter like a good housewife. Nevertheless, she went over to the window, and raised the muslin curtain that hung over the panes. At that same moment M. Darbédat left the building and Eve suddenly saw his broad shoulders. He raised his head, and blinking looked at the sky, then made off like a youngster, with long strides. 'He's overdoing it,' thought Eve, 'he'll be having that pain in his side again.' But now her hatred was almost gone: there was so little left in that head: barely even the trifling preoccupation of appearing young. And yet anger rose in her again as she saw him turn into the Boulevard Saint Germain before disappearing from sight.

'He's thinking of Pierre.' A little of their common life had broken out of the closed room, and was trailing about the streets, in the sunshine, among folk.

'Won't they ever forget we exist?'

The rue du Bac was almost deserted. An old dame, stepping carefully, crossed the road: then three girls laughingly passed. And then men, solid and grave, with portfolios under their arms, talking . . . 'Normal,' thought Eve, astonished to find such hatred in herself. A plump handsome woman ran clumsily up to a rather foppishly dressed man, who hugged her and kissed her mouth. And Eve laughed harshly and dropped the curtain.

Pierre was not singing any more, but the young woman on the third floor had sat herself down to the piano, practising something by Chopin. Eve felt calmer – she took a step towards Pierre's room, then stopped, overcome by a sense of alarm. As always, when she left the room, panic seized her at the thought that she would have to go back to it. And yet she knew perfectly well that that was the only place in which she could live, for she loved the room. With cold curiosity her eyes roved round the room, the shadowless, odourless room, while she waited for her courage to return. 'It's like a dentist's reception room.' The pink silk arm-chairs, the sofa, the stools, all were discreet and sober, benevolent even: good friends of man. And suddenly Eve began picturing grave men dressed in light suits, like those she had seen from the window, walking into the room, continuing what they were saying. They did not even bother to observe where it was they had come, they strode on firmly into the middle of the room. One, trailing an arm, let it brush the cushions, and the things that stood on the table, but did not even start at the contact. And if some piece of furniture happened to be in the way, staid as they were, these men, far from going round, would calmly move it away. But at last they sat down, still deep in their talk, and without looking round. 'A room for normals,' thought Eve. She gazed at the handle of the shut door and her throat tightened with apprehension. 'I must go back. I never leave him alone so long.'

She had to open that door: then she must wait on the threshold trying to accustom her eyes to the dark, while the room, with all its might, resisted her. She would have to conquer its resistance, and push her way to its heart. Suddenly she had a violent longing to see Pierre. How she would have liked them to make fun of M. Darbédat together. But Pierre didn't need her. Eve had no inkling of how he would welcome her. With a sort of pride she suddenly thought there was nowhere she could go. 'Normal people still think I'm one of them. But I couldn't endure being with them for an hour. This is where I feel I must live now, in there, on the other side of this wall. There, I'm not wanted.'

But now, an extraordinary metamorphosis had taken place. The light had aged, turned grey: it had grown denser like water in a flower-vase, which had been left overnight. An ancient melancholy, long forgotten by her, now because of the aged light, seemed to hover over all the objects in the room. A melancholy as of a dying autumn afternoon. Hesitantly, almost timidly, she looked round: it was all so far away. There was neither daylight, nor night-time, nor season, nor melancholy in this room. Vaguely, she recalled autumns long long ago, when she had been little. Then suddenly she stiffened, her memories made her afraid.

She heard Pierre's voice.

'Agatha! Where are you?'

'I'm coming,' she cried.

She opened the door and pushed into the room.

The dense odour of incense filled her mouth and nostrils as she widened her eyes and stretched out her hands – the scent and the darkness had for a long time now composed but one element, acrid and flocculent, as simple and familiar as air, fire or water. Circumspectly, she moved towards a pale oval which seemed hovering in the mist. It was Pierre's face. Pierre's clothes, he always wore black now since his illness, were merged in the darkness. He had thrown his head back and his eyes were shut. He was handsome to look upon. For a long time Eve gazed at the long curling lashes, then sat down by his side on a low chair. 'He seems in pain,' she thought. Little by little, her eyes grew used to the darkness. First the desk appeared, then the bed, then Pierre's own things, scissors, paste-pot, books; and then his specimens of dried flowers stuck on paper and littering the carpet near his chair.

'Agatha!'

Pierre had opened his eyes, and was looking smilingly at her.

'You know, the fork?' he was saying. 'I did that to frighten the chap. It was *almost* all right.'

Eve's fears vanished, and she laughed lightly.

'It came off splendidly,' she said, 'you had him completely bewildered.'

Pierre smiled.

'Did you see? He kept on messing it about, gripping it. The trouble is they don't know anything about handling things: they grab hold of them.'

'That's true,' said Eve.

Pierre struck his left palm lightly with his right forefinger.

'That's how they grab at things. They put out their fingers, and when they've grabbed hold of something, they clap down their hands on it and finish it off.'

He talked precipitately, mouthingly: he seemed perplexed.

'I wonder what they're after,' he said at last. 'That chap's been here before. What have they sent him for? If they want to know what I'm doing, they've only to look on the screen: they needn't even leave their houses. They make mistakes. They've got the power, but they make mistakes. I never make any myself, that's my trump card.'

'Hoffka,' he said, 'hoffka.' He waved his slender hands in front of his eyes. 'What a whore! Hoffka, paffka, suffka. Do you want any more?'

'Is it the bell?' asked Eve.

'Yes, it's gone,' he went on sternly. 'That chap, he's an underling. You know him, you went into the sitting-room with him.'

Eve made no reply.

'What did he want?' said Pierre. 'He must have told you.'

For a moment she hesitated, then answered brutally.

'He wanted to have you shut up!'

When you told Pierre the truth gently, he got suspicious. One had to bludgeon him: then he got bothered and his suspicions were paralysed. Eve preferred to deal brutally with him rather than lie to him: when she lied and he seemed to believe her, she could not help feeling slightly superior, and that made her hate herself.

'Shut me up,' Pierre repeated sarcastically. 'They're raving! What difference could walls make to me. Perhaps they imagine that that would stop me. I sometimes wonder whether there aren't two gangs of them. The real one, the negro's. And then that gang of marplots who want to stick their noses into everything, and do nothing but blunder.'

He began tapping with his hand on his arm-rests, and looked at her with an air of delight.

'Walls can be got through. What answer did you make?' he asked, turning towards Eve curiously.

'That I shouldn't allow it.'

He shrugged his shoulders.

'You shouldn't have said that. You made a mistake too – unless you did it on purpose. You should have let them put their cards on the table.'

He fell silent. Eve sadly drooped her head. 'They grab them!' How scornfully he had said that – and how true it was. 'Do I grab things too? In spite of the care I take, I believe nearly everything I do irritates him. But he doesn't say anything.' Suddenly she felt miserable, as when, at fourteen, Mme Darbédat, slim and active, would say to her: 'Anyone would think you didn't know what to do with your hands.' She dared not move, and just at that moment she felt an irresistible desire to change her position. As gently as possible she drew her feet in under the chair, barely brushing the carpet. She looked at the lamp on the table – the lamp whose base Pierre had painted black, and the chessmen. He had left only the black pawns on the chess-board. At times he would rise, go to the table, and take the pawns one by one in his hands. He talked to them, called them Robots, and in his fingers they seemed to begin to have a secret life of their own. When he had set them down again, Eve would go up and touch them too. (She felt she was being rather ridiculous.) But they had turned into mere dead bits of wood again, though there was something vague and uncapturable about them still, something like a secret awareness. 'They're his

things,' she thought, 'there's nothing of mine any more in the room.'
Once she had had some pieces of furniture, the mirror, and the little
marquetry dressing-table that had once been her grandmother's, and
which Pierre would jokingly call: *Your* dressing-table.' But Pierre had
drawn them along after him, and only to Pierre would things show
their real faces now. Eve might gaze at them for hours, but with an
unrelenting obstinacy they remained determined to deceive her, and
reveal only the simulacrum of themselves, as though she were Dr
Franchot or M. Darbédat. 'And yet,' she told herself anguishedly, 'I no
longer see them exactly as Father does. It isn't possible that I see them
exactly like him.'

She moved her knees slightly, for there were pins and needles in her
legs. Her body was tense and rigid: it hurt: she felt it was too much
alive, altogether too obvious. 'I should like to be invisible and be here:
see him without him seeing me: he doesn't need me. I'm one too many
in this room.' She turned her head sharply, and looked at the wall over
Pierre's head. On the wall threats had been written. Eve knew it,
though she was unable to read them. She often looked at the big red
flowers on the wall, until they started to dance in front of her. The
roses flared in the darkness. Generally, the threat was written close to
the ceiling, a bit to the left over the bed: but sometimes it moved. 'I
must get up. I can't . . . I can't stay sitting like this much longer.' On
the wall there were also circles of white that looked like slices of onion.
The discs began to revolve, and Eve's hands started to tremble. 'There
are times when I feel I'm going mad. But no,' she thought bitterly, 'I
can't go mad. I'm upset, that's all there is to it.'

Suddenly she felt Pierre's hand on her arm.

'Agatha,' Pierre said tenderly.

He smiled at her, but held her hand with his finger-tips in a sort of
repulsion, as though holding a crab and staying out of reach of its
claws.

'Agatha,' he said, 'how I wish I had faith in you.'

Eve's eyes closed, and her breast heaved. 'I mustn't answer, else he
won't trust me, or tell me anything.'

Pierre had released her hand.

'I love you, Agatha,' he said. 'But I can't understand you. Why do
you stay in the room all the time?'

Eve made no reply.

'Tell me why.'

'You know that I love you!' she answered abruptly.

'I don't believe it,' said Pierre. 'Why should you love me? You should hate me. I'm haunted.' He smiled, but suddenly became serious.

'There's a wall between you and me. I see you. I talk to you, but you're on the other side. What prevents us loving each other. I think it used to be easier once: in Hamburg.'

'Yes,' said Eve sadly. Always Hamburg. Not once did he ever talk of their real past. Neither Eve nor he had ever been in Hamburg.

'We used to walk by the canals. There was a lighter, don't you remember? The lighter was black: there was a dog on the deck.'

He was inventing momentarily . . . with a sly expression on his face.

'I was holding your hand: your skin was different. I believed everything you told me. Shut up!' he shouted.

He listened for a moment.

'They're coming,' he said drearily.

Eve started.

'They're coming! And I was thinking they'd never come any more.'

For three days now Pierre had been more tranquil: the statues had kept away. Pierre had a horrible fear of the statues, though he would never admit it. They did not make her afraid, but when they began to fly humming through the room, she was afraid of Pierre.

'Fetch me the Ziuthre,' said Pierre.

Eve rose and got him his Ziuthre. It was contrived of bits of cardboard stuck together by Pierre: he had made it to exorcize the statues. The Ziuthre looked like a spider. On one of the pieces of card Pierre had written 'Power over ambushes', and on another 'Black'. On a third he had drawn a laughing face, with wrinkled eyelids: that was Voltaire. Pierre took hold of the Ziuthre by one of its legs, and looked at it darkly.

'It's no use to me any more,' he said.

'Why?'

'They've reversed it!'

'You'll make yourself another.'

He looked at her steadily.

'You'd like me to,' he hissed.

Eve felt angry with him. 'Every time they come, he has warning. How does he manage it? He's never once wrong.'

The Ziuthre dangled woefully from Pierre's fingers. 'He's always got some excellent excuse why he won't use it. Sunday, when they came, he pretended it was mislaid, though I could see it perfectly well behind the inkpot, and he couldn't. I wonder if he doesn't attract them himself. You never know whether he's being honest or not.' At times

Eve had the impression that in spite of himself, unhealthy ideas and visions swarmed in on him. But at others, Pierre looked so sly, she could have sworn he was inventing it all. He's in pain? But *how much* does he believe in the statues and negro? As for the statues, I know positively that he doesn't see, but only hears them. When they pass by, he turns his head away: and yet he says he does see them and even describes them. Dr Franchot's rubicund face rose in front of her: 'But, dear lady, all madmen are liars. You're wasting your time if you try to distinguish what it is they really feel, from what they pretend they feel.' She started: 'What's Franchot got to do with all this? I'm not going to start thinking about him.'

Pierre had got up in order to throw the Ziuthre into the waste-paper basket.

'It's like you that I want to think,' she murmured. He was walking with tiny steps, tip-toe, his elbows pressed to his sides, to be as compact as possible. He returned, sat down, and looked blankly at Eve.

'We shall have to hang black round the room,' he said. 'There's not enough black in this room.'

He sat slumped in his chair, and Eve gazed sadly at the miserly body, always so ready to draw itself in, to curl itself up: the arms, the legs, the head like retractile organs. Six o'clock struck: the piano was silent. Eve sighed: the statues would not come at once, they would have to wait for them.

'Shall I put on the light?'

She would rather not wait in the dark for them.

'Do as you like,' said Pierre.

Eve switched the small desk lamp on, and a red mist invaded the room. Pierre also sat waiting.

He did not speak though his lips moved: they made two dark spots in the red mist. Eve loved these lips of Pierre's. Once they had been voluptuous and moved her deeply: but they had lost their voluptuousness now. They moved apart, quivering gently, and came together again, crushing against each other with untiring repetition. They seemed the only things that lived in that shut-off visage; they made her think of two timorous little beasts. Pierre could mumble away like this for hours, without a sound issuing from him. At times, she was all but hypnotized by the repetition of that tiny implacable motion. 'I love his mouth.' But now he never kissed her, physical contact revolted him. At night hands touched him, male hands, hard and horny, pinched all his body: women's hands with long nails caressed him foully. Often he got into bed in his clothes, but the hands slid under the clothes and plucked at his shirt. Once he heard laughter, and once swollen lips pressed on his own. It was from that night he had stopped kissing Eve.

'Agatha,' said Pierre, 'don't look at my mouth.'

Eve lowered her eyes.

'I know as well as you, that one can learn to read from a man's lips,' he continued aggressively.

His hands trembled on the arm-rest. The forefinger went rigid, and tapped thrice on the thumb, while the remaining fingers clenched themselves: it was an exorcism. 'It's beginning,' she thought. She had a longing to take Pierre in her arms.

Pierre began talking aloud, as though in a drawing-room. 'Do you remember San Pauli?'

She did not reply. Perhaps it was a trap.

'That's where I got to know you,' he said complacently. 'I got you away from a Danish sailor. We came almost to blows, but I bought the drinks, and he let us go. It was all a game.'

'He's lying: he doesn't believe a word of it all. He knows my name's not Agatha. I hate him when he's lying.' But she saw his glazed eyes and her anger melted. 'He's not lying,' she thought, 'he just can't stand any more. He feels them coming: he's talking so he shan't hear.' Pierre was clutching the arms of his chair. His face had gone livid: he was smiling.

'Such meetings are often strange,' he was saying, 'but I personally don't believe in hazard. I don't ask who sent you, I know you won't tell. In any case you were clever enough to bespatter me.'

He was talking with difficulty, in a shrill precipitate voice. There were words he could not pronounce, which came out of his mouth like some flabby shapeless substance.

'You dragged me off, right in the middle of the fair, among the black motor-car roundabouts, but past the motors there was a host of scarlet eyes which gleamed when my back was turned. I believe you were signalling to them, though you had your arm in mine, but I didn't notice. I was too engrossed in the grand ceremonies of the Coronation.'

He looked straight in front of him with wide open eyes. He passed a hand over his brow, very swiftly, with a brief gesture, talking incessantly the while: he did not want to stop.

'It was the Coronation of the Republic,' he said in a strident voice, 'a most impressive spectacle of its kind on account of the animals of every species sent by the Colonies for the ceremony. You were frightened of getting lost among the monkeys. I said among the monkeys,' he reiterated with an arrogant air, looking round. 'I *could* say among the negroes. The foetuses that glide under the table and think they're unseen, are caught out on the spot and nailed by My Eye. The watchword is "Silence",' he shouted, 'Silence: Everyone to their place, Attention! for the statues are coming!'

'That's the watchword, tralala,' he yelled, putting his hands like a trumpet in front of his mouth. 'Tralala . . . tralala!'

He fell silent and she knew that the statues had entered the room. He sat tensely, pallid and full of scorn. Eve stiffened also, and both waited silent. Someone walked down the passage: it was Marie, the 'daily', who had probably just come. Eve thought, 'I must give her some money for the gas.' And then the statues began flying around, passing between her and Pierre.

A guttural sound broke from Pierre's breast, and he buried himself in his chair, pulling his legs up. His head was turned away, and from time to time he sniggered, but beads of sweat started out on his brow. Eve could not endure the sight of his pallid cheeks, or the tremulous grimace that distorted his mouth: she shut her eyes. Gold threads began to dance on the red ground of her lids, she felt old and weighed down. Near by, Pierre was panting hard. 'They're flying, they're humming, they're bending over him now.' She felt a tickling sensation, a pressure on her shoulder and right thigh. And instinctively her body bent left, as though to avoid some unpleasant contact, as though to make way for some object, heavy and clumsy. Suddenly the floor-boards creaked, and a mad desire came over her to open her eyes and look to the right, and saw through the air with her hands. But she did nothing. She kept her eyes closed, and a harsh delight sent a shudder through her. 'I'm *also afraid*,' she thought. Everything in her seemed to be huddled for refuge in her right side. She bent towards Pierre without opening her eyes. The slightest effort would be sufficient, and for the first time she would enter that tragic world of his. 'I'm afraid of the statues,' she thought. It was a sudden blind affirmation, an incantation: with all her might she wanted to believe they were there. And she tried to make a new sense, a touching, of that anguish which paralysed her right side. In her arm, in her thigh and shoulder, she felt them passing.

The statues flew low and gently: they hummed. Eve knew they looked baleful, and that lashes grew out of the stone round their eyes: but she found it difficult to picture them. She knew too that they were not entirely alive, but that patches of flesh, warm scales, mottled their great bodies: that the stone peeled from their finger-tips, and that the palms of their hands itched. Eve could not *see* all this: she thought simply that enormous women slid up against her, solemn and grotesque, with a human expression, and the dense obstinacy of stone. 'They're leaning over Pierre —' Eve made such a violent effort over herself, that her hands began trembling — 'they're bending over me . . .' A fearful cry froze her suddenly. 'They've touched him.' She opened her eyes. Pierre had his head in his hands, he was panting. Eve felt worn out. 'A game,' she thought with remorse: 'it was only a game, not for a moment did I really believe in it. And yet during that time, he was going through agony.'

Pierre relaxed, breathing stertorously. But his pupils remained oddly dilated. He was sweating.

'You saw them?' he asked.

'I can't see them.'

'So much the better for you, they'd make you afraid. I,' he said, 'I've got used to them.'

Eve's hands went on trembling, the blood had rushed to her head. Pierre took a cigarette from his pocket and put it to his lips. But he did not light it.

'It doesn't matter to me whether I see them or not,' he said, 'but I won't have them touch me. I'm afraid they might give me pimples.'

He thought for a moment, and asked:

'Did you hear them?'

'Yes,' said Eve, 'like an aeroplane engine' (Pierre had said so himself the preceding Sunday).

Pierre smiled condescendingly.

'That's exaggerating!' he said. But he remained pallid. He looked at Eve's hands. 'Your hands are trembling. My poor Agatha, it must have upset you, but there's no need to be worried, they won't come again till tomorrow.'

Eve could not reply: her teeth were chattering and she was afraid Pierre might notice it. He looked at her steadily.

'You're very lovely,' he said, nodding. 'A pity, truly a pity.' He put his hand out swiftly, brushing her ear.

'My lovely demon! You bother me a bit: you're too lovely: it distracts my mind. If it wasn't for that recapitulation . . .'

He stopped and looked at Eve in surprise.

'That wasn't the word. It came . . . it came . . .' he said smiling vaguely. 'The other was on the tip of my tongue, and then that one came and took its place. I've forgotten what I was going to say to you . . .'

He thought for a moment and then shook his head.

'Well,' he said, 'I'm going to sleep now,' and added, in a babyish voice. 'You know, Agatha, I'm tired. I can't collect my thoughts any more.'

He threw his cigarette away and looked anxiously at the carpet. Eve slid a pillow under his head.

'You can sleep too,' he said, shutting his eyes: 'They won't come back now.'

'Recapitulation.' Pierre slept, a faint, frank smile on his face: his head hung limp, almost as though his cheek was trying to stroke his shoulder. Eve did not feel sleepy: she was thinking. 'Recapitulation.' Pierre had suddenly looked stupid, and the long whitish word had slipped out of his mouth. Pierre had looked in front of him with astonishment, as though he saw, but did not recognize the word: his lips had been open, flabby: something seemed to have broken in him. He had stammered. It was the first time that had happened to him. He had realized it though. He had said he couldn't collect his thoughts. Just then, he uttered a slight voluptuous moan, and his hand moved slightly. She looked at him with a hard look. 'How will he wake?' It tormented her. The moment Pierre slept she had to think of it, she couldn't prevent herself. She was afraid he might wake with eyes clouded, his talking incoherent. 'I'm stupid,' she thought, 'that's not for a year yet, Franchot said so.' But the feeling of anxiety would not leave her: a year, a winter, a summer, the start of another autumn. One day these features would lose their outline, he would let his jaw drop and peer through weeping half-shut eyes. Eve bent over Pierre's hand with a touch of her lips. 'I shall kill you first.'

[PNW 16, 1943]

Elizabeth Bowen

Mysterious Kôr

Full moonlight drenched the city and searched it; there was not a niche left to stand in. The effect was remorseless: London looked like the moon's capital – shallow, cratered, extinct. It was late, but not yet midnight; now the buses had stopped the polished roads and streets in this region sent for minutes together a ghostly unbroken reflection up. The soaring new flats and the crouching old shops and houses looked equally brittle under the moon, which blazed in windows that looked its way. The futility of the black-out became laughable: from the sky, presumably, you could see every slate in the roofs, every whited kerb, every contour of the naked winter flowerbeds in the park; and the lake with its shining twists and tree-darkened islands would be a landmark for miles, yes, miles, overhead.

However, the sky, in whose glassiness floated no clouds but only opaque balloons, remained glassy-silent. The Germans no longer came by the full moon. Something more immaterial seemed to threaten, and to be keeping people at home. This day between days, this extra tax, was perhaps more than senses and nerves could bear. People stayed indoors with a fervour that could be felt: the buildings strained with battened-down human life, but not a beam, not a voice, not a note from a radio escaped. Now and then under streets and buildings the earth rumbled: the Underground sounded loudest at this time.

Outside the now gateless gates of the park, the road coming downhill from the north-west turned south and became a street, down whose perspective the traffic lights went through their unmeaning performance of changing colour. From the promontory of pavement outside the gates you saw at once up the road and down the street: from behind where you stood, between the gateposts, appeared the lesser strangements of grass and water and trees. At this point, at this moment, three French soldiers, directed to a hostel they could not find, stopped singing to listen derisively to the waterbirds wakened up by the moon. Next, two wardens coming off duty emerged from their post and crossed the road diagonally, each with an elbow cupped inside a slung-on tin hat. The wardens turned their faces, mauve in the moonlight, towards the Frenchmen with no expression at all. The two sets of steps died in opposite directions, and, the birds subsiding, nothing was heard or seen until, a little way down the street, a trickle of people came out of the Underground, around the anti-panic brick wall. These all disappeared quickly, in an abashed way, or as though dissolved in the street by some white acid, but for a girl and a soldier who, by their way of walking, seemed to have no destination but each other and to be not quite certain even of that. Blotted into one shadow, he tall, she little, these two proceeded towards the park. They looked in, but did not go in; they stood there debating without speaking. Then, as though a command from the street behind them had been received by their synchronized bodies, they faced round to look back the way they had come.

His look up the height of a building made his head drop back, and she saw his eyeballs glitter. She slid her hand from his sleeve, stepped to the edge of the pavement and said: 'Mysterious Kôr.'

'What is?' he said, not quite collecting himself.

'This is –

'Mysterious Kôr thy walls forsaken stand,
Thy lonely towers beneath a lonely moon –'
                    – this is Kôr.'

'Why,' he said, 'it's years since I've thought of that.'

She said: 'I think of it all the time –

'Not in the waste beyond the swamps and sand,
The fever-haunted forest and lagoon,
Mysterious Kôr thy walls –'

– a completely forsaken city, as high as cliffs and as white as bones, with no history –'

'But something must once have happened: why had it been forsaken?'

'How could anyone tell you when there's nobody there?'

'Nobody there since how long?'

'Thousands of years.'

'In that case, it would have fallen down.'

'No, not Kôr,' she said with immediate authority. 'Kôr's altogether different; it's very strong; there is not a crack in it anywhere for a weed to grow in; the corners of stones and the monuments might have been cut yesterday, and the stairs and arches are built to support themselves.'

'You know all about it,' he said, looking at her.

'I know, I know all about it.'

'What, since you read that book?'

'Oh, I didn't get much from that; I just got the name. I knew that must be the right name; it's like a cry.'

'Most like the cry of a crow to me.' He reflected, then said: 'But the poem begins with "Not" – "*Not in the waste beyond the swamps and sand* –" And it goes on, as I remember, to prove Kôr's not really anywhere. When a poem says there's no such place –'

'What it tries to say doesn't matter: I see what it makes me see. Anyhow, that was written some time ago, at that time when they thought they had got everything taped, because the whole world had been explored, even the middle of Africa. Every thing and place had been found and marked on some map; so what wasn't marked on any map couldn't be there at all. So *they* thought: that was why he wrote the poem. "*The world is disenchanted,*" it goes on. That was what set me off hating civilization.'

'Well, cheer up,' he said; 'there isn't much of it left.'

'Oh, yes, I cheered up some time ago. This war shows we've by no means come to the end. If you can blow whole places out of existence, you can blow whole places into it. I don't see why not. They say we can't say what's come out since the bombing started. By the time we've come to the end, Kôr may be the one city left: the abiding city. I should laugh.'

'No, you wouldn't,' he said sharply. '*You* wouldn't – at least, I hope not. I hope you don't know what you're saying – does the moon make you funny?'

'Don't be cross about Kôr; please don't, Arthur,' she said.

'I thought girls thought about people.'

'What, these days?' she said. 'Think about people? How can anyone think about people if they've got any heart? I don't know how other girls manage: I always think about Kôr.'

'Not about me?' he said. When she did not at once answer, he turned her hand over, in anguish, inside his grasp. 'Because I'm not there when you want me – is that my fault?'

'But to think about Kôr *is* to think about you and me.'

'In that dead place?'

'No, ours – we'd be alone there.'

Tightening his thumb on her palm while he thought this over, he looked behind them, around them, above them – even up at the sky. He said finally: 'But we're alone here.'

'That was why I said "Mysterious Kôr".'

'What, you mean we're there now, that here's there, that now's then? . . . *I* don't mind,' he added, letting out as a laugh the sigh he had been holding in for some time. 'You ought to know the place, and for all I could tell you we might be anywhere: I often do have it, this funny feeling, the first minute or two when I've come up out of the Underground. Well, well: join the Army and see the world.' He nodded towards the perspective of traffic lights and said, a shade craftily: 'What are those, then?'

Having caught the quickest possible breath, she replied: 'Inexhaustible gases; they bored through to them and lit them as they came up; by changing colour they show the changing of minutes; in Kôr there is no sort of other time.'

'You've got the moon, though: that can't help making months.'

'Oh, and the sun, of course; but those two could do what they liked; we should not have to calculate when they'd come or go.'

'We might not have to,' he said, 'but I bet I should.'

'I should not mind what you did, so long as you never said, "What next?"'

'I don't know about "next", but I do know what we'd do first.'

'What, Arthur?'

'Populate Kôr.'

She said: 'I suppose it would be all right if our children were to marry each other?'

But her voice faded out; she had been reminded that they were homeless on this his first night of leave. They were, that was to say, in London without any hope of any place of their own. Pepita shared a two-roomed flatlet with a girl friend, in a bye-street off the Regent's Park Road, and towards this they must make their half-hearted way. Arthur was to have the sitting-room divan, usually occupied by Pepita, while she herself had half of her girl friend's bed. There was really no room for a third, and least of all for a man, in those small rooms packed with furniture and the two girls' belongings: Pepita tried to be grateful for her friend Callie's forbearance – but how could she be, when it had not occurred to Callie that she would do better to be away tonight? She was more slow-witted than narrow-minded – but Pepita felt she owed a kind of ruin to her. Callie, not yet known to be home later than ten, would be now waiting up, in her house-coat, to welcome Arthur. That would mean three-sided chat, drinking cocoa, then turning in: that would be that, and that would be all. That was London, this war – they were lucky to have a roof – London, full enough before the Americans came. Not a place: they would even grudge you sharing a grave – that was when even married couples complained. Whereas in Kôr . . .

In Kôr . . . Like glass, the illusion shattered: a car hummed like a hornet towards them, veered, showed its scarlet tail-light, streaked away up the road. A woman edged round a front door and along the area railings timidly called her cat; meanwhile a clock near, then another set further back in the dazzling distance, set about striking midnight. Pepita, feeling Arthur release her arm with an abruptness that was the inverse of passion, shivered; whereat he asked brusquely: 'Cold? Well, which way? – we'd better be getting on.'

Callie was no longer waiting up. Hours ago she had set out the three cups and saucers, the tins of cocoa and household milk and, on the gas-ring, brought the kettle to just short of the boil. She had turned open Arthur's bed, the living-room divan, in the neat inviting way she had learnt at home – then, with a modest impulse, replaced the cover. She had, as Pepita foresaw, been wearing her cretonne house-coat, the nearest thing to a hostess gown that she had; she had already brushed her hair for the night, rebraided it, bound the braids in a coronet round her hair. Both lights and the wireless had been on, to make the room both look and sound gay: all alone, she had come to that peak moment at which company should arrive – but so seldom does. From then on she felt welcome beginning to wither in her, a flower of the heart that had bloomed too early. There she had sat like an image, facing the three cold cups, on the edge of the bed to be occupied by an unknown man.

Callie's innocence and her still unsought-out state had brought her to take a proprietary pride in Arthur; this was all the stronger, perhaps, because they had not yet met. Sharing the flat with Pepita, this last year, she had been content with reflecting heat of love. It was not, surprisingly, that Pepita seemed very happy – there were times when she was palpably on the rack, and this was not what Callie could understand. 'Surely you owe it to Arthur,' she would then say, 'to keep cheerful? So long as you love each other –' Callie's calm brow glowed – one might say that it glowed in place of her friend's; she became the guardian of that ideality which for Pepita was constantly lost to view. It was true, with the sudden prospect of Arthur's leave, things had come nearer to earth: he became a proposition, and she would have been as glad if he could have slept somewhere else. Physically shy, a brotherless virgin, Callie shrank from sharing this flat with a young man. In this flat you could hear everything: what was once a three-windowed Victorian drawing-room had been partitioned, by very thin walls, into kitchenette, living-room, Callie's bedroom. The living-room was in the centre; the two others open off it. What was once the conservatory, half a flight down, was now converted into a draughty bathroom, shared with somebody else on the girls' floor. The flat, for these days, was cheap – even so, it was Callie, earning more than Pepita, who paid the greater part of the rent: it thus became up to her, more or less, to express goodwill as to Arthur's making a third. 'Why, it will be lovely to have him here,' Callie said. Pepita accepted the goodwill without much grace – but then, had she ever much grace to spare? – she was as restlessly secretive, as self-centred, as a little half-grown black cat. Next came a puzzling moment: Pepita seemed to be hinting that Callie should fix herself up somewhere else. 'But where would I go?' Callie marvelled when this was at last borne in on her. 'You know what London's like now. And, anyway' – here she laughed, but hers was a forehead that coloured as easily as it glowed – 'it wouldn't be proper, would it, me going off and leaving just you and Arthur; I don't know what your mother would say to me. No, we may be a little squashed, but we'll make things ever so homey. I shall not mind playing gooseberry, really, dear.'

But the hominess by now was evaporating, as Pepita and Arthur still and still did not come. At half-past ten, in obedience to the rule of the house, Callie was obliged to turn off the wireless, whereupon silence out of the stepless street began seeping into the slighted room. Callie recollected the fuel target and turned off her dear little table lamp, gaily painted with spots to make it look like a toadstool, thereby leaving only the hanging light. She laid her hand on the kettle to find it gone cold again and sigh for the wasted gas if not for her wasted thought. Where are they? Cold crept up her out of the kettle; she went to bed.

Callie's bed lay along the wall under the window: she did not like sleeping so close up under glass, but the clearance that must be left for the opening of door and cupboards made this the only possible place. Now she got in and lay rigidly on the bed's inner side, under the hanging hems of the window curtains, training her limbs not to stray to what would be Pepita's half. This sharing of her bed with another body would not be the least of her sacrifice to the lovers' love; tonight would be the first night – or at least, since she was an infant – that

Callie had slept with anyone. Child of a sheltered middle-class house-hold, she had kept physical distances all her life. Already repugnance and shyness ran through her limbs; she was preyed upon by some more obscure trouble than the expectation that she might not sleep. As to *that*, Pepita was restless; her tossings on the divan, her broken-off exclamations and blurred pleas had been to be heard, most nights, through the dividing wall.

Callie knew, as though from a vision, that Arthur would sleep soundly, with assurance and majesty. Did they not all say, too, that a soldier sleeps like a log? With awe she pictured, asleep, the face that she had not yet, awake, seen – Arthur's man's eyelids, cheek-bones and set mouth turned up to the darkened ceiling. Wanting to savour darkness herself, Callie reached out and put off her bedside lamp.

At once she knew that something was happening – outdoors, in the street, the whole of London, the world. An advance, an extraordinary movement was silently taking place; blue-white beams overflowed from it, silting, dropping round the edges of the muffling black-out curtains. When, starting up, she knocked a fold of the curtain, a beam like a mouse ran across her bed. A searchlight, the most powerful of all time, might have been turned full and steady upon her defended window; finding flaws in the black-out stuff, it made veins and stars. Once gained by this idea of pressure she could not lie down again; she sat tautly, drawn-up knees touching her breasts, and asked herself if there were anything she should do. She parted the curtains, opened them slowly wider, looked out – and was face to face with the moon.

Below the moon, the houses opposite her window blazed black in transparent shadow; and something – was it a coin or a ring? – glittered half-way across the chalk-white street. Light marched in past her face, and she turned to see where it went: out stood the curves and garlands of the great white marble Victorian mantelpiece of that lost drawing-room; out stood, in the photographs turned her way, the thoughts with which her parents had faced the camera, and the humble puzzlement of her two dogs at home. Of silver brocade, just faintly purpled with roses, became her house-coat hanging over the chair. And the moon did more: it exonerated and beautified the lateness of the lovers' return. No wonder, she said to herself, no wonder – if this was the world they walked in, if this was whom they were with. Having drunk in the white explanation, Callie lay down again. Her half of the bed was in shadow, but she allowed one hand to lie, blanched, in what would be Pepita's place. She lay and looked at the hand until it was no longer her own.

Callie woke to the sound of Pepita's key in the latch. But no voices? What had happened? Then she heard Arthur's step. She heard his unslung equipment dropped with a weary, dull sound, and the plonk of his tin hat on a wooden chair. 'Sssh-sssh!' Pepita exclaimed, 'she *might* be asleep!'

Then at last Arthur's voice: 'But I thought you said –'

'I'm not asleep; I'm just coming!' Callie called out with rapture, leaping out from her form in shadow into the moonlight, zipping on her enchanted house-coat over her nightdress, kicking her shoes on, and pinning in place, with a trembling firmness, her plaits in their coronet round her head. Between these movements of hers she heard not another sound. Had she only dreamed they were there? Her heart beat: she stepped through the living-room, shutting her door behind her.

Pepita and Arthur stood the other side of the table; they gave the impression of being lined up. Their faces, at different levels – for Pepita's rough, dark head came only an inch above Arthur's khaki shoulder – were alike in abstention from any kind of expression; as though, spiritually, they both still refused to be here. Their features looked faint, weathered – was this the work of the moon? Pepita said at once: 'I suppose we are very late?'

'I don't wonder,' Callie said, 'on this lovely night.'

Arthur had not raised his eyes; he was looking at the three cups. Pepita now suddenly jogged his elbow, saying, 'Arthur, wake up; say something; this is Callie – well, Callie, this is Arthur, of course.'

'Why, yes, of course this is Arthur,' returned Callie, whose candid eyes since she entered had not left Arthur's face. Perceiving that Arthur did not know what to do, she advanced round the table to shake hands with him. He looked up, she looked down, for the first time: she rather beheld than felt his red-brown grip on what still seemed her glove of moonlight. 'Welcome, Arthur,' she said. 'I'm so glad to meet you at last. I hope you will be comfortable in the flat.'

'It's been kind of you,' he said after consideration.

'Please do not feel that,' said Callie. 'This is Pepita's home, too, and we both hope – don't we, Pepita? – that you'll regard it as yours. Please feel free to do just as you like. I am sorry it is so small.'

'Oh, I don't know,' Arthur said, as though hypnotized; 'it seems a nice little place.'

Pepita, meanwhile, glowered and turned away.

Arthur continued to wonder, though he had once been told, how these two unlike girls had come to set up together – Pepita so small, except for her too-big head, compact of childish brusqueness and of unchildish passion, and Callie, so sedate, waxy and tall – an unlit candle. Yes, she was like one of those candles on sale outside a church; there could be something votive even in her demeanour. She was unconscious that her good manners, those of an old-fashioned country doctor's daughter, were putting the other two at a disadvantage. He found himself touched by the grave good faith with which Callie was wearing that tartish house-coat, above which her face kept the glaze of sleep; and, as she knelt to re-light the gas ring under the kettle, he marked the strong, delicate arch of one bare foot, disappearing into the arty green shoe. Pepita was now too near him ever again to be seen as he now saw Callie – in a sense, he never *had* seen Pepita for the first time: she had not been, and still sometimes was not, his type. No, he had not thought of her twice; he had not remembered her until he began to remember her with passion. You might say he had not seen Pepita coming: their love had been a collision in the dark.

Callie, determined to get this over, knelt back and said: 'Would Arthur like to wash his hands?' When they had heard him stumble down the half-flight of stairs, she said to Pepita: 'Yes, I was so glad you had the moon.'

'Why?' said Pepita. She added: 'There was too much of it.'

'You're tired. Arthur looks tired, too.'

'How would you know? He's used to marching about. But it's all this having no place to go.'

'But, Pepita, you –'

But at this point Arthur came back: from the door he noticed the wireless, and went direct to it. 'Nothing much on now, I suppose?' he doubtfully said.

'No; you see it's past midnight; we're off the air. And, anyway, in this house they don't like the wireless late. By the same token,' went on Callie, friendlily smiling, 'I'm afraid I must ask you, Arthur, to take your boots off, unless, of course, you mean to stay sitting down. The people below us –'

Pepita flung off, saying something under her breath, but Arthur, remarking, 'No, I don't mind,' both sat down and began to take off his boots. Pausing, glancing to left and right at the divan's fresh cotton spread, he said: 'It's all right is it, for me to sit on this?'

'That's my bed,' said Pepita. 'You are to sleep in it.'

Callie then made the cocoa, after which they turned in. Preliminary trips to the bathroom having been worked out, Callie was first to retire, shutting the door behind her so that Pepita and Arthur might kiss each other good night. When Pepita joined her, it was without knocking: Pepita stood still in the moon and began to tug off her clothes. Glancing with hate at the bed, she asked: 'Which side?'

'I expected you'd like the outside.'

'What are you standing about for?'

'I don't really know: as I'm inside I'd better get in first.'

'Then why not get in?'

When they had settled rigidly, side by side, Callie asked: 'Do you think Arthur's got all he wants?'

Pepita jerked her head up. 'We can't sleep in all this moon.'

'Why, you don't believe the moon does things, actually?'

'Well, it couldn't hope to make some of us *much* more screwy.'

Callie closed the curtains, then said: 'What do you mean? And – didn't you hear? – I asked if Arthur's got all he wants.'

'That's what I meant – have you got a screw loose, really?'

'Pepita, I won't stay here if you're going to be like this.'

'In that case, you had better go in with Arthur.'

'What about me?' Arthur loudly said through the wall. 'I can hear practically all you girls are saying.'

They were both startled – rather that than abashed. Arthur, alone in there, had thrown off the ligatures of his social manner: his voice held the whole authority of his sex – he was impatient, sleepy, and he belonged to no one.

'Sorry,' the girls said in unison. Then Pepita laughed soundlessly, making their bed shake, till to stop herself she bit the back of her hand, and this movement made her elbow strike Callie's cheek. 'Sorry,' she had to whisper. No answer: Pepita fingered her elbow and found, yes, it was quite true, it was wet. 'Look, shut up crying, Callie: what have I done?'

Callie rolled right round, in order to press her forehead closely under the window, into the curtains, against the wall. Her weeping continued to be soundless: now and then, unable to reach her handkerchief, she staunched her eyes with a curtain, disturbing slivers of moon. Pepita gave up marvelling, and soon slept: at least there is something in being dog-tired.

A clock struck four as Callie woke up again – but something else had made her open her swollen eyelids. Arthur, stumbling about on his padded feet, could be heard next door attempting to make no noise. Inevitably, he bumped the edge of the table. Callie sat up: by her side Pepita lay like a mummy rolled half over, in forbidding, tenacious sleep. Arthur groaned. Callie caught a breath, climbed lightly over

Pepita, felt for her torch on the mantelpiece, stopped to listen again. Arthur groaned again: Callie, with movements soundless as they were certain, opened the door and slipped through to the living-room. 'What's the matter?' she whispered. 'Are you ill?'

'No; I just got a cigarette. Did I wake you up?'

'But you groaned.'

'I'm sorry; I'd no idea.'

'But do you often?'

'I've no idea, really, I tell you,' Arthur repeated. The air of the room was dense with his presence, overhung by tobacco. He must be sitting on the edge of his bed, wrapped up in his overcoat – she could smell the coat, and each time he pulled on the cigarette his features appeared down there, in the fleeting, dull reddish glow. 'Where are you?' he said. 'Show a light.'

Her nervous touch on her torch, like a reflex to what he said, made it flicker up for a second. 'I am just by the door; Pepita's asleep; I'd better go back to bed.'

'Listen. Do you two get on each other's nerves?'

'Not till tonight,' said Callie, watching the uncertain swoops of the cigarette as he reached across to the ash-tray on the edge of the table. Shifting her bare feet patiently, she added: 'You don't see us as we usually are.'

'She's a girl who shows things in funny ways – I expect she feels bad at our putting you out like this – I know I do. But then we'd got no choice, had we?'

'It is really I who am putting you out,' said Callie.

'Well, that can't be helped either, can it? You had the right to stay in your own place. If there'd been more time, we might have gone to the country, though I still don't see where we'd have gone there. It's one harder when you're not married, unless you've got the money. Smoke?'

'No, thank you. Well, if you're all right, I'll go back to bed.'

'I'm glad she's asleep – funny the way she sleeps, isn't it? You can't help wondering where she is. You haven't got a boy, have you, just at present?'

'No. I've never had one.'

'I'm not sure in one way that you're not better off. I can see there's not so much in it for a girl these days. It makes me feel cruel the way I unsettle her: I don't know how much it's me myself or how much it's something the matter that I can't help. How are any of us to know how things could have been? They forget war's not just only war; it's years out of people's lives that they've never had before and won't have again. Do you think she's fanciful?'

'Who, Pepita?'

'It's enough to make her – tonight was the pay-off. We couldn't get near any movie or any place for sitting; you had to fight into the bars, and she hates the staring in bars, and with all that milling about, every street we went, they kept on knocking her even off my arm. So then we took the tube to that park down there, but the place was as bad as daylight, let alone it was cold. We hadn't the nerve – well, that's nothing to do with you.'

'I don't mind.'

'Or else you don't understand. So we began to play – we were off in Kôr.'

'Core of what?'

'Mysterious Kôr – ghost city.'

'Where?'

'You may ask. But I could have sworn she saw it, and from the way she saw it I saw it, too. A game's a game, but what's a hallucination? You begin by laughing, then it gets in you and you can't laugh it off. I tell you, I woke up just now not knowing where I'd been; and I had to get up and feel round this table before I even knew where I was. It wasn't till then that I thought of a cigarette. Now I see why she sleeps like that, if that's where she goes.'

'But she is just as often restless; I often hear her.'

'Then she doesn't always make it. Perhaps it takes me, in some way – Well, I can't see any harm: when two people have got no place, why not want Kôr, as a start? There are no restrictions on wanting, at any rate.'

'But, oh, Arthur, can't wanting want what's human?'

He yawned. 'To be human's to be at a dead loss.' Stopping yawning, he ground out his cigarette: the china tray skidded at the edge of the table. 'Bring that light here a moment – that is, will you? I think I've messed ash all over these sheets of hers.'

Callie advanced with the torch alight, but at arm's length: now and then her thumb made the beam wobble. She watched the lit-up inside of Arthur's hand as he brushed the sheet; and once he looked up to see her white-nightgowned figure curving above and away from him, behind the arc of light. 'What's that swinging?'

'One of my plaits of hair. Shall I open the window wider?'

'What, to let the smoke out? Go on. And how's your moon?'

'Mine?' Marvelling over this, as the first sign that Arthur remembered that she was Callie, she uncovered the window, pushed up the sash, then after a minute said: 'Not so strong.'

Indeed, the moon's power over London and the imagination had now declined. The siege of light had relaxed; the search was over; the street had a look of survival and no more. Whatever had glittered there, coin or ring, was now invisible or had gone. To Callie it seemed likely that there would never be such a moon again; and on the whole she felt this was for the best. Feeling air reach in like a tired arm round her body, she dropped the curtains against it and returned to her own room.

Back by her bed, she listened: Pepita's breathing still had the regular sound of sleep. At the other side of the wall the divan creaked as Arthur stretched himself out again. Having felt ahead of her lightly, to make sure her half was empty, Callie climbed over Pepita and got in. A certain amount of warmth had travelled between the sheets from Pepita's flank, and in this Callie extended her sword-cold body: she tried to compose her limbs; even they quivered after Arthur's words in the dark, words *to* the dark. The loss of her own mysterious expectation, of her love for love, was a small thing beside the war's total of unlived lives. Suddenly Pepita flung out one hand: its back knocked Callie lightly across the face.

Pepita had now turned over and lay with her face up. The hand that had struck Callie must have lain over the other, which grasped the pyjama collar. Her eyes, in the dark, might have been either shut or open, but nothing made her frown more or less steadily: it became certain, after another moment, that Pepita's act of justice had been unconscious. She still lay, as she had lain, in an avid dream, of which Arthur had been the source, of which Arthur was not the end. With him she looked this way, that way, down the wide void pure streets, between statues, pillars and shadows, through archways and colonnades. With him she went up the stairs down which nothing but moon came; with him trod the ermine dust of the endless halls, stood on terraces, mounted the extreme tower, looked down on the statued squares, the wide, void, pure streets. He was the password, but not the answer: it was to Kôr's finality that she turned.

DENTON WELCH

THE JUDAS TREE

As I was walking home from the art school one day, a rather plump, middle-aged man in shaggy tweeds passed me and then looked over his shoulder. He had a smooth round face with red veins on his cheeks, pepper-coloured hair, and a carelessly-trimmed moustache. He carried a little bunch of spring flowers – hyacinth, narcissus, daffodils – and in his other hand was a knotted walking-stick.

The first time he looked round, his face wore no expression, and it reminded me of a beefy moon or a dart-board; but when, a few yards farther on, he turned again, the skin round his eyes was crinkled into a kind and sleepy smile. He slowed down, then held out the bunch to me and said, 'Like to smell?'

I was surprised, but I bent down at once and put my nose to the cold flowers. Their rich breath filled my head. A little tingle of excitement ran through me. I waited to see what would happen next.

When I raised my head I saw that the man was looking down on me with a sort of hungry benignity impossible to resist. It was as if he were saying, 'Oh, you are young and silly and unprotected, and I am old and wise and unused. If only we two could combine!'

I felt that I had to treat him with great consideration, and this feeling threw up a slight barrier of pretence. I was a little uncomfortable.

'They are lovely,' I said, referring to the flowers. I nearly asked if he'd grown them himself, but the more I hesitated, the more inquisitive and pert the question sounded. I was tongue-tied and silent.

We were walking together over Blackheath now, near the church, and the pit where they light bonfires on Guy Fawkes' night. I expected the man to say good-bye soon and branch off in some other direction, but he stayed at my side and every now and then looked down at me. He was tall.

'Where do you go to school?' he said at last, smiling again in his disarming way.

I was nettled, but also obscurely complimented. I think I felt, 'Well, I must look simple! Nobody knows what's going on in this head.'

'I am an art student,' I said, trying not to sound stiff.

'Oh, that's interesting!' and his face lit up, as though an idea had come to him.

'Do you know what a Judas tree is?' He stared straight into my eyes, then added, very surprisingly, 'I've been a schoolmaster for thirty years, and I can always tell when a boy is lying.'

'I was going to say that I didn't know.' I felt repulsed at once by this, flashing glimpse of another side of his character. I recognized the schoolmaster's unnecessary parade, the over-emphasis.

'Well,' he said sweetly, returning to his earlier manner, 'it is a wonderful tree that bears great rose-coloured flowers; and the amazing thing is that the flowers appear before the leaves! Judas, you know, after he had betrayed our Lord, repented, and took back the thirty pieces of silver to the chief priests. But when he had told them that he had betrayed innocent blood, they gave a terrible answer; they said, "What is that to us? See thou to that." So he threw down the silver in the temple and went to hang himself. He found a bare tree, climbed up into the branches, tied the rope; then jumped. The next morning the whole tree was lighted and hung with marvellous Judas-coloured flowers. And the Judas tree, from that day to this, always bears its flowers before its leaves.'

When he had finished this story, the man's face was rapt. He seemed transported. To take him away from the dangerous subject of the Bible, I said, rather stolidly, 'Why do you call the flowers Judas-coloured?'

'Don't you know that Judas had red hair?' he rapped out. 'I've collected every picture I can lay hands on, and nearly all the painters from the early Italians downwards have given Judas red hair. Sometimes it's curly, sometimes it's straight, but it's almost always red.' Then he gave me the names of one or two famous painters who had *not* given Judas red hair. He blamed them for inaccuracy, saying that their Judases failed and had not nearly enough evil in them, because of the mistake.

'Don't you think I've proved now that Judas had red hair? Could so many painters be wrong? There must be something in it.' He looked at me sharply and anxiously, as though he wanted to make me agree.

I nodded and said, 'I expect you're right,' then thought this weak, so added what I really felt.

'It is all such a long time ago that nobody can really tell. Perhaps all the painters followed a tradition which was started by a man who hated red hair and so gave it to the villain in his picture.'

The man was infuriated. 'Of course Judas had red hair!' he thundered. I was able to picture him in front of a class at school, abusing the boys violently.

We walked on in silence. Still the man didn't leave me. I was about to turn to the right pretending that I lived in that direction, when the man, with all his fierceness gone, said: 'I'm wondering if you could do something for me, since you are obviously a clever lad.' I moved about uncomfortably in my clothes, wondering what was coming.

'Could you paint me a picture of Judas hanging dead from the Judas tree, with the beautiful rose-red flowers all round him? You could do the flowers very large, and I want Judas really dead. His tongue must be hanging out, black and swollen. It would make a wonderful picture, and I've been trying to get it painted for years.'

He looked at me with intense, excited eyes. He had begun his speech cajolingly, with the remark about the clever lad, but he ended on the same vibrant note as before. It was clear that he lived for Judas and the Judas tree.

'Won't you have a shot at it?' he pleaded when I did not answer at once. 'I could give you a great deal of help over the details. I've got some enlarged photographs of the flowers, and I know exactly how a hanged man looks. His head lolls on one shoulder just like this —' Here he stopped abruptly and, drooping his head to one side, showed the whites of his eyes and the whole length of his tongue in a hideous imitation of death.

'I could sit like this for you, if you liked,' he said, still holding the pose. I wished he would stop distorting his face, so I told him how convincing he looked and moved on. He hurried after me.

'I thought at one time of having real red hair, cut from a human being, or, if that's not possible, from a red-setter, for my Judas, but my sister, who lives with me, tells me that an oil-painting in which real materials are also used is in very bad taste. Do you agree?'

He seemed wistful, wanting me not to condemn his idea as fantastic.

'I think to have the whole picture in paint would be safer,' I said carefully; 'but I'm afraid I could never do it for you. It would be much too difficult. I wouldn't know how to begin on such a subject.'

We had almost crossed the heath. I should have gone along Chesterfield Walk to reach my rooms on Croom's Hill, but the man said: 'You *must* come home with me and see my reproductions of Judas; and if my sister's in she will give us tea.'

Again there was the tingle of excitement in me, the feeling that some sort of adventure might be unfolding. I had been growing a little restive, but this invitation reawakened my interest. I wanted to see his surroundings.

'Oh – thank you,' I said, 'I'd like just to look at your pictures, but I *mustn't* be late back.' I hoped in this way to make any sudden retreat seem necessary, not rude.

Somewhere behind the Green Man we turned down a long street of mid-Victorian yellow brick houses with dog-tooth mouldings over the doors and windows.

'We live a bit farther down, on the left,' the man said, then, realizing that he did not know my name, he demanded it in his schoolmaster's manner.

I told him and he seemed to weigh it in his mind, as if trying to assess its worth.

'Mine's Clinton,' he returned solemnly.

'Oh, we have a girl at the art school called Clinton,' I said. 'She comes to the Fabric-Painting class, and she's going to teach art.'

He frowned and looked uncertain for a moment, then he said stiffly: 'She is no relation – no relation at all. I can trace my family back to the thirteenth century.'

The last sentence, so naked, so irrelevant and disagreeable, chilled me. I said nothing.

'If they've got any books on heraldry at your art school you'll be able to look up quite a lot about my family,' he said smoulderingly, *willing* me to be awed.

I still said nothing and he began to boast about his family so outrageously that I wanted to laugh. Could he be serious? I had known nothing like it since early school days, when children vied with one another over motor-cars, the size of houses and the number of servants kept.

I was relieved when he put his key into the front door and dropped the subject of his family as abruptly as he had introduced it. We were in a dark hall now. He led me to the door of the back room, then threw it open. I saw a grand piano, a large old portfolio stand, and books in low cases, lining the walls rather meagrely. Opposite the one French window was a dilapidated brown sofa.

'Sit down, sit down,' the man said expansively. I was his guest now, no longer a chance acquaintance. He wheeled the portfolio up to me, then brought out picture after picture in which Judas appeared. Some of them were charming old prints torn from books, others were shiny 'Last Suppers' and richly-glowing 'Betrayal' scenes made for Catholic children. There were dreary photographs of great masterpieces and 'details' showing every crack in the plaster or the panel. I looked again and again at evil, twisted, avaricious features, at hyacinth curling hair, at goatee beards and at ones flowing like the little waterfalls in Japanese gardens. There was simulated love – the lips kissing while the eyes were glittering, almost radiant, with treachery. Then the torture of remorse, the last agony of realization.

But there was no picture of Judas hanged, paid out, fulfilled. For a moment I felt the lack, almost understood Mr Clinton's preoccupation with the subject.

He was sitting very close to me now, breathing on my neck as he leant over me to point with his stubby finger. I could smell juicy pipe tobacco, the animal smell of tweeds, and something between alcohol and the smell in chemist's shops. Was it the last traces of whisky, of eau-de-cologne, patent antiseptic, or medicated snuff? I tried to analyse it in this elaborate way to cover my growing uneasiness. Would Mr Clinton never move away to some other part of the room? Had he enticed me here for some criminal purpose? Was he perhaps going to try to string me up, so that he should at last have a living, kicking picture of Guilt and Retribution?

My thoughts grew so wild that in my nervousness I began to gather the reproductions together officiously and thrust them back into the portfolio. I felt that his eyes were burning into the back of my head. He said nothing. I wanted to get up and run.

'Did you like your school?' The flatness of the question came as a shock. Because I had expected strangeness, or even violence, I was bewildered. How did this man's mind work? Why at the climax did he always jump to some other subject, as if the first one no longer meant anything to him?

'Perhaps I liked it in bits,' I answered vaguely, 'but I couldn't have enjoyed it much, because I ran away.'

'You needn't imagine that I think any the better of you for that,' he said.

Blood rushed up into my face. Could he think that I was proud of running away from school? The pointless snub seemed unforgivable, until I remembered that he was a schoolmaster.

He began to tell me all about himself. He had been a housemaster at a school whose name I had not heard before. Nobody had ever run away from *his* house. He understood boys, and boys understood him. It was, I was made to realize, a great loss to the school when the ridiculous rules had compelled him to retire. He was not idle, though.

There was all this research on Judas to be done, and he was musical. Had I not noticed the Broadwood grand piano? Did I play?

'Only a very little,' I answered cautiously.

'And can you sing?'

'I was in the choir at school until my voice broke, but now I don't sing properly,' I said.

He looked at me expertly. 'Perhaps you had a good treble; but what have you got now, I should like to know? Maybe something – maybe nothing. Just come over to the piano and we'll see.'

I followed him in a hot state of embarrassment. Was I really to be made to sing 'ah, ah, ah, ah, ah, AH, AH, AH' in that shaming way? I began to sweat a little. But a part of me was pleased. I wanted to be able to sing well, and once my voice had broken no one had bothered with it. Was my adventure to end in free singing lessons? I hoped so. Clinton looked so competent on the piano-stool. I believed in him.

I began quaveringly, afraid of too much sound and of the surprising, unnatural tone of my voice.

'Louder!' he shouted.

I grew a little bolder, ascended and descended the scale, and sang particular notes which he thumped insistently, until they sounded like tom-toms in the jungle.

His hands dropped from the keyboard and there was an impressive silence for a moment; then he looked not at me, but out of the window, and said, 'I can make something of your voice. Of course, you'll have to work. You'd better come here at least twice a week.'

'Thank you so much,' I said, really grateful, 'but can you spare the time? Wouldn't it be a nuisance?'

'Nuisance! Why nuisance? It's part of my job. I've trained hundreds of lads' voices. I hate letting them go to waste.'

At this point a woman's tired, rather petulant voice called from upstairs.

'Excuse me,' the man said, leaving the piano-stool at once, 'that is my sister. I shall go up and ask her about tea.'

It was long after tea-time and I wondered what the sister would say. I heard them talking at the top of the stairs in low voices. The only clear words were the sister's irritable 'Who is it?'

I was immediately ruffled, upset, put in a false position, and I decided to leave as soon as the man returned.

I heard him running down the stairs. He burst into the room in a young way and said, between puffs, 'My sister's got one of her troublesome heads and so I've persuaded her to stay in her room, but we can go into the kitchen and forage for ourselves.' He seemed delighted about his sister's headache. He came up to me at the piano, put his hand on my shoulder and said, 'Can you boil eggs, you scoundrel, eh? I bet you coddle 'em or make them like old leather boots, but come and try, while I make toast.' He gave me several playful punches.

I was not expecting so much heartiness and good-fellowship. His changes in personality were too much for me. I had been hurt by his sister's words. And what was the cause of this sudden gaiety? Had he a sinister reason for wishing his sister out of the way in her room? All my misgivings reawoke and I longed to get away from him. It was easy to persuade myself that he was evil.

'But I really must get back,' I said, 'or they'll wonder what has happened to me.' Even if I had stayed out all night no one would have worried; but I allowed Clinton to think that careful parents were waiting for me at home.

'Can't you just stay to tea?' he asked, quite crest-fallen.

'I'm afraid not; it's getting so late.' I moved firmly towards the door and he followed me, shambling.

'You *will* try to do my picture of Judas, won't you?' he said.

He was different again – sad, deflated, almost clinging. 'And you must come here for your singing lessons.'

'Oh, thank you, I will,' I said.

We were through the dark hall and I was walking down the steps and saying good-bye over my shoulder in my haste. I smiled at him and tried to look pleased, but it was easy to see that I was escaping.

He stood under the porch disconsolately, then gave a little jerk with his hand and went in and slammed the door.

I sucked in deep breaths of air and ran up to the heath, free at last.

I saw nothing of Mr Clinton for about a month after this first meeting. I did nothing about his Judas picture and avoided going anywhere near his house. I regretted the singing lessons, but would not have braved his strangeness, his unaccountable changes of mood, and the something alarming in him, even for them.

When I saw him for the second time I was with three other students. I suddenly recognized his back. He was a few feet in front of us on the pavement. He carried no posy, but he had his walking-stick.

By turning my head away and talking earnestly I hoped to brush by unnoticed; but as I passed him I heard him call out, 'Oh, so it's you, is it?'

'Hullo!' I said, stopping and trying to put surprise and pleasure into my voice.

'What are you doing, going home?' he asked suspiciously.

'No; we're having tea together somewhere first,' I said, my eyes following the other students, who were now some yards in front.

'Have you done anything about that picture?' There was accusation in his voice.

'I haven't had a moment,' I said guiltily. 'I couldn't do that sort of thing at the school, you know. I'd have to do it at home.'

He turned sharply and saw me looking at the backs of the other students.

'Well – hadn't you better go after your friends?' he said, somehow threateningly. 'Hadn't you better leave *me* and catch *them* up?'

And in this last sentence Mr Clinton seemed to put all the waste and emptiness of his life. It was so sad that I was melted and horrified. He who had once had fifty boys to bully and befriend now had no one at all. People all smiled nervously and backed away, as I had done. How old and mad and undesirable he must be feeling!

'Why don't you cut along?' he sneered. 'Why don't you join them for a jolly tea-party? You're no use here.' He darted a venomous look at me and went on jeering at my dumb, nonplussed state. I would have stayed with him, but he was driving me away with every word.

'Yes, I must go,' I said miserably, turning my shocked, startled face to him.

But as I turned he looked away and appeared to be interested in a black boy's head and a pipe in a tobacconist's window.

'Good-bye,' I said uncertainly. He never turned.

Inexplicably wounded and humbled, I ran on to join my friends.

[*PNW* 26, 1945]

J. MACLAREN-ROSS

SECOND LIEUTENANT LEWIS

I

I'm no good at dates and I don't keep a diary; so it may have been spring or summer, 1942, I can't really remember.

I stepped into the hall of BHQ over two janker-wallahs on hands and knees scrubbing down the chequered tiles; a smell of yellow soap steamed up all around me; the doorknob of X Company office fell off with a clatter as the door itself opened. Corporal Dexter came out: shirt-sleeves and big grin, scratching his chest.

'Hey, Rossy, where'd you get to? There's an officer been round looking for you.'

'Let him look,' I said. 'I'm off duty.'

'Never 'eard of it. A soldier's on duty twenty-four hours a day.'

Dexter had a whole store of these idiotic army catch-phrases, which he repeated as though each were an epigram coined fresh by him that very moment. He was permanent orderly-sergeant, Category C, and underneath his bluffness and easy-going air he enjoyed the authority. In civvy street he had been a manufacturer of ladies' straw hats.

He said: 'Don't give a bullock what you do, meself. All I know is he said for you to report to him straightaway, soon's you come in.'

'The morning'll be soon enough,' I said. I took for granted it was one of our subalterns: the twenty-year-old school-prefect type who was always asking me how to spell something, or perhaps Lieutenant Buckley who wanted some typing done in my spare time. I was on my way again when Dexter's voice arrested me.

'Ain't one of our mob. He's a Taffy. One pip. Name of,' he looked at a pencilled scrap of paper in his hand 'Lewis. Mr Lewis. Said you was to report down the road, their HQ. Asked for you very special, by name an' all.'

He broke off to bawl out the jankermen, who'd stopped scrubbing and squatted back on their heels to enjoy our dialogue. I was intrigued. I knew of no Welsh one-pipper named Lewis, and it was curiosity, not obedience to an order, that drove me out into the evening sunshine along what had once been the marine parade, past the rusty hoops of Dannert wire cutting off the pebbly beach and the sea in which mines bobbed like buoys.

A guard on the gate of the Welsh Headquarters halted me. Mr Lewis'd be eating his dinner; Officers' Mess; third house on the left. I went in there; it seemed uninhabited: bare boards echoing to my boots, flakes of fallen plaster, wallpaper peeling off. I shouted. An orderly appeared from the kitchen with a mug of tea in his hand. He said he'd see. He disappeared up some stairs. In a few moments a young officer came running lightly down these. He wore one pip and service dress, but without his Sam Browne belt, as though he were awaiting trial by court-martial. He had a Welsh face, dark, with eyes set deep.

I came smartly to attention and saluted. '6027033, Private Ross J. reporting for duty, sir.'

To my surprise the face of Mr Lewis flushed even darker at this. He turned his head away and muttered something in a voice so low that I couldn't catch the words. I said: 'I beg your pardon, sir.'

He muttered, but more audibly this time: 'I'm Alun Lewis.' He held out his hand. In a second we were shaking hands heartily. I said: 'I'd no idea. They just said Mr Lewis and I was to report to you straightaway.'

'The fools,' he said. 'My God, isn't that typical. When you saluted I thought you were making fun of me.' He smiled, a quick boyish grin. He spoke very quickly, too, and with a strong Welsh intonation which I found difficult at first to understand. Later this wore off and I discovered it was a mark of embarrassment. He was extraordinarily shy. He said: 'But come upstairs. There's only one fellow there, the others are all out. Gone to the dance.'

We started to climb the stairs and I said: 'How did you know I was here?'

'Your padre told me. When he said your name was Ross and you were a writer, I thought you must be Hugh Ross Williamson.'

'I never thought you were Wyndham Lewis,' I said.

That set us back again; his face flushed up and he muttered something I couldn't catch. I soon learnt not to make wisecracks of that sort; they only upset him. We reached the door of the Mess and it was my turn to be embarrassed. How should a private behave when invited into the Officers' Mess? I decided it must be a social occasion and removed my cap, as if going up before the M O. This obviated the need for saluting the other subaltern whom Alun Lewis now introduced me to, and as the table was between us we didn't have to shake hands. They'd finished dinner and the orderly was clearing away. His eyes nearly fell out of his head when Lewis asked me to sit down and have some coffee. When this was served we were all at a loss. Lewis jumped up and looked out of the window. It faced on to the sea. A ship could be seen way out. We looked at this through field-glasses. But at last even the ship was exhausted as a topic of conversation and we sat down again. Cigarettes were handed round and then the other sub-altern excused himself; he had to do his tour as duty-officer.

Once he'd gone, Lewis said: 'You see, I wanted to talk to you, because I thought you could tell me about India. I'm being posted there any day now. Or is that a military secret?' He smiled.

'Not to me,' I said. 'Everyone knows your mob's bound for India. But why I should be able to tell you about it I can't imagine.'

Lewis stared at me astounded. He said: 'But surely you know India well?'

'Never been there in my life.' Then, too late, I realized. At that time I'd only had two stories printed, and both of them dealt with India – or, to be precise, Madras. I now had to explain how I had acquired my material. This story is always a let-down, and leaves people with a feeling that they oughtn't to meet writers whose stories they have read.

Lewis was no exception. He was disappointed. He said: 'I've just read another story of yours. In *Fortune Anthology*. It's not about India.'

'No,' I said. It wasn't. It was about a man of thirty seducing a girl of sixteen in a seaside hotel.

Lewis's face had begun to flush and his Welsh accent came on again. 'I've got to review the Anthology for *Tribune*. I wonder if you'll mind,' here he coughed and looked into his coffee, 'if I don't mention your story?'

'Not at all. Do you think it's so bad?'

'No, no. But you see it's about sex. I couldn't possibly say anything about it.'

'Because I don't treat sex seriously?'

He nodded. That sent me off into a denunciation. I particularly hate the idea of sex treated as a solemn fetish. I couldn't understand this attitude, which seemed to me puritanical, in a writer who had produced a fine sensual story like *The Wanderers*. It seemed like hypocrisy. It was not that, as I understood later, and Alun Lewis was not a puritan. But his deep love and respect for women, the fact that his wife was expecting a child at a time when they were about, any moment, to be separated, made him inimical to anything that savoured of a sophisticated approach to sex. We argued for a while but Lewis remained unconvinced. He coughed and kicked the table-leg doggedly. The talk switched from sex to technical problems in writing. He had a great admiration for the stories of Flying Officer X, and asked me if I knew who this was. He said he himself was writing some stories about the army and we went to his room to look at the MSS.

His room was a tiny cubby-hole with a window looking out on to a wall: no bigger and no better – except for the camp-bed and the small table piled with army pamphlets – than my own bunk at BHQ. Lewis sat down on the bed, ran his fingers through his dark hair which had just been cut: his OC had talked about curling pins and violins. Some of the pamphlets slipped off the table and lay scattered on the floor: ABCA, WAR, Battle and Weapon Training, War Office Memoranda: Lewis looked down at them with despair.

'I've got to swot all these up somehow,' he said. He'd just come back from a battle-course. It'd been hell and yet he'd enjoyed it. *This* was what he hated: the paperwork, swotting up pamphlets, reports to prepare, red-tape and routine, always something to remember that had slipped the mind; he voiced the eternal hope of the soldier. 'It'll be different out there,' and then: 'But it's a long way to go.'

He showed me two stories called that; with a third one, as yet unfinished, they were to form a trilogy. He showed me one called *Flick* and gave me a bundle of MSS. to take away and read. At this moment a knock came on the door. I thought it would be Lewis's Officer Commanding, come to give him a bullock for fraternizing with a private soldier. It wasn't. Instead it was our C. of E. Chaplain, who had been instrumental in bringing us together.

This padre once asked me as a favour not to write anything about him. I have already broken my promise, so will not say any more, except that he was one of the most intelligent and understanding men whom I ever came across during my service in the army.

The padre did not stay long, but before he knocked out his pipe and went, the constraint remaining between Lewis and myself was completely gone. We agreed to go and have one in the pub. When we got outside Lewis had to rush back in for his Sam Browne: 'I'm always forgetting the damn thing.' He walked along the street beside me buckling on the belt. My RSM was passing on the other side of the parade. He gave Lewis an eyes-right and his stiff jerky salute, imitated behind his back throughout the battalion. Lewis attempted to return the salute and the belt fell to the ground. He stooped to retrieve it while the RSM passed on stiffly disapproving in his rubber-soled shoes.

'I made a mess of that,' Lewis said ruefully, getting the Sam Browne round him at last. 'An RSM, too.'

'That's my RSM,' I said. 'Used to be a milkman.'

'Nothing against him,' Lewis said. 'That's class-distinction.'

I said: 'It's something against him when he uses his wartime authority to work off past grievances and an inferiority complex. He's more class-conscious than either of us. I bet you he votes Conservative.'

Lewis couldn't see my point, although he admitted to having had some pretty bloody sergeant-majors in his time.

Comparing notes about the sergeant-majors brought us to the pub. This was jammed to the door. It took ages to get a drink, and then they'd only Mild. We had to shout to make ourselves heard. Soldiers from Lewis's regiment kept on coming up to greet him and to offer him drinks. Eventually they shouted 'Time' and we left. Corporal Dexter, hanging on the gate chatting with the curious woman who gave us haircuts, turned and saluted. This time Lewis managed to return the compliment without dropping his stick or his service-dress cap falling off. Dexter stared after him open-mouthed. Neither of us had the army knack of surface smartness, and by military standards we must have seemed, officer and private, a pretty scruffy pair.

'Did you ever put in for a commission?' Lewis asked me.

'Failed the WOSB test,' I told him. 'Returned unsuitable.'

'I'm not certain I shouldn't have stayed in the ranks,' Lewis said. 'I thought that as an officer I'd be able to do something for the men. But one's more helpless than ever.'

The sense of helplessness and the thought of the pamphlets that remained to be swotted-up in the small airless room, while the poems, the stories, stayed unwritten: these were the things that oppressed him. Had it not been for his wife, the idea of India – the jungle, the Japs, something doing at last – would have seemed a welcome opportunity: one that I myself, being without ties, certainly envied him.

I asked how his brother officers treated the idea of his being a poet. At first they'd regarded it as rather rum, made contemptuous little jokes about Shakespeare and asked him to make up smutty limericks, but then a photograph of him was found in an old copy of *Lilliput* and the Mess was impressed. Fame could reach no higher: unless, of course, the photograph had appeared in *Men Only*. Now his writing was regarded as a harmless pastime, so long as it didn't interfere with his efficiency as an officer. It was generally hoped, however, that India would knock all that nonsense out of him.

We arrived at the door of the Mess and Lewis sighed – the pamphlets awaited him inexorably upstairs. He said: 'You must show me your stories too.'

As we were in the street I raised my hand to salute. Lewis said: 'For Christ's sake don't do that,' seized my hand and shook it. Then he doubled inside and I could hear him running up the stairs. But my RSM had observed our parting handshake from the door of BHQ where he was giving the Picquet Commander a dressing-down.

'Ah, Ross,' he said as I came up, showing in a crafty smile his greenish teeth under the clipped white moustache. 'Going up in the world, aren't you?'

'Sir?' I said.

'Consorting with officers. Who was that? Your brother?'

'A brother-writer, sir,' I said.

'Ah, that explains it; I thought something of the sort. I observed him putting on his Sam Browne belt in the street.' The RSM shook his head. 'These civilians – writers and such-like – you can't make soldiers out of 'em.'

'Sir,' I said stiffly – I was standing to attention – 'I didn't know that it came within your province to comment on the dress of commissioned officers belonging to another regiment.'

The RSM opened his mouth. He gasped, and looked round to make sure the Picquet Commander was out of hearing. His eyes narrowed but he knew I had him knackered, as the saying goes. He said: 'One of these fine days you'll go a bit too far, Private Ross, and I'm warning you.'

'Yes, sir,' I said, and went on upstairs to my office. I had meant to write a short story that evening, but I sat down and read Lewis's instead. I started with *Private Jones* and ended with *The Prisoners*. This is not a work of literary criticism and the stories have now all been published and can speak for themselves. I will say only this: that after reading them, the army stories which I myself was trying to write seemed by contrast a joke in rather bad taste. This feeling had worn off by the next morning, but I went to bed profoundly dissatisfied with myself and my work.

I sent the stories back to Lewis next day by an orderly who happened to be taking a message to the Welsh HQ. He returned with an odd story. He had accosted a fatigue party who were coal-heaving outside – why, at that time of year, I can't imagine. He asked where Mr Lewis could be found. One of the fatigue party, in shirt-sleeves and covered with coal dust, had turned and said: 'Here I am.' This had so shaken the orderly that he'd delivered the packet of MSS. without remembering to salute. I don't suppose that Lewis minded.

II

I saw him several times after that. We ate steak and chips together in a café along the sea-front, full of snobbish Wrens talking at the tops of their voices about the RAF officers who'd taken them out. I didn't show Lewis any of my stories except one which again dealt with sex, and part of a novel that I was writing. I think that to a great extent he disapproved of what I wrote. I remember him speaking once of the enormous responsibility which a writer should feel towards his characters having once called them into being. He spoke of this almost with awe.

I do not think that in civilian life we could have been friends. We were too different. Where he was genuinely humble and modest, I am arrogant and didactic. Where he felt sympathy and love, I feel anger and contempt. I have only a film-gangster's kindness towards small things – animals, children – Lewis had a deep tenderness towards life itself: a nostalgic yearning for his Welsh village, his wife, whereas I have no roots and regard family life with fascinated horror. That doesn't mean to say I am ascribing all the virtues to Lewis, to myself all the faults. I don't necessarily consider them faults or virtues in either case. We were simply of different temperaments: even our aims as writers were violently opposed. But in the army, where the strangest friendships are struck up, it was natural for us to draw together and to talk of intimate ambitions which in civvy-street – in a Soho pub or the Café Royal – we might never have discussed.

Our friendship excited much hostile comment in our respective regiments, owing to the difference in rank. Lewis, being an officer, got the worst of it. He had several open rows, whereas I only had to put up with Corporal Dexter talking about my Officer Pal and the RSM's innuendoes.

One night we were drinking in the saloon-bar of a posh hotel. Officers were staggering about with blondies and popsies in all directions. Suddenly Lewis's Officer Commanding walked in. He gave us a terrible yellow stare and said: 'Lewis, I'll see you in the Mess later.'

Lewis flushed. He was furious. Outside in the street he cursed. Later he got a blowing-up, and after that we were driven out into back streets where the O C was unlikely to see us. We used to walk aimlessly about or dodge for a drink into furtive pubs.

On the night before Lewis's mob was due to move, we sat on a rusty abandoned roller in a field of long grass. Lewis didn't talk much. He was depressed. Once he said: 'I'm not sure that I want to go really,' and later: 'But there'll be something to get to grips with out there.'

I said: 'Write to me.' We shook hands and he walked on down the road to see if they'd got his gear ready. He had his Sam Browne belt slung wrong again.

That's the last time I saw him.

'Your Officer Pal's gone then, Rossy,' Corporal Dexter said with relish next morning. 'See the Taffys've moved.'

'Yes,' I said. 'He's gone.'

He never wrote to me, or if he did I never got the letter.

In March, 1943, I was travelling to hospital under escort, for I was at the time awaiting court-martial: as the R S M predicted, I had gone a little bit too far at last. On a station bookstall I saw *The Last Inspection and Other Stories*, by A L U N L E W I S, and bought the book. I wondered how he was getting on; but not for long, as I had my own troubles and plenty of them. Much later, when I was a civilian again, I heard he'd been killed in action.

Keidrych Rhys heard the news first and rang up the War Office. They didn't know what he was talking about.

'This is the War Office.'

'I am inquiring about Second Lieutenant Lewis, believed killed in action.'

'Oh, I *see*. At first you said he was a poet or something. Why didn't you say he was an officer?'

[PNW 27, 1946]

P. H. NEWBY

KHAMSEEN

She, a plump little lady in black whose feet did not touch the ground when she sat upon her divan, was indignant at the idea. 'My servant is a dependable Berber. He is devoted to me. There is no shortage of servants for those who are prepared to pay.'

'An act of graciousness in memory of my late master, your lord and husband,' pleaded Hassan. 'I have divorced my wife and she has now no right in the child. If the woman comes she is to be told that all my rights have been made over to you. The child is yours to give or to keep, to do what you will with. I am fond of the child though it is weakly —'

The Widow silenced him. 'I know what you men are. One wife one week, another wife the next, yet another in the third week, and another in the fourth. Then you re-marry your first wife and so it goes on. Tell me,' she said, settling her jaw complacently into her many chins, 'do you think I am a fool? I treat your miserable daughter Fawzia as my own daughter, I fatten her like a chicken, I educate her, I lead her into the proper paths of life, I dress her in good clothes. What then? You marry your wretched wife again and demand the return of your daughter. It is fair neither to me nor the unfortunate child.' She looked through the open door at the child who, not venturing to enter the flat, stood scratching herself on the landing. 'However, if there is a quarrel between you and your wife I am no party to it. The child shall stay and serve me.'

At the end of the first week the Widow Hamed was startled to observe that the child Fawzia was eating as much food as Salih, the Berber servant, and herself put together. In a fortnight the girl was beginning to look her twelve years whereas previously she might have been seven or eight. The Widow Hamed had the impression that Fawzia was constituted differently from normal human beings and the gobbled rice, with no preliminary process of digestion, flowed into the cheeks and limbs like water into a goatskin.

At the end of a month Fawzia was a plump and self-possessed young woman whose special passion was to answer the telephone. At the first tinkle she would flash out of the kitchen, race along the passage and spring on to the chair under the instrument, for she was still not tall enough to reach.

'Yes, who is that? This is the house of the lady Hamed,' she would deliver in a tone of great authority and her contempt was great for those who, in telephoning, showed inexperience and nervousness so that they repeated their inquiry several times.

'This is Fawzia,' she would say, 'speaking from the house of the lady Hamed.'

The Widow was not ill-pleased. She saw to it that Fawzia was always clean and garbed her in a scarlet dress that trailed on the ground. But, given the materials, Fawzia took herself in hand. She treasured every scrap of clothing that the Widow gave her and had a washing day three times a week. She had, for a short time, attended school and now demanded books that she might learn to read. She slept on the floor in a corner of the kitchen, for Salih the Berber, a gentleman of means and independence, did not sleep on the premises. His bad Arabic amused her. He always mixed his genders and spoke to the Widow Hamed as though she were a man and of himself as though he were a woman.

Fawzia had changed so greatly that when her mother, having discovered where she lived, came to call she did not at first recognize her daughter. She was so impressed that, forgetting her real reason for coming, she could only think of enticing this fine young woman away. From now on Fatma was obsessed by the idea of once more gaining possession of her daughter; such a beautiful girl could obviously be the source of revenue and it did not occur to her, so narrow was her intelligence, that once Fawzia left the Widow Hamed's she would revert to what she had been before.

In any case Fawzia's mind was made up. 'No, I shall stay and shall not go. You left my father and me. You are old, ugly and dirty and he has forbidden me to see you. You are here in secret and I shall not go with you.'

The Widow Hamed dangled her plump legs and maintained an inscrutable neutrality. From this time on Fatma's mind was occupied with plans for kidnapping her daughter. For she planned to marry once more.

For Fawzia the Widow was not an individual living and breathing, she was part of the incomprehensible circumstance of life. It was enough for Fawzia that certain orders were given which had to be obeyed. When the Widow smiled she was not frowning or swearing; when she was swearing she was not laughing. But her laughter or her abuse was no more human than the wind when it blew dust into Fawzia's eyes or the sun that burned her skin. The Widow clapped her hands. The sound was like the crack of a small cannon. Fawzia scampered along the passage. But the Fawzia world, the flowering of consciousness that was Fawzia, lay like a frozen lake beneath the moon. The awakening did not come from the Widow Hamed.

Salih the Berber was an old man from foreign parts; even his language was different. But Fawzia found herself chattering to him with such enthusiasm that she would break off in the middle of a sentence and stare at him; the situation would hang in mid-air like a staircase in one of those derelict houses in Old Cairo. Her pause was entirely one of fear. She felt an essential part of her flowing out into the kitchen which, if she was not careful, the Berber would snap up and use for his own purposes. She found herself talking to him with such glibness that she wanted to clap a hand over her own mouth. Wasn't she doing the unmentionable thing?

Salih himself would open his thick negroid lips and put some emanation of himself into the room. In reality he was no more than forty but to Fawzia he was very, very old; he was foreign and ancient.

It was all very improper and dangerous.

If he found her with a book: 'You think to grow wise and be one of the governors of the land that you are occupied with what is marked on paper?'

Fawzia had her answer. 'Old man, do you think it is necessary to understand the thing marked on paper in order to be one of the rulers of the land?' She would have blasted him with contempt.

Instead, and before she could draw back, she found that they were talking in a new language that disturbed her. It was a language that was not made up of words though it was necessary to utter the spoken Arabic to bring it into being, just as it is necessary for the sun to shine in order to create shadow. When the Widow Hamed received lady guests in her salon and told Fawzia to make coffee the words meant an action, the action led to a certain result; the coffee made and brought in on a blue tray the power of words ceased to operate. Fawzia understood and enjoyed this limited language. But when Salih spoke the words meant something more. It was as though everything in the kitchen, the gleaming pans and the primus stove, the labelled tin of rice and sugar, even the glimpse of the busy street and the men selling paraffin and sugar-cane, everything came alive and took part in the conversation. And the rice in her belly and the fly on her face, all had developed voices of their own, such a clamour all of them talking together, such a passion they proclaimed, such a sweeping away and a lifting up that there were times when she could have fainted on her feet. Fawzia knew how to respond to orders or to abuse, she could not handle ordinary friendliness.

For this reason she did not care to talk with Salih. She was chiefly happy when sitting at the feet of the Widow and listening to her creaking corsets.

From time to time her father came to see her and sat in the corner of the kitchen where he ate whatever scraps of food it pleased the Widow to give to him. Fawzia was never particularly pleased to see him though she could never resist a little jump of excitement when she opened the door to find him there. After suddenly clutching her to his bony body he would release her and look round for what there was to eat.

One day he began to question her solemnly. 'Do you always run to the door like the wind? Or is it only when you are expecting me? I can hear you running down the passage like a wild thing. Do you recognize my ring?'

She said she always went to answer the door like that.

Hassan applied to the Widow that in future his daughter should be excused the honour of opening the door for guests. 'The woman that was my wife has plans for taking my daughter. If the little Fawzia runs to the door it will be the easiest thing for that immoral woman to catch her by the hair and drag her away.'

'Your quarrel is not my quarrel, Hassan. If the girl is seized it is not my responsibility. Is it not enough that I have taken her, dressed her in scarlet and fattened her like a fowl? Do not talk to me of these things. But I know what it will come to with you. You will marry this woman again and then all the good that I have done for Fawzia will be lost.'

Hassan warned his daughter. 'If you let this immoral woman your mother take you then I shall come and beat you until your teeth sing.'

Salih the Berber understood the conversation with difficulty, for the father spoke a vicious Cairo argot.

From now on Fawzia always looked through a judas-hole that commanded the landing before opening the door. She wanted to make sure that her mother was not standing on the other side. This was not because she was afraid of her father's threats. If she had been able to explain her caution it would probably have had something to do with the coloured caps that Salih wore. She had already made an attempt to steal one and if her mother took her away the opportunity might not come again.

She noticed it first when Salih was bending down to disengage his foot from the wet rag that he had been swishing over the floor. He was so much taller than she that normally all she could see of his headgear was a spotless white cloth wound several times round his head. She now saw that perched on the very top of his skull there was a coloured cap. She held her breath.

'You're wearing a coloured cap like I've never seen,' she remarked.

Salih straightened himself and wrung out the rag over the sink. 'In my country every man wears such a cotton cap, even the boatmen on the river.'

Although he was not looking at her and was going about his business Fawzia felt a tremor of fear. Salih's mouth always hung open. As he scrubbed away at the top of the table he hissed through his teeth. 'What manner of woman is thy mother?' he asked.

'She's got one eye,' Fawzia replied promptly, and the dear life was being called out of her.

'I've seen your father. It was your father who spoke?'

Salih did not wait for an answer to his question which was indeed not a question but a puff of incense put up into her face, his offering to the moment, to the young woman that Fawzia was, standing there. He did not look at her. He went out of the kitchen and unpegged some of the washing that was hung on the line across the back verandah.

A silver-skinned onion was lying on the window-sill, glistening in the morning sunlight, and Fawzia could not be content until she had folded her hand round its smoothness. The kitchen was still ringing with the great shout that had gone up. Fawzia did not hear it with her ears but with the core of her being. The metal pots in which they made coffee were tingling with sound.

She could not bear to be alone with Salih ever again. If it were impossible to avoid him she would not talk to him or look at him. As for the coloured caps, she could only hope that he might leave one in the bundle of clothing he left in the kitchen overnight.

The Widow Hamed trotted into the kitchen. 'Girl, I clapped, I even called. Are you deaf? Am I a mountain goat that I can dance attendance upon you? Drop that onion. I've got to eat that.'

In the middle of the Widow's abuse Fawzia smiled up into her face with such wide, unseeing eyes that the Widow caught hold of her and gave her a good shaking. Fawzia followed her back to the salon where they stood side by side watching the traffic through the window. The

Widow was aware that the child was looking at her from time to time. Self-consciousness only imposed a heavier immobility upon her marble features and all light died out of her eyes. Fawzia put out a finger and touched the glass in front of her. Her private echoing had died away and the room was filled with the sound of traffic.

'If you were to send Salih away, I could do all the work in this house, lady,' she said.

First the Widow Hamed's lips began to tremble, little pouches appeared in her cheeks, her eyes shrank. Her face turned red with a massive internal chuckle.

Some days later Salih came in from the morning's shopping and found Fawzia where she was alone.

'Your mother is downstairs and asking for you.'

'How do you know it's my mother?'

'She's as tall as a stork and she's got one eye. Besides, she asked me: "Tell my daughter, the girl Fawzia, to come to me."'

'I shall not go.'

Salih removed the shopping basket from his side where it had been strapped. Just above his left hip his white *gallabieh* was torn and soaked with blood. 'Your mother is mad for you. She is a woman with a mad spirit. She has seen that you are beautiful and thinks of nothing, night and day, but how to seize you.' Because of his extreme short-sightedness he bunched up his eyes and bent his head forward in the child's direction. There was a string of saliva running down from one corner of his mouth. Even the words that he was enunciating, uncouth and foreign as they were, did not make him any the less a blundering mute.

'There was a tall man, a Saidi, taller than your mother. He stood up close to me and pressed his knife gently into my side. There! Enough to cut but not to hurt. He told me to come up here and send you down.' He began taking the vegetables out of the basket with an indifference to the wound in his side that Fawzia herself shared. A large drop of blood splashed on his naked foot. 'I told them that your father had taken you to another house.'

She suddenly shrieked out at him – or at herself – for there was no way of asking why he had lied on her behalf. She cursed his family and his country. 'I shall complain to the Lady Hamed. Who are you to interfere with my ways and my family?'

Salih mumbled to himself and began to walk uneasily round the kitchen, but no matter where he placed himself the child turned and faced him. Her face was as crimson as the dress she was wearing. At last he went out of the kitchen and took refuge on the balcony.

Fawzia marched up the passage to interview the Widow Hamed who was taken aback by her ferocity. 'I am Fawzia and I am myself alone. My mother is below, calling for me, but I will not go, not if she waits until night comes.'

'You are what?' said the Widow incredulously.

For some weeks she was left in peace. Her mother made no further attempt to abduct her and even her father did not come. Her relations with Salih the Berber were less disturbing for after her passionate outbreak he seemed scared to talk to her. Every time she went into the kitchen and Salih invented some pretext for leaving it she burned in triumph. And the Widow had to reprimand her repeatedly for her pert, almost cheeky manner.

'There is no sugar,' she said when the Widow asked for coffee.

'No what?' The Widow allowed herself the luxury of a slight deafness.

'No su-GAR!' Her eyes sparkled to see the old lady's indignation.

She spent some time each day in the washroom dabbing at her hair with water and turning to look at her reflection in the mirror.

'The Lady wants you, Fawzia.'

She took no notice. Occasionally she bewildered him with an unexpected smile. Her ascendancy over the Berber could only be maintained, however, just so long as she did not relax in his company and allow one of those 'ghost' conversations to take place. She racked her head for taunts and insults. Only when Salih was angry did she feel that her own skin contained her. He never swore back at her but the waves of his resentment struck pleasurably against her, sheathing her, armouring her.

'Independent little bitch!' the Widow Hamed called her one day.

It was the day of the end of the world towards the latter part of the *khamseen* period. From early morning the sky had, instead of its normal blue, been a pearly opaqueness which settled down no higher than the wheeling kites. The wind rose. By the middle of the afternoon the city was blanketed by a freak sandstorm of such density that there was alarm for the Day of Judgement. The walls, chairs and tables were sweaty to the touch. Even within the shelter of the house it was as though a dozen men had been beating a dozen dusty carpets. The Widow lay on her divan with a wet handkerchief spread over her face. The windows had the brilliant amber of traffic lights. Everywhere shutters clapped, doors slammed, windows rattled. Salih lay on the floor of the kitchen with an old *gallabieh* wound round his head. Fawzia herself was excited.

The storm was beginning to lose its ruddy colour, was turning to milk and gritty air in the streets and *midans*, when there was a ring at the door and Fawzia looked through the judas-hole to find her father gesticulating on the landing. He burst in on them with a great roar of laughter, waving his arms in the air, snapping his fingers, capering, dancing, swaying from the hips, singing.

'You hashish-mad fiend,' shouted the Widow who had removed the wet handkerchief from her face.

'No, not hashish,' he declared happily. They then had time to notice that he was wearing a new gown, miraculously white. On his head was a brand new *tarboosh* that must have cost at least seventy-five piastres. He had been shaved and looked ten years younger. In his hand was a bamboo cane with which he cut the air into slices. His eyes were streaming with tears but this was only due to the grit that had lodged there. 'I'm going to be married,' he shouted like a mad creature.

He was not alone. His antics had taken up so much of their attention that they had not noticed Fawzia's mother standing with her back to the door. She also was wearing new clothes, a black dress with red facings and beads on the hem. Her eyes were heavily marked with *kohl* and there were stains of henna upon the palms of her hands. She looked at Hassan with a kind of amused contempt; then at Fawzia.

The Widow Hamed rose from her divan with the bemused desperation of the *khamseen*-afflicted. She called God, the husband, the woman, Fawzia, Salih, she called them all to witness that what she had prophesied had come to pass. The gratification almost compensated for her indignation at the cruel way that she had been served. 'So you've come to take your daughter, eh? I know!' The perspiration streamed down her face. 'After saving her from beggary and the brothel and treating her as my own daughter you, in your selfishness, in your greed and hate –' She was choked by a sense of her own clear-headedness, her anger, the clouds of dust that were still swirling round the room.

Fawzia's mother said not a word. Her one black eye was fixed upon her daughter's face and it was not removed.

Fawzia's father was indignant. He went down on his knees. He rose and twirled his cane. How had he been able to foresee that he would win thirty pounds in the State lottery and find that his wife had, all this time, been grieving for him? A man cannot live alone. A daughter belonged to her parents.

The quarrel went on. Salih prepared and brought coffee. The Widow told him to take it back again as she had no coffee to offer to the ungrateful.

'All right,' she said calmly. 'So be it. I cannot keep your daughter if you insist on taking her. It is as I foretold.' She called the girl to her and began to undo the buttons at the back of the scarlet dress. She would have stripped the girl naked and thrust her out of the door with her own hands had not Fawzia's mother started to giggle and the father to protest. He understood that Fawzia could not take away what did not belong to her but she could not walk naked through the streets. If they would wait a few minutes, not more than half an hour, he would go home and fetch a gown, or he would go into a shop and buy one; and before his wife could stop him he had opened the door and was plunging down the stairs into the *khamseen*. Her manner changed abruptly. She ran after him, waving her arms and wailing in a high tone of desperation. She leaned over the banisters and looked down into the well of the building. The scream she gave was a kind of proclamation of the desperation of her own situation. There was a sudden high cry from the depths below and when the woman, the Widow and Salih reached the entrance hall they found Fawzia's father lying on his face with a knife wound in his back. He was dead and already dusty with the *khamseen*.

It was the beginning of a week of fear. The police came and the police went. Salih could hardly be persuaded to leave the house even to go to the market. As for going home at night that was quite out of the question and the Widow Hamed, who was in any case very glad to have him on the premises, allowed him to bed-down in a spare room. Once, in answer to a ring at the door, Fawzia opened the judas-hole and saw her mother standing there. She snapped the shutter to and went to inform the Widow who began trembling, talked of telephoning for the police but eventually did nothing for fear of exposing herself to ridicule. They saw the woman, from the window, standing on the other side of the street. She looked up, their eyes met, and she smiled with a calm arrogance that seemed to reveal the extent of her power.

The three of them, the Widow, Salih and Fawzia, went to market in convoy and Fawzia's mother made a point of accompanying them, walking in the gutter at their side, saying nothing, but smiling.

'Take her, take her, take her,' the Widow whispered out of the corner of her mouth, but Fawzia's mother shook her head and continued to stare at her daughter.

Fawzia was amused. She received her mother's attentions with a genial embarrassment that was maidenly. The thought that her mother, by doing nothing at all, by merely waiting and smiling and watching was exercising such power over the wealthy Widow with her fine furniture, and over Salih with his beautiful cotton caps, could not be anything but diverting.

The Widow now quite openly wanted Fawzia's mother to take the girl away. But Fawzia's mother became increasingly distant and the Widow's alarm increased. She had taken it into her head that Fatma and the man who had murdered Hassan were now planning more than the abduction of Fawzia. Salih had told her that the tall man with the knife would undoubtedly murder them all and rob the flat.

'Fatma, my precious, how are you?' said the Widow. 'You must be sick with grief at the death of your poor husband. I have changed my mind. Fawzia may go with you – and she may keep the scarlet dress. There!' She smacked her plump hands together as though to rid them of dust. 'It is finished.'

Fatma would not consent to sit down. She held her head on one side and glanced her one eye at the ceiling. She threw up her hands in despair of deserving such generosity. 'The child is too precious to you, lady. She must not come to me unless she wants to. That would not be just.'

'Of course she wants to come to you, eh, Fawzia, my jewel?' Her hanging cheeks were waxen under the rouge. 'Tell the child how kindly you will treat her, Fatma, my love.'

Fatma was casual. 'As I've always treated her, no better and no worse. She deserves no better. She isn't even grieved for the death of her father. Look at her laughing! When she comes into my hands I shall break her.'

The Widow laughed shrilly. 'Listen to the dear woman!' She called Fawzia to her and put an arm around her. 'Always joking.' She gave her a little push. 'Go on now, go on, go with your mother.' When Fawzia hesitated the Widow lost her temper and said that was not the gratitude she expected after lavishing the very best upon her.

Fatma said she was not sure now that she wanted her daughter. The child would only be a nuisance after all, especially to someone like herself who was going to be married once more.

'I will give you a great present,' the Widow pleaded, but Fatma's one eye gleamed and she was gone.

The Widow held Fawzia responsible for the danger in which they all lay. She traced Fawzia's history from the moment she had stepped inside her door, a naked, starved, lousy maggot of a creature, up to her present proud and ignorant defiance of all human feeling in refusing to acknowledge everything that had been done for her. She smacked her soundly about the head and sent her in disgrace to the kitchen. Fawzia darted down the passage, giggling.

That evening, knowing that Salih was laying the table for the evening meal, Fawzia stole into his room and began rummaging among his belongings. The day following the murder he had brought all his possessions in a large basket, swearing that he would not leave the house again except in broad daylight. Fawzia found a spare *gallabieh*, a crimson sash, a couple of pairs of sandals, a Koran, and, what she had been searching for, three coloured caps, fitting one inside the other. She had just put her hand on them when Salih walked into the room and caught her.

He was neither surprised nor angry. 'Poor child of a dead father,' he said, 'take what you will,' and he would have pressed the coloured caps upon her but she jumped to her feet and, once more, lost her temper. There were tears of humiliation in her eyes. She said that his great age was an offence in the sight of God and gave him no right to persecute her. She ran out of the room. The only place where she could be alone was in the bedroom of the Widow herself. There she went and hid herself under the bed, feeling that she had no longer a mind but only a body or no longer a body but only a mind, a Fawzia of herself that trembled like a steel spring. She wanted to withdraw from all contact with her fellow humans but even under the bed there was a limit to her retreat. She could go no farther than the wall. Since the duststorm there had been no proper cleaning of the flat and she lay on a drift of yellow powder which, at her slightest movement, rose in the air and set her sneezing. Life had been at its best under her father's beatings and, in thanking his memory, she came for the first time to understand his departure and mourn his loss.

It was her own mother, then, who undid the buttons at the back of her dress and stripped it from her. The Widow stood by seeing herself being deprived of still one more pleasure in life. Fawzia stood in a grey shift, her black hair down to her shoulders, looking into her mother's face with calm and happy eyes. The woman had come provided.

'Take the scarlet dress as a gift,' the Widow urged, but Fatma tossed it into the corner and produced, from beneath her own voluminous robes, another scarlet dress, richer and finer by far than the one that had been discarded. The Widow admired it out of politeness and, had Fatma permitted, would have helped to adorn the child. Fawzia looked at her reflection in the tall mirror that stood in the hall. She stroked her sides complacently but was silent with admiration.

Down in the street the tall Saidi who had wounded Salih and murdered Hassan sat in an *arabiyeh*. Salih accompanied the Widow to the balcony where they looked down on the scene as Fatma and her daughter joined him. The driver was sitting on his seat holding his whip stiffly in the air, the carriage hood was down and they could see the Saidi reclining in exaggerated ease on the seat. Fatma pushed her daughter into the carriage and made elaborate preparations for climbing in herself. But still the Saidi did not move. Even when Fatma was sitting at his side and Fawzia opposite he did not stir a finger or raise his head in acknowledgement of their presence.

Some word must have been given to the driver. He began flogging his starved horses and Salih, acting on an impulse, leaned as far over the balcony as he could manage, snatched his cotton cap from his head, and tried to drop it on to Fawzia's lap.

The whiplash came back, snatched at the cap in midair, and hurled it far ahead over the heads of the trotting horses.

[*PNW* 32, 1947]

THE VALIANT WOMAN

They had come to the dessert in a dinner that was a shambles. 'Well, John,' Father Nulty said, turning away from Mrs Stoner and to Father Firman, long gone silent at his own table. 'You've got the bishop coming for confirmation next week.'

'Yes,' Mrs Stoner cut in, 'and for dinner. And if he don't eat any more than he did last year —'

Father Firman, in a rare moment, faced it: 'Mrs Stoner, the bishop is not well. You know that.'

'And after I fixed that fine dinner and all,' Mrs Stoner pouted in Father Nulty's direction.

'I wouldn't feel bad about it, Mrs Stoner,' Father Nulty said. 'He never eats much anywhere.'

'It's funny. And that new Mrs Allers said he ate just fine when he was there,' Mrs Stoner argued, and then spit out: 'But she's a damned liar!'

Father Nulty, unsettled but trying not to show it, said: 'Who's Mrs Allers?'

'She's at Holy Cross,' Mrs Stoner said.

'She's the housekeeper,' Father Firman added, thinking Mrs Stoner made it sound as though Mrs Allers were the pastor there.

'I swear I don't know what to do about the dinner this year,' Mrs Stoner said.

Father Firman moaned. 'Just do as you've always done, Mrs Stoner.'

'Huh! And have it all to throw out! Is that any way to do?'

'Is there any dessert?' Father Firman asked coldly.

Mrs Stoner leaped up from the table and bolted into the kitchen, mumbling. She came back with a birthday cake. She plunged it in the centre of the table. She found a big wooden match in her apron pocket and thrust it at Father Firman.

'I don't like this bishop,' she said. 'I never did. And the way he went and cut poor Ellen Kennedy out of Father Doolin's will!'

She went back into the kitchen.

'Didn't they talk a lot of filth about Doolin and the housekeeper?' Father Nulty asked.

'I should think they did,' Father Firman said. 'All because he took her to the movies on Sunday night. After he died and the bishop cut her out of the will, though I hear he gives her a pension privately, they talked about the bishop.'

'I don't like this bishop at all,' Mrs Stoner said, appearing with a cake knife. 'Bishop Doran – there was the man!'

'We know,' Father Firman said. 'All man and all priest.'

'He did know real estate,' Father Nulty said.

Father Firman struck the match.

'Not on the chair!' Mrs Stoner cried, too late.

Father Firman set the candle burning – it was suspiciously large and yellow, like a blessed one, but he could not be sure. They watched the fluttering flame.

'I'm forgetting the lights!' Mrs Stoner said, and got up to turn them off. She went into the kitchen again.

The priests had a moment of silence in the candlelight.

'Happy birthday, John,' Father Nulty said softly. 'Is it fifty-nine you are?'

'As if you didn't know, Frank,' Father Firman said, 'and you the same but one.'

Father Nulty smiled, the old gold of his incisors shining in the flickering light, his collar whiter in the dark, and raised his glass of water, which would have been wine or better in the bygone days, and toasted Father Firman.

'Many of 'em, John.'

'Blow it out,' Mrs Stoner said, returning to the room. She waited by the light switch for Father Firman to blow out the candle.

Mrs Stoner, who ate no desserts, began to clear the dishes into the kitchen, and the priests, finishing their cake and coffee in a hurry, went to sit in the study.

Father Nulty offered a cigar.

'John?'

'My ulcers, Frank.'

'Ah, well, you're better off.' Father Nulty lit the cigar and crossed his long black legs. 'Fish Frawley has got him a Filipino, John. Did you hear?'

Father Firman leaned forward, interested. 'He got rid of the woman he had?'

'He did. It seems she snooped.'

'Snooped, eh?'

'She did. And gossiped. Fish introduced two town boys to her, said: "Would you think these boys were my nephews?" That's all, and the next week the paper had it that his two nephews were visiting him from Eire. After that, he let her believe he was going East to see his parents, though both are dead. The paper carried the story. Fish returned and made a sermon out of it. Then he got the Filipino.'

Father Firman squirmed with pleasure in his chair. 'That's like Fish, Frank. He can do that.' He stared at the tips of his fingers bleakly. 'You could never get a Filipino to come to a place like this.'

'Probably not,' Father Nulty said. 'Fish is pretty close to Minneapolis. Ah, say, do you remember the trick he played on us all in Marmion Hall?'

'That I'll not forget!' Father Firman's eyes remembered. 'Getting up New Year's morning and finding the toilet seats all painted!'

'HAPPY CIRCUMCISION! Hah!' Father Nulty had a coughing fit.

When he had got himself together again, a mosquito came and sat on his wrist. He watched it a moment before bringing his heavy hand down. He raised his hand slowly, viewed the dead mosquito, and sent it spinning with a plunk of his middle finger.

'Only the female bites,' he said.

'I didn't know that,' Father Firman said.

'Ah, yes . . .'

Mrs Stoner entered the study and sat down with some sewing – Father Firman's black socks.

She smiled pleasantly at Father Nulty. 'And what do you think of the atom bomb, Father?'

'Not much,' Father Nulty said.

Mrs Stoner had stopped smiling. Father Firman yawned.

Mrs Stoner served up another: 'Did you read about this communist convert, Father?'

'He's been in the Church before,' Father Nulty said, 'and so it's not a conversion, Mrs Stoner.'

'No? Well, I already got him down on my list of Monsignor's converts.'

'It's better than a conversion, Mrs Stoner, for there is more rejoicing in heaven over the return of . . . uh, he that was lost, Mrs Stoner, is found.'

'And that congresswoman, Father?'

'Yes. A convert – she.'

'And Henry Ford's grandson, Father. I got him down.'

'Yes, to be sure.'

Father Firman yawned, this time audibly, and held his jaw.

'But he's one only by marriage, Father,' Mrs Stoner said. 'I always say you got to watch those kind.'

'Indeed you do, but a convert nonetheless, Mrs Stoner. Remember, Cardinal Newman himself was one.'

Mrs Stoner was unimpressed. 'I see where Henry Ford's making steering-wheels out of soybeans, Father.'

'I didn't see that.'

'I read it in the *Reader's Digest* or some place.'

'Yes, well . . .' Father Nulty rose and held his hand out to Father Firman. 'John,' he said. 'It's been good.'

'I heard Hirohito's next,' Mrs Stoner said, returning to converts.

'Let's wait and see, Mrs Stoner,' Father Nulty said.

The priests walked to the door.

'You know where I live, John.'

'Yes. Come again, Frank. Good night.'

Father Firman watched Father Nulty go down the walk to his car at the kerb. He hooked the screen door and turned off the porch light. He hesitated at the foot of the stairs, suddenly moved to go to bed. But he went back into the study.

'Phew!' Mrs Stoner said. 'I thought he'd never go. Here it is after eight o'clock.'

Father Firman sat down in his rocking-chair. 'I don't see him often,' he said.

'I give up!' Mrs Stoner exclaimed, flinging the holey socks upon the horsehair sofa. 'I'd swear you had a nail in your shoe.'

'I told you I looked.'

'Well, you ought to look again. And cut your toenails. Why don't you? Haven't I got enough to do?'

Father Firman scratched in his coat pocket for a pill, found one, swallowed it. He let his head sink back against the chair and closed his eyes. He could hear her moving about the room, making the preparations; and how he knew them – the fumbling in the drawer for a pencil with a point, the rip of the page from his daily calendar, and finally the leg of the card-table sliding up against his leg.

He opened his eyes. She yanked the floor lamp alongside the table, setting the bead fringe tinkling on the shade, and pulled up her chair on the other side. She sat down and smiled at him for the first time that day. Now she was happy.

She swept up the cards and began to shuffle with the abandoned virtuosity of an old river-boat gambler, standing them on end, fanning them out, whirling them through her fingers, dancing them half-way up her arms, cracking the whip over them. At last they lay before him tamed into a neat deck.

'Cut?'

'Go ahead,' he said. She liked to go first.

She gave him her faint, avenging smile and drew a card, cast it aside for another which he thought must be an ace from the way she clutched it face down.

She was getting all the cards, as usual, and would have been invincible if she had possessed his restraint and if her cunning had been of a higher order. He knew a few things about leading and lying back that she would never learn. Her strategy was attack, for ever attack, with one baffling departure: she might sacrifice certain tricks as expendable if only she could have the last ones, the heartbreaking ones, if she could slap them down one after another, shatteringly.

She played for blood, no bones about it, but for her there was no other way; it was her nature, as it was the lion's, and for this reason he found her ferocity pardonable, more a defect of the flesh, venial, while his own trouble was all in the will, mortal. He did not sweat and pray over each card as she must, but he did keep an eye out for reneging and demanded a cut now and then just to aggravate her, and he was always secretly hoping for aces.

With one card left in her hand, the telltale trick coming next, she delayed playing it, showing him first the smile, the preview of defeat. She laid it on the table – so! She held one more trump than he had reasoned possible. Had she palmed it from somewhere? No, she would not go that far; that would not be fair, was worse than reneging, which so easily and often happened accidentally, and she believed in being fair. Besides he had been watching her.

God smote the vines with hail, the sycamore trees with frost, and offered up the flocks to the lightning – but Mrs Stoner! What a cross Father Firman had from God in Mrs Stoner! There were other housekeepers as bad, no doubt, walking the rectories of the world, yes, but . . . yes. He could name one and maybe two priests who were worse off. One, maybe two. Cronin. His scraggly blonde of sixty – take her, with her everlasting banging on the grand piano, the gift of the pastor; her proud talk about the goitre operation at the Mayo Brothers', also a gift; her honking the parish Buick at passing strange priests because they were all in the game together. She was worse. She was something to keep the home fires burning. Yes, sir. And Cronin said she was not a bad person really, but what was he? He was quite a freak himself.

For that matter, could anyone say that Mrs Stoner was a bad person? No. He could not say it himself and he was no freak. She had her points, Mrs Stoner. She was clean. And though she cooked poorly, could not play the organ, would not take up the collection in an emergency, and went to card-parties, and told all – even so, she was clean. She washed everything. Sometimes her underwear hung down beneath her dress like a paratrooper's pants, but it and everything she touched was clean. She washed constantly. She was clean.

She had her other points, to be sure – her faults, you might say. She snooped – no mistake about it – but it was not snooping for snooping's sake; she had a reason. She did other things, always with a reason. She overcharged on rosaries and prayer books, but that was for the sake of the poor. She censored the pamphlet rack, but that was to prevent scandal. She pried into the baptismal and matrimonial records, but there was no other way if Father was out, and in this way she had once uncovered a bastard and flushed him out of the rectory, but that was the perverted decency of the times. She held her nose over bad marriages in the presence of the victims, but that was her sorrow and came from having her husband buried in a mine. And he had caught her telling a bewildered young couple that there was only one good reason for their wanting to enter into a mixed marriage – the child had to have a name, and that – that was what?

She hid his books, kept him from smoking, picked his friends (usually the pastors of her colleagues), bawled out people for calling after dark, had no humour, except at cards, and then it was grim, very grim, and she sat hatchet-faced every morning at Mass. But she went to Mass, which was all that kept the church from being empty some mornings. She did annoying things all day long. She said annoying things into the night. She said she had given him the best years of her life. Had she? Perhaps – for the miner had her only a year. It was too bad, sinfully bad, when he thought of it like that. But all talk of best years and life was nonsense. He had to consider the heart of the matter, the essence. The essence was that housekeepers were hard to get, harder to get than ushers, than willing workers, than organists, than secretaries – yes, harder to get than assistants or vocations.

And she was a S A V E R – saved money, saved electricity, saved string bags, sugar, saved – him. That's what she did. That's what she said she did, and she was right, in a way. In a way, she was usually right. In fact, she was always right – in a way. And you could never get a Filipino to come way out here and live. Not a young one anyway, and he had never seen an old one. Not a Filipino. They liked to dress up and live.

Should he let it drop about Fish having one, just to throw a scare into her, let her know he was doing some thinking? No. It would be a perfect cue for the one about a man needing a woman to look after him. He was not up to that again, not tonight.

Now she was doing what she liked most of all. She was making a grand slam, playing it out card for card, though it was in the bag, prolonging what would have been cut short out of mercy in gentle company. Father Firman knew the agony of losing.

She slashed down the last card, a miserable deuce trump, and did in the hapless king of hearts he had been saving.

'Skunked you!'

She was awful in victory. Here was the bitter end of their long day together, the final murderous hour in which all they wanted to say – all he wouldn't and all she couldn't – came out in the cards. Whoever won at honeymoon won the day, slept on the other's scalp, and God alone had to help the loser.

'We've been at it long enough, Mrs Stoner,' he said, seeing her assembling the cards for another round.

'Had enough, huh!'

Father Firman grumbled something.

'No?'

'Yes.'

She pulled the table away and left it against the wall for the next time. She went out of the study carrying the socks, content and clucking. He closed his eyes after her and began to get under way in the rocking-chair, the nightly trip to nowhere. He could hear her brewing a cup of tea in the kitchen and conversing with the cat. She made her way up the stairs, carrying the tea, followed by the cat, purring.

He waited, rocking out to sea, until she would be sure to be through in the bathroom. Then he got up and locked the front door (she looked after the back door) and loosened his collar going upstairs.

In the bathroom he mixed a glass of antiseptic, always afraid of pyorrhoea, and gargled to ward off pharyngitis.

When he turned on the light in his room, the moths and beetles began to batter against the screens, the lighter insects humming . . .

Yes, and she had the guest room. How did she come to get that? Why wasn't she in the back room, in her proper place? He knew, if he cared to remember. The screen in the back room – it let in mosquitoes, and if it didn't do that she'd love to sleep back there, Father, looking out at the steeple and the blessed cross on top, Father, if it just weren't for the screen, Father. Very well, Mrs Stoner, I'll get it fixed or fix it myself. Oh, could you now, Father? I could, Mrs Stoner, and I will. In the meantime you take the guest room. Yes, Father, and thank you, Father, the house ringing with amenities then. Years ago, all that. She was a pie-faced girl then, not really a girl perhaps, but not too old to marry again. But she never had. In fact, he could not remember that she had even tried for a husband since coming to the rectory, but, of course, he could be wrong, not knowing how they went about it. God! God save us! Had she got her wires crossed and mistaken him all these years for THAT? THAT! Him! Suffering God! No. That was going too far. That was getting morbid. No. He must not think of that again, ever. No.

But just the same she had got the guest room and she had it yet. Well, did it matter? Nobody ever came to see him any more, nobody to stay overnight anyway, nobody to stay very long . . . not any more. He knew how they laughed at him. He had heard Frank humming all right – before he saw how serious and sad the situation was and took pity – humming 'Wedding Bells are Breaking Up that Old Gang of Mine'. But then they'd always laughed at him for something – for not being an athlete, for wearing glasses, for having kidney trouble . . . and mail coming addressed to Rev. and Mrs Stoner.

Removing his shirt, he bent over the table to read the volume left open from last night. He read, translating easily: '*Eisdem licet cum illis* . . . Clerics are allowed to reside only with women about whom there can be no suspicion, either because of a natural bond (as mother, sister, aunt) or of advanced age, combined in both cases with good repute.'

Last night he had read it, and many nights before, each time as though this time to find what was missing, to find what obviously was not in the paragraph, his problem considered, a way out. She was not mother, not sister, not aunt, and ADVANCED AGE was a relative term (why, she was younger than he was) and so, eureka, she did not meet the letter of the law – but, alas, how she fulfilled the spirit! And besides it would be a slimy way of handling it after all her years of service. He could not afford to pension her off, either.

He slammed the book shut. He slapped himself fiercely on the back, missing the wily mosquito, and whirled to find it. He took a magazine and folded it into a swatter. Then he saw it – oh, the preternatural cunning of it! – poised in the beard of St Joseph on the book-case. He could not hit it there. He teased it away, wanting it to light on the wall, but it knew his thoughts and flew high away. He swung wildly, hoping to stun it, missed, swung back, catching St Joseph across the neck. The statue fell to the floor and broke.

Mrs Stoner was panting in the hall outside his door.

'What is it!'

'Mosquitoes!'

'What is it, Father? Are you hurt?'

'Mosquitoes – damn it! And only the female bites!'

Mrs Stoner, after a moment, said: 'Shame on you, Father. She needs the blood for her eggs.'

He dropped the magazine and lunged at the mosquito with his bare hand.

She went back to her room, saying: 'Pshaw, I thought it was burglars murdering you in your bed.'

He lunged again.

[*PNW* 33, 1948]

LOUIS GUILLOUX

A MAN'S NAME

Translated from the French

He would say: 'Well, shall I go? Do you agree? Am I to go?' She would answer: 'Do as you like. You must decide that for yourself.' Once she had added: 'For nearly thirty years I have done all I could for you, but here I can do nothing more. If you think you ought to go, go!'

Their discussions almost always ended with those words. Once she had said: 'Go!' he would not answer any more, but would begin to ponder, now depressed, now nervous, sometimes even angry. Always the same thing! Always this 'Go'!

That was not what he expected of her.

One day she had promised never to do anything to prevent him from going, and he had thought that strange. Prevent him? How?

'Come now, Germaine . . .'

She wasn't going to start following him in the street, to spy on him, was she? He asked no permission of her. He only wanted her to agree. But she did not. She left him free to decide, that was all.

All the same, she had never dared to say to him: 'You are free.' That would have been too cruel. He would have thought himself abandoned.

She always spoke to him in a calm tone. She was a woman who seldom lost her temper. Once, however, she had replied with a certain impatience: 'You managed quite well to decide for yourself in the beginning. You asked nobody's advice when you committed the theft . . .'

But she had not insisted.

It sometimes happened that Germaine, at the end of their arguments, hid her face in her hands, and then he did not know what to do, he felt rather ashamed of himself, he dared not look at her. He would begin to walk about the room, a nice clean dining-room with its Henri II sideboard, its salamander, its vases and cartridge shells on the mantelpiece, its gilt-framed mirror. He saw himself in the mirror. It was intolerable. What connection was there between himself and that neat, puffy little man of sixty, whose image he saw, this small, ordinary, pink head, slightly bald, this face with its large blue eyes, the big grey whiskers? And the beard on his chin. Was that he, that little bourgeois of operetta fame? Was that what he had come to? How nauseating!

So as not to see himself in the mirror, he walked to the window. Also to avoid seeing Germaine. She was sitting by the table, her hands on her face, her two slim hands, old though still beautiful. He did not want to see Germaine's white hair. When she thus hid her face in her hands, and he only saw her white hair, she looked like a very old woman. But she was the woman he had loved, for thirty years . . .

And that was what they were: an old childless couple, two little old pensioners, highly respected in the town. Was that all? He used to say to himself: 'This is what I have come to, after a whole lifetime. This is what we have come to together. And after she has loved me, saved me, I am asking this sacrifice of her. It is monstrous.'

But could he do otherwise?

— No, I cannot do otherwise, he would answer himself.

He knew well, however, that if he went there, they would send for her afterwards, for if he was guilty, she was his accomplice.

'If only she understood me! . . .'

Who could ever understand him, if not she? That passer-by, picked at random, from among those he saw walk past on the pavement? He had none to ask for advice, and neither had Germaine. Because of the circumstances, in fact, they had broken off all relations with their respective families. They had no friends.

'Germaine?'

She lowered her hands, lifted towards him her beautiful tense face, her intelligent, tired eyes.

'Understand me, Germaine . . .'

But she did not want to argue any more. She had had enough of this dialogue, which had lasted for months. Understand him? She understood, or at least pretended to. She proved it by telling him: 'Go.' However intertwined their destinies, she understood perfectly that here they could diverge. But she did not agree. She could not advise him to go. She left him free.

He said he could not 'die like that'. That was his great argument.

— Come now, Germaine, in my place . . .

— Go if you want to.

— Ah! always, always the same thing!

And he, he knew perfectly well that he would not, could not go on living like that.

In vain had he, for months, been turning the problem over and over in his mind, the result of his thoughts had always been the same, he had to go.

But he would lose her, along with himself.

– Oh, I know, she has done everything for me. And I, what have I done for her?

He reckoned he had done almost nothing for Germaine, except to allow her to profit from all that stolen money. Could that be called having done anything for her? One could say, rather: against. He had dragged her, he had let her get entangled with him in this . . . queer situation.

– We have been victims of circumstances. If . . .

And then began the unending series of 'if'. Of course, if he had not committed the theft, if afterwards he had not met Germaine in that restaurant, if they had not fallen in love, and if he had had the courage to refuse her offer . . .

That came to many 'ifs' . . . There were still more, for example: if last winter I had not been ill, if, during that illness, certain thoughts had not occurred to me, if I were not afraid to die . . .

'You should understand, though, Germaine, that I cannot die like this.'

She had answered: 'Who speaks of dying? And even if it came to that, whether it be like this, or otherwise, what does it matter?'

'You don't understand me . . .'

'And anyway, it is not at the end of thirty years one begins to own up. There are laws about that.'

As for that, that was another question, and he had also thought of that. They would suspect him perhaps of having waited so long on purpose, and he would have difficulty in proving his good faith. But he would give all the necessary facts, he would tell them about it in every detail and would offer to restore the sum.

They were not poor. Wisely, they had known how to manage their nest-egg, and how to make the most of it. Luck had always stood by them in their speculations. In spite of the changes in the value of money, they had grown considerably richer, having, for thirty years, led a tidy, modest life, an example of certain little bourgeois lives, idle in appearance, but in fact entirely governed by the fixed idea of profit. Returning the stolen money would not impoverish them much.

Besides, that side of the problem, important though it might be, remained of secondary importance. What he wanted, first of all, was to recover his name.

– My name, do you understand, Germaine, my real name.

The first time he had made this confession, Germaine had remained dumb with surprise. For all these years, there had been between them no more talk of this old business of names! He had got so well used to live under the name of Germaine's first husband. It was such luck that Germaine had just been widowed when they had met. They had loved each other right away, and he had not delayed telling her of this theft, of which they had both profited ever since. Germaine had suggested going together to a town where they would be known to none, and where he would live under her dead husband's name.

He could still hear her: 'You see, I have all the necessary papers, and even the birth certificate.' And they had begun to laugh . . .

He had accepted, they had gone off together, all had worked admirably well for thirty years. Why did he now want to spoil everything himself? She would have thought he had forgotten his lawful name.

'Your real name is not known to anyone now.'

But that was not the question! It was not because of that! Not only because of that!

'Under your real name, you have been dead for thirty years . . .'

His futile little person had shuddered with a sort of sacred terror.

Germaine had added one day:

'And as you are not even French . . .'

That day he had had something like an attack of nerves. He had begun to groan like a puppy when someone treads on its paw. Germaine had concluded from that that he was not his normal self, and that he would do something silly if not closely watched. Or, she asked herself, could he really not bear to go on living under her first husband's name? It was rather late to say so . . .

With a few, hardly noticeable, variations, it had for months always been the same conversation between them, and in between the replies, or after she had told him 'go!' the same thoughts on both sides, the same way of hiding her face in her hands, and of looking out of the window.

His real name! What childishness! No, she did not understand him. No, surely he was not his usual self. Why did he, at all costs, want to recover his real name? He had never been jealous of her first husband, he had never shown enmity against him, and he had even appeared peacefully happy to slip into the dead man's papers as into a warm garment. But then, what? Remorse?

'Perhaps.'

'You?'

'Perhaps,' he had repeated.

She had begun to laugh. It was difficult to believe. He had stolen eight hundred thousand francs, which had meant a considerable sum at the time, but he had stolen them from a bank.

'You know as well as I do that banks are protected against these sort of accidents. There is the insurance.'

And the suspicion had come to Germaine that he did not give his real reasons. Did he feel like seeking out what was left of his family? Did he want to leave his fortune to some great-nephew? Madness!

Go back to his country?

'Do you want to become Belgian again as badly as that?'

He had not replied, except to say that what was more, for thirty years he had been breaking the law about foreigners staying in France.

'Yes. And then?'

He had granted her that this did not have much importance.

'Germaine, it is not that I care so much to be in order in the eyes of the law, although I care for that very much, but what matters to me is what will happen afterwards.'

'After what? After you have gone there? After you have owned up everything to the police?'

'No,' he said, 'after I am dead.'

As he said that, he had begun to tremble from head to foot. The whole of his puffy little body trembled, his lips trembled under the white whiskers, and the small beard, he was pale, he looked as though he were going to be ill, his very eyelids quivered. He said in a sort of sigh:

'I want to die under my real name.'

'Why?' she had answered, taken in herself by the sort of idiocy of the question.

He had taken up this 'why' bitterly, as one takes up an insult.

'It seems to me that this is obvious, Germaine . . . I don't want to. No, I don't want the people who will pass through the alley . . .'

He had not finished his sentence. He was choking. Germaine was looking at him seriously, attentively. Was he in his right senses?

'What alley?' she had murmured.

With a gulp which was like a broken sob, he had said in the end:

'In the churchyard.'

A moment later he had added, almost soundlessly:

'It would seem to me as if I were buried alive.'

Then he had begun to tremble again, and he had cried and groaned:

'I don't want it. No! Germaine! They will read a name on the tombstone, and it will not be my real name! . . .'

Afterwards, another day, calm again, he had explained to Germaine that for thirty years it had not mattered to him to walk about the streets under a false name, to be greeted by people by a name which was not his own. That was easy! The difficulty of it would begin at this alley.

'I think no one could bear that, Germaine!'

She had thought for a long time and then, after yet many days, she had said to him:

'Women haven't really a name of their own. They usually find it quite easy to get used to having their husband's name.'

Was that why she understood him so little? Was that all she had to say to him?

'You don't understand me, Germaine.'

'But I do.'

'No.'

'Why do you say I don't? You have only me left in the whole world. And since I, I shall know . . .'

It seemed to Germaine that this should have sufficed to calm all his misgivings, but he had cried out:

'It is under my real name that I want to appear before God!'

The little fellow had begun to shake again the moment he pronounced the word God. He had caught a glimpse of himself in the mirror and hated himself as never before. An expression of amazing surprise had suddenly transformed Germaine's beautiful face, and he had perceived there something like a mocking smile.

'Let me be!' he had cried out. And he had left the room to go and hide somewhere, throw himself on a bed.

She had told him afterwards:

'It is not God who gave you your name!'

And did souls have to be named? Names, where did they come from? She had begun to explain to him, as to a child, that all names had, in the beginning, been nicknames. They did not come from God, but from men, often even from their malice, from the often ignorant good will of a registrar. A name, what was it? No more than a number on a door . . . What childishness! And how could it be that he cared for it even to the extent of putting everything in the balance? . . .

But why did he feel mad with horror at the thought that another name than his own would be engraved on his tombstone?

She told him:

'Listen: no one has known our secret for thirty years. If you're the first to go, nothing will be changed, since I will be here. No one will go to your grave but I. And therefore . . . If I am to go first, you can then do as you please . . .'

But he went on repeating that she did not understand him, and Germaine thought: he does not love me any more.

— She does not understand me, that means she does not love me any more, he said to himself. I am still waiting for her to say one word, but that word does not come. I cannot go there until I have convinced her. But the day she tells me: 'You cannot do otherwise and it is I who advise you to go and own up, and what is more, we shall go together, for if you are guilty, I am your accomplice,' that day everything would be perfect.

— But she will not say the word, because she does not love me any more.

People walked by in the street, all strangers. He turned round. Germaine was still resting her elbows on the table, her face behind her hands, her head bent, showing only her white hair.

He murmured:

'Germaine?'

She started, and he said:

'Well, shall I go? Do you agree? Am I to go? Say one word . . .'

He waited, shivering, in suspense, not breathing, then he made a step forward and glimpsed in the mirror the grotesque little image of the old little fellow he was, and immediately looked away. Germaine's hands slid down her lovely tense face, she fixed upon him her beautiful, intelligent and tired gaze, and they remained thus, for a long moment, looking at each other, and he felt tears come to his eyes, his arms made a small movement as if to open . . . 'Yes, she does love me, she is still the same Germaine. She loves me, she will say the word.' 'He still loves me, she thought, my God, I don't want to lose him . . .'

'Well, Germaine?'

And he made another step forward . . .

Germaine let her arms fall limply on the table. She nodded.

'What do you expect me to say to you? Do as you please. Go, if you want to.'

[PNW 37, 1949]

PAUL BOWLES

BY THE WATER

The melting snow dripped from the balconies. People hurried through the little street that always smelled of frying fish. Now and then a stork swooped down, dragging his sticklike legs below him. The small gramophones scraped day and night behind the walls of the shop where young Amar worked and lived. There were few spots in the city where the snow was ever cleared away, and this was not one of them. So it gathered all through the winter months, piling up in front of the shop doors.

But now it was late winter; the sun was warmer. Spring was on the way, to confuse the heart and melt the snow. Amar, being alone in the world, decided it was time to visit a neighbouring city where, so his father once had told him, some cousins lived.

Early in the morning he went to the bus station. It was still dark, and the empty bus came in while he was drinking hot coffee. The road wound through the mountains all the way.

When he arrived in the other city night had already fallen. Here the snow was even deeper in the streets, and it was colder. Because he had not wanted to, Amar had not foreseen this, and it annoyed him to be forced to wrap his burnous closely about him as he left the bus station. It was an unfriendly town; he could tell that immediately. Men walked with their heads bent forward, and if they brushed against a passer-by they did not so much as look up. With the exception of the principal street, which had an arc-light every few metres, there seemed to be no other illumination, and the alleys that led off on either side lay in utter blackness; the white-clad figures that turned into them disappeared straightway.

'A bad town,' said Amar under his breath. He felt proud to be coming from a better and larger city, but his pleasure was mingled with anxiety about the night to be passed in this inimical place. He abandoned the idea of trying to find his cousins before morning, and set about looking for a fondouk or a bath where he might sleep until daybreak.

Only a short distance ahead the street lighting system terminated.

Beyond, the street appeared to descend sharply and lose itself in darkness. The snow was uniformly deep here, and not cleared away in patches as it had been nearer the bus station. He puckered his lips and blew his breath ahead of him in little clouds of steam. As he passed over into the unlighted district he heard a few languid notes being strummed on an oud. The music came from a doorway on his left. He paused and listened. Someone approached the doorway from the other direction and inquired, apparently of the man with the oud, if it was 'too late'.

'No,' the musician answered, and he played several more notes.

Amar went over to the door.

'Is there still time?' he said.

'Yes.'

He stepped inside the door. There was no light, but he could feel warm air blowing upon his face from the corridor to the right. He walked ahead, letting his hand run along the damp wall beside him. Soon he came into a large dimly-lit room with a tile floor. Here and there, at various angles, figures lay asleep, wrapped in grey blankets. In a far corner a group of men, partially dressed, sat about a burning brazier, drinking tea and talking in low tones. Amar slowly approached them, taking care not to step on the sleepers.

The air was oppressively warm and moist.

'Where is the bath?' said Amar.

'Down there,' answered one of the men in the group, without even looking up. He indicated the dark corner to his left. And, indeed, now that Amar considered it, it seemed to him that a warm current of air came up from that part of the room. He went in the direction of the dark corner, undressed, and, leaving his clothes in a neat pile on a piece of straw matting, walked toward the warmth. He was thinking of the misfortune he had encountered in arriving in this town at nightfall, and he wondered if his clothes would be molested during his absence. He wore his money in a leather pouch which hung on a string about his neck. Feeling vaguely for the purse under his chin, he turned around to look once again at his clothing. No one seemed to have noticed him as he undressed. He went on. It would not do to seem too distrustful. He would be embroiled immediately in a quarrel which could only end badly for him.

A little boy rushed out of the darkness toward him, calling: 'Follow me, Sidi. I shall lead you to the bath.' He was extremely dirty and ragged, and looked rather more like a midget than a child. Leading the way, he chattered as they went down the slippery, warm steps in the dark. 'You will call for Brahim when you want your tea? You're a stranger. You have much money . . .'

Amar cut him short. 'You'll get your coins when you come to wake me up in the morning. Not tonight.'

'But, Sidi! I'm not allowed in the big room. I stay in the doorway and show gentlemen down to the bath. Then I go back to the doorway. I can't wake you.'

'I'll sleep near the doorway. It's warmer there in any case.'

'Lazrag will be angry and terrible things will happen. I'll never get home again, or if I do I might be a bird so my parents will not know me. That's what Lazrag does when he gets angry.'

'Lazrag?'

'It is his place here. You'll see him. He never goes out. If he did the sun would burn him in one second, like a straw in the fire. He would fall down in the street burned black the minute he stepped out of the door. He was born down here in the grotto.'

Amar was not paying strict attention to the boy's babble. They were descending a wet stone ramp, putting one foot before the other slowly in the dark, and feeling the rough wall carefully as they went. There was the sound of splashing water and voices ahead.

'This is a strange hammam,' said Amar. 'Is there a pool full of water?'

'A pool? You've never heard of Lazrag's grotto? It goes on for ever, and it's made of deep warm water.'

As the boy spoke, they came out on to a stone balcony a few metres above the beginning of a very large pool, lighted beneath where they stood by two bare electric bulbs, and stretching away through the dimness into utter dark beyond. Parts of the roof hung down like grey icicles. Amar looked about in wonder. It was very warm down here. A slight pall of steam lay above the surface of the water, rising constantly in wisps toward the rocky ceiling. A man dripping with water ran past them and dived in. Several more were swimming about in the brighter region near the lights, never straying beyond into the gloom. The plunging and shouting echoed violently beneath the low ceiling.

Amar was not a good swimmer. He turned to ask the boy: 'Is it deep?' but his guide had already disappeared up the ramp. He stepped backward and leaned against the rock wall. There was a low chair to his right, and in the murky light it seemed to him that a small figure was close beside it. He watched the bathers for a few minutes. Those standing at the edge of the water soaped themselves assiduously; those in the water swam to and fro in a short radius below the lights.

Suddenly a deep voice spoke close beside him. He looked down as he heard it say: 'Who are you?'

The creature's head was large; its body was small and it had no legs or arms. The lower part of the trunk ended in two flipperlike pieces of flesh. From the shoulders grew short pincers. It was a man, and it was looking up at him from the floor where it stood.

'Who are you?' it said again, and its tone was unmistakably hostile.

Amar hesitated. 'I came to bathe and sleep,' he said at last.

'Who gave you permission?'

'The man at the entrance.'

'Get out. I don't know you.'

Amar was filled with anger. He looked down with scorn at the little being, and stepped away from it to join the men washing themselves by the water's edge. But more swiftly than he moved, it managed to throw itself along the floor until it was in front of him, when it raised itself again and spoke.

'You think you can bathe when I tell you to get out?' It laughed shortly, a thin sound, but deep in pitch. Then it moved closer and pushed its head against Amar's legs. He drew back his foot and kicked the head, not very hard, but with enough firmness to send the body off balance. The little creature rolled over in silence, making efforts with its neck to keep from reaching the edge of the platform. The men all looked up, an expression of fear on their faces. As the little creature went over the edge it yelled. The splash was like that of a large stone. Two men already in the water swam quickly to the spot. The others started up after Amar, shouting: 'He hit Lazrag!'

Bewildered and frightened, Amar turned and ran back to the ramp. In the blackness he stumbled upward. Part of the wall scraped his bare thigh. The voices behind him grew louder and more excited.

He reached the room where he had left his clothing. Nothing had changed. The men still sat by the brazier talking. Quickly he snatched the pile of garments, and struggling into his burnous, he ran to the door that led into the street, the rest of his clothes tucked under his arm. The man in the doorway with the oud looked at him with a startled face and called after him. Amar ran up the street barelegged toward the centre of the town. He wanted to be where there were some bright lights. The few people walking in the street paid him no attention. When he got to the bus station it was closed. He went into a small park opposite, where the iron bandstand stood deep in snow. There on a cold stone bench he sat and dressed himself as unostentatiously as possible, using his burnous as a screen. He was shivering, reflecting bitterly upon his poor luck, and wishing he had not left his own town, when a small figure approached him in the half-light.

'Sidi,' it said, 'come with me. Lazrag is hunting for you.'

'Where to?' said Amar, recognizing the urchin from the bath.

'My grandfather's.'

The boy began to run, motioning him to follow. They went through alleys and tunnels, into the most congested part of the town. The boy did not bother to look back, but Amar, being uneasy, turned occasionally to glance behind him. They finally paused before a small door at the side of a narrow passageway. The boy knocked vigorously. From within came a cracked voice calling: '*Echkoon?*'

'*Ana!* Brahim!' cried the boy.

With great deliberation the old man swung the door open and stood looking at Amar.

'Come in,' he finally said; and shutting the door behind them he led them through the courtyard filled with goats into an inner room where a feeble light was flickering. He peered sternly into Amar's face.

'He wants to stay here tonight,' explained the boy.

'Does he think this is a fondouk?'

'He has money,' said Brahim hopefully.

'Money!' the old man cried with scorn. 'That's what you learn in the hammam! How to steal money! How to take money from men's purses! Now you bring them here! What do you want to do? Kill him and get his purse for you? Is he too clever for you? You can't get it by yourself? Is that it?' The old man's voice had risen to a scream, and he gestured violently in his mounting excitement. He sat down on a cushion with difficulty and was silent a moment.

'Money,' he said again, finally. 'Let him go to a fondouk. Take him to the hammam. Why aren't you there?' He looked suspiciously at his grandson.

The boy clutched at his friend's sleeve. 'Come,' he said, pulling him out into the courtyard.

'Take him to the hammam!' yelled the old man. 'Let him spend his money there!'

Together they went back into the dark streets.

'Lazrag is looking for you,' said the boy. 'Twenty men will be going through the town to catch you and take you back to him. He is very angry and he will change you into a bird.'

'Where are we going now?' asked Amar gruffly. He was cold and very tired, and although he said to himself that he did not really believe the boy's story, he wished he were out of the unfriendly town.

'We must walk as far as we can from here. All night. In the morning we'll be far away in the mountains, and they won't find us. We can go to your city.'

Amar did not answer. He was pleased that the boy wanted to stay with him, but he did not think it fitting to say so. They followed one crooked street downhill until all the houses had been left behind and they were in the open country. Presently the path led down a narrow valley, and joined the highway at one end of a small bridge. Here the snow was packed down by the passage of vehicles, and they found it much easier to walk along.

When they had been going down the road for perhaps an hour in the increasing cold, a great truck came rolling by. It stopped just ahead and the driver, an Arab, offered them a ride on top. They climbed up and made a nest of some empty sacks. The boy was very happy to be rushing through the air in the dark night. Mountains and stars whirled by above his head and the truck made a powerful roaring noise as it travelled along the empty highway.

'Lazrag has found us and changed us both into birds!' he cried when he could no longer keep his delight to himself. 'No one will ever know us again.'

Amar grunted and went to sleep. But the boy watched the sky and the trees and the cliffs for a long time before he closed his eyes.

Some time before morning the truck stopped by a spring for water. In the stillness the boy awoke. A cock crowed in the distance, and then he heard the driver pouring water. The cock crowed again, a sad, thin arc of sound away in the cold murk of the plain. It was not yet dawn. He buried himself deeper in the pile of sacks and rags, and felt the warmth of Amar as he slept.

When daylight came they were in another part of the land. There was no snow. Instead, the almond trees were in flower on the hillsides as they sped past. The road went on unwinding as it dropped lower and lower, until suddenly it came out of the hills upon a spot below which lay a glittering emptiness. Amar and the boy watched it and said to each other that it must be the sea, shining in the morning light.

The spring wind pushed the foam from the waves along the beach; it rippled their garments landward as Amar and the boy walked by the edge of the water. Finally they found a sheltered spot between rocks, and undressed, leaving their clothes on the sand. The boy was afraid to go into the water, and found enough excitement in letting the waves break about his legs, but Amar tried to drag him out further.

'No, no!'

'Come,' Amar urged him.

Amar looked down. Approaching him sideways was an enormous crab which had crawled out from a dark place in the rocks. He leapt back in terror, lost his balance, and fell heavily, striking his head against one of the great boulders. The boy stood perfectly still watching the creature make its cautious way toward Amar through the tips of the breaking waves. Amar lay without moving, rivulets of water and sand running down his face. As the crab reached his feet, the boy bounded into the air, and in a voice made hoarse by desperation, screamed: 'Lazrag!'

The crab scuttled swiftly behind the rock and disappeared. The boy's face became radiant. He rushed to Amar, lifted his head above a newly-breaking wave, and slapped his cheeks excitedly.

'Amar! I made him go away!' he shouted. 'I saved you!'

If he did not move, the pain was not too great. So Amar lay still, feeling the warm sunlight, the soft water washing over him, and the cool, sweet wind that came in from the sea. He also felt the boy trembling in his effort to hold his head above the waves, and he heard him saying many times over: 'I saved you, Amar.'

After a long time he answered: 'Yes.'

[*PNW 39*, 1950]

FOUR

THE CRITICAL ESTIMATE

STEPHEN SPENDER

BOOKS AND THE WAR

Tragedy and some Modern Poetry

Are we living in a tragic age? Why is not the suffering and violence of today being reflected in great tragic works of art?

These are questions which in one form or another are often asked. The more I think about them, the less easy do I find an answer.

In order to answer them, it is necessary to have a clear idea of the nature of tragedy. Tragedy involves more than suffering and violence. It involves a belief in life and also a belief that principles and values for which human beings live may triumph over death and destruction.

A tragic situation is essentially a conflict between good and evil principles in which the principle which is destroyed is, at the same time, purified and separated from the human drama, so that it is born again in the mind of the spectator.

Whether tragedy exists as a form of art in an age is a comment not only on the artists living at the time but also on the age itself, which is the audience of works of art. For poets and artists are the interpreters of the deepest conflicts within the life of their time, and of the principles which lie below the surface of social life.

Tragic art cannot exist without a tragic situation; and that situation, unless it is simply a repetition of themes copied from the past, must depend on the beliefs and the spiritual struggles in the minds of the artist's contemporaries who are his audience. The 'tragic situation' is in life itself, it is not invented by the artist, though it may require great inventive genius to be able to draw it from the hidden soul of mankind.

Thus the greatest tragedies are dramatized interpretations of beliefs about the nature of existence which are common to a civilization. Classical Greece, Elizabethan England, the Court of Louis XIV, all had poets who produced tragedies expressing a view of man in situations which the audience recognized as valid and fitting into their conception of life.

The Greek hero, by chance or through arrogance, defied the gods and drew down on himself nemesis. The Greek audience knew that the 'dark furies' would come and strike down the 'son of carnage'. To believe that a play about the fall of a tyrant was true to life, they had to believe in a system of fates outside and beyond human control. Without this belief, the vengeance of the gods would be merely 'wishful thinking', like articles on astrology 'proving' that Hitler is doomed to fall at such and such a date.

To a modern audience, a modern *Macbeth* would also be 'wishful thinking', because most people are more impressed by the achievements of science than by the working out of a fate which makes certain the fall of a tyrant in control of all the resources of modern science. Today Macbeth would be assisted by a ministry of propaganda and a Gestapo. The manoeuvres of Birnam wood would not take him by surprise, as he would be accustomed to camouflage. A scientific view of life would free him of the superstitious fears that haunted Macbeth. Of course, he might nevertheless live within a tragic situation. That is exactly where the creative genius of the artist comes in, to discover the modern equivalents for the generalizations which are true of the human situation in the present and the past. The true poet does this; the false poet dishes up the old situations without realizing that they have ceased to apply to reality, and therefore are no longer true to life. The old situations remain true only in their old settings. When one sees a past play one unconsciously enters into the mental environment of the past, suggested by words and atmosphere, which make the imagination live in the moral beliefs of another age.

Possibly the greatest opponent of tragic art is the modern materialist view of life, whether this be held by fascists, communists or liberal democrats.

Unamuno, the Spanish Catholic philosopher, recognizes this in his book, *The Tragic View of Life*, by insisting on the irrationality of religion and refusing to compromise with reason by reconciling Catholicism with science. The communists, who are open materialists, also recognize it. In an interesting essay called 'A Marxist Interpretation of Literature', in the symposium *The Mind in Chains*, Edward Upward maintains that writers in the future socialist state will no longer regard tragedy – the contemplation of the defeat of man – as the most effective and serious literary form. This is revealing, for only a convinced materialist would regard tragedy as the contemplation of the defeat of man. To the mind that sees a significance in this life beyond the struggle for existence and for social gain, tragedy is the spectacle of the triumph of man's spirit within material defeat.

But to the materialist there are only material successes and failures. Failure which admits of no possibility of future triumph is defeat complete and irreversible, and inconsolable: that is all there is to be said about it. On the other hand, when the struggle over 'the forces of reaction' has been won, and when the problems of distributing the benefits of man's triumphs over nature and the capitalists have been solved, then humanity enters into a new era in which failure, defeat and suffering need not be contemplated. Incidentally, Mr Upward – who, working within his limitations, is a critic of great integrity – says that socialism, having rejected the most spiritual form of art – tragedy – will adopt the 'fairy story' on 'a higher, a scientific level', 'celebrating the triumph of man over danger and difficulties'. This is again revealing. The basis of fairy stories is belief in magic. Whether or not tragedy is superseded, an art of magical legends seems a step backwards rather than forwards. Yet Mr Upward is very shrewd in indicating that a belief in the power of science to solve spiritual conflicts by altering material circumstances corresponds to a belief in the wave of a magic wand, or flying carpets.

It may be objected that the class struggle provides subjects for tragedy. The defeat of the Spanish Republic, for example. Yet, artistically speaking, this is only a tragedy if one is able to accept the defeat as final and believe that it was a triumph, not of some future Spanish Republic, but actually of the spirit of those who were defeated. Tragedy accepts defeat. If the audience has an eye on the future triumphs of another Republic, the play is propaganda (and such propaganda might indeed be magnificent material), inciting the audience to reverse the tragedy and change it on the stage of life into a material triumph.

The materialism of the communists is a reaction to and a product of the materialism of the society which they are trying to overthrow. Unamuno, who is not a politician at all, recognizes this by being thoroughly opposed to the materialism of all modern forms of society. The difference between the communists and their materialist opponents in their aesthetic theories is that writers like Upward are honest and realistic in their grasp of the situation in art, and their opponents are muddled and dishonest. This does not mean that the methods of the communists are scrupulous in practice, but at least they have a radical grasp of what they are doing. The materialism of socialists can afford to be honest because, although it is amoral and materialistic, it happens to have a great act of social justice on its side. Their opponents, who are equally materialistic, cannot afford to be so honest because they are upholding a system of social injustice, and therefore they cannot afford to throw away metaphysical arguments which surround their own aims with vagueness and offer their impoverished opponents spiritual consolations.

So that we get a very curious situation. The critics like Edward Upward who stand for social justice call themselves materialists, which indeed they are. The people who defend a socially unjust system, and who live within a society which puts the materialist considerations of a small minority before every other interest, talk a great deal about justice and other virtues. At the back of this, both sides tacitly recognize a kind of bar of human justice at which they plead their cause. Equally, both sides act with nothing but material aims of class in mind, and believe in nothing but material triumphs and failures. The audience of ordinary people in the world, realizing that the protagonists in the struggle for power and wealth have nothing but material aims in mind, that they judge events entirely by material success and failure, and submit the world to a kind of reign of terror beyond which there seems no appeal, naturally have little faith in the working out of any moral system beyond the seizing of power by one or other group of people who think in terms of nothing except power. There is little room in the modern world for a belief in spiritual triumphs over unmitigated material failures. The defeated in modern history look as if they will be as completely wiped off the records as the Etruscans who, having been 'liquidated' by the Romans, left nothing but a few tombs, some inscriptions which no one can decipher, and a reputation for vice.

The fact that triumphs of the spirit do take place all round us in the lives of individuals, in groups of people, and even in nations, is regarded as extraordinary and quixotic. It does not altogether fit in with our view of life. And yet perhaps it is more like life than all the aims of capitalism and all the aims of communists.

Possibly the tragic view of life would by now have indeed disappeared, were it not for the disastrous circumstances of our lives, which contradict all our rationalism and all the triumphs of science. It would be some consolation to be able to regard these disasters as tragic, and not just as so much waste thrown on to a slag heap.

A consolation perhaps, perhaps also a dangerous temptation. A materialist society, without any belief in triumphs of spiritual values over total worldly defeat, yet hankers after the consolation of tragedy without the triumph of the spirit. For tragedy is a triumph, it is a triumph of the spirit over disaster.

Without this triumph, tragedy falls into a mere insistence on despair, suffering, defeat, ultimate disaster, the necessity of violence and the conclusion of life in darkness and horror. E. M. Forster points to the dangers of this catastrophic view of life in his excellent pamphlet *Nordic Twilight*. The pattern of much German history, in which the rest of Europe has become involved, is the Wagnerian myth of the triumph of the gods followed by their twilight and downfall. Possibly a tragic view of life is dangerous, says Mr Forster, because it creates an atmosphere of disaster.

From what I have said, it will be evident that the view of life in Wagner's opera cycle is not tragic, but catastrophic. All the same, Mr Forster's remark is a real contribution to this discussion because it suggests that when we are faced with great unresolved material problems, we cannot afford the luxury of the tragic view of acceptance of defeat. In our present circumstances, we cannot contemplate defeat at all, not even if we believe in a spiritual triumph. Something else emerges from this. The great periods of tragic art have been triumphant moments in human history, classical Greece, the Renaissance, Elizabethan England, the reign of Louis XIV. Perhaps Mr Upward is wrong. For perhaps it is in his moments of triumph that man needs to contemplate failure and defeat, in order to humble himself, whereas in times of great material difficulty he must think only of overcoming disaster.

Nevertheless, it is defeats which provide the material of tragedies, even if they cannot be written at the time. Sometimes, as in Greek tragedy, these defeats belong to the past and are associated with certain great families, and well known events. With Racine, it is possible that they are anticipations of the future, and that he was conscious of the great disasters that were going to befall the French monarchy.

If the tragedies of our own time are ever written in the future, what situations in contemporary life will be found to have been tragic? I think that there are two. The first is the situation of the individual, believing in justice, who is defeated by the forces of centralized political power. Note that I cannot say 'the just man', because there is no basis of agreement about the nature of justice. Both sides do not recognize the same principle, which one side is destroying in the other. One individual believes in something which society rejects. This is the tragedy of the upholders of liberal justice all over Europe. The tragedy of judges who refuse to believe that justice serves the ends of the omnipotent State, of scientists who refuse to conform to the myth of the superiority of one race and the inferiority of others, of Christians who refuse to abandon their religious freedom. The spectacle of the individual in conflict with a blind and unbelieving social system is as tragic as the spectacle of the individual in conflict with a blind fate. In the past, the audience could identify themselves with the man against fate: can they identify themselves with the man against a materialist society?

I think that in their hearts the vast, censored audiences to the unwritten tragedies in the concentration camps do identify themselves, unwillingly even, with the brave spirits who have been tormented and destroyed by the machinery of the totalitarian state.

This brings me to my second tragic situation which is really only the logical development of the first. It is that the tragic situation of today is the situation of humanity itself: humanity with its faith in moral systems and religions shaken, at the mercy of the demonic forces of a machinery which it has itself invoked. These machines have fallen everywhere into the hands of a self-interested minority who themselves are unable to control forces of war and economic disaster which they develop.

In this situation, perhaps we laugh and attempt to build up a great macabre comedy like Céline's *Voyage au Bout de la Nuit*, or perhaps we see man in a civilization which has developed far beyond any previous one, yet forced back on to the ultimate truths of his own nature, hunger, fear, love, humanity itself. This is the ordinary man, the citizen, the soldier, in the present war. But if we look at the great man at the head of affairs, he is also a victim. For making every allowance for the unprecedented powers which machinery has given him, he is still doomed to die, and his nature is not altered by the impassivity of machinery itself. He is liable to make mistakes, he is liable to grow tired, his soldiers are liable to become slack and demoralized, in spite of all wonders of organization, and all modern inventions.

This relation of modern man to the modern environment is not so much a tragedy as the statement of a tragic situation. It might indeed crystallize into a tragedy, if having been forced back on to his humanity man became really human, instead of remaining half a product of the machine age, with the mind of a machine. Doubtless individuals do at times reflect, in suffering, the truth of the situation. Politicians are too full of humbug to do so, but individuals do. It is in the passive suffering of people themselves that one sees the tragic situation.

The phrase 'passive suffering' is an extremely significant one. When the poet W. B. Yeats compiled, shortly before his death, an anthology,

The Oxford Book of Modern Verse, he refused to print the poems of certain poets writing during the last war, because they reflected an attitude of 'passive suffering'. The writer, usually an officer, identified himself with the suffering of his men. Yeats objected to this passive attitude which did not triumph – as he expressed it – in a dance over the corpses of the war.

It is interesting that one of the best communist critics, Christopher Caudwell, in his book *Illusion and Reality*, takes up almost the same position as Yeats the political reactionary and aristocrat. He condemns the kind of war poetry which weakens the determination of people to fight, by playing on their sense of pity. Unamuno, the Catholic, also criticizes the fashionable tendency to be sentimental about the horrors of war. Caudwell (whose real name was Christopher St John Sprigge) was killed fighting for the Spanish Republic. Neither Unamuno nor Yeats fought in any war nor seems to have been particularly distinguished for bravery. This contrast between the lives and deaths of Caudwell and Cornford, Unamuno and Yeats, is a striking example of the difference in practice between the materialism of communists and the romantic idealism of reactionaries.

Yeats's criticism, which was aimed at the war poetry of Owen, naturally offended a great many people. Yet I think that his attack on this kind of war poetry expresses a point of view which ought to be discussed. The same people who dismiss it impatiently would admit that Yeats himself wrote great poetry. But if he did so, it is largely because he applied to his work a discipline of arrogance, deliberate egoism, and a refusal to give way to feelings of pity.

Yet, great as Yeats's poetry was, there is something which prevents it from having the universal appeal of the greatest poetry. In spite of its fine music, it is bleak and cold. It stands up magnificently like a bare mountain, with a few ruins on it, perhaps, covered with such vegetation and inhabited with such life as can endure an icy, though passionate, climate. Modern as the form of the poetry is, the emotions and ideas have a rigid aloofness from modern life. Yeats wrote by saving himself from the mud of Flanders and the mud of the common mind of his time. He is an isolated figure who achieved greatness. Other poets may admire him, but they cannot follow him, because he does not wrestle with the problem of interpreting the surrounding life of his time into poetry. He is only himself.

Owen, on the other hand, dwells in the worst hell of modern life – the war of 1914–18. The best defence of his poetry is that it tells the truth. The picturesque rhetoric of aristocrats and communists who now see war as noble falls before the immediate truth which his poetry communicates. If the truth is unpalatable for some because they do not wish bloodthirsty methods of gaining their ends to be deplored, and to others because they have a view of war derived from the age of chivalry which they do not wish dispelled – then it is for these to alter their critical standards so as to include unpalatable truths.

Because Owen's poetry seemed truthful to younger writers in post-war years, it influenced them. Perhaps some of it is open to the charge of excessive emotionalism, which appeals to us through the piteousness of the situation as much as through the poetry:

'Let the boy try along this bayonet-blade
How cold steel is, and keen with hunger of blood;
Blue with all malice, like a madman's flash;
And thinly drawn with famishing for flesh.'

This criticism might also in some degree apply to the situations in 'Futility', 'Conscious' and 'Mental Cases'. The subjects are so horrifying that it is difficult for the poetry to add much feeling to a mental image of this suffering humanity. However, the great virtue of Owen's poetry lies in an occasional power of detachment which is almost cold, considering how close the poet was to his subject-matter:

'My soul looked down from a vague height with Death,
As unremembering how I rose or why,
And saw a sad land, weak with sweats of dearth,
Gray, cratered like the moon with hollow woe,
And pitted with great pocks and scabs of plagues.'

Here objectivity is achieved by the effect of physical distance from the scene of battle. In another poem the effect of distance is achieved by a cold power of analysis:

'One time he liked a blood-smear down his leg,
After the matches, carried shoulder-high.
It was after football, when he'd drunk a peg,
He thought he'd better join. – He wonders why,
Someone had said he'd look a god in kilts,
That's why; and maybe, too, to please his Meg;
Aye, that was it, to please the giddy jilts
He asked to join. He didn't have to beg;
Smiling they wrote his lie; aged nineteen years.
Germans he'd scarcely thought of; all their guilt
And Austria's, did not move him. And no fears
Of Fear came yet.'

The poem *Miners* is a vision of the workers who hew the coal, which takes the mind far into the past and deep into the earth:

'My fire might show steam-phantoms simmer
    From Time's old cauldron,
Before the birds made nests in summer,
    Or men had children.'

The poem *Asleep* transcends the war in a vision of the order of the universe:

'Whether his deeper sleep lie shaded by the shaking
Of great wings, and the thoughts that hung the stars,
High-pillowed on calm pillows of God's making
Above these clouds, these rains, these sleets of lead,
And these winds' scimitars;'

These quotations show that Owen was far more than a poet who expressed morbid feelings of excessive sympathy with suffering and of self-pity. He was capable of viewing the war from a distance, much as Hardy viewed the Napoleonic Wars in *The Dynasts*. He could rise to a vision, half-serious, half-ironic, of a divine order of the universe. He was sensitive to aesthetic beauty, and also, in the rich texture and imagery of his verse, to traditional influences (Keats in particular).

A part of Yeats's criticism falls to the ground, but nevertheless the main charge, that Owen's poetry does triumph in the dance over death, remains true. Actually the Great War did produce poetry by Graves and Blunden which, in its metres, at least, is dancing. But this poetry is singularly uninteresting and compares badly with other work by these writers. It is only Owen's, and some of Sassoon's, poetry which makes one feel the impact of a genuine experience of the truth of the war.

If there is poetic truth in Owen's work it is useless for criticism to ignore this and dismiss his poetry on account of the poet's attitude. Perhaps, indeed, the attitude is faulty; and future readers may find themselves less interested in some of this poetry than we, who are close to the event, find ourselves. Nevertheless, I believe that there will be an increment of genuine achievement which criticism will have to account for, and which cannot be dismissed.

Yeats's criticism is too much a defence of his own poetry to be just to Owen. For his own poetry lacks exactly the qualities of humanity and wide sympathy which we find in Owen. His insistence on the dance dehumanized his poetry and made it somewhat remote. His critical standards neglected some aspects of poetry, such as the lament and the elegy. Unamuno, with a greater sensibility than Yeats, praises despair; and Rilke, the greatest modern German poet, in one of the finest of his letters written during the Great War, exclaims that one, just one person, ought to go out into the 'hopeless, flag-hung city' and cry out against the horror of the war. Wilfred Owen was that one person.

Such poetry is not tragedy; it is, rather, a tragic statement. There are moments in Shakespeare when the tragedy melts into something quieter, less violent, and deeper than tragedy: 'But yet the pity of it, Iago! O, Iago, the pity of it, Iago!' *Othello* could not be created from such passive suffering as this, and yet it underlies the whole theme.

It seems unlikely that humanity in the democratic countries – if the tragedy in which we live is not just the conflict between ideologies – has yet attained to the degree of purification necessary for tragedy. But nevertheless the tragic situation exists, just as it does in Wilfred Owen's poetry. And if our deepest poetry, in Rilke, in Eliot, in Owen, is the poetry of lament, who can say that this does not contain springs of joy? Because when suffering touches ultimate truth we are not far from the terrible joy of the last scene of *Othello* when Emilia, the vital, simple-hearted and worldly shrew, refuses to be prevented from telling the truth:

'I care not for thy sword; I'll make thee known
Though I lost twenty lives.'

Indeed, if Yeats had troubled to read it, Owen's preface to his poems contains the best answer to him. 'The Poetry is in the pity. Yet these elegies are to this generation in no sense consolatory. They may be to the next. All a poet can do today is to warn. That is why the true poets must be truthful.'

[*PNW* 4, 1941]

C. V. WEDGWOOD

POETS AND POLITICS IN BAROQUE ENGLAND

The restlessness of the seventeenth century is a massive restlessness, reflected in gigantic convolutions of stone and tempestuous statuary. In Western Europe this was perhaps the most unhappy century until our own time, and it is closer to our own than any other in the causes of that unhappiness. Between the joyous experimentalism of the sixteenth century and the intellectual serenity of the eighteenth, it interposes a period of bewilderment: a time (like ours) in which man's activities had outrun his powers of control.

The change from a land to a money basis for society, and the conflict between state and individual were important elements in the unrest of the time, but they were not its fundamental cause while the apparent struggle between Catholic and Protestant was a mere pendant of political issues. A mental conflict stronger than the material quarrels which set Europe's entangled dynasties and growing nations against each other divided the mind of the individual against itself: the struggle between reason and revelation.

Fascinatingly, slowly, the planets had begun to move in the sixteenth century. The solar system became apparent through the eyes of Copernicus. When Galileo, in the early seventeenth century, set the world itself spinning, the Holy Office stepped in; too late. Only a few years afterwards William Harvey discovered a yet more intimate circulation, that of the blood in the human body. The static world dissolved in motion.

But at the beginning of the seventeenth century, the ordinary educated man lived, as he had lived for the past thousand years, by revelation. The day-time of the faith was over, but the sun had not set: far and fading, it was still the light men knew. Saint Teresa was newly dead, and very newly canonized. Men had seen miracles, and were to see them for some years more. The curtains had not yet been drawn and the artificial lamps of reason lit. There was the deceptive conflict of the inward and the outward light. Not until the latter half of the century was a renewed and circumscribed security to be found whose foundation was the *cogito ergo sum* of Descartes.

The political storms which blew up over Europe at this time were not physically more horrible than those which had gone before, but they were more demoralizing. In the sixteenth century men had known very well what they were doing, whether they were poisoning rival princes in Italy, or harrying silver fleets in mid-Atlantic. It was a cocksure century. The seventeenth century was not. An anxious or resigned uncertainty, a doubt embracing both motives and aims obscured men's minds. Witchcraft and witch-hunting rose in horrible crescendo; astrology gained fantastic hold, extraordinary religions sprang up like mushrooms.

It is significant that only in the victorious, comfortable Dutch republic did a highly realist school of painting develop. Elsewhere the artist – with few exceptions – transmutes or subordinates reality. Even as sharp an observer as Callot handles his *Misères de la Guerre* with a light and airy line. *Simplicissimus*, the nightmare novel of the Thirty Years' War, was not written until a generation later, could not have been written . . . Compare the neat, topographical drawings done by Hollar when he accompanied Lord Arundel on an embassy to Germany at the height of the conflict, with the horrified jottings of Lord Arundel's secretary. The artist has deliberately closed his eyes. Compare also the symbolic grandeur of Rubens' painting of the Habsburg leaders meeting on the eve of the battle of Nördlingen: below, well-fed symbolic figures of the Danube and its tributaries, above the graceful young princely generals, Spanish and Austrian, their cloaks and love-locks streaming in the wind, their left hands doffing one the plumed sombrero, the other the Hungarian bonnet, their right hands clasped in brotherly greeting; behind each in artfully dissimilar groups the idealized officers of their staff; and beneath their clasped hands the distant spire of Nördlingen church. Tomorrow will be fought the battle in which ten thousand men will die and the scattered remnants of a routed army carry disease and vermin from the Lech to the Rhine.

In civilizations, as in human beings, recognizable phenomena signalize certain periods. In periods of transition an inward uneasiness is often expressed by affectations designed to conceal it; baroque performed this function in the civilization of Western Europe, bridging the gap between the crude assurance of the Renaissance and the polished assurance of the eighteenth century. All would ultimately yield again to man's control: science would be organized, the passions embanked, the arts regulated, religion reduced to formula; but in the meantime thoughts were directionless and men unhappy.

To this general oppression, a further weight was added in England.

The young northern country of between three and four million inhabitants had recently come thrusting forward among the powers of Western Europe, had gained one or two spectacular successes against the gigantic power of Spain and suffered some ignominious checks. Her people, or rather her educated classes, accepted the former as the most natural thing in the world and blamed convenient scapegoats for the latter.

The phenomenal vigour and precocity of the Elizabethans had created a false expectation among their successors. The English knew already that they were the chosen people, their habitation a demi-paradise, their prowess by sea and land unmatched, their swords ever drawn and ever victorious in just causes. The deceits, the shifts, the betrayals, the total eclipse of the seventeenth century shook their faith in almost everything except their country. The King, the Commons, the idle rich, the idle poor, the gentry, the City – you could take your choice which to blame, much as you can today. But nobody seems to have recognized the simple fact that England, with a quarter the population of France and a third that of Spain, with few discovered resources, with all her wealth in private hands, could not maintain the position she had intermittently reached under Elizabeth.

The total insignificance of their country in the European scene was all the harder for the average Englishman to understand, since it went with a period of comparative economic prosperity at home. One should not pay too much attention to the perennial English complaint that everything was going to the dogs, nor to evidence of local depressions. Local depressions there are always. Still less should one be misled by the poverty of the Crown; wealth was in private hands, and the Crown's powers of taxation were so limited that it had no means of tapping the wealth of the community either in its own or the public interest. But great wealth there certainly was, and the things which should – but do not always – go with wealth: a growing interest in the arts and education, leisure for thought and the cultivation of the graces.

Nor were wealth and civilization confined to the capital. England, a small country, was beginning to be fairly well-roaded; communications improved, posts were instituted. If London continued to be the only town of first-class importance, and the two universities the sources from which the intellectual life of London was fed, innumerable country houses were the centres of local constellations of talent. Everything points to a period of comfort and ease such as the Elizabethans had hardly known.

All the more inexplicable, therefore, to contemporaries was the insignificance of their country in European politics. The independent gentry who stalwartly refused to give loans to the Crown were the first to throw up outraged hands when bankrupt preparations for war ended in disaster. 'Since England was England she got not so dishonourable a blow . . .' The causes for which they cared were being betrayed and defeated on the continent of Europe, while their Government did nothing, or, fatally, too little. Puzzled, indignant, conscience stricken, some of them volunteered in foreign armies. Others stayed at home and blackguarded their rulers. Still, others justified the inglorious epoch, though for the wrong reasons:

White Peace (the beautifull'st of things)
Seems here her everlasting rest
To fix, and spreads her downy Wings
    Over the Nest:

As when great Jove, usurping Reign,
From the plagu'd World did her exile,
And ty'd her with a golden Chain
    To one blest Isle:

Which in a Sea of plenty swam
And turtles sang on every Bough,
A safe retreat to all that came
    As ours is now.

Thus Sir Richard Fanshaw, in 1630, a moment when religious liberty and the Protestant cause had been wiped out almost to the shores of the Baltic. Two years later, when the King of Sweden had smashed the Catholic armies back to the Danube and the younger generation in England strained at the leash to join in, another courtier, Thomas Carew, took up the refrain:

. . . What though the German drum
Bellow for freedom and revenge, the noise
Concerns not us, nor should divert our joys;
Nor ought the thunder of their carabins
Drown the sweet airs of our tun'd violins.

But it was not 'white Peace the beautifull'st of things' any more in the 1630s than in the 1930s; it was a wretched, uneasy peace with a bad conscience, and the tuned violins quivered with foreboding.

Foreboding as much of inward as of outward disaster. The signs of political unrest in this country where the turtles were singing on every bough were apparent to anyone not blinded by its material prosperity. Church, State and society suffered from a succession of insignificant or unsuitable leaders. Intelligence was not lacking, but something — confidence, style, character, even — was. The prestige of the Crown would hardly have survived any successor to Elizabeth; James I, who might have been a distinguished eccentric don, was clearly impossible. His son Charles acquired a tragic pathos at his latter end, but was not, reigning, an impressive king. The Archbishops were little better: Bancroft portentous, not impressive, Abbot, cantankerous and bigoted (having shot a beater while hunting, he was ultimately suspended for manslaughter: an unreassuring thing to happen to the Archbishop), and last of all fussy little Laud, trotting briskly round snuffing out abuses. Society shook with the kind of scandals that had either been concealed, or been carried off with more style, in the days of Elizabeth: the Essex divorce, the Overbury murder trial, the case of Lord Audley, the prosecution of Lady Purbeck for adultery.

Small things, but educated England was a small, inbred society. This smallness gave importance to single personalities, and a negative importance to the lack of them.

A political crisis was evidently approaching at terrific speed. The government could not continue bankrupt in the 'sea of plenty'. Either the Crown must find means to tap the wealth of the country, or it must cede its authority to those who could. The same crisis had already broken in most European countries. Kings who could not be masters were liable to become victims. King James might survive; King Charles was obviously doomed. From Elizabeth's death in 1603 until 1630 the situation built up towards the crisis. Then came ten years of postponement when Charles threw the opposition out of gear by refusing to call Parliament. It was never anything but an unexpected interlude, and never — except to those who were wilfully blind — appeared as anything else. The inevitable clash was postponed for a decade, the unrestful, mock-happy thirties.

Ten years the world upon him falsely smiled
Sheathing in fawning looks the deadly knife —

Fanshawe again, writing of the King his master; but he might be speaking for many of his contemporary poets, for the whole of his precocious generation.

The combination of spiritual unrest with material comfort — a combination never again so strikingly apparent until our own time — seems to be in England at least a fruitful one for poetry. The astonishing harvest of the second quarter of the seventeenth century has, reckoned in numbers alone, rarely been equalled. But of this great population of poets very few made an attempt to grapple with the problems of their times. The recurring note is, if worldly, insouciance; if unworldly, retreat.

The two obvious exceptions, Milton and Marvell, were both to be found among the opponents of the King. Milton is too complicated and individual a genius to conform to any general rules, but in Marvell, born in 1621 and maturing as a poet during the most restless and disastrous years of the century, many of the characteristics of the Cavalier poets are apparent. He was unlucky by so narrow a margin in missing the interlude of the thirties:

The forward youth that would appear
Must now forsake his Muses dear
Nor in the shadows sing
His numbers languishing.

Tis time to leave the books in dust
And oil the unuséd armour's rust . . .

Unhappy 'forward youth', Marvell was only twenty-one when war broke out. The sense of threatened happiness was never more graphically expressed than in his

But at my back I always hear
Time's wingéd chariot hurrying near:
And yonder all before us lie
Deserts of vast eternity.

He, too, could retreat at times from the pressure of the world to embroider prettily on country themes. There are his glow-worms.

Ye Country Comets, that portend
No war, nor prince's funeral
Shining unto no higher end
Than to presage the grasses fall
Ye glow-worms, whose officious flame
To wandering mowers shows the way . . .

Evidently close kin to Herrick's glow-worms whose services were called in to light Julia to bed. Yet the bedrock of his poetry is not retreat, but acceptance and understanding. It is only necessary to compare the fearless political grasp displayed in his celebrated *Horatian Ode on Cromwell's Return from Ireland* with, for instance, Abraham Cowley's welcome to Charles I after the first abortive Scots War. Marvell manages to compress a whole political theory as well as an extremely striking aperçu of the situation into his lines: Cowley makes no attempt to write anything but good verse. Neat and accomplished the empty phrases ring:

Others by war their conquests gain
You like a god your ends obtain
Who when rude chaos for his help did call
Spoke but the word and sweetly order'd all . . .

The King had in fact been forced to yield to the Scots rebels without fighting because he realized in time that he had no army with which to fight them. Two years later, when he risked a war, the results were so disastrous that even Cowley had no words for them.

But the poets were mostly on the King's side. The reason can hardly have lain in the patronage afforded by the Court to literature. It was notoriously poor. The truth was that the poets of this period, however young and fashionable, belonged to the *arrière*, not to the *avant garde*. Their whole trend of thought reached back into a receding past, away from the cold and probing realism, both in thought and politics, which was gradually submerging the older world. They were in fact anti-political, just as the King's view was anti-political – an attempt to do without politics, not an attempt to reform them. This, in the political field the fatal weakness of the King's side, was its attraction for them, and its charm for posterity.

Revealed religion had dominated the dying world, and revealed religion is the refuge of one large group of these poets, the impregnable fortress into which they retreated from the anxious pressure of the time. Donne, from whom the poetic inspiration of his successors was partly derived, stands outside the group. He was thirty by the time Elizabeth died, and like all who reached manhood in that more robust epoch, his torments came mostly from within. There is no retreat in his religious verse, rather a fierce grappling with the mysteries of dogma and the hideous reality of death. He does not, like the later metaphysical poets, soar into the Empyrean, or abandon himself in feminine surrender to the arms of God. The earth is solid under him.

His successors, without exception, are in flight before the world; escape is their only message, whether they speak with the pellucid ingenuousness of Herbert, the lofty sweetness of Vaughan, the ecstasy of Crashaw, the liquid fluency of King, the vibrating rapture of Quarles. Occasionally and far off, one catches the echo of the world without:

But hark! My pulse like a soft drum
Beats my approach, tells thee I come.
And slow howe'er my marches be,
I shall at last sit down by thee.

The military simile has a hint of menace in King's peaceful elegy on his wife.

Each individual case is, of course, different. George Herbert, of noble birth, forsook the prospect of a worldly career for quiet at Bemerton; Henry Vaughan, a simple doctor in remote Brecknock, had little opportunity to know the world; Francis Quarles, who had been a courtier and travelled abroad, knew from what he was retreating; Henry King and Richard Crashaw felt the wind of politics at its keenest, the former losing his bishopric and, worse still, his library, the latter his Cambridge fellowship. King's quiet conscience and sweet disposition made his troubles the easier, and Crashaw, who died in poverty on pilgrimage to Loreto, had found in the Catholic faith shelter from the blast.

Quarles, describing only his individual case, gives reason for them all:

Like to the Artick needle, that doth guide
    The wand'ring shade by his magnetick pow'r,
And leaves his silken Gnomon to decide
    The question of the controverted hour;
First franticks up and down, from side to side,
    And restless beats his crystall'd Iv'ry case
    With vain impatience, jets from place to place,
And seeks the bosom of his frozen bride;
    At length he slacks his motion, and doth rest
His trembling point at his bright Poles' beloved brest.

Ev'n so my soul, being hurried here and there,
    By ev'ry object that presents delight,
Fain would be settled, but she knows not where;
    She likes at morning what she loathes at night;
She bowes to honour; then she lends an eare
    To that sweet swan-like voice of dying pleasure,
    Then tumbles in the scatter'd heaps of treasure;
Now flatter'd with false hopes; now foyl'd with fear
    Thus finding all the world's delights to be
But empty toyes, good God, she points alone to thee.

Less secure than his total retreat from the world was the mere country retreat of Herrick, who lacked the quality of mind necessary for more arduous contemplation than that of violets. Not that he contemplated violets with much assiduity (he had at first bitterly resented being cut off from the gaieties of the capital). A close observation of nature is markedly absent from his, as from most, contemporary verse. He evokes the colour and the climate of the English summer with what proves to be on examination an astonishing vagueness of accurate detail. Therein lies his genius. Comfortably settled at Dean Prior in Devonshire, well connected, by nature and breeding contentedly obsequious ('Great Caesar' he apostrophizes the minuscule Charles I and wreathes verses like garlands round the baby Duke of York) – he was in a position to bury his head, not in the sand, but in a bank of wild flowers. He sang as he himself said

> of Maypoles, hock-carts, wassails, wakes,
> Of bridegrooms, brides and of their bridall cakes.
> I write of Youth, of Love and have Accesse
> By these to sing of cleanly wantonesse.

'Cleanly wantonesse' – but for a few coarser outbursts at the expense of personal enemies – does indeed hit off Herrick very neatly. But his gifts, nourished on a diet of material, if simple, pleasures could not apparently contend with adversity. Driven out of his rectory, he was pleased at first with the prospect of returning to London, but things were not what they had been, his Great Caesar beheaded, his pretty Duke of York in exile, and well on the way to becoming the far from pretty James II. The honeysuckle talent withered.

The fact was that in the seventeenth century – as in our own – escape was impossible. There is matter for reflection in the fact that its major poet, Milton, went out to meet the political problem of his time and to some extent subdued it to his verse. With few exceptions the others, when caught, were caught unwillingly. For there was no escape: not in contemplation at Little Gidding, not in the common rooms of Oxford and Cambridge, not in the rectories of Devonshire or the country mansions of the Cotswolds, least of all in the gardens of Whitehall. It was the politician's century, and the poet was already being pushed away, driven back, as it were, into his own society. Hence the flourishing of cliques, the Oxford clique with Will Cartwright, the Cambridge clique with Cowley and Crashaw, the 'sons' of Ben Jonson, the Whitehall clique of gentry. Hence the private jokes, the adulation of friends, the lampooning of enemies, the sly topical scandals and oblique references which make great tracts of their verse incomprehensible.

The false forward spring of the thirties brought on the flowering of innumerable talents; verses flowed gracefully from a hundred fluent quills, Carew, Davenant, Waller, Godolphin, Lovelace, Townsend, Habington. They were all quiet-needing talents, born in rich soil and germinated by showers of applause. Flowering in the sunshine of the thirties their delicate blossoms were later to fall unquickened or hang withered on the bough. But they were most of them, however short their bloom or few their verses, something more than mere fashionable practitioners of *vers d'occasion*. The anthological immortality of so many of their lyrics – an immortality which makes them too hackneyed for quotation – is itself a tribute to the astonishing felicity of their touch. 'Go lovely Rose', 'The lark now leaves his watery nest', 'My dear and only Love' – each is unique, each perfect. Artificial in design, their poetry is yet unforced. Its effortlessness makes it at first glance seem almost too easy. There is nothing, not even observation, to give body to their works. Their natural phenomena are almost always wrong. Even gardens, a form of tamed and sophisticated nature in which they delighted, they never closely observed or accurately described. Yet at times their poetry seems all compact of sunlight and green lawns, of bright flowering borders and the white-thorn hedgerows of an English spring. Marvell's bees go to bed in the tulips, a freak of nature equalled by Lovelace's grasshopper snugly tucked up in a carved acorn. Their convention was not the laboured convention of accuracy. They relied on the rightness of sound and rhythm, and the associations which one happy phrase can call to mind. Their appeal is through the senses to the imagination, never laboriously to the inward eye which was Wordsworth's bliss of solitude but emphatically not theirs.

Imagination was their refuge, as faith was that of the metaphysical poets: imagination so strong that in most of them the poet and the man led separate lives. Some intrigued at Court, some planned a *coup d'état*, some when war came raised troops of horse, many distinguished themselves in the field and more in the dangerous parts of spies and messengers. Their experience of life was vivid, harsh and dangerous, anxious and despairing, the experience of the defeated. Not a breath of it reaches their verse, unless it be a soft melancholy like that of a summer evening: life is short, beauty is shorter, and the cool shadow of not unwelcome death lengthens across the garden.

The *carpe diem* theme recurs in innumerable variations. Light-hearted in Cowley's

To-day is ours, what do we fear?
To-day is ours, we have it here.
Let's treat it kindly that it may
Wish at least with us to stay.

Didactic in Herrick's 'Gather ye Rosebuds', *moqueur* in Jordan's irrefutable statement that his mistress 'will be damnable mouldy a hundred years hence', faintly menacing in Jasper Mayne's

Time is the feather'd thing,
And, whilst I praise
The sparklings of thy looks and call them rays,
Takes wing,
Leaving behind him as he flies
An unperceivéd dimness in thine eyes.

But apart from this general preoccupation with the shortness of time, they search after beauty rather than truth, manner and not matter. Occasionally, but very occasionally, genuine personal feeling forces a way through. Cowley's lament for his friend William Harvey opens on a note almost harsh with pain:

It was a dismal and a fearful night,
Scarce could the Morn drive on th' unwilling light,
When sleep, death's image, left my troubled breast
By something liker death possessed,
My eyes with tears did uncommanded flow
And on my soul hung the dull weight
Of some intolerable fate.
What bell was that? Ah me! Too much I know.

But this is the exception. For death, however keenly felt, as for love, however genuine, there were the accepted patterns, the tender, plaintive strain, the Grecian vegetation, the mourning shepherds. Life could only be met on these terms, feeling only expressed under the customary disguises. From the country peace of Bemerton George Herbert mildly protested:

Is it no verse, except enchanted groves
And sudden arbours shadow coarse-spunne lines?
Must purling streams refresh a lover's loves?
Must all be vail'd, while he that reads, divines,
Catching the sense at two removes?

George Herbert could dispense with such veils. The 'sweet and vertuous soul' had made peace with heaven and had no more to fear on earth. He was lucky, too, in dying before the crisis of the time.

But for those who must go on living in the world, the pretence was essential. Like Milton, they knew about the 'two-handed engine at the door'. Unlike Milton, they were not on terms with it. So while the King's government went finally bankrupt, while the Scots overran the northern counties, while Strafford was beheaded in front of a gigantic crowd of jubilant spectators, and the little Archbishop escaped by a back way from the mob, and the King fled the capital and the Queen fled the country, and after a hundred and fifty years of peace England was at war with herself, these poets were imploring Amarantha to unravel her hair, giving the nightingale winter quarters in their lady's throat, asserting that birds and flowers mistook her coming for the dawn, with a hundred other irrelevancies.

When the assumed mood breaks down, it gives place to a venomous or ribald parody of itself. Equivocal words and a whole alphabet of symbols invest the pretty gallantries with other meanings. Most of these poets are adept at disguising obscenity; Suckling's sleight of hand is positively insolent. From his brilliantly accomplished verse, indeed, a savage, go-getting, tomorrow-we-die materialism emerges almost naked. Gambler and society playboy, he never had any doubt of the fate in store for the lilies of the field, planned to have his good time and had it. Whether or not he killed himself, preferring poison to starvation, is a matter of indifference; but he died in Paris and in poverty during the opening months of the Civil War. The first whiff of gunpowder had been enough for him.

His fellows, more sympathetic for that reason, cultivated their wilful blindness to the end, their 'careless heads with roses bound' within the doomed walls of Basing House or besieged Oxford, in the shadow of the firing party and the block. Montrose, like Raleigh, was rhyming on the eve of execution. Nor did they mean, as one literal-minded editor has thought, that roses were commonly twined in their hair. The roses were their still lovely imaginings, though the draught whistled under the door in the fireless prison, and a querulous wife with a sheaf of unpayable bills was the material out of which they conjured Althea whispering 'at the gates'.

Theirs was a mental, not a physical shrinking. Few of them actually failed in courage. Suckling, not unexpectedly. Waller, too; sensitive and vain, with most of his relations on the Parliament side, he fancied himself as an orator in the House of Commons. Later, becoming involved in a plot to betray London to the King, he lost his nerve and betrayed his associates instead, an act which forty subsequent years of blameless life could not altogether wipe out.

The soul's dark cottage, batter'd and decay'd,
Lets in new light through chinks that time hath made,

he was to write long after, in a poem whose eighteen lines sum up perhaps more perfectly than anything else in the English language the mistakes of youth and the regrets of age.

But Davenant was knighted for valour by the King and employed on dangerous missions. Falling into Parliamentary hands, he was only saved from execution, as some thought, by the intervention of Milton. Cowley, expelled like Crashaw from Cambridge, entered the Queen's service as a secretary and was employed as a confidential agent during the Commonwealth. It did his talent no good. He was never to fulfil the promise of his radiant teens. Sidney Godolphin was killed in a skirmish at Chagford; Cartwright died of camp fever in overcrowded Oxford; Montrose was hanged in Edinburgh; Denham, Cleveland, Lovelace, Fanshawe, all were active for the King, and all were dispossessed, imprisoned or exiled.

In debts, defeat and hunger their voices fade out. A few naturally carried over the tradition, with the remains of their lives, into the ensuing period. The individual always exists to blur the lines which historians for convenience must draw precisely. Traherne, born late in the 1630s, closes the exquisite cycle which began with Quarles. The Restoration brought with it the triumph of the scientific approach, the foundation of the Royal Society, and the cynical shelving of moral values which accompanied the new outlook. Smooth, ingenious and satirical was the new and more ordered expression of the poetic impulse. Fantasy and faith were alike dead: they had been the last expression of the nation's wondering and ingenuous adolescence, of a time when men still saw themselves midway between the beasts and the angels. Henceforward man was lord of creation: there was nothing he would not know. The limitless world, inexplicable and impressive, dwindled to the compass of his mind. Descartes, Boyle, Newton – the physical and mental map regained its contours. Men knew once more where they were and whither they were going, but their fancy would never again range so freely, and no one again would say

I saw Eternity the other night
Like a great ring of pure and endless light.

[PNW 21, 1944]

WALTER ALLEN

HENRY GREEN

'The pink decade' the 1930s have been christened, but in spite of the
sneer, for any writer of the thirties to have been non-political, to have
aimed at pure art, is in a way itself suspect; and Henry Green is one of
the very few pure artists among the novelists of the thirties. His second
novel, *Living*, pre-dated Auden's first book of verse by a year, and
reading it when it appeared one was excited by it in much the same
way as one was by Auden, one cannot say wrongly because it was
impossible to foresee his next novel, *Party Going*, written between
1931 and 1938. The subject-matter of *Living* gave him, as it were,
honorary membership of a movement in writing to which he never
truly belonged; but in 1929 it was the subject-matter, life among
Birmingham factory workers, that fascinated. In the novelty of the
material, while one admired the style one saw it as little more than
eccentricity, an attempt to express new subject-matter in a new way;
for already emphasis had passed from technique to content. But with
the publication of *Party Going* one could no longer see it that way; in
it it became clear that Green stood apart from what had become the
contemporary movement, that he was an artist in an older sense, in a
way that Flaubert and George Moore and Joyce were artists, men
whose main preoccupation was with style. For such writers material
was of course not unimportant: Flaubert has for so long been summed
up in a single sweeping phrase *le mot juste*, that it is necessary to
remember that *Bovary* and *L'Éducation Sentimentale* are magnificent
social documents just as *Ulysses* is an excellent *vade mecum* to Dublin.
But for the pure artist, with his preoccupation with methods of
expression, subject is of secondary importance in that he sees it as
existing mainly as the vehicle for a method of expression; and as
Flaubert followed up the study of provincial life that is *Bovary* with
the archaeological reconstruction of *Salammbô*, so Green could write
first a novel of working-class life in Birmingham and then a novel
about wealthy irresponsibles which, considered in terms of content
alone, should be trivial and is anything but that.

It is anything but that because of its style. In *Pack My Bag*, Green has stated his idea of the function of prose:

> Prose is not to be read aloud but to oneself at night, and it is not quick as poetry, but rather a gathering web of insinuations which go further than names however shared can ever go. Prose should be a long intimacy between strangers with no direct appeal to what both may have known. It should slowly appeal to feelings unexpressed, it should in the end draw tears out of the stone.

That is obviously no description of prose as it is written by most of the best contemporary writers, by Isherwood and Orwell and Graham Greene. Prose has become colloquial and direct, has returned to Dryden and Defoe and Swift. We no longer object, with Johnson, that the 'rogues never hazard a metaphor'; but Green hazards them continually, and to such an extent has the plain style conquered that, reading the Sunday reviewers, you might be pardoned for inferring that *Party Going* was the work of an illiterate. Beneath this apparent naïvety, the occasional superficial resemblance to the Stein stutter, his prose is a prose carefully wrought, highly sophisticated and highly mannered, the most distinctive prose in contemporary writing. Whereas the basis of most modern prose is the simple sentence (to take an extreme instance, there is only one relative clause in Halward's story *Arch Anderson*), each paragraph of Green is planned and built up as carefully as the octave of a sonnet. Take the following, from *Pack My Bag*:

> Later, when the accident I have described disrupted me, I felt, and it is hard to explain, as though the feelings I thought I ought to have were hurting me. I was as much alone as any hunted fox. Only as my feelings turned and doubled in their tracks to the loud blast of news each cable brought, as conscience the huntsman cast my feelings forward and then back until the fox I was was caught, bowled over at last into genuine surrender, there was something desperate in the noise, the howling at my heels. At this distance the noise of the pack is stilled, their music as it is called comes from over the hill, the huntsman, now an older man, blows his horn gently, and the note, now so distant it is no louder than a breath to bring forgotten embers to a glow, is a shame remembered, a run across familiar country.

Green is, in fact, to use Connolly's word, a Mandarin; of a new kind certainly, but none the less a Mandarin.

Or there is another way in which Green's distance from his contemporaries may be measured. Compare him, for instance, with Calder-Marshall, a writer of much the same social class and education, and one of the leading theorists of contemporary fiction as well as a characteristic practitioner. His style, more violent than Isherwood's and Orwell's since it is based on Joyce and the shock-tactics of Wyndham Lewis, is akin to theirs in that it aims at direct expression. His progress, one may say, has been from psycho-analysis to social realism, from Freud to Marx; so that his books are the record of a personal development which has also been the typical development of a generation. His work, then, forms a continuum. Green's does not in any such way; with the exception of his first novel, *Blindness*, written while he was still at school, it is not at all the record of a personal development. He is aloof from his material in a way that Calder-Marshall is not; and he is untouched, as a writer, by contemporary ideas whether political or psychological. Lawrence defines the novel somewhere as a 'thought adventure', and for the majority of writers this is true. But Green – and this is another sign of the pure artist – appears to be quite apart from his work, outside it; it is not a series of disguised chapters of autobiography.

His prose is, I think, a poetic prose. It was so conventionally in *Blindness*, a first novel of no more than average promise, though the theme, a literary and Etonian adolescent going blind and adjusting himself to blindness, is ambitious. There, the writing, the descriptions of nature in which the book abounds, are Georgian: Rupert Brooke is just round the corner and John Drinkwater may drop in at any moment. But after Eton and Oxford Green went to work in his Birmingham foundry. He started his novelist's career with one great advantage over his middle-class contemporaries: as the boss's son, with an inherited interest in a foundry, he could move, as it were, up and down the social scale as he pleased. In order to write about working-class life, as in *The Nowaks*, Isherwood had to go to Berlin; but Green could go to Birmingham.

In his Bordesley foundry he worked on the floor for some months, writing *Living* in his spare time. The difference between *Blindness* and *Living* is as startling as the difference between Oxford and the Coventry Road must have been to the author. The title of the book is itself defiant, as though Green had discovered life for the first time. No working-class writer could have written the book; the author's delighted sense of novelty is carried over to the reader, and it is significant that it has had no apparent influence on working-class writers apart from James Hanley, who owes something to its style in his *Stoker Bush*. The theme is now a familiar one: the displacement of labour by reorganization and the infatuation of a girl who wants marriage and children before anything else with a young man who finally, and comically, deserts her. But it remains, after twelve years, the best novel of factory life written by an Englishman.

But *Living* is not, as one interpreted it when it first came out, primarily a realistic novel. Green escapes, sometimes through a poetry of incident, sometimes through a daring arrangement of words which may be called poetic, often through both at once, the bounds of narrow realism that have confined most writers of working-class life in this country and trembles on the verge of symbolism. As an example of what I mean by poetry of incident the following passage may be quoted:

> Then, one morning in iron foundry, Arthur Jones began singing. He did not often sing. When he began the men looked up from work and at each other and stayed quiet. In machine shop, which was next iron foundry, they said it was Arthur singing and stayed quiet also. He sang all morning.
>
> He was Welsh and sang in Welsh. His voice had a great soft yell in it. It rose and rose then fell again and, when the crane was quiet for a moment, then his voice came out from behind noise of the crane in passionate singing. Soon each one in this factory heard that Arthur had begun and, if he had two moments, came by iron foundry shop to listen. So all through that morning, as he went on, was a little group of men standing by door in the machine shop, always different men. His singing made them all sad. Everything in iron foundries is black with the burnt sand, and here was his silver voice yelling like bells. The black grimed men bent over their black boxes . . .
>
> Everyone looked forward to Arthur's singing, each one was glad when he sang, only, this morning, Jim Dale had bitterness inside like girders, and when Arthur began singing his music was like acid to that man and it was like that girder was being melted and bitterness and anger decrystallised, up rising up in him till he was full and would have broken out – when he put on coat and walked off and went into town and drank . . .
>
> Still Arthur sang and it might be months before he sang again. And no one else sang that day, but all listened to his singing. And that night son had been born to him.

That is a good sample of Green's style in *Living*: bare, repetitive, harsh, angular, sometimes deliberately clumsy, an admirable medium for the expression of the blackness and din of a foundry. Green tells us in *Pack My Bag* that in the Oxford English School he failed to learn Anglo-Saxon; but whether by design or not, the prose of *Living* is an Anglo-Saxon prose, many of its devices, the omission of the definite article, the emphatic 'that', are Anglo-Saxon devices, and one suspects that Sweet's *Old English Reader* had a greater influence on Green than he knew.

As an example of the tendency towards symbolism I would quote the way in which the background of drab streets and public parks is dominated by the flights of homing pigeons, as though Green himself, writing at the window of an upper room, were endlessly fascinated by their flight. Any conscientious realist might have put in the pigeons as part of his detail. But Green makes much more out of them than this. They recur again and again throughout the book, sometimes in simple description, sometimes as images for the working of the characters' minds. They are symbolic at once of escape, of the life beyond the labyrinths of brick, and the attachment to home and the familiar scene. This use of something approaching symbolism gives *Living* a unity underlying its formal structure; and such passages remain in the mind in 'a gathering web of insinuations'.

In *Party Going,* as the subject-matter lessens in importance – it is the world of Evelyn Waugh, with a difference – so the style becomes more rotund and involved and the symbolism deepens. A party of what would once have been called bright young people are going to France as the guests of an absurdly rich young man; they meet at the station, fog holds up the train, and they are marooned in the upper rooms of the station hotel, while the hordes of workers waiting for trains below, singing community songs, thicken until they threaten to swamp the hotel itself. What Hollywood calls the 'plot-line' is as simple as that. Symbolism, concrete in its imagery, stirs the mind with the richness of its implications, and if it can be translated into definite terms, into a prose meaning, is symbolism no longer. A case in point is the incident – its repercussions run through the book – of the spinster aunt at whose feet a dead pigeon tumbles in the station entrance; she picks it up, takes it to the ladies' lavatory and washes it, and makes it up into a brown paper parcel. The discovery disturbs the party, as it disturbs the reader; the incident is funny, but it is more than that, and its meaning cannot be paraphrased. To account for its effect one is forced back, as Forster was when discussing the nature of Lawrence's genius in *Aspects of the Novel*, on some such word as prophetic.

Party Going is a comic novel; it can rest, I believe, on the same shelf as the best of Firbank. But it is on its symbolism that I have preferred to concentrate, since it seems to me, as a symbolic novel, so much more successful than anything the English disciples of Kafka have written. The difference between it and Upward's *Journey to the Border,* for instance, seems to me the difference between symbolism and allegory. *Journey to the Border* can be paraphrased, it is 'about' something, a moral can be extracted as you can extract no moral from Kafka: in the little streets down by the docks there is a small newsagent's where you can buy the *Daily Worker*. Upward's is one of the most exciting novels produced during the last decade; yet in the end the book fails, the excitement fizzles out, the explanations begin, the reader is let down. The moral is not commensurate with the excitement that has been generated in the imagination. More than any book of the decade it shows the dangers that beset the imaginative writer who is also a political writer. *Party Going* may be much less worthy from a left political view, and it is certainly less ambitious, but it succeeds as Upward's does not, and is original in that it derives from the author alone. You may see it as an exposure of futility and as a satire on people with wealth but without responsibility; or you may read it simply as a comic novel. It is all these; and something more; obstinately itself and irreducible to a single moral. Again Green's own phrase, 'a gathering web of insinuations', best describes its effect.

Pack My Bag is a slighter work than the two which preceded it, though the style is richer and more consciously poetic. It is right, I think, to see it as a substitute for a novel; it is a crisis book written in 1938 and 1939. Green calls it a 'self-portrait', and though it is a book that nobody interested in modern writing must miss, one reads it primarily for the light it throws on Green as an artist. The content is ordinary enough: other people have described expensive prep schools and the pleasures and trials of hunting and fishing; and Eton is now a familiar scene. But, like the novels, it is an original book. Autobiographies of childhood and adolescence, whether avowedly autobiographical or ostensibly fiction, fall generally into two kinds. There is the report on experience, the intellectual, analytical, almost clinical study, like *Lions and Shadows* or Connolly's *A Georgian Boyhood*, in which the author attempts to answer the question, 'How did I come to be the man I am?'; and there is the attempt to recreate the past in itself, without reference to the author's present state, as in Spender's *The Backward Son*. In either case the writer looks as far as possible at himself as though he were somebody else. Green makes no such attempt. 'It is all wrong,' he writes, 'to try to recreate days that are gone. All one can do is search them out and put them down as close as possible to what they now seem.'

The result is a highly subjective, highly personal book. His Eton days cover, for instance, much the same period as *A Georgian Boyhood*, which may almost be read as a gloss on *Blindness* and *Pack My Bag*, but the pictures of Eton are so different as to be pictures of worlds that appear to have nothing in common. It is significant that Eton is not even given its name. The book portrays one isolated human being as child, schoolboy and undergraduate, and so strong is the sense of isolation that one feels the author's withdrawal to be deliberate. There is no trace of any concern for ideas, any preoccupation with society and the individual's relation to it.

During the war Green has been in the Fire Service and the theme of his novel *Caught*, published two years ago, is life in the AFS before and during the early part of the blitz on London. It remains by far the best novel dealing with that period. Green has added to his equipment as a novelist by achieving a complete mastery of the eddies and convolutions of working-class speech, seemingly endless, maddeningly repetitious, thick with qualifications and explanations, lit up with 'swear words like roses in their talk'. Out of a series of such conversations he made his surprising tour-de-force the short story called 'The Lull', which appeared in the Summer, 1943, *New Writing and Daylight*. In snatches of flat, often pointless conversation he expresses a whole range of characters and the boredom they feel. The result is a strange poetry, the kind of poetry achieved by an artist like Beaton in his blitz photographs or that a brilliant film director sometimes discovers in shots of the sordid and banal. Green's ear and the camera's eye are alike in making familiar things new, and that, for Dr Johnson, was a definition of poetry.

This aspect of Green's art is strongly brought out in *Caught*. But there is much more to *Caught* than that alone. *Caught* is an organic growth. Picasso has said of himself and his work, 'I do not seek, I find,' and that is applicable to much of Green's work. Many of his most characteristic achievements, what the eighteenth century would have called his beauties, have the air of *objets trouvés*, things found, not contrived. With most novels one knows pretty well what is going to happen, and why. One may be presented with a moral problem, and the interest depends upon the subtlety and fairness with which it is worked out. Or if the life described in the novel is one familiar to the reader, the interest lies in the light which the author is able to throw on the already known; one seeks, in a way, a confirmation. With other novels, those of Huxley or Isherwood, for instance, what interests primarily is the personality of the writer, which unites the most diverse scenes and incidents of the story. With a novelist like Graham Greene, again, one is fascinated by the playing out of what one recognizes as an extraordinarily compelling personal myth.

But in *Caught*, as in Green's fiction as a whole, there is another quality, not easily defined. One is moved obscurely, as by some kinds of poetry in which the meaning is never clear and can never be wholly clear. Which is to say that Green's novels arise from a layer of consciousness deeper than that from which fiction usually emanates; one is aware at one and the same time of several strata of meanings. Events are never simple or single in Green's world; they have their symbolic meanings too.

This is apparent both in *Caught* and *Loving*, whose common theme has been described as 'an emotional Black Hole of Calcutta'. For what exactly is *Caught* about? Life in the Fire Service. The lives of men and women held in unwelcome proximity for too long and with too little to do, gossip-ridden and corroded by suspicion. The mutual distrust of the working-class man and the middle-class man. The overwhelmingly disastrous effect of sudden authority and hero-worship combined on a man totally unprepared for them. In part, an account of the first night-raids on London; in part, a father's puzzled devotion to his son and a brother's puzzled devotion to his sister. All these go to make *Caught*, but all these, as it were, simultaneously, fused together, so that no one strand can be isolated and drawn out without the whole fabric perishing. From one point of view *Caught* is a tragi-comedy of misunderstanding; everyone talks at length, but there is no communication. There is no communication between the middle-class auxiliary Roe and his five-year-old son, as there is none between the principal antagonists Roe and his officer Pye, whose lunatic sister abducted Roe's son. The title summarizes the book; it is the incomprehension and incommunicability of Kafka played out in a naturalistic setting, and the tangle of thwarted understanding and frustrated urge to communicate can be resolved only by the death of Pye by suicide and the liberation of the auxiliaries from their 'emotional Black Hole' by enemy planes bombing the docks.

Green's titles have a particularly organic relation to his novels: *Blindness, Living, Party Going, Caught, Loving*. When Jane Austen wrote a novel called *Pride and Prejudice* the theme of that novel was precisely pride and prejudice, just as Fielding's *Tom Jones* is about a young man named Tom Jones. The relation between contemporary titles and contents is more esoteric: *Eyeless in Gaza, All the Conspirators, England Made Me, The Horse's Mouth*, all these are ironical comments rather than titles in the old sense. Isherwood called his autobiography *Lions and Shadows*, using the title of a novel he had planned but not written; in other words, the titles were interchangeable. One has heard that in Gaza an Arab bookseller had his window stocked with Mr Huxley's novel, thinking it a guidebook to the town. He had a literal mind, but not more so than our own eighteenth-century novelists or Henry Green. Thus, Green's latest novel, *Loving*, is summed up by the title: it is about loving; not love, but the condition expressed by the verbal noun. As almost every character in *Caught* is caught, so practically every character in *Loving* is in a state of loving. Again, as in *Party Going* and *Caught*, the characters are set in a confined space, marooned, as it were, on a desert island too small for them in the midst of the great world from which they are cut off. The desert island of *Loving* is a castle in Eire staffed almost entirely by English servants who do not venture outside the grounds for fear of the neutral Irish. The period is that of the blitz; they are well out of it, glad of it, and guilty about it. The castle, like the fire station of *Caught*, and the hotel rooms of *Party Going*, is a web of gossip, intrigue, scandal and misunderstanding, though the novel throughout is written in terms of pure comedy. As in *Caught*, the whole book revolves round one nuclear incident: 'Mrs Jack', the daughter of the owner of the castle, is surprised one morning in bed with her lover by a housemaid. It is the beginning of the end; everything follows from that. From then on it is inevitable that Raunce, the butler, and Edith, the housemaid, should run away together to England.

Though on a smaller scale than *Caught*, it represents in some ways an advance on it. It is much more closely knit, and in many ways Raunce is a more subtle character than Pye, because Mr Green is continually surprising us with new facets of his character. At first he seems to be nothing more than a petty fiddler, then a hypocrite, then a lecher. As facet after facet is revealed we realize that he is more complicated than our preconceived notion had allowed for, that he is that rare creation the character in the round, who surprises disconcertingly, as people do in life. But Green is the enemy of preconceived notions of character.

Green has now written five novels. They are all very different, not only from the works of any other novelist writing today, but from each other. Among the ranks of contemporary writers he is as much on his own as Miss Compton Burnett, but every novel he writes is unpredictable, which can scarcely be said of Miss Burnett's. He has, perhaps, the most completely original vision of any writer of his generation. That alone is not enough to make a good novelist, but when it is combined, as in Green, with technical mastery and the resources of a virtuoso, it is enough to make him, if not the best, certainly the most exciting novelist writing in England today.

[PNW 25, 1945]

EDWIN MUIR

THE NATURAL MAN AND THE POLITICAL MAN

The history of the modern novel is the history of the disappearance of man as religion and humanism conceived him. Instead, there has emerged a new species of the natural man firmly dovetailed into a biological sequence and a social structure. This new natural man is capable of improvement but, unlike the natural man of religion, has no need for regeneration. He is simply a human model capable of indefinite improvement on the natural plane; the improvement depending ultimately on the progress of society, and of things in general.

Towards the end of last century it was fashionable to call this new natural man 'the thinking animal', and he has since been called 'the unique animal'. He follows a natural development from birth to death, and since this is all that is allowed him, it is important that he should pass through all its stages — childhood, adolescence, love, maturity — in a manner closely corresponding to the requirements of nature; otherwise he will be 'frustrated' or 'distorted'. His upbringing, his surroundings, his ideas, should be as 'natural' as possible. If they are, the expectation is that he will turn out to be satisfactory.

But in practice it is discovered that he is never quite satisfactory, that some residue of frustration or distortion always remains in him. This residue is taken to be due to the imperfection of our political and social system, and under a perfect constitution it is assumed that it would disappear. The corollary of the natural man is consequently the political man: the man conscious that something must be done collectively by all natural men, or a majority or an effective minority of them, in order that an opportunity may be given to every natural man to develop his natural potentialities in the most natural way conceivable.

The difference between this new natural man and the natural man of myth and religion and humanism is quite simple. The first natural man was not regarded as human in the complete sense until he put on the spiritual man; he had to be made anew by a process which did not enter into the rest of the biological sequence. This process was conceived symbolically as a re-birth, a spiritual act by which man was integrated into his true image and became conscious of his unique place in the world and in time. We may conceive this new man as being grafted on the natural man, or as being innate in the natural man and seeking to emerge from him into complete humanity. In either case, as the new man can exist only in the body of the old, his co-existence with the old implies a moral struggle in the centre of the individual, a struggle which determines in all sorts of ways his struggle to adapt himself to society or society to himself, but is different in its intimacy, its unavoidability, and its apparent lack of utilitarian causation. This fundamental moral struggle within the individual was for many centuries accepted as the essential character of man. This being suspended between good and evil by a law inherent in his nature is the man of Dante and Shakespeare, and of Balzac and Tolstoy. He occupies a country of his own with unique rights and needs, quite apart from the biological sequence.

During a number of generations the frontiers of that country have been crumbling away. For the separate autonomous drama of mankind we have gradually substituted a natural process. The result has been a reduction of the image of man, who has become simpler, more temporal, more realistic, and more insignificant.

The difference between man as he was conceived by Christian theology, by Dante, Milton, Pascal, and the tragic poets of England and France in the sixteenth and seventeenth centuries, and man as he is understood in different ways by Mr H. G. Wells, D. H. Lawrence, the early Aldous Huxley, Mr Ernest Hemingway, M. Henri de Montherlant, and a great number of popular middle-brow novelists – for the most important point about the new conception is that it has become the popular conception – is difficult to define, though obviously great. One way of expressing it is by saying that to the traditional man the individual's life was a conflict, and that to the modern man it is a development. The conflict has been stated in various terms; but the formulation of it which is closest to our own ways of thinking and most readily understandable by us is that which we find in Milton and Racine: the conflict is a conflict between reason and passion or impulse. This formula was accepted as valid throughout the seventeenth and also a great part of the eighteenth century, though in a somewhat mechanical way; reason and impulse tending to become categories instead of vital principles in the individual.

The Romantic Movement reinstated impulse, but it also did something else; it tended to identify reason with impulse; it substituted for the old conflict a sort of mystical co-operation. France, with its capacity for stating everything rationally, first became conscious of the implications of the new attitude. By a succession of writers from Madame de Stael to George Sand and Alfred de Musset the impulses were declared to be sacred, and more reasonable than reason itself. This phase, strewn with the wrecks of spontaneous love affairs, illustrated by a confused crowd of anonymous Byrons and Chateaubriands, did not last for very long. But it left behind it, in spite of its failure in practice, the assumption that reason and impulse worked in co-operation; and if this was so, there was nothing left for the individual but to develop. This conclusion was merely implicit in the work of the romantics; it was not formulated until much later. It required for its formulation certain theories drawn from Darwin, and particularly the idea of evolution applied to the life of the individual. The old conflict was gone, or was hidden away. Darwin and the orthodox economists taught man the necessity for adaptation; Spencer and the Utopians opened before him the endless possibilities of evolution. The adaptation was a present need; the evolution, a future contingency. But at the same time the adaptation was a changing adaptation, for the environment of man was changing, and therefore to adapt oneself was to evolve. That the evolution might have no moral principle, that the environment of man might change for the worse instead of for the better, was not at that time seriously considered.

To contemplate man's image of himself changing and catch the stages of the change is almost as difficult as to imagine visually the process by which the countless animal species developed from a few simple prototypes. The idea of man current at any one time is not a homogeneous one; old conceptions linger on; new ones which may prevail later tentatively appear. The idea that man's life is a development, and part of a greater development which is essentially political or sociological, not moral or religious, was bound to lead to the conclusion that this development could be controlled, and that human life could be conditioned to a great extent, given the power and the equipment. Today we can see this theory being applied on a large scale in two countries, in Russia, on the whole beneficially, and in Germany, disastrously. For this theory man becomes a subject who responds in a more or less calculable way to certain things such as encouragement, suggestion, the carefully thought-out system which is called propaganda, intimidation, display, rubber truncheons, and in general all the varieties of greed and fear. As man is a creature with a natural development, entirely contained in his environment, all that is needed is to decide the terms within which he shall develop. Once these are settled by a sufficiently powerful group, men can be used with calculable accuracy.

This is a theory which could have been founded only on the new natural man developing within an environment in a calculable way, without any effective inward struggle, or any permanent conception of a desirable life, or any personal striving to realize it. If the theory does admit that such obstacles to its working exist, it regards them as foolish, since they ignore the reality of *things*; such things as the power of the state, tanks, shells, concentration camps, and such things also as the natural man's appetites, vanities, angers, fears and hatreds, which can always be easily aroused, and which, even with a little direction, can become irresistible. Consequently what has gradually been brought into prominence by the religion of development is the primacy of *things*, and it finds its fulfilment in the theory that men can be conditioned by things. Control things and you control mankind. In this conception the moral struggle which possessed the imagination of other ages, and was strong even a century ago, recedes into irrelevance, and becomes like one of those vestigial organs in the body which no longer perform any useful function, but exist merely to plague us: a sort of vermiform appendix.

It is easy to note the reduction of the image of man in contemporary politics, for there it presents itself in flesh and blood and works out logically in contempt for human freedom and for human life, things which always go together. To see it in contemporary literature is more difficult. Perhaps it may be best seen in a drastic simplicity. In his book *Modernes*, M. Denis Saurat makes the generalization that in French literature the classical writers of the seventeenth century exalted reason, the Romantics of the nineteenth century emotion, and certain contemporary writers sensation. This generalization traces the graph of the modern fall of man. It is a descent from complexity to simplicity, from the civilized to the primitive.

An idea of the change in our attitude to human life may be had by comparing any character in Dickens with any character in the early work of Mr Ernest Hemingway. Dickens was a very emotional writer, but he still knew that there was in the individual a struggle between impulse and reason. He was not a religious writer, but his characters still lived on a plane which was partly spiritual and partly natural. Mr Hemingway's characters live on the natural plane alone. The two gunmen in his short story, 'The Killers', are mechanical murderers, and their victim a mechanical murderee; they are all equally conditioned; and there is nothing to be said about them, except that they evoke the kind of pity one might feel in watching some hunting beast pulling down and killing its prey. The whole story is astonishingly natural from one point of view, and astonishingly unnatural from another, for after all the characters are not animals but merely men thinking and feeling and acting in an extraordinarily circumscribed way. The murderers have no remorse; the victim has no feeling except animal resignation. The immediate lust to kill, the immediate dread of being killed, are all that remain. There is nothing but sensation.

Turn from this to Dickens. Jonas Chuzzlewit too is a murderer, but he never suggests to our minds the picture of an animal armed with a gun or a knife; he remains a human being with thoughts and emotions, horrible enough, certainly, yet drawn from the general fount of human thought and emotion. In his short story Mr Hemingway is sure of only one thing, the immediate sensation, and being a scrupulously honest writer, he confines himself to that and leaves out thought and emotion as much as possible. He starts with the natural man following his needs, suffering from his frustrations as a wounded animal might suffer. And starting from that, it was impossible for him to reach the world of emotions and thoughts, for they are a legacy from the traditional man and are determined by beliefs which assume that man is not natural in the same sense as an adder or an ape is natural.

Mr Hemingway began to write in the years of disillusion which followed the last war, and the natural man he describes is therefore the frustrated natural man. Probably no one else has described more vividly the horror of the natural man's life when he is driven and goaded and denied natural satisfaction, and retires into himself to lick his wounds or seeks forgetfulness in drink or sex. For many years Mr Hemingway went on describing the frustrated natural man, articulate only in violence or in sensual experience. Then he discovered that the frustrated natural man was not enough, and that he must transcend himself and become the political man. This was the discovery of a whole generation, not of Mr Hemingway alone; what makes it particularly interesting in his case is that we can see it taking place in his work. He began with the undirected revolt of *Fiesta*; he attained the disciplined revolt of *For Whom the Bell Tolls*, with its glorification of the republican struggle in Spain. The man Mr Hemingway describes in this book is still the natural man, fighting and lusting. He has merely added a few words to his vocabulary; the words liberty, fraternity and equality. They are sufficient in themselves to give him an aim beyond his appetites; but his way to them is still the way of the natural man; and only by fighting and killing can he achieve a world where there will be nothing to hinder his natural development, no obstacle, no frustration. The goal of all men has miraculously risen before him; although he has acknowledged nothing but sensation, three ideas have announced themselves to him; but they are in a different world from his world, and can be reached only in a different way from his way. They can be reached only by thought and emotion and the action which follows from them, while all that he can offer is sensation, a sort of *appetite* for liberty, equality and fraternity which drives him to batter down all that stands between him and them without knowing that, even if he were to gain them, he could not, as he is, enjoy them. This incompatibility between the natural man and his political aims makes Mr Hemingway's later work sentimental in a curious way; it is as if we saw Caliban looking for a moment through the eyes of Prospero, and, without Prospero's rod, swearing to perform Prospero's miracle with his naked fists. This sentimentality of violence is implicit in the work of all writers who conceive Utopia as a kingdom to be taken by storm. Mr Hemingway's first frustrated men were far more real.

The frustrated natural man was a popular, almost a typical, figure in the fiction after the last war, when hope and belief were at their lowest ebb. Some of the writers who wrote about him then have since given him up and turned elsewhere for a more adequate conception of man; Mr Aldous Huxley, for example. But those who stuck to him and tried to educe something positive from him were finally left with no choice but to turn him into the political man. And when the natural man becomes political, there seems to be only two directions in which he can advance: towards Communism or towards Fascism. The man who thinks of himself developing within an environment, without any deep-rooted resistance, will ultimately prefer that the terms of his development should be laid down unmistakably, so that a clear channel may be provided for his impulses. In following these impulses he knows the only kind of freedom which he can know; and as that freedom seems infinitely dear to him in prospect, he is prepared even to die for it. Communism and Fascism, which both believe in the natural man, provide a channel for his impulses, in the one case a channel which may lead him to live better, in the other a steep road rushing steadily downwards, where he will bury himself entirely in nature in a sort of sacred frenzy. When the inward struggle of the individual is regarded as irrelevant such things as these can be achieved; the one thing which cannot be achieved is liberty.

Communism, by postulating the natural man and using him as he is, with his needs and his desires, tries to teach him; there are transcendental implications in Communism, no matter how carefully communists may rule them out. Fascism is far more radically involved with the natural man, and rests upon him entirely. It does not look beyond him, but glorifies him, sees in him the sole hope of the future, and regards the spirit, the intellect and the higher uses of the senses merely as diseases marring his natural perfection. The two modern writers who have described the natural man most penetratingly and eloquently, D. H. Lawrence and Henri de Montherlant, are therefore almost of necessity Fascists by implication. They are not pre-eminently political in their attitude. In Lawrence we have a fierce exposure of the squalor of our industrial civilization, and in Montherlant a contempt for all the shams of the age and a ruthless assertion of the right of the natural man to go his own way. They both criticize society from the point of view of the natural man. Lawrence's criticism of Industrialism is that it frustrates even the simplest natural impulses, and sex in particular, the central impulse: the criticism is valuable because it is fundamental. Against the synthetic monstrosity of modern life he sets the values of blood and soil, the first natural values, essential because natural. But having affirmed them, he turns against what he calls 'the white consciousness', the bloodless consciousness of the spirit; and whether he does this because it is spirit or because it is diseased spirit it is impossible to say. He preferred the primitive, for he felt that only the primitive, in a world he hated so much, was still sound. He was outraged by the Christian counsel to love your neighbour, and retorted that hate was often more honest and salutary; for hate was an instinctive discharge of energy, and in a world which lived mainly by routine, any instinctive discharge was to him its own justification. He asserted all the impulses of the natural man, love, hatred, anger, cruelty, scorn, and found a mystical meaning in the working of the impulses. He found in them too a sort of mythology, not unlike the mythology which the Nazis have invented, though far less heavy and tedious, since he was a writer of genius. He wanted mankind to start again at the beginning, in a state beyond good and evil, and never reach the Fall. He would have been satisfied if man could be born properly once. The question is whether man can be born properly once, and therefore whether Lawrence's gospel was nothing but a dream. He saw that our senses and impulses were frustrated at every point by the life we live; he wanted a state in which they would function naturally, without distortion. He saw that such a state would be better than our present one. He believed that this state could be reached by a sort of mystical assertion of the natural man; here again he forestalls the Nazis. But the Nazis themselves have shown to what a belief of this kind leads; to violence, persecution, cruelty, war and, in the last resort, slavery. For the natural man is violent, quarrelsome, greedy, and also, since he has no inner resistance, easily subjugated.

Montherlant's picture of the natural man is more sophisticated. His natural man has attended fashionable parties on the Riviera, and knows all the tricks of the social life. At the same time he has the greatest contempt for society and is by conviction anti-social. He is much more formidable than Lawrence's natural man; for he has examined the life of the spirit and sardonically dismissed it. He scorns the world in which he lives, a world of dupes; but he has no wish to change it; he is content that he himself should live the infinitely preferable life of a very clever, unusually honest, and terrifically vital natural man. He is exclusive; he insists on his privileges. If he has a counterpart in the Fascist movement, it is among the leaders who use the beliefs of the ordinary man for their own purposes, and see through the mythology while exploiting it.

The importance of Lawrence and Montherlant is that they draw with unusual honesty the consequences of a belief in the natural man. These consequences are very different from those which his original sponsors expected. The believers in evolution thought that the natural man contained within himself endless potentialities of improvement; and their faith was ultimately founded on a mystical belief in the necessary tendency of things to go on improving for all time: it was founded on a faith in things. Man had merely to develop; and his development was guaranteed by the beneficial development of things, which was certain. Then it was discovered that man was not a single term in the equation, that some men were fitted to lay down, within the human sphere, the conditions on which man should develop, and that others were fitted only to observe those conditions. For the first was reserved the actual conduct of human policy; for the second, a mythology that would please or inspire them, and make them eager to obey and ready to lay down their lives. Human life thus became a thing completely contained in an environment, and therefore a thing to which the imagination of the writer could give no ultimate significance, since there was not in it even the pretence of choice, even the day-dream of freedom. If the life of the individual is a development, then that development is simple and inevitable. If the life of the individual is a conflict, then that conflict implies a choice and the choice, complexity, and complexity, the existence of more in human life than can be compressed into a formula. What has taken place in literature is a simplification of the idea of man, connected with this notion of natural process and development. The simplification is a general tendency; literature has not initiated, but merely reflected it; and only those writers who are deeply rooted in tradition, and possessed with the idea of time, have been able to make headway against it; such writers as Proust, James Joyce and Virginia Woolf, to confine ourselves to the novelists: there are similar figures in poetry. The obsession of such writers with tradition was called out by this human crisis. But Lawrence, Hemingway and Montherlant are completely in the modern convention. They definitely accept the new leaf which history has turned, the leaf on which the present war is being written. They themselves write on that leaf, and the first words written on a new leaf, even by genius, are never new but merely primitive, a repetition of words written on the first leaf of all, before civilization began, with the few precarious modifications which have been wrought since by civilization on the material fabric of life.

[*PNW* 26, 1945]

David Magarshack

Chekhov and his Producers

Anton Chekhov, the only name among Russian dramatists really familiar to the English playgoer, has gained so firm a hold on the English stage that it may not be amiss to ask how far Chekhov plays in their English guise really represent what Chekhov wrote and, more particularly, what Chekhov wanted to express by an art he took to only late in life.

Before turning to an analysis of Chekhov's art as a playwright, however, something ought to be said about the belief, unfortunately widely held both in England and America, that the chief characteristic feature of his plays is inaction. This belief has become so deeply rooted, for reasons that will become apparent later on, that in a recent American translation of Chekhov's plays, a footnote to Chekhov's stage direction in *The Seagull* – the action takes place on Sorin's country estate – informs the reader quite blandly that it is ridiculous to speak of action in a Chekhov play since its main characteristic is inaction. What has been chiefly responsible for this idea, or at any rate for the idea that a Chekhov play is characterized by lack of action, is the intrinsic nature of the drama of Chekhov which is quite different from the drama of direct action to which we are accustomed. The main characteristic of a Chekhov play is not inaction, but indirect action, that is to say, it is not a play in which nothing ever happens, but one in which the main dramatic action does not happen on the stage. *The Seagull*, for instance, is full of the most dramatic incidents. Its hero attempts to commit suicide, and in the end does commit suicide. Its heroine runs away from home, is disowned by her rich parents, is seduced, has an illegitimate child and the child dies, is abandoned by her lover, and, generally, experiences one disaster after another, any one of which would have been enough to make a full-length play. In addition, we have no less than five love affairs, and a multiplicity of themes tacked on to the main theme, which would have provided several plots for any ordinary playwright. But – and this is what is so characteristic of a Chekhov play – none of these highly dramatic incidents takes place on the stage. What we see is merely how these incidents shape and influence the lives of the characters. Now, far from being invented by Chekhov or being characteristic only of his art as a playwright, this drama of indirect action is the oldest type of drama in existence, namely, Greek drama. To say that it lacks action is to misunderstand the very nature of dramatic action, which finds its highest expression in repose, in a pause, in inner rather than in outer movement. An actor who stands still on the stage is not inactive. On the contrary, he should be more active in such a pose than when, for instance, lighting a cigarette or making love to the heroine. A faint smile can be more shattering in its dramatic effect than firing a pistol or transfixing your enemy with a sword. But, of course, it is quite true that since the Elizabethans modern drama has been mainly of the direct action type. Nor must the fact be overlooked that when Chekhov began writing plays, he was anxious to write plays of the usual type, that is, plays of direct action. His first two plays, *Ivanov* and *The Woodsprite*, were of that type, and it was his failure in what might be called the ordinary type of drama, due chiefly to the fact that he was not a man of the theatre, that drove Chekhov to take up the older drama of indirect action. This transition from one type of play to another can be plainly seen when we compare *The Woodsprite* with *Uncle Vanya*. In *The Woodsprite*, which is merely an earlier version of *Uncle Vanya*, the main character is Dr Astrov, who bears the name of Khrushchov, and who in the end marries Sonia. Uncle Vanya, who in Chekhov's first version of the play appears rather characteristically under the name of Uncle George (Chekhov did not change his surname Voynitsky), shoots himself in the last act but one instead of firing at *and* missing the old professor. The whole play does not revolve round the character of Uncle Vanya, but round Astrov's or Khrushchov's attempts to reclaim his land by afforestation (hence his nickname Woodsprite). Helen, the young wife of the elderly professor, runs away from her husband after Voynitsky's suicide (in the first version, too, Voynitsky is in love with her), but returns to him, as a good wife should, in the last act, which has the most artificial happy ending a great playwright ever contrived. Chekhov published *The Woodsprite* in a magazine in 1890, but later withdrew it from the list of his published plays and would not allow any theatre to perform it. One can't help feeling that the unusually gloomy ending of *Uncle Vanya* is due chiefly to Chekhov's unhappy experiment with the happy ending of *The Woodsprite*. Be that as it may, the fact remains that, having failed in his attempts to write plays of direct action, that is to say, plays in which, to use Granville Barker's definition of a

Shakespearean play, nothing of any dramatic significance ever happens off stage, but every important incident takes place in full view of the audience, Chekhov turned to indirect action plays, which, as has already been pointed out, belong to a much more ancient type of drama.

Indeed, what is so characteristic of a Chekhov play is that it possesses the main elements of Greek drama through which the function of action is expressed. These are: the 'messenger' element, the function of which is to tell the audience about the chief dramatic incidents that take place off stage (in a direct action play the 'messenger' element is, as a rule, a structural flaw); the arrival and departure of certain characters in the play round which the chief incidents that do occur on the stage are grouped; the presence of a chorus which, as Aristotle points out, 'forms an integral part of the whole play and shares in the action'; further, the most powerful element of emotional interest in indirect action plays, which is also their main instrument for sustaining suspense and arousing surprise, and which Aristotle calls 'peripetia', a theatrical term that, by the way, is in common use in Russian, meaning the reversal of the situation leading up to the dénouement – Aristotle defines it as 'a change by which the action veers round to its opposite, subject always to the rule of probability or necessity'; and, finally, the last element – background.

Let us examine these elements a little more closely and see how they are used by Chekhov and, what is perhaps more important, how a producer can use them to discover the main themes and, particularly, the ruling idea of a Chekhov play.

The 'messenger' element is perhaps the most difficult one to manage satisfactorily, that is to say, without distracting the attention of the audience from the dramatic action on the stage; and Chekhov's great art as a playwright is best revealed in the superb way in which he manages his 'messenger' scenes. A good illustration of this is the opening scene of *The Three Sisters*, where the messenger part is divided between the three heroines, the narrative being used in addition for the delineation of character, and in the opening scene of *The Cherry Orchard*, where Chekhov uses the same method. The remarkable fact about *The Seagull* is that Chekhov completely dispenses with the 'messenger' element in the first three acts, using it only in the fourth act, where Dr Dorn's and Konstantin Treplyov's narratives rather tend to impede the (supposedly absent) action.

The arrival and departure element in a Chekhov play is so well known that it is hardly necessary to enlarge on it. It is, as a matter of fact, the only element a producer makes full use of as a function of action.

It can hardly be claimed, however, that he does justice to the chorus element which is one of the most characteristic features of a play of indirect action, although in a modern play of this type it may be disguised by the fact that instead of having a special actor for the part, as in the Greek plays, it is usually assigned to one or more of the characters. Chekhov manages the chorus parts in his plays with consummate skill. Indeed, he makes the comments of the chorus on the life of the characters and its moral judgement truly an integral part of the play, as Aristotle urged the Greek playwrights to make them. For he distributes the chorus element among several of the characters who, as it were, assume the mantle of the chorus always at the right moment, when, that is, their inner life suddenly overflows in a flood of words, or sometimes even in sound, as, for instance, the famous tum-tee-tum of Vershinin and Masha in *The Three Sisters*. It is this spontaneous and almost palpable transformation of thought into speech that is perhaps the most subtle expression of dramatic action in a Chekhov play, which, if not treated as such on the stage, is liable to transform the chorus parts in a Chekhov play into static, isolated, and disconnected statements of opinion.

The most important element of emotional interest in the drama of indirect action is *peripetia*, the reversal of situation which, as Aristotle says, 'arises from the internal structure of the plot so that what follows should be the necessary or probable result of the preceding action'. Aristotle illustrates this element by a reference to *Oedipus* where, he writes, 'the messenger comes to cheer Oedipus and free him from his anxiety about his mother, but by revealing who he (Oedipus) is, produces the opposite effect'. This is the simplest and, no doubt, the most effective example of peripetia. In modern plays of the indirect action type, however, this element assumes much more subtle forms, and it is not an infrequent occurrence for even an experienced producer to misinterpret it and ruin the play. This is what actually happened with the first Moscow Art Theatre production of *The Seagull*, at least in the opinion of the only man who matters, namely, Chekhov.

The Moscow Art Theatre production of *The Seagull*, as is well known, was a great success, and not only launched this theatre on the road to international fame, but was also responsible for the fact that Chekhov, who had made up his mind to give up writing for the stage after the failure of *The Seagull* in Petersburg, changed his mind and gave us his last three great plays. But the success of *The Seagull* in Moscow was due to all sorts of causes, and not in the least to the fact that Stanislavsky, who was mainly responsible for its production, realized that the most essential condition for the success of a play of this sort is to give a physical expression to the action inherent in its dialogue. That was why in his first productions of Chekhov's plays, Stanislavsky cluttered up the stage with all sorts of objects in order to force the actor to *act* his dialogue by making it impossible for him to move without *doing something*.

The revival of *The Seagull*, however, was a failure, and the play never regained its popularity on the stage of the Moscow Art Theatre and was taken off its repertoire after only forty-five performances, as compared with the 635 performances of *The Cherry Orchard*, the 334 performances of *The Three Sisters*, the 320 performances of *Uncle Vanya*, and even the 110 performances of *Ivanov*, during the five seasons between 1898 and 1906.

Chekhov himself never saw the performance of *The Seagull* at the Moscow Art Theatre. He only saw it at the beginning of May, 1899, after his arrival in Moscow from Yalta, at a performance specially arranged for him. Olga Knipper, who later became Chekhov's wife and who played Arkadina in the first performance of *The Seagull*, has given us this account of Chekhov's behaviour after the last act of the play: 'Chekhov, the mild, well-mannered Chekhov, walked on the stage with his watch in his hand, looking very pale and grave, and declared in a very firm voice that everything was excellent, only "I suggest that my play should end with the third act: I will not permit you to play the fourth act!"' And Knipper ends her account with these surely highly significant words: 'Chekhov was very excited and told us that the fourth act was not from his play.'

What happened to make Chekhov so excited and threaten such drastic action *after* the great success of his play? What happened was that the two producers, Stanislavsky and Nemirovich-Danchenko, failed to appreciate the importance of the peripetia element in the play, and this failure to appreciate one of the most significant elements in the drama of indirect action is also responsible for the singular lack of success of *The Seagull* on the Russian stage in general.

Where does the element of peripetia come in in *The Seagull*? It comes in in the inner development of the character of the protagonists of the play – Konstantin and Nina – and it has nothing whatever to do with their unhappy love affair. In Konstantin's case it deals with his most powerful passion – his desire to become a great writer; in Nina's case it deals with her most powerful passion – her desire to become a great actress. The whole play, in fact, deals with one of the most important problems in art – what makes a creative artist? The symbolism of the play expressed in the 'seagull' theme, applies only outwardly to Nina. It is only a poetic way of expressing the very common fact of life, namely, the destruction of beauty by people who do not see it and are not even dimly aware of it, so that they do not know what a terrible crime they commit. Konstantin shoots down the seagull just because he has nothing to do; Trigorin nearly ruins Nina's life and her stage career just because of a chance meeting, a selfish whim, a passing infatuation; Arkadina tramples on and utterly destroys the spark of genius in her son because she is entirely unaware of it and, indeed, quite incapable of appreciating it.

Let us examine in greater detail how this element is worked out by Chekhov in his two characters. In the first act we find Konstantin talking very confidently, and indeed almost hysterically, of the new forms in art, but in the last act we see a complete reversal of the situation: Konstantin becomes more and more convinced that, as he says, 'it isn't old or new forms that matter; what matters is that one should write without thinking of any forms at all, and that whatever one has to say should come straight from the heart'. When one considers how much his belief in new forms of artistic expression meant to Konstantin and how truly dramatic Chekhov has made this passionate desire of his to prove to everybody and, above all, to his mother, that he was right in holding such a belief, this sudden acknowledgement of his mistake is perhaps one of the most tragic moments of self-illumination in all Chekhov plays, foreshadowing, as it does, the inevitable tragedy that is to take place so soon. Chekhov has here invested a purely literary theme with the attributes of high drama, providing, through the element of peripetia, one of the greatest surprises in the whole play, and the failure of a producer to realize the dramatic significance of this, and to bring it out in the performance must inevitably mar the play as a whole.

But the element of the reversal of the situation is even more important in the case of Nina. At the beginning of the play, Nina, who is to be the sole performer in Konstantin's 'advanced' play, is very excited about her coming appearance on the stage, hoping to impress Arkadina, a famous actress, and, above all, Trigorin, a celebrated novelist and playwright, whose writings she admires and with whom, in fact, she is already in love. Her mild girlish affair with Konstantin bores her, and it is with unconcealed reluctance that she allows him to kiss her.

A little digression on the nature of the two kisses in the play may not be out of place here. In the first act Nina's kiss is not only reluctant; it must reveal to the audience in a flash the true nature of her feelings for Konstantin, whose play she despises and whose theories on art make no impression on her whatever. Nina's second kiss in the third act is her first *real* kiss, and must reveal to the audience that, so far as she is concerned, it is not just a young girl's 'crush' on a middle-aged celebrity, but true love. This is only another instance of how extraordinarily dramatic the action of the play is.

When the moment of Nina's appearance on the stage comes, her utter inexperience and nervousness practically kill Konstantin's play even before Arkadina's unfortunate interjection after Dr Dorn had taken off his hat to mop his brow. Nina's total inexperience of the stage is of vital importance here, if we are to appreciate the change in her acting of the first part of Konstantin's play in the last act, and believe in her, as Chekhov undoubtedly wants us to, as a future great actress. It is, however, usual for the actress playing Nina to recite her monologue in a way that leaves no doubt in the mind of the spectator that it is an accomplished actress who is doing it. This is what actually happened at the first performance of the play at the Alexandrinsky Theatre in Petersburg, which was such a frightful flop. Chekhov pointed out at the time to Kommissarzhevskaya, the great Russian actress who played Nina, that 'Nina is a young girl who finds herself for the first time on a stage, who suffers from stage-fright, and is very nervous.' The significance of this remark seems to have escaped the producers, and the play is still acted, on the English stage, at any rate, in a way that does not bring out Nina's inexperience as an actress, an oversight that is bound to result, as we shall see presently, in the distortion of the main theme of the play.

In the fourth act Nina comes back an entirely different person from the girl we have seen in the first three acts. A complete reversal of the situation has occurred: Nina has become an actress, and is on the way to becoming a great actress. The amazing fact is that this reversal of the situation is completely overlooked by producers, who thereby reduce the whole level of the play to a sentimental love story that has gone wrong, and that in spite of the well-known fact that Chekhov loathed sentimentality of any sort.

What is the theme of the play as they see it, so far as Nina is concerned? The late Professor Elton, in a paper on Chekhov, gives this conventional summing up of Nina's character which is so typical of an English production of the play: 'Nina', he writes, 'is a stage-struck girl, who has been blandished by the second-rate celebrated author Trigorin, and misled into the wrong profession. She becomes an actress and finds she is a poor one.' Professor Elton does not tell us who has misled Nina into the wrong profession or what justification there is for the view that Nina considers herself a poor actress. The whole point of the play, surely, is that Konstantin, starting with his grandiose ideas about the great name he was going to make for himself as a writer, at last realizes that he is a failure; while Nina, who makes such a frightful mess at the very start of her stage career, at last realizes that she is on the way to becoming a great actress, and that, moreover – and this is of course the great message of the play – only he can become a great artist who does not allow himself to be discouraged by disasters in his private life and who knows how to endure suffering and transmute it into art. This point is of the utmost importance to the understanding of *The Seagull* as well as of Chekhov, who, whatever the believers in the Chekhov 'legend' may think or say, was certainly not a prophet of resignation.

Indeed, in the fourth act Nina, distracted as she is, makes it quite clear that she is not the silly girl Stanislavsky had taken her to be when, at the beginning of his career, he produced *The Seagull*.

'I'm different now,' she tells Konstantin. 'I'm a real actress now. I enjoy my acting. I revel in it. The stage intoxicates me. When I'm on it, I feel that I am beautiful.' And she finishes her long speech with this avowal of her faith in art: 'Now I know, my dear, now I understand that in our calling, whether we are writers or actors, what really matters is not fame, nor glory, nor any of the things I used to dream of. What matters is knowing how to endure, how to bear your cross – and have faith. I have faith, and that is why nothing can hurt me so much any more, and when I think of my calling, I am no longer afraid of life.'

To which Konstantin at once replies sorrowfully that she, Nina, has found her true purpose in life, while he is still lost in a maze of images and dreams.

Here, therefore, we have a complete reversal of the situation, and Chekhov, indeed, immediately proceeds to prove to the audience that Nina is not boasting about her being a good actress by making her recite part of her soliloquy in Konstantin's play. It must be obvious that if Nina's rendering of the words of the play within the play does not differ from her first rendering of them, the whole dramatic significance of the peripetia element is lost, and the main theme of the play ruined into the bargain.

Nina's last speech, no doubt, requires the finest possible acting because of her rapid changes of mood, the sudden pangs of agony she suffers when she discovers that Trigorin, whom she still loves, is in the next room, and the poignant memories which her visit to Sorin's country-house awaken in her, but that does not alter the fact of her complete transformation, of her spiritual rebirth, and of her faith in herself as an actress.

Their failure to grasp the significance of the peripetia element in the play resulted in a complete misinterpretation of this important scene by Stanislavsky and Nemirovich-Danchenko, and afterwards in Chekhov's declaration that the fourth act was not from his play. After the success of the play Nemirovich-Danchenko wrote to Chekhov that the actress who played Nina was the weakest in the cast. 'It was partly Alexeyev's fault [Stanislavsky was Alexeyev's stage name],' he wrote, 'for confusing her by making her play a kind of a silly fool. I got angry with her and told her to go back to her first lyrical way of acting. So she got all muddled up.' But how is an actress not to get muddled up if, instead of having her part interpreted to her intelligently, she is told to act 'lyrically'?

How is it that Stanislavsky and Nemirovich-Danchenko were guilty of such a blunder? So far as Stanislavsky is concerned, he himself afterwards confessed that he did not understand *The Seagull*. The play, he told his fellow producer, Nemirovich-Danchenko, appeared to him 'a sort of half and half, the passions not effective, and the characters incapable of supplying the actors with good stage material'. Stanislavsky was then at the very beginning of his career as producer and actor and he showed, according to Nemirovich-Danchenko, an unmistakable predilection for the classics, or, in other words, for the drama of direct action. As for Nemirovich-Danchenko, he had a profound admiration for Chekhov's genius and without his encouragement and constant badgering Chekhov would most probably have stuck to his decision not to write any more plays, but he seems to have missed the point of Nina's last speech for the same reason as many another Russian producer, right up to the present day, seems to have missed it. The cause of this curious misunderstanding shows how one word is sometimes enough to mislead a producer. Nina finishes her long speech in the last act with a strongly evocative word which, unfortunately, is more commonly used with a different connotation from that in which Chekhov used it. What Nina says is,

Ya veruyu ee mnye nye tak bol'no, which is more likely to convey the meaning of 'I believe in God and nothing can hurt me so much any more' than what Chekhov undoubtedly meant, namely, 'I have faith and that is why nothing can hurt me so much any more', the noun *vera* and the first person singular of its verb *veruyu* being most commonly used in the sense of religion and 'I believe in God'. This religious tinge of the phrase, especially as it is preceded by another religious metaphor of bearing the cross, had the unfortunate result of distorting Nina's meaning, and one can't help feeling that Stanislavsky's direction to the actress to play Nina as though she were a silly fool was due to this. It is only quite recently that Russian critics have begun pointing out that the whole significance of Nina's speech lies in the word *veruyu*, that is to say, in her profession of faith in her art.

The misinterpretation of this scene by Stanislavsky and Nemirovich-Danchenko, due to their failure to grasp the importance of the peripetia element, also led them to delete one of the most pregnant sentences in Nina's speech: 'I am a seagull – no, that's not it – I am an actress – yes, that's it!'

If one single word could produce an association of ideas conflicting with those the author wanted to convey and in this way endanger the continuous success of a play, what can happen to a Chekhov play when his dialogue has to be entirely transfused into the medium of another language? What can and does happen to Chekhov plays in English translations will become apparent if we consider the nature of Chekhov's dramatic dialogue. It can be taken as an axiom that the difference between a playwright's and a novelist's dialogues is that the words put into the mouths of his characters by a playwright, to be spoken by actors from the stage, must be a great deal more evocative than those used by a novelist in his dialogue. For unless the dialogue of a playwright is 'dramatic' in the sense that it can hold the attention of the spectator in spite of the fraction of time it takes the actor to say his words, it might as well have remained unspoken. This very simple fact is not always grasped by a novelist who decides to turn playwright, very often simply because he is incapable of differentiating between dramatic and undramatic dialogue. Chekhov, however, not only grasped the importance of dramatic dialogue; realizing that his type of play of indirect action demands a kind of dialogue that is even more evocative than the dialogue of the writer of plays of direct action, he took great pains to intensify the evocative powers of the words he used in his plays. An example which even those who do not know Russian should be able to follow will perhaps best explain this. In *The Cherry*

Orchard, Yepikhodov, the book-keeper on Mrs Ranevsky's estate, is a broadly drawn farcical character of a conceited halfwit who imagines himself a highly educated man because he possesses the bovine patience to wade through 'learned' books he has not the brains to understand. A character like that is not difficult to draw, and, indeed, has been drawn in every conceivable way in English, French, and Russian drama. But the way Chekhov has drawn him by the dialogue he makes him use is typical of Chekhov's dramatic dialogue in general. To begin with, the book Chekhov makes Yepikhodov read is a book that had been a best-seller in Russia for years and that everyone in the audience could be presumed to have read. It is *The History of English Civilization*, by Henry Thomas Buckle, which enjoyed a tremendous popularity in Russia towards the end of the nineteenth century and is mentioned not only in the works of Chekhov, but also in those of Dostoyevsky and other great Russian novelists. What Chekhov does next is highly characteristic. Instead of parodying Yepikhodov's 'learned' fatuities, he simply takes typical sentences out of Buckle and strings them together so as to fit them into the play, conveying at the same time the utter idiocy of the prig of a book-keeper. Some turns of Yepikhodov's speech seem to have puzzled many an anxious English student of the original text of Chekhov's play, but anyone who takes the trouble to read a page or two of Buckle's *History* need be puzzled no longer, for all those turns of speech are there as large as life. What Chekhov did in the case of such a broadly farcical figure as Yepikhodov, he did in a much more subtle way in the case of all his characters, that is to say, he enormously intensified the evocative powers of their speeches by a prodigal use of 'literary echoes' from Russian classics that were so familiar to his audience that they were sure to evoke a whole swarm of sensations similar to those his characters experienced, and in this way make his audience apprehend emotionally the state of mind of his characters. A good example of this is Masha's repetition of two lines from Pushkin's poem *Russlan and Lyudmila* at the end of the first act of *The Three Sisters*. No translation of these two lines, torn from a context that is completely unfamiliar to an educated Englishman or American, can possibly convey Masha's mood when she dimly perceives the stirrings of a great passion in her and is annoyed with herself for mumbling words the significance of which she is as yet unable to grasp. There are hundreds of less obvious, though scarcely less important, instances of that kind. But these 'literary echoes', translated as they stand, as they invariably are translated, are bound to give rise to a feeling that not only Chekhov's characters, but Russians in general, are a very curious kind of people. Unfortunately, the idea that Chekhov's plays are full of quite harmless but crazy people, due to the inability of the translator to recognize, let alone cope with, the 'literary echoes' in the text of his plays, is further magnified by a producer's inability to deal with the 'chorus' element which is so typical of a Chekhov play. This is also true of the peripetia element which is the main *functional* element in a Chekhov play and, as such, is usually suggested in its title. It is, that is to say, the key to the discovery of the ruling idea of the play and of what Stanislavsky calls its 'through-action', or the main theme that forms, as it were, its backbone. Even a superficial analysis of *The Cherry Orchard* will show how the peripetia element, if logically studied in the development of the Lopakhin–Ranevsky part of the plot, can deepen a producer's understanding of the psychology of the main characters of the play.

The last element in the play of indirect action, which ought to be kept in mind when dealing with a Chekhov play, is its background.

By 'background' I do not mean what the Russians call *byt*, that is to say, the characteristic details of everyday life of the Chekhov characters, which every producer of his plays must have at his finger-tips, anyhow. What I mean is the background against which Chekhov places his plays and which lends additional depth to them. This background will, as a rule, be found to be another well-known play, for instance *Hamlet* in the case of *The Seagull*, or Ostrovsky's *Forest* in the case of *The Cherry Orchard*. It was W. B. Yeats who observed that 'the old playwrights took old subjects, and did not even arrange the subject in a new way, because they were absorbed in expression, that is to say, in what is most near and delicate'. Chekhov certainly did arrange the old subject in a new way, but he too preferred to choose an old subject as the background of his plays because, like the old dramatist, he was absorbed in expression, in what was most near and delicate.

As a rule, this background is always present in a Chekhov play, though it may not be always so easy to detect. In *The Seagull*, however, it is very prominent, indeed. There is, for example, 'the play within the play', which, as in *Hamlet*, comes to an abortive end because of the storms it arouses. But, as a matter of fact, the very first line in the play, spoken by Medvyedenko to Masha, 'Why do you always go about in black?' gives us the clue to the presence of this characteristic element. It is the *Hamlet* motif which manifests itself in all sorts of delicate variations, rising to a crescendo just before the curtain goes up on the play within the play in the first act and again in the Arkadina–Konstantin scene in the third. In the first act, indeed, Chekhov comes out into the open and reveals to the spectator not only the relationship between Arkadina and Trigorin, but also between Arkadina and her son Konstantin by two quotations from *Hamlet*. Arkadina, the famous actress, who, as Chekhov pointed out at one of the rehearsals of the play in Petersburg, is 'a foolish, mendacious, self-admiring egoist', does not dream that when she turns mockingly to Konstantin and recites Queen Gertrude's lines –

O Hamlet speak no more;
Thou turn'st mine eyes into my very soul;
And there I see such black and grained spots
As will not leave their tint –

her son, who deeply resents her relationship with Trigorin, would turn furiously on her and her lover with Hamlet's withering words –

Nay, but to live
In the rank sweat of an enseamed bed,
Stew'd in corruption, honeying and making love
Over the nasty sty.

Konstantin's 'mother fixation', in fact, was as great as Hamlet's, and as disastrous to him in the end. This first outburst prepares us also for his pathetic, 'Why, oh why, mother, are you so much under the influence of that man?' in the third act, just when he should, surely, have encouraged his mother to take Trigorin away from Nina, an outburst which clearly shows how deep-seated this 'fixation' was.

The importance of these two quotations from Hamlet for the development of the inner action of the play is obvious enough. Yet we find that some translators of the play leave out Konstantin's Hamlet lines altogether, while Constance Garnett substitutes for them the utterly irrelevant lines – 'And let me wring your heart, for so I shall, if it be made of penetrable stuff,' which shows a complete confusion in the mind of the translator and no awareness at all of the importance of the *Hamlet*, or rather Gertrude–Hamlet, theme in the development of the play.

These are therefore the main basic elements through which the functions of action are expressed in a Chekhov play. Where Chekhov's genius as a playwright, however, finds its most brilliant expression is in the entirely original form he gave to the indirect action type of drama by a completely new and infinitely subtle combination of its basic elements, and it is in this sense that Chekhov can be said to be one of the greatest innovators in modern drama. As for the almost limitless scope Chekhov's dramatic art gives to the actor and producer, I can only quote Stanislavsky who towards the end of his life said that though he had acted a certain part in a Chekhov play hundreds of times, he always discovered new depths in it whenever he came to act it again.

[*PNW 37*, 1949]

J. C. HALL

EDWIN MUIR: AN INTRODUCTION

I

Edwin Muir is a serious writer whose achievement is broadly acknowledged but whose actual work has been strangely neglected. His poems, for instance, appear in few anthologies, and I know of no adequate interpretation of his work. This is all the more surprising when we consider how much attention has been paid to many of his contemporaries; and how, on the face of it, his work would appear to reflect certain recent literary trends. I say 'reflect' deliberately, for Muir cannot be said to represent any modern school or clique. He is an essentially individual writer, whose innate distrust of 'personalities' partly explains, perhaps, why after thirty years we still have to discover his work for ourselves. He has published some dozen volumes of poetry and criticism (including a most illuminating study of the novel), three novels, an autobiography, a biography of John Knox, and various books on Scotland. He is also, with his wife, a gifted translator, whose translations of Kafka in particular have been largely responsible for introducing that extraordinary genius to English readers. It is as a poet, I think, that Muir has done his most characteristic work, and this essay is therefore mainly an introduction to his poetry. But first I would like to say something about Muir himself, for a writer's background often helps us to understand certain aspects of his work. This is certainly so in Muir's case, and we are fortunate in having his own account of the first thirty-five years of his life in *The Story and the Fable*,* a book of great beauty and honesty of feeling.

Muir was born in 1887 in Orkney. His father came of farming stock, and he grew up in the raw, vivid atmosphere of the farmyard – 'a carnival of birth and death', as he calls it. For company Muir had three brothers, two sisters, and a much older cousin, Sutherland, a remarkable character whose habits were 'a great danger to the young women of Wyre, Rousay and Egilsay'. Sutherland appears in Muir's

* *The Story and the Fable* (Harrap, 1940).

novel of the Scottish Reformation, *The Three Brothers*,* and it was perhaps in tribute to his originality that Muir gave the fictitious character not only very much the same role, but also the same name, as that of his childhood companion.

Muir's description of his childhood among the islands is a brilliant piece of writing both for the picture it gives us of Orkney at that time and for its deeply sympathetic study of a child's mind. He was a sensitive boy and these early years, happy though they often were, were also full of doubt and strain for him. No doubt this was partly due to the fact that his father was constantly having to move from farm to farm owing to the exactions of the landlord (the 'Little General' of one of his poems). Gradually a sense of discouragement settled on the family; one by one the brothers and sisters broke away to try their fortunes elsewhere, until finally only Edwin and his sister Clara remained to help their parents. Eventually the father, worn out by the desperate struggle, packed up the family belongings and moved to Glasgow. Muir was fourteen at the time.

This move to Glasgow called for a power of adaptation which was beyond many of the members of this simply-bred family. 'The first few years after we came to Glasgow', writes Muir, 'were so stupidly wretched, such a meaningless waste of inherited virtue, that I cannot write of them even now without confused grief and anger.' One by one the members of the family were carried off by death: first the father from sheer exhaustion, then Willie by consumption, Johnnie by a tumour on the brain, and finally his mother by some obscure disease. The futility, the bitter sense of loss, of these years lies heavily upon this part of his autobiography and is reflected, too, in his novels. In *The Three Brothers*, for instance, Sandy's death from consumption clearly echoes Willie's fate; while in *Poor Tom*† Muir gives us an almost undisguised account of the appalling disease which had reduced Johnnie to a helpless cripple. These two novels are not, I think, altogether satisfactory in themselves, but the note of personal tragedy underlying them gives them a certain undeniable power.

Muir stayed in Glasgow for eighteen years and during this time worked at a remarkable variety of jobs: as office clerk, chauffeur's assistant, and, for two fantastic years, as a clerk in a bone-factory. His descriptions of these jobs and of the people he met give us a fascinating picture of the life of a big city and particularly of Muir's intellectual

* *The Three Brothers* (Heinemann, 1931).
† *Poor Tom* (Dent, 1932).

interests at this time – his conversion to Socialism, his discovery of the *New Era*, and his passionate absorption in the work of Heine and Nietzsche, who seemed to offer him some sort of compensation for the squalid life he was leading.

When the war came Muir, whose health had suffered under the stress of experience, was passed unfit for active service and took a job in a ship-building office, devoting much of his spare time to the National Guilds movement. About this time, too, he began to write, and, although the aphorisms he published in the *New Age* appeared to him later merely as a reflection of his mental confusion, they did at least bring him into contact with other writers. These were his happiest years in Glasgow, but a new phase in his life was soon to begin. In 1919 he married Willa Anderson and moved to London.

Muir has called his marriage (to which he has paid touching tribute in some recent poems) the most fortunate event of his life. It helped him to face up at last to the vague fears that had weighed him down more and more during his life in Glasgow. Shortly after his arrival in London he began treatment with a psycho-analyst, and his account of the analysis is one of the most interesting chapters in his book. I will not attempt to describe it here, but read within its context it clearly reveals how deeply this painful experience altered the course of his life, enabling him to climb out of the dark despairs and frustrations of his early years. And – what is important for us – it released those creative forces without which he could never have developed as a writer.

II

The Story and the Fable was published in 1940, but (with the exception of a few extracts from a later diary) it does not carry us beyond 1922. Muir felt he could not write with sufficient clarity of later occurrences – a decision we may regret, for it leaves us with no record of his career as a writer. Nevertheless, it is not difficult to see why Muir chose to break off at this point; it was a natural turning-point in his life. 'I was thirty-five then,' he writes, 'and passing through a stage which, if things had been different, I should have reached ten years earlier. I have felt that handicap ever since. I began to write poetry at thirty-five instead of twenty-five or twenty.' Does this mean that an artist necessarily loses by developing late? In Muir's early work there are many of the faults of diction which we associate with a younger poet, but there is also a considerable gain in psychological perception. Indeed it reveals very clearly the imaginative depths opened up by his analysis. His strange symbolical novel *The Marionette*,* in which the father tries to rehabilitate his feeble-witted son by encouraging him to work out his conflicts in games with dolls and marionettes, could have been written, one feels, only by someone for whom this drama had more than a merely intellectual significance. And perhaps it is worth noting here that Muir's analysis, though beneficial, was not complete; he broke it off after nine months to go abroad. Whether or not we regard this as adding to the significance of his work, Muir has certainly acknowledged the therapeutic value of art and shown how in one poem ('Ballad of Hector in Hades') he worked out, quite spontaneously, a childhood terror.†

The Story and the Fable is a title that leads us immediately to the heart of Muir's thought. 'In themselves,' he writes, 'our conscious lives may not be particularly interesting. But what we are not and can never be, our fable, seems to me inconceivably interesting. I should like to write that fable, but I cannot even live it; and all I could do if I related the outward course of my life would be to show how I have deviated from it.' This double vision of life haunts Muir, and his work is an attempt to understand it by means of dreams and other subconscious activities. Muir describes a great many dreams in his autobiography, and this is certainly one reason why we should read it before approaching his poetry. In this respect Muir can be said to reflect a tendency in modern literature – the attempt to find poetical form for psychological concepts. Faced with this task the modern poet has explored the world of myth, but how tedious, how drily intellectual, many of these explorations are! Muir succeeds where others fail because this approach is integral to his vision of the world and goes back deep into his childhood, to the Orkney 'where there was no great distinction between the ordinary and the fabulous; the lives of living men turned into legend'. At that time the fable was real to him; but later the distinction grew greater and to bridge that gulf his mind turned to metaphysics.

This, then, the destiny of the human soul, is at the centre of Muir's work. 'Our minds are possessed by three mysteries: where we come from, where we are going, and, since we are not alone, but members of a countless family, how we should live with one another.' Muir has

* *The Marionette* (Hogarth Press, 1927).

† Rilke, when faced with the possibility of psycho-analysis, refused 'this operation, this great clearing-up which is not done by life'. He sought a solution in his art, and the *Elegies* and *Sonnets* are, surely, his justification.

called one of his volumes of poems *Journeys and Places*, and this aptly describes his preoccupation. For the history and evolution of mankind is most easily conceived of as an endless journey through Time, which we can begin to understand only in certain recognizable stages or 'places'. 'One or two stages in it I can recognize; the age of innocence and the Fall, and all the dramatic consequences which arise from the Fall. But these lie behind experience, not on the surface; they are not historical events; they are stages in the fable.' We are helped to understanding through our own experience, for each man does in a sense re-enact the fable in his life. First, there is the coming to birth, described most beautifully in 'The Voyage':

That sea was greater than we knew.
   Week after week the empty round
Went with us; the Unchanging grew,
   And we were headed for that bound . . .

Our days were then – I cannot tell
   How we were then fulfilled and crowned
With life as in a parable,
   And sweetly as gods together bound.

Delusion and dream! Our captain knew
   Compass and clock had never yet
Failed him; the sun and stars were true.
   The mark was there that we should hit.

And it rose up, a sullen stain
   Flawing the crystal firmament.
A wound! We felt the familiar pain
   And knew the place to which we were sent.

The crowds drew near, the toppling towers;
   In hope and fear we drove to birth;
The dream and a truth we clutched as ours,
   And gladly, blindly stepped on earth.

Then comes the timeless age of childhood when 'the earth, the houses on the earth, and the life of every human being are related to the sky over-arching them; as if the sky fitted the earth'.

My childhood all a myth
Enacted in a distant isle;
Time with his hour glass and his scythe
Stood dreaming on the dial,

And did not move the whole day long
That immobility might save
Continually the dying song,
The flower, the falling wave.

('The Myth')

Muir perfectly understands this stage, which yet must be broken as
contradiction enters life and earth and sky are dislocated 'as if the
frame of things were ruptured'. Then 'archaic fevers' begin to shake
the blood and some ancient burden falls upon the soul.

The fathers' anger and ache
Will not, will not away
And leave the living alone,
But on our careless brows
Faintly their furrows engrave
Like veinings in a stone . . .

The angers will not away.
We hold our fathers' trust,
Wrong, riches, sorrow and all
Until they topple and fall,
And fallen let in the day.

('The Fathers')

This need to 'let in the day', to understand oneself and through oneself
the life of mankind, is the eternal quest of the soul.

In our search for understanding we are constantly thwarted by
Time. Time is the great protagonist in Muir's spiritual drama, the
enemy before whose advance all vision disintegrates, all action is
transformed. Muir's poems are indeed what one of his titles suggests,
'Variations on a Time Theme', for it is Time's despotic presence that
haunts his pages.

Here at my earthly station set,
    The revolutions of the year
Bear me bound and only let
    This astronomic world appear.

Yet if I could reverse my course
    Through ever-deepening yesterday,
Retrace the path that led me here,
    Could I find a different way?

('The Stationary Journey')

This is an ultimate question, to which the poet returns again and again. The idea of predestination has always fascinated Muir (witness his interest in Calvinism and his early devotion to Nietzsche), but it has become increasingly clear that the negation of human will is no part of his philosophy. If he has shown us, more starkly than any other writer, mankind closed in the grip of Time and Change, it is surely to underline the immensity of the struggle for liberation which is behind all spiritual endeavour.

Forward our towering shadows fall
Upon the naked nicheless wall,
And all we see is that shadow-dance.
Yet looking at each countenance
I read this burden in them all:
'I lean my cheek from Eternity
For Time to slap, for Time to slap.
I gather my bones from the bottomless clay
To lay my head in the light's lap'.

('The Human Fold')

This image of the aspiring spirit runs through even the most forbidding of Muir's poems. If the struggle is bitter, it is because Time has robbed us of the ability to recognize the truth for which we seek.

We hurried here for some such thing and now
Wander the countless roads to seek our prize,
That far within the maze serenely lies,
While all around each trivial shape exclaims:
'Here is your jewel; this is your longed-for day',
And we forget, lost in the countless names.

('The Prize')

The soul is lost and yet it knows there must be a way. It is not surprising, then, that Muir should have been drawn to Kafka, of whom he writes:* 'The image of a road comes into our minds when we think of his stories; for in spite of all the confusions and contradictions in which he was involved he held that life was a way, not a chaos, that the right way exists and can be found by a supreme and exhausting effort, and that every human being in fact follows some way, right or wrong.'

* *Essays on Literature and Society* (Hogarth Press, 1949).

·III

Edwin Muir is a metaphysical writer whose work calls, therefore, for a rather special perception of its qualities. Outwardly unassertive, it has throughout a subdued passion of its own: intellectual, yet springing, we cannot doubt, from deep emotional experience. It is true that Muir is a poet of certain limitations; but these very limitations give his work a single-mindedness and formal clarity which are all too rare in poetry today. Reading his work over twenty-five years we discern little development in the usual sense of the term; rather an ever deeper exploration of a single theme, a gradual discovery of meaning. In this, perhaps, Muir is closer to European than English ways of thought. We have already seen how he has illuminated his own work in writing of Kafka. Here is a passage from his essay on Hölderlin in the same collection:

The imagination in Hölderlin's poetry is obviously related to dreams. It is not the kind of imagination which deals with ordinary experience — for instance, the life around it — but has its subject-matter given to it in a quite different way, somewhat as the subject-matter of a dream is given in sleep. It has, therefore, very little specifically to do with the contemporary world, like a good deal of romantic poetry and almost all mystical poetry. Or at most it regards the contemporary world as the Old Testament prophets regarded it; that is, in general terms, as falling short of its vision. This imagination is unlike any other kind; for while it works with greater freedom than ordinary imagination, one can hardly say on what it works: the ancestral racial dream material of which Jung speaks, or the delusive desires of mankind in all ages.

A brief examination of Muir's imagery will show how relevant this criticism is to his own work.*

Although Muir is not a religious poet in the narrow sense, his poetry is nevertheless informed with deep religious feeling. He recognizes the validity of Biblical imagery and has often used it in his work. In 'Variations on a Time Theme' for instance, mankind's eternal quest finds symbolic expression in the Israelites' long wanderings in the wilderness. In 'Moses' he gives us a vivid picture of the great leader surveying the promised land from Mount Pisgah and yet blind to what must come after — the great disasters, exiles, and migrations which laid waste the promised land and gave rise to the ghettos of Europe. But

* Although his poetry has some points in common with Jungian psychology, there is nothing to suggest that Muir is a follower of Jung. True poetry of this type derives from forces within the poet, not from psychological theory — a point worth emphasizing in this age of 'psychological' criticism.

perhaps the most fundamental image of this type in Muir's poetry is that of the Fall. For the Fall is clearly of archetypal importance in the fable, a macrocosm of each individual's fall from childhood grace of which we spoke earlier.

What shape had I before the Fall?
  What hills and rivers did I seek?
What were my thoughts then? And of what
  Forgotten histories did I speak

To my companions? Did our eyes
  From their foredestined watching-place
See Heaven and Earth one land, and range
  Therein through all of Time and Space? . . .

The ancient pain returns anew.
  Where was I ere I came to man?
What shape among the shapes that once
  Agelong through endless Eden ran?

                          ('The Fall')

These lines come from a poem which is in effect a condensed version of a remarkable vision which Muir had at the time of his analysis. It is interesting, therefore, to set it beside that part of the vision which clearly points back to the same stage of evolution.

All that I remember next is wandering through a rough woodland country interspersed with little brown rocks, where there were troops of low-browed, golden-haired, silent creatures somewhat like monkeys, and seeing in the distance a procession of white-robed female figures slowly passing as if to silent music. I wandered there, it seemed to me, for a long time. I remember coming to what I thought was the green, mossy trunk of a fallen tree; as I looked I saw it was a dragon, and that it was slowly weeping its eyes into a little heap before it . . .

Psychologically, this strange passage is most interesting; but here I am concerned only with its bearing on his imagery. Commenting on the passage Muir suggests that the white-robed figures wandering among the animals have a prophetic significance, as if 'long before man appeared on the earth he existed as a dream or prophecy in the animal soul'. This intimate relation between man and the animal world is something we are now only obscurely aware of. 'The age that felt this connection between men and the animals was so much longer than the brief historical period known to us that we can scarcely conceive it. In that age everything was legendary, and the creatures went about like characters in a parable of beasts . . . They were protagonists in the first sylvan war, half human and half pelted and feathered, from which rose the community and the arts. Man felt guilty towards them, for he took their lives day after day, in obedience to a custom so long established that no one could say when it began.' Such ideas of necessity and guilt no longer consciously trouble us; and yet these natural forces are still working in our unconscious minds, held down by the weight of civilization, and if they break through it will be in a modified or distorted form.

Muir has found a brilliant symbol for this concept in heraldry. For the heraldic image seems to bridge the past and the present and express in a vivid way the intellectualization of natural forces which has taken place in modern life.

Who curbed the lion long ago
And penned him in this towering field
And reared him wingless in the sky?
And quenched the dragon's burning eye,
Chaining him here to make a show,
The faithful guardian of the shield?

A fabulous wave far back in Time
Flung these calm trophies to this shore
That looks out on a different sea.
These relics of a buried war,
Empty as shape and cold as rhyme,
Gaze now on fabulous wars to be.

                              (*Variations*, X)

This sort of imagery, with its interplay of static and dynamic ideas, is peculiarly suited to Muir's thought.

The covenant of god and animal,
The frieze of fabulous creatures winged and crowned,
And in the midst the woman and the man –

Lost long ago in fields beyond the Fall –
Keep faith in sleep-walled night and there are found
On our long journey back where we began.

                              ('The Covenant')

All the creatures in Muir's work are clothed in this heraldic light; they move across his dreams, but it is significant that they are rarely creatures of nightmare. They are natural denizens of the poet's universe, and Muir has woven them into a background of legendary scene and drama which gives his poetry something of the strange, timeless quality of a tapestry.

The Fall, then, is the central point in the fable. Behind him the poet sees the dim, receding vistas of Adam's world; before him 'man's long shadow driving on', in its eternal quest for the lost godhead. If the poet is to transcend his own circumstances he must enter imaginatively into the great legendary and historical situations of the past. We have already seen how Muir has used Biblical imagery for this purpose; in other poems he goes to different sources. There is, for instance, a group of poems written round the idea of the fallen town or citadel, betrayed and brought to ruin by Time and the human agents of Time. The archetype of this situation is the fall of Troy, which appears again and again in Muir's work. In another brilliantly conceived poem, 'Then', he gives us a picture of the first anonymous upheavals of life:

There were no men and women then at all,
But the flesh lying alone,
And angry shadows fighting on a wall
That now and then sent out a groan
Buried in lime and stone,
And sweated now and then like tortured wood
Big drops that looked yet did not look like blood . . .

If there had been women there they might have wept
For the poor blood, unowned, unwanted,
Blank as forgotten script.
The wall was haunted
By mute maternal presences whose sighing
Fluttered the fighting shadows and shook the wall
As if that fury of death itself were dying.

Elsewhere he takes as his theme a personal crisis in the life of some great character; Tristram, for instance, or Oedipus, whose guilt seeks expiation in the innocence from which it came:

I have wrought and thought in darkness,
And stand here now, an innocent mark of shame,
That so men's guilt might be made manifest
In such a walking riddle – their guilt and mine,
For I've but acted out this fable. I have judged
Myself, obedient to the gods' high judgment,
And seen myself with their pure eyes, have learnt
That all must bear a portion of the wrong

That is driven deep into our fathomless hearts
Past sight or thought; that bearing it we may ease
The immortal burden of the gods who keep
Our natural steps and the earth and skies from harm.

('Oedipus')

In one of his finest poems, 'Hölderlin's Journey', Muir tries to answer imaginatively the question that still baffles literary historians: What happened to drive Hölderlin mad during his mysterious journey across France to Germany in the summer of 1805? While he was making this journey, his beloved Diotima was dying in Frankfurt, and in this poem Muir suggests that Hölderlin had a sudden premonition of her death and that this unhinged his mind.

Perhaps already she I sought,
  She, sought and seeker, had gone by,
And each of us in turn was trapped
  By simple treachery.

The evening brought a field, a wood.
  I left behind the hills of lies,
And watched beside a mouldering gate
  A deer with its rock-crystal eyes.

On either pillar of the gate
  A deer's head watched within the stone.
The living deer with quiet look
  Seemed to be gazing on

Its pictured death – and suddenly
  I knew, Diotima was dead,
As if a single thought had sprung
  From the cold and the living head.

In this image, so complex and yet so wonderfully lucid, Muir seems to me to symbolize the theme which runs through all his work – the ambivalence of human life. Man seeking in man sought, man immortal in man mortal, the story and the fable – out of this duality springs suddenly the 'single thought' from which poetry is made.

[PNW 38, 1949]

JOHN LEHMANN

THE LIFE OF THE PRODIGAL SON

At one time in my life I wanted to write poetry above all things, and I went to Vienna to devote myself to it. I don't quite know why I chose Vienna – I am sure the reasons I gave myself and others at the time only partly expressed the truth – but it seems to me now that I was drawn on by obscure impressions of childhood, things told me or overheard by me or seen in picture books, and sustained by the thought that I should be absolutely alone. And one of the few books I took with me, perhaps the one I was most careful to pack, was an English translation of Rilke's *Notebook of Malte Laurids Brigge*.

It was not my first acquaintance with this extraordinary book, which I now think one of the most original and beautiful books of the twentieth century; I had already, at various times, dipped into it, and I had already fallen under the spell of Rilke's poetry that has worked so powerfully on my generation; but I was now going to immerse myself in it under the conditions in which it demands to be read: in solitude, in a strange city, and with poetry in my head. It stayed with me, my favourite reading, all that late summer and autumn. Much of it I found hermetic, even incomprehensible, and impossible to relate to any central pattern; for it demands not only some knowledge of Rilke's own life to explain its riddles, but also a marriage of experience and ideas of which I was still too young to be aware. Again and again, however, I came upon passages that enthralled and haunted me, and one passage in particular that I read and re-read and tried to absorb into myself with all my assimilative powers of mind, the passage in which Malte describes how to be a poet:

Verses amount to so little when one begins to write them young. One ought to wait and gather sense and sweetness a whole life long, and a long life if possible, and then, quite at the end, one might perhaps be able to write ten good lines. For verses are not, as people imagine, simply feelings (we have these soon enough); they are experiences. In order to write a single verse, one must see many cities, and men and things; one must get to know animals and the flight of birds, and the gestures that the little flowers make when they open out in the morning. One must be able to return in thought to roads in unknown regions, to unexpected encounters, and to partings that had been long foreseen; to days of childhood that are still indistinct, and to parents whom one had to hurt when they sought to give one some pleasure which one did not understand (it would have been a pleasure to someone else); to childhood's illnesses that so strangely begin with such a number of profound and grave transformations, to days spent in rooms withdrawn and quiet, and to mornings by the sea, to the sea itself, to oceans, to nights of travel that rushed along loftily and flew with all the stars – and still it is not enough to be able to think of all this. There must be memories of many nights of love, each one unlike the others, of the screams of women in labour, and of women in childbed, light and blanched and sleeping, shutting themselves in. But one must also have been beside the dying, must have sat beside the dead in a room with open windows and with fitful noises. And still it is not enough yet to have memories. One must be able to forget them when they are many, and one must have the immense patience to wait until they come again. For it is the memories themselves that matter. Only when they have turned to blood within us, to glance and gesture, nameless and no longer to be distinguished from ourselves – only then can it happen that in a most rare hour the first word of a poem arises in their midst and goes forth from them.

This seemed to me then one of the most wonderful, releasing statements about poetry that I had ever read. It is, I can now see, an ideal which might lead to the writing of a great deal of very bad poetry, unless corrected by what one might call the *grammarian's* attitude which had been in fashion in the circles I moved in at Cambridge and directly after: the view that the first essential for the poet is to be able to think clearly and to use words precisely, and to express a certain intellectual energy in his views by his wit, in the sense of the term defined by T. S. Eliot. If the ultra-romantic view was responsible for a great deal of showy nonsense, this grammarian's view, admirable in its due place and proportion, was in danger, if slavishly followed, of producing mere arid exercises, the purely masculine without that feminine and intuitive element which is essential to poetry; all the more arid and marginal if the poet had also come under the influence of the equally fashionable 'clinical' view, which insisted that poetry was the resolution in words of obscure psychological tensions in the mind of its author. Rilke's words, so eloquent, so simple and so evocative, avoiding so carefully the exalted peaks of the claims made by the great romantics such as Shelley, seemed to me to present exactly what was missing in these views: a vision of how poetry was created or should be created in our post-romantic age, not by taking great themes and giving them the noblest treatment one was capable of, but by allowing the whole of experience, of years of thought and feeling and observation to be distilled in the depths of one's imagination, un-forced and unhurried, to form this precious fluid. And, above all, it presented a design for the dedicated life a poet should lead, not merely for his working hours but for the whole preparation of himself before and between those (perhaps very brief) periods.

This ideal, of a life devoted to poetry, planned to provide the opportunity for every kind of experience that might nurture the poetic being and avoid every experience and entanglement that might be destructive to it, was grand enough when Rilke wrote the *Notebook* before the first world war. It is grander, in fact it is heroic now, when the wars and revolutions of our age have destroyed the old Europe – in which leisure was possible even if only for the more fortunate classes and those to whom they acted as patrons – and when the cancerous development of state control and interference has created an environment where everything conspires to ruin the inner life.

The fulfilment of the inner life was Rilke's own supreme object, and the passion with which he endowed Malte. Almost the last words in the *Notebook* are:

Long ago he had detached himself from the accidents of fate to which men cling, but now even whatever of pleasure and pain were necessary lost their spicy after-taste and became pure and nourishing to him. From the roots of his being there sprang the sturdy, evergreen plant of a fertile joy. He was wholly engrossed in learning to handle what constituted his inner life; he wanted to omit nothing, for he doubted not that his love dwelt and grew in all this. Indeed, his inward serenity went so far that he resolved to overtake the most important of those things which he had hitherto been unable to accomplish, the things he had simply allowed to slip past while he waited.

The *Notebook* itself can be described as the record of how Rilke learnt, in the first period of his life as a poet, to 'handle his inner life': it is a distillation of experience, through the invented character of the young Danish poet, that follows remarkably faithfully the prescription for a poet's life Rilke gives within it. All the wanderings, both over Europe and inside his own world of thought, all the emotions and spiritual struggles, all the provocative outward events and inward imaginative discoveries of six years of Rilke's life are mirrored in Malte's notebook; and the history of its development is a fascinating study of his creative processes at work.

We know from Maurice Betz, with whom Rilke collaborated in the French translation of the *Notebook* during his stay in Paris in 1925, that the original germ was Rilke's discovery of a book called *The Diary of a Priest*, by Sigbjörn Obstfelder, a young Norwegian writer who had come to live in Paris and died there at the early age of thirty-two. Rilke read this story of the struggles of a tormented soul to find God, a pursuit that ends in madness, at a time when his enthusiasm for anything Scandinavian was at its height; and the fact that Obstfelder had, like Rilke, been a stranger alone in Paris as a young man, made a special bond of sympathy. Rilke seems to have been haunted by the Norwegian from the beginning: and in the end his imaginative occupation of his life became so intense that he speaks of Malte as if he were a living person, always beside him; who was, as it were, dictating the book. 'I must not advance beyond him and his suffering too far,' he says in a letter to his wife in 1908, 'otherwise I will no longer understand him.' It is always in this strain that he speaks of the book; and his description of the sudden sprouting of the seed that Obstfelder's work had planted in his mind is like the account of a spiritual possession. Maurice Betz reports Rilke as telling him the story as follows:

At that time I was in Rome. I had been living for several months in a little studio which had been lent me in the park of the Villa Strohl-Fern. The Italian spring disappointed me by its undue haste, and my reading of Jacobsen awakened my longing for that Northern country where I knew no one except the good Ellen Key, to whom I had dedicated *The Stories of God*. I wrote a series of dialogues between a young man and a young girl who confide their little secrets to each other. The young man told the girl a great deal about a Danish poet, a certain Malte, whom he had known and who died young in Paris. The girl wanted to know more about Malte, and the young man was indiscreet enough to tell her that his friend had left a diary, while he admitted that he himself had never looked into it yet. The girl begged him to let her see it. I succeeded in keeping her waiting for several days by various subterfuges, but her curiosity increased and in the end she began to build up her own picture of Malte. I realized that it was not permissible for me to offer resistance any longer, and so I interrupted the dialogue and began to write Malte's own diary without troubling any more with the subsidiary personages who had led me to him almost against my will.

From that moment in 1904, the *Notebook* was always in Rilke's mind; and from 1906 to 1910, with occasional intervals of a few weeks or months when Malte's problems became too difficult for him to solve and he had to turn away from the 'heavy, heavy book', it was his major preoccupation as a writer. During that time he was restless and dissatisfied, with frequent breakdowns in health, always moving from one place to another, but experiencing new scenes and making new friends – among them, one of the most important in his whole life, Rodin – the stimulus of which can be traced again and again in the *Notebook*. There was, first of all, the excitement of getting to know

Denmark, the country he was to make Malte's own. It is probably true, as Countess Wydenbruck suggests in her book,* that the friends he made during these years among the North German Lutheran nobility, were as important, or even more important than his brief experiences of Denmark itself, in providing him with material for building up the background of Malte's family. Nevertheless, the Danish visit was responsible for at least one of the most striking and characteristic passages in the *Notebook*, where the young Malte and his mother visit the family of the Schulins, the great central wing of whose manor-house has recently been burnt down. Rilke describes the arrival by sleigh, in darkness and snowstorm:

One might have imagined one saw the church tower on the left, but suddenly the outline of the park wall appeared, high up, almost on top of us, and we found ourselves in the long avenue. The tinkling of the bells no longer ceased abruptly; it seemed to hang in clusters right and left on the trees. Then we swung in and drove around something, passed something else on the right, and came to a halt in the centre.

Georg had quite forgotten that the house was no longer there, and for all of us at that moment it was there. We ascended the front steps that led up to the old terrace, and only wondered at finding all in darkness. Suddenly a door opened below and behind us on the left, and someone cried, 'This way!' at the same time lifting and swinging a dim lantern. My Father laughed: 'We are wandering about here like ghosts,' and he helped us down the steps again.

'But still there was a house there just now,' said Mother . . .

The actual experience from which this episode was created is related in a letter to Lou Andreas Salomé in December, 1904. He describes how he went to visit his Danish friend Ellen Key in a lonely country house that belonged to her brother:

We found ourselves in the courtyard, enclosed by the small lateral wings of the château. But there, where four flights of steps ascended with a great effort from the deep snow of the courtyard to the terrace, on which a balustrade with ornamental vases appeared to herald the château itself, there was nothing except a few snow-covered shrubs and a grey, glimmering sky, against which I could distinguish snowflakes falling through the twilight. I had to remind myself that the building no longer existed, that I had been told how it had burnt down to the ground years ago, but still I could not help feeling that there must be something there, that the air behind the balustrade was not the same as the air around, but was still divided into passages and rooms and a great central hall, a high, empty, forsaken, twilit hall . . .

* *Rilke: Man and Poet*, a book to which I am indebted for more than I can say in the preparation of this study.

Thus the actual description in the *Notebook* is taken almost exactly from Rilke's own experience at Oby, but he transforms and enlarges it by making it pass through the wondering mind of a small boy who, quickly taking up the hint dropped by his Mother, is overcome by the idea of this phantom house, tries to slip away to see it again, and *believes* in it in spite of the laughter of the others: '"Of course they only go when it is not there," I thought contemptuously: "If Mother and I lived here, it would always be there." Mother looked distraught, while the others were all talking at once. She was certainly thinking of the house.'

Another striking example of Rilke's way of refashioning the experiences of these years to make them part of the *Notebook* is the passage towards the end, where Malte is once more reminded of Abelone, vividly and with a new insight, by a girl he meets at a salon one afternoon in Venice. The famous description of Venice, not 'the soft, narcotic Venice' that is the illusion of the 'somnolent foreigners', but the real Venice of winter that reveals itself when they have gone, 'awake, brittle to breaking-point, and not in the least dream-like: this Venice willed into being in the midst of nothing and set on sunken forests, created by force, and in the end so thoroughly manifest', 'this inventive state that bartered the salt and glass of its poverty for the treasures of the nations', was directly inspired by the winter he spent in the city in 1907. The same images occur in a letter he wrote to his wife at the time, and in the poem *Spätherbst in Venedig* which he published in *New Poems*:

Aber vom Grund aus alten Waldskeletten
steigt Willen auf: als sollte über Nacht
der General des Meeres die Galeeren
verdoppeln in dem wachen Arsenal . . .

Even more fundamental to the purpose of the book was the vision of Paris he conjured up, in the opening passages, out of his early experiences when he went there for the first time in 1902, and his later impressions in 1907, when he shut himself up in his room in the Rue Cassette and worked at the *New Poems*, the book on Rodin and the *Notebook* itself throughout the summer and autumn. Again, nothing could be less sentimental than the vision this poet, who has so often been accused of sentimentality, created of Paris: for him it seemed always to be a city of macabre happenings, of suffering and poverty (except when he thought of it as the home of Rodin):

People come here, then, to live? I should rather have thought that they came here to die. I have been out, and I saw hospitals. I saw a poor fellow stagger and fall. People gathered round him: so I was spared the rest. I saw a pregnant woman. She dragged herself heavily along a high, warm wall, now and again groping for it as if to assure herself it was still there . . .

These are the opening words of the *Notebook*, and they set the tone for all that comes after. His very first letter to his wife from Paris, in 1902, records the same impression, and shows that Malte's, that Obstfelder's nightmares had been his own: 'I am appalled at the great number of hospitals here. Legions of sick people, armies of dying men, populations of corpses – I have never felt this as strongly in any other city.' Even the man with St Vitus's Dance appears first of all as a person actually observed and described in one of his letters a year later. And the harrowing episode of the medical student in the room next door, whose eyelid refused to stay open and who in his misery and nervous exhaustion stamped up and down while a noise repeated itself 'the noise made by any round, tin object, such as the lid of a canister when it slips from one's grasp' – this, too, came directly out of his own experience, while he was working at the *Notebook* in the Rue Cassette.

All these scenes, these moments of intense imaginative apprehension, Rilke was able to work into the fabric of the *Notebook*, while preserving the thematic wholeness of the book, with an art that reveals itself as more consummate with every reading. The method he had chosen, the apparently random record of an intimate journal, allowed him considerable latitude; and as he later admitted to Maurice Betz, his idea of giving it the air of incompleteness that the journal of the dead Obstfelder might well have had, so took possession of him that he did not even collect all the fragments he had written at one time or another for use in it. But the book is one: as a poem of loneliness and suffering, of death in all its mysterious and terrible aspects, the spiritual voyage through a haunted darkness of a young man who strives to recapture the beauty and meaning of his childhood; and to fulfil what he had left there incomplete and unsatisfied, by reliving his memories and using all his maturer powers to understand where and why he had failed to answer all the demands of heart and imagination made on him. The *Notebook* was to Rilke a 'heavy, heavy book', causing him such disturbance and exhaustion of spirit, because it was a delving into his own failures in the inner life; and yet, unlike Malte, he finally surmounted these failures – to a miraculous degree by the very fact of writing out Malte's suffering. 'The creative artist is not permitted to select or to turn away from any form of existence,' he wrote in an illuminating letter on Baudelaire's poem *La Charogne* in October 1907, 'surely among his earlier works there must be some where he overcame himself with a mighty effort, right to the utmost limits of love. Beyond this surrender lies saintliness, beginning with small things, the simple existence of a love that has passed the test, and, without boasting, approaches everything.' He was about to make that surrender himself, and the anticipation of it lies in what follows: 'Suddenly (for the first time) I understood Malte Laurids's fate. Is it not that the ordeal was too great for him, that he could not pass the actual test, though he was theoretically convinced of its necessity, so much so that he sought it out instinctively until it haunted him? The book of Malte Laurids, once it is written, will be nothing but the story of this insight, exemplified in one for whom it was too mighty . . .'

It was this insight which drew Malte to the story of the Prodigal Son, which forms part of the great coda to the *Notebook*, and out of which Rilke made one of the most beautiful of his shorter poems. Rilke and Malte then become one in what was perhaps the crucial spiritual problem of the poet's earlier years. 'It will be difficult to persuade me,' writes Malte, 'that the story of the Prodigal Son is not the legend of one who did not want to be loved. When he was a child everybody in the house loved him. He grew up knowing nothing else, and as a child he became accustomed to their tenderness. But as a growing boy he sought to lay aside these habits . . . what he then desired was that inner indifference of spirit, which, sometimes, of an early morning in the fields, seized him so unalloyed that he began to run, that he might have neither time nor breath to be more than a transient moment in which the morning became conscious of itself.'

The impulse which, obscurely but so intensely, racks the Prodigal Son, is surely the deep instinct of the artist in one of its many disguises – the artist who must, as he becomes conscious of being an artist, learn to apprehend everything for himself and create his own universe before he can go back to the allegiances and habits of his childhood, so as to be strong enough to treat with them on equal terms. The desire not to be 'more than a transient moment in which the morning becomes conscious of itself' is not unlike Keats's idea that a poet must be capable of being everything and nothing and has no identity, and his confession that 'if a sparrow comes before my window I take part in its existence and pick about the gravel'. The similarity becomes even more striking when Malte goes on to describe, in a passage evidently inspired by Rilke's own holiday in Provence in the spring of 1909, the shepherd's life of the Prodigal Son: 'That was the time which began with his feeling himself a part of the universe and anonymous, like a lingering convalescent. He did not love unless it were that he loved to live. The lowly affection of his sheep did not weigh upon him; like light falling through clouds it dispersed itself about him and gleamed softly on the meadows. In the innocent track of their hunger he strode silently across the pastures of the world. Strangers saw him on the Acropolis; and perhaps he was for a long time one of the shepherds in Les Baux, and saw the petrified age outlast that lofty race which, despite all its acquisition of sevens and threes, could not master the sixteen rays of its star . . .'

With Rilke, however, the mood of the Prodigal Son was not simply the impulse of the artist to become anonymous; it was at the same time the struggle against loving and being loved, a struggle that had in the end to be abandoned because the complete person, the complete artist (like Baudelaire) learns to love and be loved without shrinking, and the Prodigal Son (not Malte, but Rilke himself) comes home at last. These two themes are intertwined in the *Notebook*; but the book is even more than the exploration of the artist's need to lose himself and the Prodigal Son's attempt to escape love, because Rilke's unique poetic faculty makes out of all the gropings within the spirit and journeyings in the outer world, a demonstration of his extraordinary sensibility so vivid and convincing that one feels one has acquired a new kind of perception. One actually *sees* with him a woman, too suddenly disturbed in her private thoughts, leaving her face in her hands and exposing something flayed and terrible to the onlooker; and one actually comes to think of death as a being that possesses (has always, in a slow process of growth, possessed) the dying creature and finally enacts its own individual drama: 'one *had* it, and that gave one a singular dignity, a quiet pride'. And more than that, with its movement from Malte's own childhood reminiscences, the way of life in the old country houses, to his wanderings in the great cities, and from them to recreations of legends and famous moments of history, it achieves an evocation of the ancient Europe, a four-dimensional evocation of a haunting resonance and depth. How deliberately this was in Rilke's design, one cannot be sure, but once one has observed how as an artist he loves to present symbols and drop hints within his work of what the work as a whole is fulfilling, one remembers in this connection the picture at the end of the *Notebook* of the sage, the older man who has travelled much in his youth and has long been considered eccentric, as the light burns late in his study:

He does not always remain bent over his pages; he often leans back and closes his eyes on a line he has read again and again, and its meaning passes into his blood. Never before has he been so certain of the ancient past. He could almost smile at the generations that have mourned it as a lost drama, in which they would have liked to play a part. Now he instantly understands the dynamic significance of that early world-unity, which was something like a new and simultaneous gathering up of all human labour . . .

In writing the *Notebook* Rilke felt, in a strange way, that he was exploring deeper even than in the poetry he had written hitherto. In his letters we find him talking of going back to the 'discipline of writing verses' and seeking renewal in nature, so that the inner world from the depths of which the *Notebook* was emerging should be 'strengthened and tautened by the influences of the external world' – as if his poetry, compared with his prose, was part of that external world; and in a letter to Rodin, in December 1908, he says: 'In writing poetry one is always helped, and even carried along, by the rhythm of external things – the waters, the winds, the night. But to acquire the rhythms of prose one must go deep down into oneself and find the anonymous and manifold rhythms of the blood.'

It was indeed out of these depths that the *Notebook of Malte Laurids Brigge* was created, and because Rilke was courageous and persistent enough, in spite of illness and misery and the resistance of the wounded memory, to explore them fully, it stands out, ever more clearly as the years go by, as a masterpiece. No book of our time is more passionately dedicated to the inner life, more completely infused with the belief in the primacy of the imagination, of the poetic way of apprehending life; and as the threat to all that means increases like the deafening roar of a flight of super-bombers in the sky, so we instinctively reach out to hold such precious things closer to us.

[PNW 39, 1950]

JOHN WAIN

AMBIGUOUS GIFTS

Notes on a Twentieth-Century Poet

I was sorry to see that the *Sewanee Review*, having occasion in a recent issue to mention William Empson in its 'Notes on Contributors', set him down baldly as 'British critic'. One knew that criticism was a more profitable activity than poetry, but this seems to indicate that it is also more durable. In an age when nine out of ten people who bother about literature do so because they are drawing a salary for it, it may well be that criticism will be read and remembered while poetry is forgotten, for criticism breeds fresh criticism more easily than poetry breeds fresh poetry; but in Empson's case it would be a pity if he were known simply as the 'ambiguity' man, and not as a poet. Of course it is the penalty of silence – he has published nothing in verse since *The Gathering Storm* in 1940 – and in these scribbling days, out of print is out of mind. The position is made all the more difficult by the fact that Empson, as poet no less than as critic, has very firm local associations, and that these associations have themselves ceased to count for much. He was always placed, rightly or wrongly, as a product of the Cambridge English school: certainly the influence of Richards is very evident in *Seven Types*, and the professor repaid his pupil's compliment by quoting his poetry in lectures. What is more, Empson was one of the early contributors to *Scrutiny*, besides being one of the two young poets singled out by Dr Leavis to be publicly congratulated in *New Bearings* (the other was Ronald Bottrall, who, it seems, has since been sent back to the bottom of the class – see *Scrutiny* for spring 1947). I do not wish to imply that Empson's association with these teacher-critics is any reason why he should be neglected, but when a writer begins his career by closely identifying himself with one par-ticular movement, he is likely to be left high and dry when that movement has spent itself. This is true to some extent of all the poets who were breaking new ground in the Thirties; the conditions (social, political and literary) which did so much to form their characteristics, have vanished, leaving them without any source of nourishment, and a little beyond the age at which it is possible to make a major adjustment. It is true that Messrs Spender, Auden, Day Lewis, and

MacNeice are still more or less firmly in possession of the public ear, but that is really due to the mediocrity of the younger poetic generation; they are likely to stay in fashion, however little they have to say, simply because their juniors have even less. Still, it is depressing to see poets carrying on from sheer force of habit, and one of the reassuring things about Empson is that, having produced two very remarkable volumes of verse before the rot set in, he has since had the wisdom to hold his peace, even though this means being described in American reviews as 'British critic'.

I shall have some more positive claims to make for Empson's poetry, but first we must see it in its historical setting.

I

The trouble with the Thirties, as a literary epoch, is that they happened a long time ago. As I write this I have to keep remembering that Empson is nearly twenty years my senior, and that *Seven Types of Ambiguity* came out when I was just learning to read nursery rhymes. It is thus an act of the historical imagination to discuss such matters as the storm that blew up over the use, in verse, of the names of machinery and other 'anti-poetic' material (as if Arthur Hugh Clough, with his fondness for railway imagery, had not already started it anyway). All one can say at this distance of time is the obvious thing, that it is useful, like any other material, when it is properly assimilated, and not lugged along in the form of compulsory equipment. Many ludicrous failures could be listed, but they are usually cases where such imagery was slapped on with a trowel. Take Mr Day Lewis's lines on the death of a friend:

Was so much else we could have better spared —
Churches, museums, multiple stores: but the bomb
Fell on the power-house: total that eclipse.
He was our dynamo, &c &c.

Here the symbolism is (quite literally) useless; the poet would have lost nothing by saying simply that the most gay and vital person of his acquaintance was dead. Empson never jars like this. He places concrete for abstract in a way that, even in its least exciting passages, is recognizable as English poetry.

Law makes long spokes of the short stakes of men.
Your well fenced out real estate of mind
No high flat of the nomad citizen
Looks over, or train leaves behind.

What is more, when he introduces scientific or mechanical imagery, he does so because it has a genuine function in the poem; whereas Auden, for instance, is clever at placing such imagery at the fringe of the poem, where it can do small harm and little good. When he writes

O all the instruments agree
The day of his death was a dark, cold day

the *frisson* is really coming from the second line, which might be as old as *Beowulf*; the bit about the instruments is just there to look chic and contemporary.

But this question is really part of a bigger one, into which we must go more fully. How far ought scientific ideas to be incorporated into poetry? Poets, from Wordsworth on, have been better at talking about the relevance of science than actually doing anything about it, and this seems to be one of the ways in which Empson has made a real advance. It is worth noticing that in both prose and verse his mind flies to the scientific for analogy and metaphor. In his prose it is merely irritating. *Seven Types* is not really impregnated with the scientific spirit, despite its title; it is a collection of *aperçus* based on a method of analysis inaugurated by Riding and Graves in *Survey of Modernist Poetry*. But the reek of the laboratory was so strong in the author's nostrils as he wrote that we have to endure a barrage of not very illuminating asides like 'Here as in recent atomic physics there is a shift in progress' or 'having fixed the reaction, properly stained, on a slide, they must be able to turn the microscope on it with a certain indifference and without smudging it with their fingers'. In *Some Versions of Pastoral* we are even told that 'Milton's evasive use of language . . . has the squalid gelatinous effect of ectoplasm in a flashlight photograph'. At all events this is probably not a mere affectation, since Empson started as a mathematician and probably knows a certain amount of science as well; but in the attempt to bring scientific ideas into poetry, it is not enough to know what you are talking about. James Thomson had read up quite a lot of eighteenth-century physics, but when he came to introduce it into *The Seasons* the result is rather forced.

What art thou, frost? – and whence are thy keen stores
Derived, thou secret all-invading power,
Whom even the illusive fluid cannot fly?
Is not thy potent energy, unseen,
Myriads of little salts, or hooked, or shaped
Like double wedges, and diffused immense
Through water, earth, and ether?

Who cares? The fact is that it is useless merely to *describe* in verse the things of which science tells us, while to introduce them in the form of simile and metaphor when the poem is really about something quite non-scientific is not much better. The only way to treat such material is to form it into a series of conceits on which the general meaning of the poem can be made to turn. This was Donne's way, and it is Empson's. In *The World's End* he uses the perfectly straightforward idea that, since space is 'curved', there is no such thing as the end of the world; you are always beginning your journey afresh, and so the world is a more oppressive prison than you ever suspected.

Apples of knowledge and forgetful mere
From Tantalus too differential bend.
The shadow clings. The world's end is here.

In the same way *Arachne* is not really about either soap-tension, or molecular structure, or the habits of water-spiders. These things are pivots on which a tragically sardonic love-poem is made to turn; the whole thing is a triumphant *tour de force* which culminates with a simultaneous application of all the available symbols to a pair of human lovers:

We two suffice. But oh beware, whose vain
Hydroptic soap my meagre water saves.
Male spiders must not be too early slain.

Empson wrote this poem at, or before, the age of twenty-three (he was born in 1906 and this appeared in *Cambridge Poetry 1929*); and even those who are not attracted to the poem – it can be found in *The Oxford Book of Modern Verse* – will agree that to express such a complexity of ideas in a metre as tight as *terza rima*, and in language entirely suited to its purpose, is a good enough start for a poetic career.

II

Another distant echo from the past is the question of 'obscurity'. Nowadays one of two things will generally happen; either a poem will offer little or no difficulty, because its readers have grown up reading that kind of poetry and do not have to make the awkward crossing from one kind of reading to another; or it may be really obscure, in the bad sense, because the poet does not want to be understood, in which case no one will find it worth the effort to protest. As regards prose, where obscurity really is intolerable, Cyril Connolly's remark seems all that is required: 'A writer who thinks himself cleverer than his readers will write simply; one who is afraid they are cleverer than he, will make use of mystification; good style is arrived at when the language chosen represents what the author requires of it without shyness.' As regards verse, the issue is not so simple. For one thing, the author is not always so certain what it is that he is requiring of his language: he is giving the wagon a push to see how far it will roll by itself. This sounds dangerously close to a defence of 'romanticism' in the bad sense, or even a rationalization of automatic writing, but in reality it is true even of the poet with a firm intellectual grasp – indeed it is precisely this that makes such a grasp necessary. It is harder to produce an accurate statement than a careless rapture, harder still to combine the two, yet poetry *is* this combination. Tired of it though we all are, the question of 'obscurity' forces itself on our attention in discussing a poet whose blurb describes him as 'the most brilliantly obscure of modern poets': unfortunately Empson's own statement on the subject is itself of uncertain significance. In his Note on the Notes to *The Gathering Storm* he says, 'partly they are meant to be like answers to a crossword puzzle; a sort of puzzle interest is part of the pleasure you are meant to get from the verse, and that I get myself when I go back to it'. Obviously this is not wholly serious, any more than the Preface to Graves's *Poems 1938–45*, about the islanders who took in each other's washing, is wholly serious; but neither is a good enough joke to be that and nothing more. One has to take Empson's remark about puzzles at least partly in good faith, because it really represents a feature of his mind; a 'puzzle interest' is evidently part of the pleasure he gets from all poetry. *Some Versions* is constantly saying this; 'Milton's language about stars contains two puzzles about them', the Darwinian passages in *Alice in Wonderland* are 'tantalizing', and so forth. Indeed, his two books of criticism are valuable chiefly as a very telling attack on the idea that we understand what we read.

In any case, it is usually best to obey any instructions from a poet as to how his work should be approached. If Empson's work is advertised as 'obscure', and he himself speaks of 'puzzle-interest', it would obviously be dishonest in a critic not to make some attempt to see what this means in practice. As a specimen of his more cryptic vein, I here quote in full *The Teasers* (*Gathering Storm*, p. 38).

Not but they die, the teasers and the dreams,
  Not but they die,

and tell the careful flood
To give them what they clamour for and why.

You could not fancy where they rip to blood,
You could not fancy
                    nor that mud
I have heard speak that will not cake or dry.

Our claims to act appear so small to these,
Our claims to act
                    colder lunacies
That cheat the love, the moment, the small fact.

Make no escape because they flash and die,
Make no escape
                    build up your love,
Leave what you die for and be safe to die.

To begin with the form: it is a blend of originality and imperfection. The first stanza suggests a real lyrical discovery – a metre one does not remember to have seen elsewhere, and a beautiful one. The rhyme scheme, *dreams – die – flood – why*, is a normal quatrain which justifies the broken second line. The second stanza goes one better with *blood – fancy – mud – dry*, which is stricter, and moreover carries on the rhyme from *flood* in a way that suggests *terza rima*. Stanza 3 carries on the improved form well, though no further effort is made to carry on a rhyme from the preceding stanza; but the whole thing crumbles in the fourth with a lame *die – escape – love – die*. The form, in fact, is typically Empsonian: the brilliant discovery of a minor verse-form which exactly suits its content, and then the uncertainty which keeps him swinging between unresolved possibilities, and finally the collapse into random shapelessness. As with rhyme, so with metre. The second line, a decasyllabic in stanza 1, octosyllabic in stanza 2, shapeless nothing in stanza 3, and octosyllabic again in stanza 4. Does this matter? Emphatically yes, in a lyric poem twelve lines long. For one thing, it renders the whole poem suspect. Is it worth trying to decipher the meaning of a poet who is so little interested in the problem of expressing himself that he cannot be bothered to sustain a simple metrical form for four stanzas together?

Now for this 'meaning'. When people refuse to talk about the 'meaning' of a poem, in the sense of its paraphrasable content, I take it that what they are objecting to is the idea that a poem has one meaning (the 'right' one) and no other. Nowadays we have reached such a pitch of sophistication that no one would confess to so naïve a view: each reader makes his own poem, we assure each other, on the basis of the words provided for him by the poet. This would be all very well if it did not lead to so widespread a neglect of a poem's paraphrasable content; the feeling seems to be that if this content is different to each reader, there is no point in bothering about it: whereas of course the mere fact that a poem varies from reader to reader makes it all the more imperative for each reader to work out for himself the exact 'meaning' of every poem he comes across. One risks a lot by coming into the open on matters like these, but here is my paraphrase of the poem in question.

The teasers and dreams are our inward afflictions and aspirations – in Bacon's noble phrase, the 'desires of the mind'. These desires, though they die and are merged with the undiscriminating stream of existence ('the careful flood' – possibly with an underlying reference to Styx) are still so much more important than the 'colder lunacies' – the disciplined and regulated actions – that it is useless to try to evade them (rendering 1. 13 as 'do not, merely because they flash and die, seek to escape them'). Grouped about this hub of meanings is a riot of subsidiary meanings; to enumerate them would be a lengthy business and best done afresh by each reader. The second stanza, for example, seems to rely wholly on suggestion, and it is possible to deduce (or devise) at least a dozen 'logical' meanings for it, but its function seems to be more like that of a simile or metaphor: intensification and, in a roundabout way, illustration. The poem appears to collapse into negation in the last stanza; if you abandon what you would normally be defending, you will be safe – to die, i.e. you will gain nothing. I shall be told, of course, that I have entirely missed the point, but it were better to be wrong than to follow the common critical practice of refusing to make an attempt. Besides which, the poem is not mentioned in the Notes which occupy sixteen pages of the volume, and must therefore be assumed to lie at the mercy of the reader.

III

Partly for the reasons I have given, Empson has often been called 'metaphysical'; and on this side, too, his work needs some historical comment.

During the last twenty-five years the seventeenth century has been much in the air, and apologists for 'modern' poetry have found the appeal to Donne and the late Shakespeare a very useful weapon (we are not forced, like the French, to choose finally between the present and the past in our poetic theory). Yet, while it is legitimate to defend intellectualized and elliptical poetry by calling on the 'metaphysicals', the theory is, after all propaganda, and must be modified when the shouting has died down. This, evidently, is not yet: in 1948 English reviewers could still hail Cleanth Brooks's ten-year-old *Modern Poetry and the Tradition*, which argues along these lines, as if it were the last word on its subject. How much twentieth-century poetry, examined in cold blood, really resembles Donne or Marvell? I should say that only John Crowe Ransom, Robert Graves since 1926, and possibly the early dandified Eliot, ever consistently recalled the metaphysical way of setting about poetry. Whether the theory about 'dissociation of sensibility' is true or not, that particular blend of thinking and feeling has been very rare since 1700, and the claim that it has been revived in our own time does not bear much examination: Auden, for instance, has not been blending them at all, but slipping from one to the other – hence the utter lack of repose and certainty even in his best work. For the rest, there are a few traces of Donne, but generally through one of the conventional intermediaries – Hopkins, Browning, Eliot himself – and there the matter rests. So that, historically speaking, the renascence of (in any precise sense of the word) 'metaphysical' poetry boils down to a few poems by a few poets.

Empson, however, is one of these poets. It is not easy to define metaphysical poetry, but obviously there are two features which distinguish it at once – a kind of general modernity which leads poets to bring in current ideas and current language, and a strong, at times almost perverse, desire to follow the argument wherever it leads the poem. Donne's poetry has no more 'conceits' in it than anyone else's, but the conceits are taken seriously and allowed to lead the poem from one point to another. It is this trait which links Empson most firmly to the seventeenth century. Witness the pursuit of the idea in these lines:

All those large dreams by which men long live well
Are magic-lanterned on the smoke of hell;
   This then is real, I have implied,
   A painted, small, transparent slide.

These the inventive can hand-paint at leisure,
Or most emporia would stock our measure;
   And feasting in their dappled shade
   We should forget how they were made.

And so the argument goes on developing until, like some great glittering, tortured poem of Donne or Crashaw, it seals our assent with the measured rhetoric of the last stanza.

Imagine, then, by miracle, with me
(Ambiguous gifts, as what gods give must be),
    What could not possibly be there,
    And learn a style from a despair.

I speak of 'measured rhetoric'; and indeed it would be impossible to assess Empson's achievement without some reference to the slow, heavy fullness of his lines; they seem to me a miraculous blend of the colloquial immediacy of Donne and the immense weight of Hopkins; and in the middle of a quiet, meditative poem he will suddenly introduce lines of an enormous Marlovian grandeur –

Wait, to be fathered as was Bacchus once,
Through men's long lives, that image of time's end.

Of course no landscape is made up entirely of peaks; Empson has published, even in his small output, a number of pieces that are too slight to be worth sustained attention – *Just a Smack at Auden* and *Your Teeth are Ivory Towers* would be good if made up extempore at a party – while

This passive style might pass perhaps
    Squatting in England with the beer,
But if that's all you think of, what
    In God's name are you doing here?

is a little too prattling. At the other end of the scale is the over-elaboration of a poem like *Bacchus*, which requires six pages of notes ('A mythological chemical operation to distil drink is going on in the first four verses') and seems hardly worth the fuss. But he has, after all, written at least a dozen poems which pass every known test of greatness: and who has done more?

Whether Empson will ever write any more poetry is not my business. If he does, it will be interesting to see whether the landslide in English literary taste has left us with a public capable of appreciating him. For the plain fact is that many of the reputations which today occupy the poetic limelight are such as would crumble immediately if poetry such as Empson's, with its passion, logic, and formal beauty, were to become widely known. If the day ever comes when poems like *This Last Pain*, *To an Old Lady*, *Manchouli*, *Note on Local Flora*, are read and pondered, and their lessons heeded, it will be a sad day for many of our punch-drunk random 'romantic' scribblers. But I suppose it never will.

[*PNW* 40, 1950]

ACKNOWLEDGEMENTS

(These pages constitute an extension of the copyright page)

Acknowledgement is gratefully made to the following for permission to reprint the works contained in this anthology:

Walter Allen, *Henry Green* (PNW 25), copyright by Walter Allen 1945. Reprinted by permission of the author and David Higham Associates Ltd.

W. H. Auden, *Lay Your Sleeping Head* (PNW 3) and *The Novelist* (PNW 10), copyright by W. H. Auden 1941. Reprinted by permission of Faber & Faber Ltd.

George Barker, *Channel Crossing* (PNW 40), copyright by George Barker 1950. Reprinted by permission of Faber & Faber Ltd.

Earle Birney, *The Road to Nijmegen* (PNW 26), copyright by Earle Birney 1946. Reprinted by permission of the author.

Elizabeth Bowen, *Mysterious Kôr* (PNW 20), copyright by Elizabeth Bowen 1944. Reprinted by permission of Curtis Brown Ltd, London, and Jonathan Cape Ltd.

Paul Bowles, *By the Water* (PNW 39), copyright by Paul Bowles 1950. Reprinted by permission of Ed Victor Ltd.

Jocelyn Brooke, *The Blanket* (PNW 29), copyright by Jocelyn Brooke 1947. Reprinted by permission of the Estate of Jocelyn Brooke and A. M. Heath & Co. Ltd.

Norman Cameron, *El Aghir* (PNW 22), copyright by Norman Cameron 1944. Reprinted by permission of the author and The Hogarth Press.

Demetrios Capetanakis, *Detective Story* (PNW 13), *Abel* (PNW 16) and *The Isles of Greece* (PNW 20), copyright by Demetrios Capetanakis 1942, 1943 and 1944. Reprinted by permission of Devin-Adair Publishing Co., Connecticut, USA.

John Cornford, *Huesca* (PNW 2), copyright by John Cornford 1941. Reprinted by permission of the Estate of John Cornford and Carcanet Press Ltd, *Understand the Weapon, Understand the Wound: Selected Writings of John Cornford*, ed. Jonathan Galassi, Carcanet Press Ltd, 1976.

Odysseus Elytis, *The Age of Blue Memory* (PNW 31), copyright © by Odysseus Elytis 1947, 1981. English translation copyright © by Nanos Valaoritis 1947, 1981. Reprinted by permission of Anvil Press Poetry Ltd.

Roy Fuller, *Royal Naval Air Station* (PNW 13) and *The Green Hills of Africa* (PNW 16), copyright by Roy Fuller 1942 and 1943. Reprinted by permission of the author.

David Gascoyne, *The Writer's Hand* (PNW 7), copyright © by David Gascoyne 1941, 1965. Reprinted by permission of the Oxford University Press, *Collected Poems* ed. Robin Skelton, Oxford University Press, 1965.

Denis Glover, *Convoy Conversation* (*PNW* 16), copyright © by Denis Glover 1943, 1981. Reprinted by permission of the Estate of Denis Glover and the Richards Literary Agency.

Henry Green, *Mr Jonas* (*PNW* 14), copyright by Henry Green 1942. Reprinted by permission of the Hon. Mrs Henry Yorke.

Graham Greene, *Men at Work* (*PNW* 9), copyright by Graham Greene 1941. By permission of William Heinemann Ltd and The Bodley Head.

J. C. Hall, *Edwin Muir: An Introduction* (*PNW* 38), copyright by J. C. Hall 1949. Reprinted by permission of the author.

Michael Hamburger, *Two Poems: From the Note-book of a European Tramp* (*PNW* 34), copyright by Michael Hamburger 1948. Reprinted by permission of the author and John Johnson Ltd.

H. T. Hopkinson, *I Have Been Drowned* (*PNW* 2), copyright by H. T. Hopkinson 1941. Reprinted by permission of the author and Richard Scott Simon Ltd.

Christopher Isherwood, *A Berlin Diary* (*PNW* 1), copyright by Christopher Isherwood 1940. Reprinted by permission of Curtis Brown Ltd, London.

Denys L. Jones, *Cain in the Jungle* (*PNW* 28), copyright by Denys L. Jones 1946. Reprinted by permission of the author.

Laurie Lee, *Thistle* (*PNW* 28), copyright by Laurie Lee 1946. Reprinted by permission of A. D. Peters & Co. Ltd.

John Lehmann, *The Sphere of Glass* (*PNW* 20), *The Nightmare* (*PNW* 26) and *The Life of the Prodigal Son* (*PNW* 39), copyright by John Lehmann 1944, 1945 and 1950. Reprinted by permission of the author and David Higham Associates Ltd.

Rosamond Lehmann, *When the Waters Came* (*PNW* 3) and *For Virginia Woolf* (*PNW* 7), copyright by Rosamond Lehmann 1941. Reprinted by permission of the author and the Society of Authors.

Alun Lewis, *Ward 'O' 3 (b)* (*PNW* 18), copyright by Alun Lewis 1943. Reprinted by permission of Mrs G. M. Lewis.

F. G. Lorca, *Song* (*PNW* 7), copyright by F. G. Lorca 1941. Translation copyright by J. L. Gili and Stephen Spender 1941. Reprinted by permission of Laurence Pollinger Ltd.

Louis MacNeice, *Brother Fire* and *The Springboard* (*PNW* 16), copyright by Louis MacNeice 1943. Reprinted by permission of Faber & Faber Ltd, *Collected Poems*, and David Higham Associates Ltd.

David Magarshack, *Chekhov and his Producers* (*PNW* 37), copyright by David Magarshack 1949. Reprinted by permission of Mrs M. Magarshack.

James Michie, *Arizona Nature Myth* and *The Robin and the Lark* (*PNW* 40), copyright by James Michie 1950. Reprinted by permission of the author and Chatto & Windus Ltd.

J. E. Morpurgo, *The Pipes* (*PNW* 22), copyright by J. E. Morpurgo 1944. Reprinted by permission of the author.

Jiří Mucha, *Alexey the Cook* (*PNW* 16), copyright by Jiří Mucha 1943. Translation copyright by Ewald Osers 1943. Reprinted by permission of the author and translator and The Hogarth Press, *The Problems of Lieutenant Knap*.

Edwin Muir, *The Natural Man and the Political Man* (*PNW* 26), copyright by Edwin Muir 1945. Reprinted by permission of Mr Gavin Muir.

P. H. Newby, *Khamseen* (*PNW* 32), copyright by P. H. Newby 1947. Reprinted by permission of David Higham Associates Ltd.

Norman Nicholson, *Shortest Day, 1942, For the New Year* and *Waiting for Spring, 1943* (*PNW* 17); *Five Minutes* and *Gathering Sticks on Sunday* (*PNW* 35); copyright by Norman Nicholson 1943 and 1948. Reprinted by permission of the author and David Higham Associates Ltd.

George Orwell, *Shooting an Elephant* (*PNW* 1), copyright by George Orwell 1940. Reprinted by permission of the Estate of Sonia Brownell Orwell and Secker & Warburg Ltd.

Boris Pasternak, *The Thrushes* (*PNW* 30), copyright by Boris Pasternak 1947. Translation copyright by George Reavey 1947. Reprinted by permission of the Pasternak Trust.

William Plomer ('Robert Pagan'), *Happy Days* (*PNW* 3) and *A Recent Discovery* (*PNW* 33), copyright by William Plomer 1941 and 1948. Reprinted by permission of the Executors of the William Plomer Estate.

J. F. Powers, *The Valiant Woman* (*PNW* 33), copyright by J. F. Powers 1948. Reprinted by permission of A. M. Heath & Co. Ltd.

V. S. Pritchett, *A Sense of Humour* (*PNW* 1), copyright by V. S. Pritchett 1940. Reprinted by permission of the author and Chatto & Windus, *Collected Stories*.

Henry Reed, *Chrysothemis* (*PNW* 26), copyright by Henry Reed 1945. Reprinted by permission of the author.

Alan Ross, *Night Patrol* (*PNW* 25), copyright by Alan Ross 1945. Reprinted by permission of the author.

William Sansom, *Through the Quinquina Glass* (*PNW* 14), copyright by William Sansom 1942. Reprinted by permission of Elaine Greene Ltd.

Frank Sargeson, *A Great Day* (*PNW* 5), copyright by Frank Sargeson 1941. Reprinted by permission of Penguin Books (N.Z.) Ltd, *The Stories of Frank Sargeson*.

Jean-Paul Sartre, *The Room* (*PNW* 16), copyright by J.-P. Sartre 1943. Translation copyright by John Rodker 1943. Reprinted by permission of Librairie Gallimard.

Iain Scott-Kilvert, *Four Poems from Cavafy* (*PNW* 32), copyright by Iain Scott-Kilvert 1947. Reprinted by permission of the author.

E. J. Scovell, *Return from the Beach* (*PNW* 37), copyright by E. J. Scovell 1949. Reprinted by permission of the author.

Edith Sitwell, *Girl and Butterfly* (*PNW* 20), copyright by Edith Sitwell 1944. Reprinted by permission of David Higham Associates Ltd.

John Sommerfield, *The Way We Live Now* (*PNW* 4), copyright by John Sommerfield 1941. Reprinted by permission of the author.

Bernard Spencer, *On a Carved Axle-Piece From a Sicilian Cart* and *On the Road* (*PNW* 32); *At the Courmayeur* and *The Boats* (*PNW* 37), copyright by Bernard Spencer 1947 and 1949; copyright © Mrs Anne Humphreys 1981. Reprinted by permission of Oxford University Press, *Collected Poems* ed. Roger Bowen.

Stephen Spender, *Books and the War* (*PNW* 4), copyright by Stephen Spender 1941. Reprinted by permission of A. D. Peters & Co. Ltd and Random House Inc. *No Orpheus, No Euridice* (*PNW* 17) and *A Trance* (*PNW* 18), copyright by Stephen Spender 1943. Reprinted by permission of Faber & Faber Ltd, *Collected Poems*.

ACKNOWLEDGEMENTS

George Stonier ('Fanfarlo'), *Shaving Through the Blitz* (*PNW* 5), copyright by George Stonier 1941. Reprinted by permission of Edward Spender.

A. S. J. Tessimond, *The British* and *The Neurotics* (*PNW* 24), copyright by A. S. J. Tessimond 1945. Reprinted by permission of Hubert Nicholson.

Terence Tiller, *Shop Window* (*PNW* 13) and *Double Weather* (*PNW* 31), copyright by Terence Tiller 1942 and 1947. Reprinted by permission of the author and Chatto & Windus.

John Wain, *Ambiguous Gifts* (*PNW* 40), copyright by John Wain 1950. Reprinted by permission of the author.

C. V. Wedgwood, *Poets and Politics in Baroque England* (*PNW* 21), copyright by C. V. Wedgwood 1944. Reprinted by permission of the author.

Denton Welch, *The Judas Tree* (*PNW* 26), copyright by Denton Welch 1945. Reprinted by permission of David Higham Associates Ltd.

Diana Witherby, *Casualty* (*PNW* 22), copyright by Diana Witherby 1944. Reprinted by permission of the author and H. F. & G. Witherby Ltd.

Every effort has been made to contact and obtain permission from copyright owners of works contained in this anthology, but in some cases without success. The editor and publisher wish to thank those whose permission it has not proved possible to obtain, and apologise for the absence of acknowledgement above.